Law, Populism, and the Political in Central and Eastern Europe

This book addresses the variety of right-wing illiberal populism which has emerged in Central and Eastern Europe (CEE).

Against the backdrop of weak institutional traditions, frequent and profound transformations, and deep historical traumas affecting the law, politics, economy, and society in the region, the book critically examines the entanglements of legality in the region's transformation from state socialism to neoliberalism and Western-style democracy. Drawing on critical legal theory, as well as legal history, legal theory, sociology of law, history of ideas, anthropology of law, comparative law, and constitutional theory, the book goes beyond conventional analyses to offer an in-depth account of this important contemporary phenomenon.

This book will be of interest to legal researchers, especially of a critical or socio-legal perspective, political scientists, sociologists and (legal) historians, as well as policy makers seeking to understand the regional specificity and deeper roots of Central and Eastern European illiberal populism.

Rafał Mańko is Research Affiliate at the Central European University Democracy Institute, Budapest (Hungary), and legal researcher at the European Parliamentary Research Service, Brussels (Belgium).

Adam Sulikowski is full Professor of Legal Theory and Philosophy of Law at the Faculty of Law, Administration and Economics of the University of Wrocław, Poland.

Przemysław Tacik is Assistant Professor at the Institute of European Studies of the Jagiellonian University of Kraków, Poland, and Director of the Nomos: Centre for International Research on Law, Culture and Power.

Cosmin Cercel is Assistant Research Professor in Law at Lazarski University in Warsaw, Poland.

Law, Populism, and the Political in Central and Eastern Europe

Edited by
Rafał Mańko, Adam Sulikowski,
Przemysław Tacik, and Cosmin Cercel

Birkbeck
LAW PRESS

First published 2024
by Birkbeck Law Press
4 Park Square, Milton Park, Abingdon, Oxon OX14 4RN

and by Birkbeck Law Press
605 Third Avenue, New York, NY 10158

Birkbeck Law Press is an imprint of the Taylor & Francis Group, an informa business

British Library Cataloguing-in-Publication Data
A catalogue record for this book is available from the British Library

Library of Congress Cataloging-in-Publication Data
Names: Mańko, Rafal, editor. | Sulikowski, Adam, editor. | Tacik, Przemysław, 1985- editor. | Cercel, Cosmin Sebastian, 1982- editor.
Title: Law, populism, and the political in Central and Eastern Europe / edited by Rafał Mańko, Adam Sulikowski, Przemysław Tacik, and Cosmin Cercel.
Description: New York : Birkbeck Law Press, 2024. | Includes bibliographical references and index.
Identifiers: LCCN 2023034213 (print) | LCCN 2023034214 (ebook) | ISBN 9781032623405 (hardback) | ISBN 9781032624501 (paperback) | ISBN 9781032624464 (ebook)
Subjects: LCSH: Law--Political aspects--Europe, Cental. | Law--Political aspects--Europe, Eastern. | Populism--Political aspects.
Classification: LCC KJC432 .L39 2024 (print) | LCC KJC432 (ebook) | DDC 349.43--dc23/eng/20231002
LC record available at https://lccn.loc.gov/2023034213
LC ebook record available at https://lccn.loc.gov/2023034214

ISBN: 978-1-032-62340-5 (hbk)
ISBN: 978-1-032-62450-1 (pbk)
ISBN: 978-1-032-62446-4 (ebk)

DOI: 10.4324/9781032624464

Typeset in Sabon
by Deanta Global Publishing Services, Chennai, India

Contents

About the Contributors

Mikhail Antonov is Professor of Law at the Faculty of Law of the National Research University Higher School of Economics in Saint Petersburg. He holds two PhDs in law from the Saint Petersburg State University and from the University of Leiden and is the author of *Formalism, Decisionism, and Conservatism in Russian Law* (2021). His research interests focus on the history of legal and political thought and the relations between law and religion. Recent publications include 'Russia's Conservative Challenge to Human Rights in Europe' in *Religious Diversity, State, and Law. National, Transnational and International Challenges* (2023), 'Leon Petrażycki and Georges Gurvitch: Normative Facts as a Litmus Test for Political Convictions' in *Leon Petrażycki: Law, Emotions, Society* (2022) and (jointly with Paul Robinson) 'In the Name of State Sovereignty? The Justification of War in Russian History and the Present' *The Justification of War and International Order: From Past to Present* (2021). He was a fellow at the Institute of Eastern European and Comparative Law of the University of Cologne (2019–2020) with the financial support of the Alexander von Humboldt Foundation.

Mátyás Bencze is Professor of Legal Theory and Sociology of Law at the Széchenyi István University, Győr (Hungary) and Senior Research Fellow at the Institute for Legal Studies, Centre of Social Sciences (Hungary). He has participated in numerous research projects concerning the functioning of judiciary and his current research focuses on the relationship between law and populism in Hungary. His recent publications include 'Everyday Judicial Populism in Hungary' (2022) 47(1) *Review of Central and East European Law* 37; 'Judicial Populism and the Weberian Judge—The Strength of Judicial Resistance Against Governmental Influence in Hungary' (2021) 22(7) *German Law Journal* 1282; 'Explaining Judicial Populism in Hungary – a Legal Realist Approach' (2020) 25 *Iuris Dictio* 83.

Cosmin Sebastian Cercel is currently Assistant Research Professor in Law at Lazarski University in Warsaw (Poland) and previously he was Associate Professor in Law at the University of Nottingham. His research focuses on genealogies of law and politics with specific reference to twentieth-century continental legal history. He is the author of *Towards a Jurisprudence of State Communism: Law and the Failure of Revolution* (2018), a monograph analysing the jurisprudential aspects of state communism, and has co-edited *Law and Critique in Central Europe: Questioning the Past, Resisting the Present* (2016) as well as *States of Exception: Law, History, Theory* (2020). His recent publications include: 'Mapping the State of Siege: Law, Crisis and the Antinomies of Liberal Legality' (2022) 12(2) *Romanian Journal of Comparative Law* 193; 'Law, Politics, and the Military: Towards a Theory of Authoritarian Adjudication' (2021) 22 *German Law Journal* 192. In January 2023 he received a Consolidator Grant from the European Research Council (ERC) and will be employed as Professor at Ghent University from September 2023 to research the history of emergency legislation during the last century in Europe with a view to offering a legal historical explanation of how the experience of emergency has shaped constitutional and political cultures across Europe in the past century.

Peter Čuroš is Assistant Professor at the Polish Academy of Sciences in Warsaw. He received his PhD in law at the Pavol Jozef Šafárik University in Košice on the basis of a thesis on *The Right to Disobey: Civil Disobedience*. From 2016 to 2019, he was Assistant Professor at the PJ Šafárik in Košice. He led there a program on professional ethics and taught mandatory courses on 'Legal Ethics' and 'History of Legal Thought'. Between 2019 and 2022 he held a post-doctoral position at the University of Oslo, where, in the project 'Judges under Stress: the Breaking Point of the Judicial Institutions,' he focused on Central and Eastern Europe, researching the core concepts of the judicial profession. He investigated from the point of view of the critical legal theory, how different political regimes consider these concepts and what qualities they expect from their judges. He was also a visiting scholar at the Washington and Lee University School of Law (2015–2016), with the research areas of professional ethics and professional responsibility and a visiting scholar at the International Institute of Sociology of Law in Oñati (2021–2022). His work in progress focuses on critical legal theory, legal education, and legal ideology in Central and Eastern Europe.

Saygun Gökarıksel is Assistant Professor in Sociology at Boğaziçi University, Istanbul (Türkiye) and a member of the School of Social Science at the Institute for Advanced Study at Princeton, New Jersey (USA). He holds a PhD from City University in New York (USA), an MA from the Jagiellonian University, Kraków (Poland), and a BA from Boğaziçi

University (Türkiye). His research and writing engage the themes of law, history, and politics, especially transitional justice and human rights, from a critical legal, historical, and political anthropological perspective. His current research examines the reckoning with the communist past of Poland in particular and in Eastern Europe more generally, with a focus on law, violence, archive, memory, and neoliberal and right-wing authoritarianism. His writings and commentaries have appeared in a number of journals and fora across Eastern Europe, the Middle East, and the US including 'Beyond Transparency: The Communist-Era Secret Police Archives in Postsocialist Eastern Europe' (2020) 41(3) *Archives and Records* 236, 'Facing History: Sovereignty and the Spectacles of Justice and Violence in Poland's Capitalist Democracy' (2019) 61(1) *Comparative Studies in History and Society* 111, and (with Umut Türem) 'Banality of Exception: Law and Politics in "Post-Coup" Turkey' (2019) 118(1) *South Atlantic Quarterly* 185. He is currently working on a book manuscript which offers a critical ethnographic perspective on Polish lustration in the context of post-socialist neoliberalisation, liberal legalism, and authoritarian populism.

Karolina Kocemba is Max-Weber Post-Doctoral Fellow at the Law Department of the European University Institute, and Post-Doctoral Fellow at the University of Wrocław, Faculty of Law, Administration and Economics, where she is co-investigator in a research project on "Women as Subjects of Constitutional Rights in Central and Eastern Europe" funded by the National Science Centre, Poland (*Narodowe Centrum Nauki*) (project no. 2021/41/B/HS5/01421, principal investigator: Dr. habil. Anna Śledzińska-Simon). Previously, she was a researcher at the Centre for Legal Education and Social Theory, University of Wrocław, where she defended her PhD thesis in the sociology of law on *Interactions in Spaces of Legal Education* devoted to the spatial influence on interactions in places of legal education (mainly in Poland but compared to the law faculties in the Czech Republic, Netherlands, and Australia). At the same university, she graduated with two Master's degrees in law and administration. She is also a graduate of the International Master in Sociology of Law of the Oñati International Institute of Sociology of Law, Oñati (Spain). In her work, Karolina focuses on women's rights, constitutionalism, strategic litigation, legal education, and sociology of law. At the EUI, she is examining constitutional litigation undertaken to limit women's rights in CEE countries in the populist moment. Her research object is the actors' participation in constitutional cases on women's rights and their legal strategies and arguments. She is analysing the participation of actors, especially right-wing organisations and churches, the type of participation, their legal strategy and arguments, and convergence with the arguments in the Constitutional Courts' rulings. Karolina mainly taught sociology of law classes for law students (MA) and co-led a three-year seminar series on strategic litigation at the University of Wrocław. Karolina was also a teacher and tutor of the Empirical Legal Research course in the International EDELNet+ PhD Training Programme.

Rafał Mańko is Research Affiliate at the Central European University Democracy Institute, Budapest (Hungary) where he is a member of the Rule of Law Working Group and legal researcher at the European Parliamentary Research Service, Brussels (Belgium), where he specialises in the rule of law and private law. Previously, he was a fellow at the Centre for the Study of European Contract Law (CSECL) (later renamed to Amsterdam Centre for Transformative Private Law, 'ACT') at the University of Amsterdam (the Netherlands). In his academic work as a critical legal theorist, Rafał blends legal philosophy, sociology of law, and comparative legal history to study the multifaceted relationships between law, ideology, and the political, with a particular focus on legal interpretation and adjudication, on the one hand, and the resilience of legal forms despite political transformations, on the other. Rafał received his Master's degree in (Roman) law from the University of Warsaw, followed by a PhD in law from the University of Amsterdam and a Habilitation in law (Dr. habil. degree) from the University of Wrocław. He is the author of over 100 scholarly publications, including two monographs in Polish, *Private Law in the European Union: Perspectives for the Future* (2004) and *Towards a Critical Philosophy of Adjudication: The Political, Ethics and Legitimacy* (2018). He has co-edited three volumes, including *Law and Critique in Central Europe: Questioning the Past, Resisting the Present* (2016), *Law, Space and the Political: An East-West Perspective* (2019), and *Legal Scholarship and the Political: In Search of a New Paradigm* (2020), as well as contributed to edited collections published by Routledge, Cambridge University Press and Hart. He has recently been a guest lecturer at the Academy of European Law in Trier and a visiting scholar at the Oñati International Institute for the Sociology of Law. His most recent publications include 'Judicial Decision-Making, Ideology and the Political: Towards an Agonistic Theory of Adjudication' (2022) 33 *Law and Critique* 175, '*Sententia Non Existens*: A New Remedy Under EU Law?' (2022) 59(4) *Common Market Law Review* 1169 (with Przemysław Tacik) and 'Legal Survivals and the Resilience of Juridical Form' (forthcoming in *Law and Critique*).

Alexandra Mercescu is Lecturer at the Faculty of Law at the West University of Timişoara (Romania) where she teaches comparative public law, legal philosophy, and academic writing. She is also Affiliated Researcher at the Centre for Legal Education and Social Theory of the University of Wrocław (Poland) and a board member of the Central and Eastern European Forum of Young Legal, Political and Social Theorists. She holds a Master's and a PhD from Sorbonne University (obtained in 2016). Her thesis – *Pour une comparaison des droits indisciplinée* – was awarded 1st prize of the Centre français de droit comparé (an award granted annually in France since 1957). Her academic career has benefited from research stays or exchanges at the Swiss Institute of Comparative Law (as a Van Calker Scholar), Max-Planck-Institute for European Legal History, and Oñati Institute for the Sociology of Law. Alexandra publishes in English, French, and Romanian. Her doctoral work appeared with the leading Swiss publisher Helbing Lichtenhahn in the "Grundlegendes Recht" collection. She is the editor of *Constitutional Identities in Central and Eastern Europe* (2020) and co-editor (with Simone Glanert and Geoffrey Samuel) of *Rethinking Comparative Law* (2021).

Michał Stambulski is Assistant Professor in Legal Theory at the Erasmus School of Law, Erasmus University Rotterdam where he teaches Master's-level courses on international law and global governance, the rule of law, and human rights and a 2023 Emile Noël Global Fellow at the Jean Monnet Center for International and Regional Economic Law and Justice, New York University. He holds a PhD in law from the University of Wrocław. Previously he was executive director at the Centre for Legal Education and Social Theory at the University of Wrocław, Poland, and a visiting scholar at the Faculty of Law of the University of New South Wales, Australia, and Oñati International Institute of Sociology of Law, Spain. His research interests include philosophy of politics and legal theory, constitutionalism, populism, and legal education. He is the author of a monograph (in Polish) entitled *Message from the Emperor: The Concept of Law in Analytical and Post-Analytical Theory* (2020). He is also co-author of three reports from empirical studies conducted on different stages of legal education in Poland. His recent publications deal with the problems of constitutional populism, legal mobilisation, and strategic litigation in Central and Eastern Europe. During his time at the Jean Monnet Center, Michał worked on a project on the intersection of constitutional ethnography and the sociology of legal knowledge.

Adam Sulikowski is full Professor of Legal Theory and Philosophy of Law at the Faculty of Law, Administration and Economics of the University of Wrocław, Poland. He is the author of *Postliberal Constitutionalism: The Challenge of Right-Wing Populism in Central and Eastern Europe* (2023), and has co-edited *Law and Critique in Central Europe: Questioning the Past, Resisting the Present* (2016), *Legal Scholarship and the Political: In Search of a New Paradigm* (2020), and *New Perspectives on Legislation: A Comparative Approach* (2020). He has also published (in Polish) two monographs on postmodern theory of constitutional law *Constitutional Discourse: The Triumph and Crisis of Modern Episteme* (2011) and *The Contemporary Paradigm of Constitutional Justice and the Crisis of*

Modernity (2008), as well as a monograph (in Polish) on *Post-Humanism and Jurisprudence* (2013). His recent journal publications include 'The Return of Forgotten Critique: Some Remarks on the Intellectual Sources of the Polish Populist Revolution' (2020) 45 *Review of Central and Eastern European Law* 376.

Przemysław Tacik is Assistant Professor at the Institute of European Studies of the Jagiellonian University of Kraków, Poland, and Director of the Nomos: Centre for International Research on Law, Culture and Power. A philosopher, lawyer, and sociologist by education, he holds PhDs in philosophy (2014) and international law (2016). He has been Visiting Scholar at several universities (Columbia University, SUNY at Buffalo, Université de Nice, Université Paris-1, Université d'Orléans, Universität Heidelberg, Max-Planck-Institut für ausländisches öffentliches Recht und Völkerrecht, Universität Salzburg, the Higher School of Economics in Moscow, and Universidade de Lisboa). He received a scholarship from the French government (2018), a scholarship for the best young researcher awarded by the Polish Ministry for Science and Higher Education (2018–2020), and a DAAD scholarship (2020). In his academic work, he combines both philosophical and legal perspectives, attempting to approach them from an interdisciplinary angle. His main fields of interest are: in philosophy – contemporary philosophy, Jewish philosophy, and animal studies; in law – critical legal studies, international law, human rights law. He has authored five books as well as over 40 articles and one translation of a poetry volume (from French to Polish). His most recent publications are *A New Philosophy of Modernity and Sovereignty: Towards Radical Historicization* (Bloomsbury 2021) and *Deconstructing Self-Determination in International Law. Sovereignty, Exception, and Biopolitics* (Brill 2023).

Introduction

Law, Populism, and the Political in Semi-Peripheral Central and Eastern Europe*

Rafał Mańko, Przemysław Tacik, and Cosmin Cercel

0.1 Addressing the Spectre of Populism in Central and Eastern Europe

There is a spectre haunting academic discourse on Central and Eastern Europe, the spectre of "populism." In Derridean terms, a spectre is 'a phenomenon situated somewhere between the subjective conscience of the person to whom the specter appears and the (rationally dubious and yet somehow credible) reality of the ghost's claims,' it is 'not just a product of the "haunted" person's imagination'; its very 'appearance ... is a call to change,' and indeed, it 'usually heralds a profound change and a serious crisis.'[1] In this sense, populism both as a *theoretical concept*, increasingly invoked in academic writings on law and politics in Central and Eastern Europe, and as a *social reality*, structured around ethnonationalist and conservative ideological projects and challenging the status quo of liberal legality, is a genuine spectre. It is 'suspended in the past' of the region's traditions of right- and left-wing authoritarianism, and thereby 'a reminder of something ... that was already there,' but, 'at the same time, [it] is inseparable from the future—it *provokes what could come to pass*.'[2] The present edited collection seeks to engage, on the terms of critical legal theory, with this spectre in the specific context of populism's relationship to law and the political, the latter understood, in the spirit of Chantal Mouffe, as structural social agonism.[3]

* All views expressed in this chapter are entirely personal and do not purport to present the position of any institution.

1 Adam Sulikowski, *Postliberal Constitutionalism: The Challenge of Right-Wing Populism in Central and Eastern Europe* (Abingdon: Routledge, 2023), 91–2. Cf. Jacques Derrida, *Specters of Marx* (London: Routledge, 2006).

2 Sulikowski, *Postliberal*, 92. Emphasis added.

3 Chantal Mouffe, *On the Political* (London-New York: Routledge, 2005). Cf. Michał Paździora and Michał Stambulski, 'The Politics of Legal Theory and Education' in Adam Sulikowski, Rafał Mańko, and Jakub Łakomy, *Legal Scholarship and the Political: In Search of a New Paradigm* (Warszawa: CH Beck 2020), 42–4.

DOI: 10.4324/9781032624464-1

The notion of "populism" is undoubtedly an elusive and essentially contested one,[4] but its relatively agreed-upon common core seems to revolve around the political technique of opposing the "healthy people," on behalf of which a populist leader purports to act, to the "corrupt elites" which the populists claim to struggle against.[5] However, as Bojan Bugarič has recently shown,[6] there are many varieties of populism, depending on local specificities, including the relation of populists to constitutional democracy (authoritarian vs. democratic populism), their broader ideological commitments (conservative vs. progressive populism), their origins (anti-system populism vs. populism of long entrenched political groups), to mention but a few dimensions differentiating the various instantiations of what scholars place under the almost catch-all label of "populism."

The "populism" that interests us in the present volume, however, is not an abstract form of some kind of "populism *in genere*" (if it could be distilled, which is itself open to discussion),[7] but specifically the *Central and Eastern European variety* of populism which, as Paul Blokker rightly argues, is characterised *inter alia* by its conservative ideological commitments and the challenge it poses to liberal constitutionalism in what can rightly be described as authoritarian tendencies and an illiberal ideological backbone.[8] As Michał Stambulski asserts, Central and Eastern European populism is, furthermore, characterised by its conscious engagement with constitutional discourse, leading him to speak of a 'constitutional populism.'[9] Adam Sulikowski goes even further pointing out that even 'the most radical circle within the ruling majority' in Poland 'clearly identifies with the nomocratic ideology and the arguments that emanate from this group are, to use Rorty's terminology, rooted in the lexicon of the rule of law.'[10] CEE populism is, therefore, a conundrum of sorts, ridden by profound paradoxes at its very core.

These paradoxes can, however, be explained or at least contextualised within the specific historical and geographical conjecture in which CEE populism emerged, namely the 1989 transformation from actually existing

4 Krzysztof J. Kaleta, 'Populizm konstytucyjny a realizacja zasady suwerenności ludu' [Constitutional Populism and the Realisation of the Principle of Popular Sovereignty] in Piotr Grzebyk, *Prawo w epoce populizmu* (Warszawa: Scholar, 2023), 105–6. See also Chapters 1 and 2 in this volume.

5 See, e.g., Bojan Bugarič, 'Populist Constitutionalism – Between Democracy and Authoritarianism' in Martin Krygier, Adam Czarnota, and Wojciech Sadurski (eds), *Anti-Constitutional Populism* (Cambridge: Cambridge University Press, 2022), 30–1.

6 Ibid. 36–41.

7 Ibid. 36.

8 Paul Blokker, 'Conservative Populism in Defiance of Anti-Totalitarian Constitutional Democracy' in Krygier et al. (eds), *Anti-Constitutional*.

9 Michał Stambulski, 'Constitutional Populism and the Rule of Law in Poland' in Krygier et al. (eds), *Anti-Constitutional*, 337.

10 Sulikowski, *Postliberal*, 114.

socialism to capitalism-*cum*-liberal constitutionalism, on the one hand, and the semi-peripheral condition of the region, itself inherited from a historical *longue durée*, on the other. Both of these features jointly have favoured the phenomenon of legal transplants, especially in the area of constitutional law, flowing into the region from the West, and more specifically from continental Western Europe. In this very context, the current populist backlash can be conceptualised as a reaction to those legal transplants and the way in which they have actually been functioning in the local, semi-peripheral conditions, and, more broadly, as a form of contestation of the way in which the post-1989 transition occurred in its economic, political, and juridical dimensions.[11] It should not be forgotten that today's CEE populist leaders were, in fact, active mainstream politicians at the time of transformation, and their political programmes and practices are, to a large extent, the voicing of their discontent with the modalities of a transition which they not only witnessed, but also partly co-determined.[12]

The purpose of the present introductory chapter is to set the scene for the ten topical interventions that follow by offering an overarching background narrative on the semi-peripheral condition of Central and Eastern Europe, impacting upon its legal and political culture, against the backdrop of which the current right-wing populist tendencies have emerged. We first focus on the potential of a critico-juridical engagement with authoritarian populism, including certain methodological aspects (section 2), followed by a closer look at the semi-peripheral status of the region, including the significance of legal transplants and the CEE's problematic relation to legal form (section 3), all placed in the broader historical context of CEE's weak traditions, frequent transitions, and deep traumas (section 4). Following that, in section 5, we unpack the logic and structure of the book, introducing the ten chapters that follow.

0.2 Critical Jurisprudence and the Threshold of Populism

0.2.1 Populism as the Lacanian "até"

Looked at with the benefit of hindsight, populism emerges as a threshold between two regimes of historicity[13] that have marked our experience of thinking and doing law. After two years during which seemingly the world

11 Cf. Blokker, 'Conservative,' 306. See also Adam Czarnota, 'Populist Constitutionalism or New Constitutionalism' (2019) 11(1) *Krytyka Prawa* 43.

12 Blokker, 'Conservative,' 304–27. Cf. Adam Czarnota, 'Rule of Law as an Outcome of Crisis: Central-Eastern European Experiences 27 Years after the Breakthrough' (2016) 8(2) *Hague Journal on the Rule of Law* 311.

13 François Hartog, *Régimes d'historicité: Présentisme et expériences du temps* (Paris: Seuil, 2003).

stood still under the strain of COVID-19, when chancelleries and law-officials across the world battled the pandemic through legal means,[14] by a flurry of emergency measures,[15] while actively trying to pursue the opposite with the same emergency measures in order to appease the markets and keep the economy going,[16] populism might have seemed to be somehow a trifling concern. After all, what would be the significance of the alleged, perceived, or real violations of constitutional process when there is an effective suspension of the very process ongoing, primarily grounded in necessity? After the era of global constitutionalism, when constitutional transplants were circulating across the globe, it seems that we are living in the dawn of open dissent to the constitutional form and armature of the liberal consensus, with a global circulation of illiberal activism and governmentality. Central and Eastern Europe has not been the exception, as evidenced by its rising variety of right-wing, neo-authoritarian,[17] deeply illiberal[18] populism in the region. New forms of political subjectivity, ideological interpellation, as well as political praxis have emerged in the shadow of COVID-19 and subsequent emergencies, reminding us that a state of exception is always fertile ground for reconstructions of sovereignty, alongside ideologies of blood and soil.[19] This sense of crisis, already haunting polities of the global North from the early 2000s – while being a constant effective reality, and almost an existential condition for the rest of the world under the rule of capitalism – has unavoidably affected our normative universe, and has fuelled, to unprecedented levels, an already existing malaise with legality. We can find traces articulating this boredom with liberal legality from all sides of the politico-legal spectrum, as well as coming from all layers of society. Populism is, in this context, precisely the tipping point, the ideological trope that signals and marks the entry into a new normative universe. Here the Lacanian concept of *atè*,[20] the

14 See, e.g., Piotr Szymaniec, 'Law in Times of the Pandemic' (2021) 96 *Acta Universitatis Lodziensis – Folia Iuridica* 99.

15 David Fraser, 'Afterword: Emergencies, Exceptions, Legalities' in Cosmin Cercel, Gian-Giacomo Fusco, and Simon Lavis (eds), *States of Exception: Law, History, Theory* (Abingdon: Routledge, 2021), 203–11; Sulikowski, *Postliberal*, 97–101.

16 Cosmin Cercel, 'Pandemic, Exception and the Law: Notes on the Shattered Nomos of Europe' (2021) 96 *Acta Universitatis Lodziensis – Folia Iuridica* 83.

17 Przemysław Tacik, 'A New Popular Front, or, on the Role of Critical Jurisprudence under Neo-Authoritarianism in Central-Eastern Europe' (2019) 89 *Acta Universitatis Lodziensis – Folia Iuridica* 31.

18 Cf. Mirosław Michał Sadowski, 'Law and Collective Memory in the Service of Illiberalism. Through the Looking-Glass: Transformation or a Reactionary Revolution?' (2021) 18(1) *Kraków International Studies* 107; Sulikowski, *Postliberal*, 66–88.

19 Cf. Fraser, 'Afterword,' 204–5.

20 Jacques Lacan, *Le séminaire, livre VII: L'ethique de la psychanalyse* (Paris: Seuil, 1986).

in-between of bodily and psychic finitude, the *non-death* and lack of life,[21] the limit preventing the second death, becomes useful in approaching the symbolic space described by *populism* within legal studies. For Lacan, reader of Sophocles, 'beyond *atè* we could stay only for a brief period of time, and it is there that Antigone strives to go.'[22]

Read through these lenses, as a signifier of a specific historical moment, populism is the limit, the quilting point between the era of the "end of history" and history's brutal return, the proper name for the break between the era of the judicialisation of politics and that of overt emergencies, *or worse*, of a normalised,[23] permanent state of exception,[24] which, perhaps, 'has haunted and will eternally (and inevitably) haunt the legal form.'[25] As *atè*, populism designates the limit of an ultimate transgression, and as such the space beyond it.[26] This is the source of all the theoretical, and subsequent political difficulties entailed by this essentially political phenomenon that had yet to find its *droit de cité* within legal studies.[27] Approached as a marker of a historical conundrum whose signs are retrospectively becoming clearer, populism appears as the distorted transgression towards the ruin of the constitutional status quo. Beyond it, lies the menacing figure of overt authoritarianism of all sorts, the repressed historical material of the age of the extremes.

0.2.2 For a Critique of Populism in Central and Eastern Europe

As already recalled above in reference to Bojan Bugarič and Paul Blokker, the actually existing populisms of Central and Eastern Europe have been of the right-wing, conservative, and statist variety, rather than partaking in the tradition of emancipatory and progressive projects. This does not, at least purely theoretically, exclude the possibility of a "left populism," advocated by Chantal Mouffe,[28] but for various reasons pertaining to the historical conjecture of the Central and Eastern European region, no meaningful populism of this kind has appeared following the 1989 transformation. Whatever the hypothetical chances of the emergence, at some indefinite point in the future, of a progressive and democratic variety of populism in Central and Eastern

21 Slavoj Žižek, *Looking Awry: An Introduction to Jacques Lacan through Popular Culture* (Cambridge, MA: MIT Press, 1991), 21–2.

22 Lacan, *Le séminaire, livre VII*, 305.

23 Rafał Mańko, Przemysław Tacik, and Gian-Giacomo Fusco, 'Introduction: The Return of the Exception' (2021) 96 *Acta Universitatis Lodziensis – Folia Iuridica* 7, 9.

24 Sulikowski, *Postliberal*, 93.

25 Mańko, Tacik, and Fusco, 'Introduction,' 10.

26 Žižek, *Looking Awry*, 25.

27 See Chapter 2.

28 Chantal Mouffe, *For a Left Populism* (London: Verso, 2018).

Europe, the actually existing illiberal and authoritarian populist movements of the present cannot be considered as a *pharmakon*,[29] a cure, albeit a dangerous one, for the failures and the misery of contemporary constitutional democracies in the region. Rather, as spectres of authoritarianisms of the past, they should be seen as 'inseparable from the future' and could 'provok[e] what could come to pass.'[30]

This opens the question of the status of a critical legal reaction to the populist challenge. When opposing the rise of authoritarianism from within a critical legal position, one should not turn a blind eye on the numerous complicities, proclivities, and affinities that the purportedly liberal status quo entertained and continues to entertain with its putative Other. Transgressions of the constitutional process were not invented by the populists, the effective suspension of constitutional protections under the war on terror, militarism, the rise of securitisation, diffuse racism in policing, sentencing, and immigration policies, have all been there under the status quo. The national populists just brought this politics to the fore, a move that is important, in signifying a next stage in the rise of authoritarianism, but one should not belittle the existence of these ready-made legal and institutional practices, let alone the economic causes of the present series of crises.[31] While one would be tempted to call for a "popular front" strategy[32] before the unleashed authoritarian Behemoth, we should not lose sight of the complicities that brought about this situation. Not being silent about the conditions that enabled the authoritarian turn in Central and Eastern European politics and exposing the failures and limits of the hegemonic neoliberal legality should not be confused with a call for a regression – returning legally and politically to the era of Empires and nation-states cannot be on a critical legal agenda unless one resolutely falls back on the commitments for a progressive radical politics. It is therefore necessary, in the light of this grave situation, to be able to grasp the making of the current authoritarian turn, and to engage within a history of the present by seizing what has made an eruption within the otherwise humdrum life of the law.

0.2.3 Beyond Affirmative Amnesia

Adam Sulikowski has coined the term "affirmative amnesia" to deal with the disappearance of critical legal instruments from the jurisprudential toolbox

29 Dimitrios Kivotidis, 'The Pharmakon of Democracy: General Will and the People in the Context of the Greek Referendum' (2018) 27(6) *Social & Legal Studies* 755.

30 Sulikowski, *Postliberal*, 92. Emphasis added.

31 Michael Wilkinson, *Authoritarian Liberalism* (Oxford: OUP, 2021), 262–7.

32 Tacik, 'A New.'

following the fall of actually existing socialism.[33] Instead, after 1989, the myth of an apolitical jurisprudence was embraced, founded on 'interpretive passivity and obedience' of lawyers, a position whose genealogy can be traced back to Catholic theology[34] on the one hand, and inscribed into the broader climate of "scientism" on the other.[35] This debilitating post-theological approach as 'fidelity to the rules and the text itself'[36] has been in crisis ever since the populist onslaught on the status quo of liberal legality. Interestingly, the right-wing populists themselves, as populists-in-opposition, were keen to tap into the treasure trove of critical legal theory in search of convenient instruments to criticise institutions they had not yet managed to seize.[37] Even more paradoxically, populists-in-power have been equally quick to dump the critical legal toolbox and engage into formalism as usual[38] to justify their decisions and claim the legitimacy of their power. In doing so, populism-in-power:

> seeks to reconstruct political neutrality by ensuring the loyalty of lawyers and legal experts to political power, which is considered a more reliable and legitimate factor (axiologically, ethically and pragmatically) for establishing the post-theological rules of juristic discourse than demoliberal-expert abstractions.[39]

In tackling the emergent populist legality from the perspective of critical jurisprudence, particular emphasis must be placed, first and foremost, on fidelity to the progressive, emancipatory inner core of critical theory, which is an essential foundation and condition precedent of any kind of genuinely

33 Adam Sulikowski, 'Apolitical Jurisprudence: Crisis of an Idea and the Phenomenon of Populism' in Sulikowski, *Legal Scholarship*, 2.
34 Adam Sulikowski, 'Law After the Death of God: Jurisprudence and Some Assertions of the Contemporary Philosophy' in Andrzej Bator and Zbigniew Pulka (eds), *A Post-Analytical Approach to Philosophy and Theory of Law* (Berlin: Peter Lang, 2019), 182–4.
35 Adam Sulikowski, 'The Crisis of Traditional Legal Theory: A Diagnosis and View into the Future' in Andrzej Bator and Zbigniew Pulka (eds), *Legal Theory and Philosophy of Law: Towards Contemporary Challenges* (Warsaw: Scholar, 2013), 231.
36 Sulikowski, 'Apolitical,' 7.
37 Adam Sulikowski, 'The Return of Forgotten Critique: Some Remarks on the Intellectual Sources of the Polish Populist Revolution' (2020) 45 *Review of Central and East European Law* 376.
38 Cf. Alan Uzelac, 'Survival of the Third Legal Tradition?' (2010) 49 *Supreme Court Law Review* 377; Zdeněk Kühn, *The Judiciary in Central and Eastern Europe: Mechanical Jurisprudence in Transformation?* (Leiden-Boston: Martinus Nijhoff, 2011); Rafał Mańko, 'Weeds in the Gardens of Justice? The Survival of Hyperpositivism in Polish Legal Culture as a Symptom/Sinthome' (2013) 7(2) *Pólemos* 207.
39 Sulikowski, 'Apolitical,' 16.

critical legal thinking.[40] In this vein, rather than exposing, in the spirit of legal positivism, that populists-in-power do not respect the "letter of the law" (a problematic concept in itself, assuming an *a priori* access to meaning without interpretation[41]), we should rather show how, in concrete reality, populist reforms, including reinterpretations of the constitution, impinge on fundamental human freedoms, such as reproductive rights.[42] Second, it is a focus on the *critique of legal ideology*, understood as exposing the actual ideological stakes behind populist legal devices.[43] These stakes may, in fact, be hidden, as populists often seek to present their dark neo-authoritarian tendencies masquerading in the costumes of genuine democrats, inspired by the need to restore "true" democracy to the "authentic" people. A *genealogy of legal institutions*, allowing the exposure of the darker legacies hidden behind innocently framed legal innovations, such as the 'extraordinary complaint' introduced into Polish law in 2017 under the pretext of defending human rights, but in fact aimed at allowing to undermine legal certainty in the name of executive intervention in court proceedings, is a telling case.[44] Third, and in connection with the two aforementioned aspects, is the focus on a *profoundly realist* approach to the law, understood as exposing the actual workings of populist legality, its effective implications for the political (social antagonisms), rather than satisfying oneself with the face value of populist legal texts.

These three broad methodological guidelines can help unmask the formalist hypocrisy of populists-in-power and expose the actual implications of populist legality which, in the name of a deepened democracy, in fact imposes upon citizens a narrow, ethnonationalist-*cum*-obscurantist ideological blueprint. In fact, the populist moment of crisis of liberal legality when 'the masks have fallen,'[45] can open a window of opportunity for advancing the project of critical legal theory more broadly, and avoiding the pitfalls of

40 Duncan Kennedy, *A Critique of Adjudication {fin de siècle}* (Cambridge, MA: Harvard University Press, 1997), 5. Cf. Max Horkheimer, 'Traditional and Critical Theory' in idem, *Critical Theory: Selected Essays* (New York: Continuum Press, 1999) 188–234; Costas Douzinas and Adam Gearey, *Critical Jurisprudence: The Political Philosophy of Justice* (Oxford: Hart, 2005), 241–4.

41 Cf. Jakub Łakomy, 'Critique of Legal Interpretation: Hermeneutic Universalism, Interpretative Communities, and the Political' in Sulikowski et al. (eds), *Legal Scholarship*, 95–116.

42 See Chapter 4.

43 Cf. Andrew Halpin, 'Ideology and Law' (2006) 11(2) *Journal of Political Ideologies* 153; Rafał Mańko, 'Legal Form, Ideology, and the Political' in Sulikowski et al. (eds), *Legal Scholarship*, 17–40.

44 Tadeusz Zembrzuski, 'Extraordinary Complaint in Civil Proceedings under the Polish Law' (2019) 1 *Access to Justice in Eastern Europe* 31.

45 Adam Sulikowski and Mateusz Wojtanowski, 'The Polish Constitutional Court Crisis: Some Remarks on the Political, Liberalism and Culture' in Béla Pokol and András Téglási (eds),

juristic hypocrisy.[46] This is, inter alia, an occasion to address also the more difficult questions, which have not been hitherto tackled in juristic discourses, such as the 'drawbacks and costs of installing (demo-)liberalism in the region in a very neoliberal version,' on the one hand, and the 'lack of rootedness of institutions,'[47] on the other – two aspects which cannot be addressed outside the specific context of Central and Eastern Europe as a semi-peripheral space – an issue that we address in the next section.

0.3 Central and Eastern Europe as a Semi-Peripheral Politico-Juridical Space

0.3.1 Central and Eastern Europe and Theories of Peripherality and Post-Colonialism

As Polish sociologist Tomasz Zarycki notes, Fukuyama's "end of history" was supposed to be also an 'end of geography [and] more broadly, was supposed to end the significance of historico-cultural context in the analysis of political or economic phenomena.'[48] The current crisis of the world order established in 1989, and specifically the illiberal populist challenge to the constitutional foundations of that order, calls for returning to classical notions of peripherality in the analysis of the juridico-political ramifications of populism in Central and Eastern Europe, even if it has to be admitted that one of the difficulties in applying the centre-periphery discourse to Central and Eastern Europe lies in the fact that term "peripherality" is considered as, at the very least, derogatory.[49]

Whenever Europe is theorised as an ideological construct, Central and Eastern Europe remains the odd one out, being a 'no man's land between West and East.'[50] Not distanced enough from the Western centre[51] to be easily pigeonholed as "the East" – which could be safely relegated to the position of "the Other" locked in a binary opposition with the centre – it is also too distinct to be unproblematically reabsorbed into the Western understanding

---

Die stufenweise Entstehung des juristokratischen Staates (Budapest: Dialóg Campus, 2019), 193.

46 Sulikowski and Wojtanowski, 'The Polish Constitutional Court,' 194. Cf. Pierre Bourdieu, 'Les juristes, gardiens de l'hypocrisie collective' in François Chazel and Jacques Commaille (eds), *Normes juridiques et régulation sociale* (Paris: LGDJ, 1991), 95–9.

47 Sulikowski, *Postliberal*, 115.

48 Tomasz Zarycki, *Peryferie: Nowe ujęcie zależności centro-peryferyjnych* [The Peripheries: A New Approach to Centre-Periphery Dependences] (Warszawa: Scholar, 2009), 19.

49 Zarycki, *Peryfierie*, 23–6.

50 Jan Sowa, *Fantomowe ciało króla: Peryferyjne zmagania z nowoczesną formą* [The King's Phantomal Body: Peripheral Struggles with Modern Form] (Kraków: Universitas, 2011), 15.

51 The concept of the "West" used here and throughout the book is, of course, a construct of the Central European perspective and relates to what Immanuel Wallerstein calls the "core" of the capitalist world-system.

of Europeanness. As a result, Central and Eastern Europe experiences the position relative to what world-systems theory describes as semi-periphery. Immanuel Wallerstein, who theorised it from his economics-centred point of view, described semi-peripheries in the following manner:

> The semiperiphery, however, is not an artifice of statistical cutting points, nor is it a residual category. The semiperiphery is a necessary structural element in a world-economy. These areas play a role parallel to that played, *mutatis mutandis,* by middle trading groups in an empire. They are collection points of vital skills that are often politically unpopular. These middle areas (like middle groups in an empire) partially deflect the political pressures which groups primarily located in peripheral areas might otherwise direct against core-states and the groups which operate within and through their state machineries. On the other hand, the interests primarily located in the semiperiphery are located outside the political arena of the core-states, and find it difficult to pursue the ends in political coalitions that might be open to them were they in the same political arena.[52]

In Wallerstein's account, semi-peripheries are a necessary product of the transforming global economy that, at each of its formations, produces middle areas as a means of keeping proper peripheries at bay. These regions act both as an enticement to the peripheries and a buffer that assures their proper distance from the centre. In more symbolic terms, semi-peripheries are exposed to a very complex game of self-identification through an ambiguous reference to the Big Other of the centre. In this zone the alluring symbolic force of the centre is too palpable to be omitted in the construction of identity; at the same time, it produces counterreactions that call for local resistance in symbolic terms. Consequently, semi-peripheries experience strong tidal forces that make the constitution of their identity and self-perception inherently unstable. In a historical perspective, semi-peripheral regions – with Central and Eastern Europe being a telling example – are usually in-between zones falling under the hegemony of either the centre or the peripheries.

The history of the 20th and 21st century demonstrates deep patterns of CEE's oscillation between the "West" and the "East" in approximately 20–40 year cycles. Domination of the West after 1918 and the help of the *Entente* in state-creation was gradually replaced with centrifugal forces in the 1930s. After 1945 much of the region was hegemonised by the USSR, although centrifugal forces appeared also in relation to this form of domination (early, as in the case of Yugoslavia, or later, as in Romania after

52 Immanuel Wallerstein, *The Modern World System I. Capitalist Agriculture and the Origins of the European World-Economy in the Sixteenth Century* (Berkeley: University of California Press, 1974), 349–50.

1971). Finally, 1989 brought about one more turn, this time to the West. Nonetheless, the appearance of illiberal regimes since 2010 once again demonstrated the volatility of hegemonies imposed on the region. Yet what seems particularly significant is not only the rhythm of transformations in formal hegemony over this region, but also the fact that each hegemonic constellation is neither stable nor complete; the tidal force of the other binary pole cannot be eliminated. Hence, the properly Central European dreams of being 'the stolen part of the West' under actually existing socialism (according to Kundera's famous portrayal[53]) or the contemporary resurgence of anti-Western sentiments under liberal hegemony.

The colonial experience – and post-colonial studies – have been influential in diagnosing the Central and Eastern European condition.[54] One of the useful concepts in this context is colonial mimicry theorised by Homi Bhabha as:

> the desire for a reformed, recognizable Other, as a subject of a difference that is almost the same, but not quite. (...) [T]he discourse of mimicry is constructed around an ambivalence; in order to be effective, mimicry must continually produce its slippage, its excess, its difference. The authority of that mode of colonial discourse (...) is therefore stricken by an indeterminacy: mimicry emerges as the representation of a difference that is itself a process of disavowal. Mimicry is, thus the sign of a double articulation; a complex strategy of reform, regulation and discipline, which "appropriates" the Other as it visualizes power. Mimicry is also the sign of the inappropriate, however, a difference or recalcitrance which coheres the dominant strategic function of colonial power, intensifies surveillance, and poses an immanent threat to both 'normalized' knowledges and disciplinary powers.[55]

Central and Eastern Europe constitutes itself in relation to the Other: through its mimicry that produces inevitable excess and instability that accompany disciplinary practices allowing for self-constitution. In Lacanian terms, the West is for Central and Eastern Europe properly *le grand Autre* (the Big Other). On the one hand, it is desired and its desire is demanded – Central Europe plays before its ultimate spectator, awaiting recognition and approval. On the other hand, Central and Eastern Europe knows that the West – precisely like the Big Other in Lacan – has an inherent lack:[56] it cannot see and

53 Milan Kundera, 'The Tragedy of Central Europe' (1984) 31(7) *New York Review of Books* 33.

54 See, e.g., Larry Wolff, *Inventing Eastern Europe: The Map of Civilization on the Mind of the Enlightenment* (Stanford, CA: Stanford University Press, 1994).

55 Homi Bhabha, *The Location of Culture* (London-New York: Routledge, 1994), 122–3.

56 Cf. Jacques Lacan, *Le Séminaire. Livre X – L'angoisse* (Paris: Seuil, 2004), 33.

record the truth that a semi-peripheral region recognises from its position. The contemporary challenge posed to liberal constitutionalism might be read as obscene debunking of a discourse that from a semi-peripheral perspective appears as ravaged by an inherent flaw that makes it illusionary. Mimicking the Western Big Other and, at the same time, suspecting that its values, discourses, and practices are a lure, determine the oscillation in which Central European identity constitutes itself.[57] This inherent instability is particularly visible in post-transition times, when the pressure to adopt Western patterns was particularly strong and rapidly applied. To a great extent it pertains to the legal dimension of the transition: if the law (especially constitutional law) is a symbolic system that constitutes a medium of statal self-definition and self-constitution, it must reveal the semi-peripheral oscillation.

Tomasz Zarycki underlines that relations with the centre are particularly important for the elites of the periphery, given that these contacts constitute for them an essential form of social capital.[58] The role of an intermediary between the periphery and the centre, including in the symbolic-cultural dimension, can become, for the peripheral elites, an important source of their social position.[59] This applies, of course, to legal elites which have been engaged from the very outset as the juridical enablers of the transformation from actually existing socialism to capitalism, not least as activist constitutional court judges and politically engaged constitutional scholars.[60] Indeed, it is the 'unholy alliance between the intellectual elite and the markets that is perhaps at the core of the vagaries of the post-communist transformation,'[61] based on a 'mainstream "knowledge-power complex" (...) formed around the belief that universal Western liberal modernity' was all that is needed.[62]

It is in this precise context that CEE legal elites have become the object of targeted populist backlash, epitomised by the hostile takeover of the Polish Constitutional Court and its staffing with judges with little constitutional experience but all-too-vivid political convictions.[63] The Court, 'previously hailed by the liberal doctrine as a stronghold of impartiality, independence and loyalty to the Constitution (...) was now denounced (...) as elitist,

57 Cf. Cosmin Cercel, Alexandra Mercescu, and Mirosław Michał Sadowski (eds), *Law, Culture and Identity in Central and Eastern Europe: A Comparative Engagement* (Abingdon: Routledge, forthcoming in 2023).

58 Zarycki, *Peryferie*, 182.

59 Ibid.

60 Adam Sulikowski, 'Government of Judges and Neoliberal Ideology: The Polish Case' in Rafał Mańko, Cosmin Cercel, and Adam Sulikowski (eds), *Law and Critique in Central and Eastern Europe: Questioning the Past, Resisting the Present* (Oxford: Counterpress, 2016).

61 Cercel 'Destruction,' 25.

62 Sulikowski, 'Government,' 27.

63 Mirosław Wyrzykowski, 'Experiencing the Unimaginable: The Collapse of the Rule of Law in Poland' (2019) 11 *Hague Journal on the Rule of Law* 417.

postcommunist and politicised.'[64] At the same time, as Adam Czarnota notes, in the CEE 'populists in power treat constitutions, at least rhetorically, quite seriously, especially as sources of their own legitimacy.'[65] This was certainly facilitated by the fact that following the Court's hostile takeover, it became a loyal partner of the executive and legislative powers, controlled by the same right-wing coalition, endorsing their key decisions and refraining from exercising authentic constitutional review.[66]

However, one ought to be mindful not to fall prey to the mirror palace of reflection and (mis)recognition between the supposed centre and the periphery within this particular relationship. True, the core of today's right populism in Central and Eastern Europe owes much to this particular position, of being the "odd one out," neither fully a periphery, nor the centre, but this condition needs not to be essentialised as a matter of an unchanging, stable identity, if ever there was one. Furthermore, we should not forget that the political economy of the region, alongside the symbolic and libidinal economy of investments and recognition between the centre and its margins, between the coloniser and the colonised, are part of a material historical history that quilts both economy and cultural signification.[67]

0.3.2 Legal Transplants as the Juridical Aspect of Peripherality

In strictly juridical terms, the *definiens* of peripherality is the position taken by a jurisdiction with regard to the global flow of legal models: the centre is where legal forms are produced, the (semi-)periphery is where those forms are then transplanted.[68] If, perhaps, Wallerstein's distinction of periphery and semi-periphery could be given a certain content within the sphere

64 Przemysław Tacik, 'Polish Constitutional Identity under the Illiberal Turn' in Alexandra Mercescu (ed.), *Constitutional Identities in Central and Eastern Europe* (Berlin: Peter Lang, 2020), 168.

65 Adam Czarnota, 'Sources of Constitutional Populism – Democracy, Identity and Economic Exclusion' in Krygier et al. (eds), *Anti-Constitutional*, 497.

66 Tacik, 'Polish Constitutional,' 167.

67 Cf. Mitchell A. Orenstein and Bojan Bugarič, 'Work, Family, Fatherland: The Political Economy of Populism in Central and Eastern Europe' (2020) 29(2) *Journal of European Public Policy* 176. See also Damjan Kukovec, 'Hierarchies as Law' (2014) 21 *Columbia Journal of European Law* 131; idem, 'Law and the Periphery' (2015) 21 *European Law Journal* 406.

68 Cf. Gianmaria Ajani, 'By Chance and Prestige: Legal Transplants in Russia and Eastern Europe' (1995) 43(1) *American Journal of Comparative Law* 93. See also Rafał Mańko, 'Legal Transfers in Europe Today: Still "Modernisation Through Transfer"?' in Paulina Bieś-Srokosz, Jacek Srokosz, and Ewelina Żelasko-Makowska (eds), *Mutual Interaction Between Contemporary Systems and Branches of Law in European Countries* (Częstochowa: Podobiński Publishing House, 2017), 139–56; Michał Gałędek, 'Introduction: Modernisation, National Identity, and Legal Instrumentalism' in Michał Gałędek and Anna Klimaszewska

of the juridical, this could be through the distinction of how exactly legal transplants operate in these two respective zones of global legal culture, especially with regard to the active or passive role of local legal elites, the degree of adjustment of legal transplants to local needs and conditions, and finally with regard to the degree of the unquilting of legal form from legal substance. True, as Alan Watson claimed, legal borrowing is a ubiquitous vehicle of legal development,[69] nonetheless the intensity and one-sidedness of legal transplants, characteristic for peripheral legal development, is striking.[70] However, legal transplantation, especially if done involuntarily, hastily, and unreflexively can also lead to problems. First, it could hamper the symbolic relation between the law and the society it governs, preventing legal form from being capable of becoming an expression of the collective identity.[71] A further problem potentially posed by legal transplantation is its possible implication in terms of symbolic violence and an articulation of hegemonic relations within the juridical,[72] whereby the 'passive recipients' of involuntary legal transfers[73] enjoy a 'patronized status,'[74] – exacerbating the periphery's nature of a properly 'post-colonial space.'[75]

(eds), *Modernization, National Identity and Legal Instrumentalism: Studies in Comparative Legal History*, vol. 1: *Private Law* (Leiden-Boston: Brill-Nijhoff, 2020).

69 Alan Watson, *Legal Transplants: An Approach to Comparative Law* (2nd ed., Atlanta: University of Georgia Press, 1993).

70 Rafał Mańko, 'Being Central European, or Some Reflections on Law, Double Peripherality and the Political in Times of Transformation' in Tomás Gábriš and Ján Sombati (eds), *Central and Eastern Europe as a Double Periphery* (Berlin: Peter Lang, 2020), 19.

71 Cf. Jiří Přibáň, *Legal Symbolism: On Law, Time and European Identity* (Aldershot: Ashgate 2007), 25.

72 Rafał Mańko, Martin Škop, and Markéta Štěpáníková, 'Carving Out Central Europe as a Space of Legal Culture: A Way Out of Peripherality?' (2016) 6(2) *Wroclaw Review of Law, Administration and Economics* 4, 21.

73 Esin Örücü, 'A General View of "Legal Families" and of "Mixing Systems"' in Esin Örücü and David Nelken (eds), *Comparative Law: A Handbook* (Oxford: Hart, 2007), 176; Esin Örücü, *Critical Comparative Law: Considering Paradoxes for Legal Systems in Transition* (Alphen: Kluwer, 1999), 31. Cf. Hans-Wolfgang Micklitz, 'Prologue: The Westernisation of the East and the Easternisation of the West' in Michal Bobek (ed.), *Central European Judges Under the European Influence: The Transformative Power of the EU Revisited* (Oxford: Hart, 2015), 5.

74 Jiří Přibáň, "From 'Which Rule of Law?' to 'The Rule of Which Law?': Post-Communist Experiences of European Legal Integration' (2009) 1 *Hague Journal on the Rule of Law* 337, 352.

75 Alexandra Mercescu, 'Introduction: From Country to Country, from Time to Time, Questions and Answers of Self and Other' in Mercescu (ed.), *Constitutional Identities*, 16.

0.3.3 *Legal Form in the Semi-Periphery: A Problematic Relationship*

All this leads to a deeply problematic relation to legal form which, being usually transplanted and often considered as foreign, becomes, within the (semi-)periphery, the object of a peculiar dialectic between formal legality and actual normativity. Is it not an accident that the theory of normative pluralism was first advanced by a jurist from the periphery, Eugen Ehrlich, who lived and worked in the outermost eastern province of Austro-Hungary, Bukowina?[76] Ehrlich's emphasis on the actual legal life, his insistence on the precedence of informal (or pre-juridical) normativity over formal law, the underlying feeling about the externality of legal form to society,[77] is something which could be closely linked to the transplantation of legal form. Take also the peculiar universe of Kafka, another Central European par excellence, which is constituted of parallel and competing normative universes, and of uncertain rules of recognition, or rather *Grundnormen.*[78] Behind the emancipatory façade of separation of powers, of equal protection under the law, and of civil liberties, lay the positive reality of informal hierarchies of status, ethnos, and race, the rivalries of ethnic and national allegiances, as well as the survival of royal prerogative.

These experiences from the age of Empires did not disappear with their breakdown. In fact, the experience of actually existing socialism, with its peculiar relationship with legal form, contributed to the perpetuation of Central and Eastern Europe's specific *nomos.*[79] In a telling passage, Mikhail Antonov explains the reality of the Soviet legal experience – a peculiar form of "legal realism" – in the following terms:

> In practice, (…) when the provisions of a formal legal code (….) collide with the principles set out in the moral codes (e.g., the Moral Code of the Builder of Communism) or the CPSU Program), nothing guarantees that the former would prevail even in the courts. Moreover, the validity (binding force) of law in this logic was conceived as dependent on how powerholders appreciate the expediency of applying legal norms in a given case.

76 Incidentally, Leon Petrażycki – a Polish-Russian sociologist of law working in St Petersburg and later Warsaw – also focused a great deal of his research on the opposition between formal and informal law, the latter thematised in his works as 'legal intuition.' See, e.g., Edoardo Fittipaldi and A. Javier Treviño (eds), *Leon Petrażycki: Law, Emotions, Society* (Abingdon: Routledge, 2023).

77 Eugen Ehrlich, *Fundamental Principles of the Sociology Law* (Abingdon: Routledge, 2017), 35–6.

78 Giorgio Agamben, 'K' in Justin Clemens and Nicholas Heron, *The Work of Giorgio Agamben: Law, Literature, Life* (Edinburgh: Edinburgh University Press, 2008), 13–27.

79 Used here to signify normativity beyond and outside the legal form of *lex* and *ius*. Cf. Jerzy Zajadło, 'The Concept of *Nomos* – Some Remarks' (2020) 12(3) *Critique of Law* 143, 159.

> If in the opinion of judges and other law officers individual rights did not fit this appreciation, predictably these rights would hardly win any legal protection. Surely, in the avalanche of ordinary mundane cases this reasoning was not applied, though in "high-profile" cases such "objective needs" could be referred to as grounds for exception.[80]

The Kelsenian pyramid of legal acts – with the constitution at its apex, and ministerial ordinances, circulars, and executive decrees at the bottom – was fundamentally reversed under actually existing socialism. It was the constitution that was at the very bottom, virtually never applied directly by the courts and devoid of any greater significance in the sphere of law-in-action, and the inner, unpublished ministerial circulars – the so-called 'mimeo law' (*prawo powielaczowe*)[81] – which determined the actual way that public officials acted and decided, was placed *de facto* at the apex of the real legal order.

The tradition of "mimeo-law" and "telephonic law" are not something than can quickly and entirely disappear from the collective memory of a post-socialist peripheral society.[82] The overarching feeling of a mismatch between the (official) legal form and the (unofficial) "living law" is, in the semi-peripheral CEE, something persistent,[83] leading to the ever present capacity of juridical signifiers to become unquilted, at the most unexpected moments, from their signifiers and by the instability of the inner relation keeping together legal form and substance. These features have come to the fore following the 1989 transformation, but have repeated themselves with great force in the guise of populist legality.[84] As a result, the CEE semi-periphery becomes the site of a permanent Agambenian carnival, where the power of legal form is suspended and neutralised.[85] After all, as Adam Sulikowski points out, '"smashing the legal system" was from the outset a priority in the program of the United Right' in Poland as 'was also the case in Hungary, where Fidesz's ideologists and the constitutionalists who supported them wrote clearly and emphatically about the need to break up the juristocracy or the judgeocracy.'[86] The phenomenon of populist illiberal legality in Central

80 Mikhail Antonov, 'Legal Realism in Soviet and Russian Jurisprudence' (2018) 43 *Review of Central and East European Law* 483, 500.

81 Cf. Jolanta Jabłońska-Bonca, *"Prawo powielaczowe": studium z teorii państwa i prawa* ['Mimeo Law': A Study in the Theory of State and Law] (Gdańsk: Wydawnictwo Uniwersytetu Gdańskiego, 1987).

82 Cf. Chapter 8 in this volume.

83 Cf. Karol Muszyński, *Polityka regulacji zatrudnienia w Polsce: Kryzys ekonomiczny a destandaryzacja stosunków pracy* [Employment Regulation Policy in Poland: Economic Crisis and Destandardization of Labour Relationships] (Warszawa: Scholar, 2019), 68.

84 See Chapters 4 and 5.

85 Cf. Giorgio Agamben, 'What is a Destituent Power?' (2014) 32 *Environment and Planning D: Society and Space* 65 at 70.

86 Sulikowski, *Postliberal*, 112.

and Eastern Europe can, therefore, be considered as a symptom of the semi-periphery's troubled relationship with legal form, and the fact that populists notoriously oppose the legal form to a putative popular feeling of justice[87] could be seen as a deeply culturally embedded symptom.

0.4 Weak Traditions, Frequent Transitions, Deep Traumas

Even if it is true that the current trend of populist onslaught is part of a global trend, it has nonetheless taken a particular form within the context of Central and Eastern Europe. This context is marked by three elements which we consider particularly relevant here: first, *weak institutional traditions*, especially as regards the political and legal institutions; second, *frequent transitions*, often of a revolutionary character, occurring within short intervals of time, in general more frequently than in the West; and third, *deep traumas* left behind by wars, revolutions, and brutal socio-economic transformations.

0.4.1 Weak Traditions

Obviously, revolutions and transformations are not a unique feature of Central and Eastern Europe. Nonetheless, if we look closer at the traditions of statehood, at the time when each of the nation-states in the region was created and how long are its uninterrupted institutional traditions, we will note that they are, as a rule, relatively shorter than in the Western European countries of the Centre. With the exception perhaps of Hungary which, although in personal union with Austria, continued to exist as a distinct entity, all other CEE countries have emerged, as independent states, no earlier than at the end of the 19th century, but most of them only in the 20th century, with the peaceful breakup of Czechoslovakia and bloodbath in Yugoslavia marking the last moment of eruption of new sovereign entities in the region. Frequent and sometimes radical border changes, as effected after World War I (for instance the Trianon Treaty) and after World War II (for instance, the moving of Poland hundreds of kilometres to the West) also contributed to the uprooting of institutions, which had to be planted on entirely new soil (such as the "Regained Lands" in post-1945 Poland, or Transylvania incorporated into Romania in 1918). Relatively short traditions of statehood impact upon the relatively weaker institutional traditions of the legal infrastructure, such as court systems or law faculties. In turn, a weak cultural embeddedness

87 Zbigniew Cywiński, 'Głos ludu: dla kogo równość i czyja sprawiedliwość? Socjologicznoprawne refleksje o populizmie' [Voice of the People: Equality for Whom and Whose Justice? Socio-Legal Reflexions on Populism] in Grzebyk (ed.), *Populizm*, 81.

of the institutional order is one of the factors favouring the emergence of populism.[88]

0.4.2 Frequent Transitions

If shorter traditions of stable statehood were not enough, Central and Eastern Europe has also experienced, over the span of barely a century, no less than six profound politico-juridical and socio-economic transitions. The *first transition* was the one from the age of Empires (Austro-Hungarian, German, Russian) to the age of inter-War nation-states, many of which emerged on the map of Europe for the first time. Initially, they were predominantly democratic liberal but, in a decade or so, all of the countries of the region (save for the ill-fated Czechoslovakia) experienced a *second transition*, this time from liberal democracy to right-wing authoritarianism, emergency powers, or even dictatorship, incidentally not unlike many countries in Western Europe at the time.

Following the deep trauma of World War II, all countries in the region – in contrast to Western Europe – embarked upon the experiment of building state socialism, which entailed a *third transition* of political, economic, and legal institutions, much more profound in all respects from the first two transitions. The ambiguity of this third transition cannot be overemphasised and it is revealed in the uncertain status of the countries of Central and Eastern Europe: as "people's republics," they were either the result of bourgeois democratic forms of liberation in cooperation with socialist forces, or they have been just liberated directly.[89] In both cases, the result was similar: the "revolution" was one which was imposed from above, it was not intrinsic to social formation, insofar as the revolutionary situation was somewhat artificial[90] – determined by the wartime conditions. One could even speak, following Andrzej Leder of a "dreamt-through revolution,"[91] whose putative subject was not even conscious of the revolutionary moment.

The socialist period was, however, not a monolith, but rather was marked by regular popular outbursts – of 1956 and 1968, or of 1980 – all of which contained a popular element that has been positively downplayed both by the Soviet hegemon and by Western anti-communism, for obvious reasons. Let us note here that the Prague spring started as a matter of conflict between the communist parties within the Warsaw bloc over the autonomy of each communist party to take its own path towards communism.[92] The brutal

88 Cywiński, 'Głos ludu,' 79.
89 H. Gordon Skilling, 'People's Democracy in Soviet Theory I' (1951) 3 *Soviet Studies* 16.
90 Felipe García Casals, 'Theses on the Syncretic Society' (1980) 9 *Theory and Society* 233.
91 Andrzej Leder, *Prześniona rewolucja* (Warszawa: Wydawnictwo Krytyki Politycznej, 2014).
92 Dan Stone, *Goodbye to All That: A History of Europe since 1945* (Oxford: OUP, 2014), 96.

repression in Budapest and Prague, revealed not only the limits of the autonomy of local communist parties, but also the essential fracture within the type of communism in Central and Eastern Europe. The Solidarity revolution of 1980, brought brutally to a halt by the Martial Law imposed on 13 December 1981, was aptly described as a properly proletarian movement, aiming to hold the Party to account for its failure to live up to the promises of Marxism.[93] To increase the paradoxical character of this situation, one should add that the Martial Law as such paved the way to neoliberal transformation and it was under its shield that the first elements of the rule of law (constitutional court, ombudsman) were built.

This brings us to the *fourth transition*, when, after 45 years of the state-socialist experiment, all countries of the region embarked upon a transformation towards capitalism, fitted with a superstructure of liberal democracy and the rule of law, within the framework of states which regained their sovereignty from the Soviet hegemon.[94] Once again, independent institution-building was taking place, but already in the early 1990s the direction of integration with the European Communities began to dictate the form and content of law and the outlook of legal institutions.

Indeed, most countries of the region joined the European Union in 2004, 2007, or 2011, and the outstanding ones are candidates for membership. Accession to the EU – which can be described as the *fifth transition* – meant the need to accept the voluminous *acquis communautaire*, a legal heritage developed in Western Europe since 1951, that is over the time-span of over five decades, which had to be implemented into the legal systems of Central and Eastern European "new Member States" within about a decade or so, separating association and accession agreements. Joining the Union entailed a profound intake of legal transplants, a pattern already well-known in the semi-peripheral region. Judges who, until 1989, were dependent on the communist party, who only since 1990 were learning how to function as an independent branch of government in a state under the rule of law, were now asked to also become Union judges, applying EU law and national law, making preliminary references to the ECJ, and taking into account the principles of primacy, direct effect, or proportionality.

The populist onslaught, represented by the rule of United Right in Poland and Fidesz in Hungary, given its profound impact upon the *de iure* (Hungary) or *de facto* (Poland) constitutional design, can be described as a *sixth transition*, marked by profound EU-sceptic sentiments, fuelled by ethnonationalist

93 Rafał Mańko, '"Our Fatherland has found itself on the verge of an abyss...": Poland's 1981 Martial Law, or the Unexpected Appearance of the State of Exception under Actually Existing Socialism' in Cercel et al. (eds), *States*, 140–66.

94 See, e.g., Kazimierz Z. Poznański, *Constructing Capitalism: The Reemergence of Civil Society and Liberal Economy in the Post-Communist World* (Boulder, CO: Westview Press, 1992).

and conservative-clerical ideology. All in all, six juridico-political transitions, often with profound socio-economic and cultural implications, are a lot over the timespan of less than a century (counting from 1918), and certainly quantitatively but also qualitatively more than experienced at the same time in Western Europe.

0.4.3 Deep Traumas

Profound transitions do not come about without deep traumas. The first transition, from the age of Empires to new CEE nation-states, not only occurred on the ashes of World War I, but also frequently was the outcome of local wars, for instance, the Hungarian-Romanian-Czechoslovak war quelling the Hungarian Revolution, the Polish-Soviet War, or the wars in the Baltics.[95] During World War II, which represents a threshold preceding the emergence of state socialism, Central and Eastern Europe was positively turned into a site of genocide,[96] with catastrophic consequences that have shaped the politics, law, and the memory of the region until today. Whereas Nazi occupiers smashed the statehood of Poland or, to an extent, of Czechoslovakia, the Red Army smashed the social structures of feudal land ownership and capitalist structures of industry and commerce. Although millions of workers and peasants could now accede to education and culture and were clearly the beneficiaries of the revolution from above,[97] we must not forget the trauma of the former elites, many of whom did not survive the War, targeted by the occupiers seeking to annihilate the human substance of independent statehood.

The transition from actually existing socialism to capitalism was not a bloody one, but still, for many people, traumatic. Hasty privatisations,[98] mass layoffs, the sudden deterioration of life conditions not backed by a welfare state, contributed to a deeply traumatic memory of the post-1989 transformation among many belonging to the Central and Eastern European working classes.[99] Liberal freedoms and the rule of law, dear to the intellectual and legal elites, meant little to those who struggled to feed their children.

If the transition from socialism to capitalism was a deep trauma for many within the working class, the on-going populist transition is a trauma for the liberal elites. Mirosław Wyrzykowski, former judge of the Polish

95 Enzo Traverso, *Fire and Blood: The European Civil War, 1914–1945* (London: Verso, 2017), 71–5.

96 Omer Bartov, 'Eastern Europe as the Site of Genocide' (2008) 80 *Journal of Modern History* 557.

97 See, e.g., Wiesław Żółtkowski (ed.), *Zrozumieć PRL* [Understanding People's Poland] (Warszawa: Muza, 2012).

98 See, e.g., Liviu Damşa, *The Transformation of Property Regimes and Transitional Justice in Central Eastern Europe* (Cham: Springer 2016).

99 See, e.g., Jane Hardy, *Poland's New Capitalism* (London-New York: Pluto Press, 2009).

Constitutional Court, describes what has been happening in Poland as an occurrence of the "unimaginable,"[100] Wojciech Sadurski, a Polish-Australian legal sociologist, speaks of a "constitutional breakdown."[101] At the same time, however, Bojan Bugarič points out that '[c]onstitutional courts and other rule of law institutions in Central and Eastern Europe always lacked the necessary support of genuinely liberal political parties and programs, leaving the courts vulnerable to attacks from populists.'[102] Liberal rule of law institutions also did not find much social legitimacy, being focused on abstractly framed liberal rights rather than pressing social issues.[103] The Polish case is notable here, with the Constitutional Court's attempts to gain popular legitimacy through pro-social decisions coming too late and offering too little.[104]

It is precisely in this *longue durée* historical context of weak institutional traditions, frequent and profound transformations, and deep traumas affecting both the masses and the elites (although not necessarily on the same occasions), that the spectacle of right-wing illiberal populism is unfolding today in the Central and Eastern European semi-periphery. At the same time, we must not forget that what is now a trauma for the liberal elites, constitutes an important legitimising factor in the eyes of the masses, enjoying symbolic recognition of their resentments.[105]

0.4 Structure of the Book

The present volume consists of ten topical interventions, inspired broadly by critical legal perspectives, looking into various aspects of the current populist upsurge in Central and Eastern Europe in its relation to the juridical. The first two chapters by Przemysław Tacik and Cosmin Cercel set the theoretical scene. In Chapter 1 on 'Populism, Legal Studies, and CEE: Some Meta-Reflections' Tacik reconstructs the *episteme* in which concepts like "populism" emerged and gained traction, noting that it is determined by a set of partly overlapping oppositions, in which liberal "legality" (identified with the rule of law) is opposed with populist "politics" and Western Europe is contrasted with the post-socialist CEE region. In Chapter 2 entitled 'Against

100 Mirosław Wyrzykowski, 'Experiencing the Unimaginable: The Collapse of the Rule of Law in Poland' (2019) 11 *Hague J Rule Law* 417.

101 Wojciech Sadurski, *Poland's Constitutional Breakdown* (Oxford: OUP, 2019).

102 Bojan Bugarič, 'Central Europe's Descent into Autocracy: A Constitutional Analysis of Authoritarian Populism' (2019) 17(2) *International Journal of Constitutional Law* 597, 614.

103 Jacek Srokosz, 'The Influence of Americanisation on Polish Philosophy of Law and Legal Practice After 1989' in Sulikowski et al. (eds), *Legal Scholarship*, 166.

104 For details, see Chapter 3.

105 Cf. Maciej Gdula, *Nowy autorytaryzm* [The New Authoritarianism] (Warszawa: Wydawnictwo Krytyki Politycznej, 2018).

"Populism": Critical Legal Studies and Authoritarian Politics in Central and Eastern Europe' Cercel subjects the notion of "populism" to a further theoretical critique, considering it to be a 'failed epistemic device,' entangled as it were 'in a specific arrangement of power and knowledge that operates as a positive stopgap for grasping the social and political phenomena structurally supporting authoritarian politics in relation to law.' Drawing on psychoanalytical metaphors, Cercel urges legal scholars to return to an analysis of law as politics, and going directly to the heart of the matter which he thematises as nothing else than "post-fascism."

With this threshold, the book passes from theoretical reflection on historical entanglements of legality in CEE to more focused case studies of particular CEE countries. Instead of aspiring to present comprehensive "national reports," we rather aim to present exemplary problems of CEE legality. Taken together, they offer a dynamic, multi-perspective account of legal vicissitudes in this part of Europe. This section opens with Adam Sulikowski's Chapter 3 on 'The Polish Constitutional Court in the Grip of Neoliberalism' which exemplifies the typical historical sequence of legalities in CEE: the Court was established during the last phase of socialist legality, and, following the transformation, it became a crucial enabler of the new liberal legality (legitimising privatisations and delegitimising workers' rights), before trying to embark, just before its populist takeover, on a belated pro-welfare turn. The topic of constitutionalism and rights is continued in Chapter 4 by Karolina Kocemba and Michał Stambulski who offer a critical analysis of the Polish right-wing populists' complex relation to human rights. They claim that the populists are restricting rights stemming from liberal legality, such as LGBT rights, reproductive or asylum seekers' rights, at the same time as social rights are being actively reinforced. Rafał Mańko's Chapter 5 on '*Exceptio Popularis*: Resisting Illiberal Legality,' takes a step back from the constitutional developments in Poland in order to offer a new juridico-political concept which could explain the phenomenon of unilateral suspension of Constitutional Court judgments through the non-publication of their operative part. Drawing on Benjamin and Agamben, he offers the theory of "minor state of exception" as a theorem allowing to thematise the people's effective intrusion into constituted regimes of legality.

The subsequent three chapters draw on case studies from Romania, Hungary, and Slovakia. In Chapter 6 on 'Constitutional Signalling in Neoliberal Times: A Romanian Perspective,' Alexandra Mercescu offers an alternative history of the role that a constitutional court may play in a post-socialist country. In her detailed case studies, she shows how the application of constitutional law – especially of proportionality tests – injects ideological content into a purportedly neutral legal form. Instead of neutrality, the case studies demonstrate how undecisive the Court was when faced with complicated topics of economic policy so much so that it tried to deliver a message palatable, at least in part, to actors of all political hues. The critique of the particular blend of neoliberal policies and legal ideology in CEE countries continues in Chapter 7 by Mátyás Bencze entitled '"Law Is Not Politics" – the Role of the Liberal View on Law in the Rise of "New Populism."' By presenting an elaborate historical panorama, Bencze traces back the roots of autonomisation of the law in Hungary to transformations of socialist legality. Emancipation of jurisprudence from the grasp of Marxist orthodoxy led to its self-grounding and professionalisation. This, in turn, offered a convenient segue into the new, liberal regime, which drew an ideological thick line between law and politics. The Hungarian Constitutional Court in particular donned the cloak of professionally neutral arbiter basing its decision only on law, even though its political biases could be easily demonstrated. This paved the way for an instrumental use of legal realism by populists, who reinvigorated the political context of legality for their own purposes. In Chapter 8 entitled '"Who Stands in the Mirror and Who Stares Back – Tradition of Populism in Slovakia' Peter Čuroš employs philosophical and psychoanalytical discourses in order to grasp the emergence of populism in CEE, as evidenced by the case of Slovakia. Seeking the roots of populist tendencies in the crisis provoked by post-modern depoliticised liberal politics, he identifies deep patterns in the history of CEE countries, demonstrating how periods of liberal constitutionalisation alternate with authoritarian rule that typically dismantles judicial independence.

The final two chapters focus on the place of right-wing, conservative collective memory and the legacy of the communist past. Thus, in Chapter 9, 'Judicializing Communism: Transitional Justice and Nationalist Populism in the Uneven Time-Space of Eastern Europe' Saygun Gökarıksel explores the role of law and the mechanisms of transitional justice in the criminalisation of communism, taking Poland as a case study. Mikhail Antonov's Chapter 10 on 'Russian Conservatism and Populism: Between the Legal and the Political,' written back in 2020, focuses on similarities and differences in the emergence of identitiarian and conservative narratives in the CEE and Russia, concluding that the common socialist past and peripherality vis-à-vis the West might be the deeper roots of the populist wave. A strong point of Antonov's analysis is the concept of "populism-in-law" which, instead of analysing how populists instrumentalise the law for the sake of power, grasps how 'ideological narratives are used to gain approval of the population for laws.'

The book ends with concluding remarks by Adam Sulikowski and Rafał Mańko who, drawing on the common themes of the chapters, make a final plea for a region-specific methodological approach with regard to the critique of populism and law in the Central and Eastern European semi-periphery.

Chapter 1

Populism, Legal Studies, and CEE

Some Meta-Reflections

Przemysław Tacik

1.1 Introduction

In a glimpse of purely phenomenological perception, the concept of populism – regardless of how problematic it is in itself[1] – has invaded legal studies in recent years.[2] It has been elevated to the position of a key that opens the door to understanding how law is mired in politics and how politics can backlash against the futile attempts of the legal system to depoliticise itself. It has been frequently used in order to account for politico-legal transformations in Central-Eastern and South-Eastern Europe. Other countries of the world, such as the US under Trump, Brazil, or the Philippines, have equally been classified as resorting to "populist" measures. The stunning career of this term may be deplored, as a sign of how impoverished our thinking on relations between law and politics has become. Numerous other terms, such as "illiberalism,"[3] only wait in line to take the place of "populism," still troubled by its vagueness and ideologically dubious origins.[4] "Populism," apart from being a codename that liberal politics uses for all measures and

1 Zoran Oklopcic, 'Imagined Ideologies: Populist Figures, Liberalist Projections, and the Horizons of Constitutionalism' (2019) 20 *German Law Journal* 201.

2 Paul Blokker, 'Populism as a Constitutional Project' (2019) 17 *International Journal of Constitutional Law* 536; Oran Doyle, 'Populist Constitutionalism and Constituent Power' (2019) 20 *German Law Journal* 161; Gábor Hálmai, 'Is There Such Thing as "Populist Constitutionalism"? The Case of Hungary' (2018) 11 *Fudan Journal of the Humanities and Social Sciences* 7; Lucian Bojin and Alexandra Mercescu, 'Protests in Romania: Civil Society, Populism and Civic Constitutionalism' in Alexandra Mercescu (ed.), *Constitutional Identities in Central and Eastern Europe* (Berlin: Peter Lang, 2020), 209–23; Luigi Corrias, 'Populism in a Constitutional Key: Constituent Power, Popular Sovereignty and Constitutional Identity' (2016) 12(6) *European Constitutional Law Review* 6.

3 Laurent Pech and Kim Lane Scheppele, 'Illiberalism Within: Rule of Law Backsliding in the EU' (2017) 19 *Cambridge Yearbook of European Legal Studies* 4; András Sajó, 'The Rule of Law as Legal Despotism: Concerned Remarks on the Use of "*Rule of Law*" in Illiberal Democracies' (2019) 11 *Hague Journal on the Rule of Law* 376.

4 Gábor Attila Tóth, 'Constitutional Markers of Authoritarianism' (2019) 11 *Hague Journal on the Rule of Law* 37, 41–2.

DOI: 10.4324/9781032624464-2

tactics that escape its repertoire, is helplessly overused and turned into a political label. Yet at the same time the rise of this concept may be welcomed as a step towards undermining the all-too-easy understandings of the law inherited from the epoch of uncontested neoliberal hegemony.[5] In this vein, the very emergence of "populism" in legal studies is a sign of its need to address the link between the legal and the political. Even without imposing any methodological judgments, the presence of this notion already at the heart of legal scholarship must be recognised as a sign of its repoliticisation.

Nonetheless, the concept of populism in legal studies is like a thorn in a human body. Although it has already earned its *droit d'asile*, it still remains a term loosely borrowed from political studies and political discourses.[6] Consequently, legal scholarship is externally determined: just as populism itself is an irruption of the political at the heart of liberal depoliticisation, so, does its concept constitute an intervention from the outside into the logic of legal studies? If so, we might claim that by using the concept of populism legal studies not only confront a real political antagonism that it connotes, but address *their own complex relationship both to the political and to political studies*. The emergence of a crossover field of populist studies, where legal and political scholarships freely meet, mirrors – in a sense – the clash of liberal politics with its rules of what can be politicised and what cannot with the populist irruption that blurs hitherto existing distinctions.

Still, the principal problem with legal studies taking up this term is the fact that it is rarely used in a thought-out manner. It rather seems that legal scholarship absorbed it in order to tackle the political onslaught on the stronghold of liberal legality which aimed to preserve politics in a circumscribed field.[7] In other words, "populism" is a concept developed precisely in order to create a

5 See Cosmin Cercel, 'The Destruction of Legal Reason: Lessons from the Past' (2019) 89 *Acta Universitatis Lodziensis – Folia Iuridica* 15.

6 Jan-Werner Müller, *What Is Populism?* (Philadelphia: University of Pennsylvania Press, 2016); Cas Mudde, Cristobal Rovira Kaltvasser, *Populism: A Very Short Introduction* (Oxford: OUP, 2017); Cristobal Rovira Kaltvasser, Paul Taggart, Paulina Ochoa Espejo, Pierre Ostiguy, *The Oxford Handbook of Populism* (Oxford: OUP, 2017); Benjamin De Cleen, Jason Glynos, Aurelien Mondon, 'Critical Research on Populism: Nine Rules of Engagement' (2018) 25 *Organization* 649; Benjamin De Cleen, Yannis Stavrakakis, 'Distinctions and Articulations: A Discourse Theoretical Framework for the Study of Populism and Nationalism' (2017) 24 *Javnost-The Public* 301; Paris Aslanidis, 'Is Populism an Ideology? A Refutation and a New Perspective' (2016) 64 *Political Studies* 88; Yves Mény, Yves Surel, *Democracy and the Populist Challenge* (London: Palgrave, 2012); Jasper Muis, Tim Immerzeel, 'Causes and Consequences of the Rise of Populist Radical Right Parties and Movements in Europe' (207) 65(6) *Current Sociology Review* 909; NW Barber, 'Populist Leaders and Political Parties' (2019) 20 *German Law Journal* 129; Axel Mueller, 'The Meaning of "Populism"' (2019) 45(9–10) *Philosophy and Social* 1025.

7 For an excellent map of terms that have been used in legal studies in order to address the ongoing transformations see: Tom Gerald Daly, 'Democratic Decay: Conceptualising an Emerging Research Field' (2009) 11 *Hague Journal on the Rule of Law* 9.

buffer separating the doctrine from challenges of populism as a real phenomenon. It often lacks not only the empirical rigidity with which this concept is used in political science, but – even more importantly – a deepened theoretical background on the relationship between the political and the legal that is required in order to adequately understand "populism." If populism itself is a confounding phenomenon that blurs and undermines existing politico-legal frameworks, its conceptual representation is no less troublesome. The real populism is, in fact, a pack of political measures and ideological gestures of family resemblance (in Wittgenstein's understanding) that, however, share one trait: they are described negatively, through their anti-liberal edge. Analogously, the concept of populism, as used in legal scholarship, is a protean notion knit together mainly by being posited as *negative vis-à-vis the (liberal) autonomy of the legal*. Hence it cannot be used non-reflectively: its reabsorption into legal studies is more a symptom rather than an adoption of a "tranquil" concept, to use Hegel's terminology. Before phenomena like "populist legality" are analysed, the concept itself requires a critique.

To make the situation even more complex, European legal scholarship is chiefly focused on CEE populism – with its two frontline countries, Hungary and Poland, that openly chose the path of building their own respective versions of hybrid illiberalism. If we set aside – for the time being – the reasons why it was CEE that proved the weakest link in the chain of liberalism, this geopolitical imbalance produces a rather unfortunate type of gaze: Western, mainly liberal academia, looking at the illiberal East of Europe. Combined with the axis depoliticised v. the political, it pigeonholes CEE in the role of the raw political Borduria that opposes the fortress of legally curbed Western liberal legality. The post-dependence context in these analyses is inevitable; if we are not to be duped by clichés that reproduce geopolitical dominance, "populism" needs to be seen as mired in regional hierarchies of power.

To sum up, populism is a concept deeply entrenched in the ongoing ideological fight that takes place both in politics, the field of law and the academia. The term is as far from being "neutral" as possible: its usage reproduces hierarchies of power and imagery of the Western liberal legality. No one will deny that in contemporary Europe some deep transformations take place that remould the relations between the political and the legal. But the concept with which these transformations are described is not a transparent tool, but part of the struggle. With an inspiration of Foucauldian geological metaphors, it may be claimed that "populism" lies at the tectonic rift between the waning liberal hegemony, on which the independence of the law (and, consequently, of legal scholarship) is pegged, and the anti-liberal irruption of the political that still seeks a name and a form for itself. By using this term, we are sucked into the long chain of skirmishes between these two blocks that aim to present themselves as consolidated, in between which *tertium non datur*. The task of the critique is to see how "populism" is a term that cuts across the political, the legal, and the academic, revealing – at the same time – their deep entanglements.

The aim of this chapter is to provide some key meta-reflections on "populism," both as a concept and a phenomenon that nags at contemporary CEE and SEE. I will begin with a critical overview of the term itself in its entrenchment in political struggles of contemporary Europe. Then I will attempt to identify the current episteme in which "populism" as a concept is blocked, producing some popular legal myths. Finally, a new term – the European legal war – will be proposed in order to address contemporary populism in all its complexity, including its geopolitical dimension.

1.2 Populism as an Overdetermined Floating Signifier in the Field of Political Struggle

Contemporary populism in Europe (especially in CEE and SEE) eludes simplistic definitions; abundant use of the term in legal studies coupled with simultaneous proliferation of related or intentionally synonymic terms, tainting it with more pejorative connotations (such as "illiberalism"[8] or "authoritarianism"[9]) makes it notoriously vague. Contrariwise, designates the concept of the "populist regime" are much easier to determine with Hungary under the Fidesz' rule and Poland under the Law and Justice as the typically adduced examples. Naturally, contemporary populism in CEE is clearly of right-wing hue and thus shares many traits with authoritarian regimes and movements of the interwar period and fascist affiliation:[10] nationalism, strong leadership, xenophobia, scepticism towards universal egalitarian political projects, scapegoating (including persecution of ethnic and sexual minorities) and anti-elitism.[11] Yet the concept of "populism" is neither an umbrella term for them nor their replacement. Its protean nature is a curse for those who expect strong definitions, but a blessing for those who

8 Gábor Halmai, 'An Illiberal Constitutional System in the Middle of Europe' (2015) 14 *European Yearbook of Human Right* 497; Gianluigi Palombella, 'Illiberal, Democratic and Non-Arbitrary? Epicentre and Circumstances of a Rule of Law Crisis' (2018) 10 *Hague Journal on the Rule of Law* 5.

9 Attila Ágh, 'The EU polycrisis and hard populism in East-Central Europe: From the Copenhagen dilemma to the Juncker paradox' (2017) 13 *Politics in Central Europe* 7; Veronika Nagy, 'How to silence the lambs? Constructing authoritarian governance in post-transitional Hungary' (2017) 15 *Surveillance & Society* 447; Daniel R. Kelemen, 'Europe's Other Democratic Deficit: National Authoritarianism in Europe's Democratic Union' (2017) 52 *Government & Opposition* 211.

10 Cosmin Cercel, 'The Destruction,' 15–30.

11 Takis S Pappas, 'Populists in Power' (2019) 30(2) *Journal of Democracy* 70; David Prendergast, 'The Judicial Role in Protecting Democracy from Populism' (2019) 20 *German Law Journal* 245, 246–52; Andrea Pin, 'The Transnational Drivers of Populist Backlash in Europe: The Role of Courts' (2019) 20 *German Law Journal* 225, 227–30.

prefer a symptomal lecture and try to understand academic concepts not as neutral tools, but part of hegemonic transformations within the politico-legal field.

The first thing we need to observe is the condition of structural overdetermination (in the Althusserian understanding[12]) of the term "populism." On the one hand, it means too much: it seems currently able to encompass almost every form of active non-liberal movements, provided that they are relatively recent and still in progress. The reason for it is that "populism" seems to denote processes rather than stable governmentalities; the elements of active development and struggle for self-definition seem to distinguish it from ossified authoritarianisms. For example, one would hardly claim that North Korea or the Chinese People's Republic are populist regimes. The structure of their authoritarian governmentalities is based on principles that predate the rise of contemporary populisms. In order for the term "populism" to be used in contemporary discourse, its denotation must remain in an active relationship with liberal governmentality, usually negating it or denying certain of its elements. But as long as this condition is met, "populism" is an unusually versatile term, comprising various discrepant forms of anti-globalist and anti-(neo)liberal transformations. At the same time, it means too little: its vagueness and difficulty in operationalisation have been ritually deplored by the academia (admittedly, by political sciences rather than legal scholarship). This brings us to the conclusion that "populism" remains an overdetermined term. It does not mean that it should be rejected; but in order to use it, we need to be aware of its character.

Second, contemporary populism exhibits a few traits that make it problematic to believe in the historical continuity of this phenomenon. Numerous (quite classic) theorisations attempt to present it as existing at least since the French Revolution, if not since ancient Rome.[13] Not denying that there are some family resemblances between possible historical "incarnations" of populism, it should be asserted that contemporary populism remains specific to the point that the assumption of an easy historical continuity might be a fallacy. This structural break is introduced by what in previous decades was known as *the condition of postmodernity*,[14] and now, with the benefit

12 Althusser borrowed this term from Freud in order to explain the specificity of Marxist (chiefly Marx's and Lenin's) contradiction in contrast to Hegel's dialectics. See Louis Althusser, 'Sur Marx et Freud' in *Écrits sur la psychanalyse. Freud et Lacan* (Paris: STOCK/IMEC, 1993), 224-225.

13 See for example Roger Eatwell, 'Populism and Fascism' in *The Oxford Handbook on Populism*, 363–82.

14 See Jean-François Lyotard, *The Postmodern Condition* (Manchester: Manchester University Press, 1984); Fredric Jameson, *Postmodernism, or, the Cultural Logic of Late Capitalism* (Durham: Duke University Press, 1991); David Harvey, *The Condition of Postmodernity* (Malden & Oxford: Blackwell, 1990).

of hindsight, may be described as virtual turbocapitalism producing a right-wing travesty of the notion of modernity.[15] Based on the so-called new media and virtualisation of discourse – now built on inescapable irony, parody, and recycling of signifiers – the new populism plays on the repertoire of historical elements in order to produce fleeting discursive constellations that ideologically veil struggles for power.[16] The image of a contemporary populist is that of a clown – either deliberately adopted, as in the case of Trump and Duterte (although pioneered by Berlusconi), or emerging from the pompous spectacle of sabre-brattling and muscle-flexing that sharply contrasts with the complexity of the modern world (as in the case of Orbán and Kaczyński). In this sense, contemporary populism is 'really existing postmodernism' that produces a permanent Baudrillardian spectacle that successfully covers the real of class struggle and geopolitical hegemonies.[17]

This condition *makes contemporary populism a phenomenon that parasites on the history of liberal – authoritarian struggles.* As argued by Enzo Traverso,[18] contemporary right-wing populist movements develop in the reality of post-fascism: they are neither fascist (as a historical determination) nor usually neo-fascist (apart from some rather marginal groups). In the postmodern condition the solid formations of fascism or Nazism become dismembered into pieces that may be arbitrarily re-assembled. The post-fascist formations combine rhetorical gestures and institutional arrangements of actual fascism with elements of liberal governmentality. Their in-built ironical and parodical qualities make the ideological layer further distanced from the level of measures actually undertaken.

15 As Göran Thorborn noticed, 'Although the intellectual wave of postmodernism has now subsided, the right-wing revival of modernity persists. The contamination of social Darwinism by Fascism is being pushed under the rug, while globalization is staged as the survival of the fittest alone, free from Spencerian pacifism and accompanied instead by a loud neo-imperial drumbeat. The "modern" is becoming the property of liberal reaction. "Modernizing" the labour market usually means more rights for capital and employers. "Modernizing" social services usually means the privatization of and cuts to public services. "Modernizing" the pension system generally means fewer rights for old people. ...Were socialist modernism a species, it would be almost extinct." Göran Thorborn, *From Marxism to Post-Marxism?* (London & New York: Verso, 2008), 32.

16 Mudde and Rovira Kaltwasser, *Populism*, 108.

17 As Maurizio Ferraris noted already in 2009, 'La dissoluzione dei fatti nelle interpretazioni e del mondo nel testo ha anticipato non il mondo emancipato di cui parlevano Nietzsche e i postmoderni, ma il populismo e l'autoritarismo.' Maurizio Ferraris, *Documentalità. Perché è necessario lasciar tracce* (Bari-Roma: Laterza 2009) 85–6.

18 Enzo Traverso, *The New Faces of Fascism. Populism and the Far Right*, tr. D. Broder (London & New York: Verso, 2019) 10–20. See also Mikkel Bolt Rasmussen, 'Postfascism, or the Cultural Logic of Late Capitalism' (*Third Text*, vol. 32, no. 5–6, 2018) 682–8.

For this reason, it may be problematic to speak of re-traditionalisation[19] in "really existing populisms":[20] much as they return to arrangements predating liberal democracy (for example the clear supremacy of the executive over the judiciary), they still build hybrid regimes[21] with a selection of liberal elements, picked *à la carte*. *Nota bene*, the "returns" that these regimes play with have as their objects not only the pre-WWII authoritarian gestures, but also the socialist period. In this respect, inner inconsistencies of CEE populisms are striking.[22] Polish populists in particular mastered the revival of some practical elements of the Polish People's Republic: the informal top role of the party in the political system, trumping the official hierarchy of institutions, priority of the executive, inapplicability of constitutional norms (which have been effectively modified by sub-constitutional laws that cannot be repealed despite their incompliance with the Constitution because the Constitutional Court is a marionette of the ruling party), poor quality of legislation, always supplemented with the "political will" that motivated it and "should" guide the institutions which apply it. Alongside these political transformations, Polish populists revived some ideological gestures from the socialist period, such as praising state property, anti-elitism, anti-Western resentments as well as permanent scapegoating. As a result, 'the really existing populism' is an unorthodox blend: although generally it is symbolically and ideologically located on the far-right, it combines elements of different breed. Analogously to pre-WWII fascisms, CEE populisms conceive of themselves as "traditionalist revolutions",[23] turning the purported reestablishment of the past with violent and active transformations.

Quite clearly, the current populisms cannot be isolated from the postmodern foundations they flourish upon. "Populism" does not connote an unambiguous set of practices, but rather a volatile field of practices and rhetoric that readily mingles past and contemporaneous elements to reach its goals. *Therefore, it seems more substantiated to take 'populism' for a floating signifier in a discursive practice that oscillates between the academic field and political involvement.* As a consequence, beyond the Weberian spirit

19 See Андрей Медушевский, "Конституционная ретрадиционализация в Восточной Европе и России" (2018) 122(1) *Сравнительное конституционное обозрение* 13.

20 See Attila Ágh, 'Cultural War and Reinventing the Past in Poland and Hungary: The Politics of Historical Memory in East-Central Europe' (2016) 45 *Polish Political Science Yearbook* 32.

21 Halmai, 'An Illiberal,' 512; Tóth, 'Constitutional Markers,' 41–2.

22 Attila Antal, 'Communist Populism in Hungary' (2018) 40(4) *Society and Economy* 622.

23 See Balázs Jarábik, 'From Belarus to Hungary: Lessons from a Traditionalist Revolution' in Péter Krasztev and Jon Van Til (eds), *The Hungarian Patient. Social Opposition to an Illiberal Democracy* (CEU Press, 2015) 319–24.

of value-neutral scientific analysis,[24] "populism" inextricably quilts three dimensions: (1) political auto-identification (usually through repudiation of the term "populist") by the regime, (2) descriptive discursive practice of politics and mass media, and (3) academic reflection. The current academia borrows this term from its socio-political environment and cannot make it artificially rigid without losing the overdetermination preserved in the designation as "populist." This imbroglio deprives scholars of the possibility to study populist regimes "objectively" by requiring them to self-position on the political map.

As a consequence, the lines of political division are reproduced in academia that addresses the "problem" of populism. Inevitably, scholarly discourses are biased towards the status quo. As long as they believe to portray populism in a neutral, objective way, but lack substantial dialectical critique, they use languages and perspectives of the undermined liberal hegemony. The aura of academic disengagement and neutrality – a crucial element in the Weberian ideal of social sciences – posit the existing scholarship at another front of the struggle for which "populist governmentality" is one name. Political science often seems to harbour a myth of being able to operationalise populism without demonstrating its own position.[25] Legal studies, however, are afflicted by an even more problematic entanglement. As long as they cultivate the liberal vision of the political entirely curbed by the legal, they reproduce the exact position against which populism is directed. Consequently, their independence both from the political and from political studies poses a significant obstacle on their way to critically grasp the ongoing transformations.

1.3 Populism in a Blocked Episteme

To make the situation more complicated, academic analysis of relationships between populism and legality are shaped by the very particular conditions of a transitory *episteme* – to borrow Foucault's term – in which we are currently located. This *episteme* seems to be determined by an entanglement between two powerful discourses: (1) the crumbling, but still potent discourse of liberal constitutionalism, whose hegemony managed to identify each constitutionalism with its liberal form; (2) identification of populism with raw, anomic, or anti-legal political force. The interaction of these two discourses produces some banal diagnoses of contemporary populism

24 See Max Weber, *Science as a Vocation* in *The Vocation Lectures*, tr. by Rodney Livingstone (Indianapolis and Cambridge: Hackett, 2004), 14–31.

25 See Paris Aslanidis, 'Is Populism an Ideology? A Refutation and a New Perspective' (2016) 64 *Political Studies* 88; Benjamin De Cleen, '"Flemish Friends, Let Us Separate!": The Discursive Struggle for Flemish Nationalist Civil Society in the Media (2015) 22(1) *Javnost – The Public* 37.

as "legal nihilism" or pure politics against the rule of law.[26] The power of liberal constitutionalism still lures us into believing that populist legality is no legality whatsoever,[27] or that populist constitutionalism simply does not exist[28] instead of being a paradoxical and incoherent real phenomenon. To sum up, this entanglement deforms and dislocates the field of knowledge on populism and legality. In a nutshell, neither liberal constitutionalism is a universal form of curbing politics, nor is populism just its counterpart based only on the political.

Being determined by the currently dominating *episteme* and the above-described entanglement, *we should avoid the artificial opposition between "real legality" imagined by liberal constitutionalism (construed as purportedly neutral metaregulation of politics*[29]*) and "illegal politics" epitomised by populism.* This opposition is part of political struggle and geopolitical hierarchies (in which "Western" liberal legality is confronted with "Eastern" inherent propensity for authoritarianism). Populism in its relations with contemporary multi-level legality is a thick web of interrelated legal and political acts that cannot be simply subsumed under the label of "pure" anomic politics. Moreover, the geopolitical context of domination and (semi-)peripherality must be part of analysis not as a final *explanans*, but as one of many layers that determine populism as a multi-level backlash against the politico-legal project of liberalism.

The clash of two forms of power-knowledge described above is prone to luring us into unfortunate myths that aim to explain contemporary populism. These myths may be traps for "both sides," that is liberal scholars and politicians as well as populist ones. They provide some answers, but constructed by cutting corners which require critical approach. In what follows I address three big myths, but naturally there are many more minute *idola* which recur in legal scholarship and politics.

The first myth assumes that populism can be identified with legal nihilism, that is a belief in the inexistence or inutility of the law. On the level of constitutional law, such identification entails the assumption that "populist constitutionalism" is a *contradictio in adiecto* that cannot exist. There is already

26 See Marta Bucholc, Maciej Komornik, and Peter Oliver Loew, 'Die PiS und das Recht: Verfassungskrise und polnische Rechtskultur' (2016) 66(1–2) *Osteuropa* 79.

27 This gesture is analogical to the vision of legal inexistence of Communist regimes in popular post-1989 theorisations. See Cosmin Cercel, *Towards A Jurisprudence of State Communism: Law and the Failure of Revolution* (Abingdon: Routledge, 2018).

28 Gábor Hálmai, 'Is there Such Thing,' 7–8. Nonetheless, see other approaches in: David Landau, 'Abusive Constitutionalism' (2013) 47 *UC Davis Law Review* 189.

29 Melissa Crouch, 'Constitutionalism After Authoritarian Rule' (2019) 11 *Hague Journal on the Rule of Law* 349, 350.

an increasing volume of scholarship on "populist constitutionalism,"[30] but this term is still received with suspicion, just as if by using it the actions of populist governments against the rule of law were condoned. Nevertheless, it should be taken for a neutral descriptive term: no matter which objections we can raise against particular arrangements that populisms introduce, they have produced some populist constitutionalisms which demand closer scrutiny. Legal nihilism, if it has ever existed, should rather be linked with revolutionary attempts to establish a space free from the law, as in the October Revolution for example,[31] and not the reactionary populisms of EU member states. We need to look beyond the identification of constitutionalism with liberal constitutionalism: it is a trite thing to say that there were, are, and probably will be properly constitutional forms of non-liberal hue. The task of the critique is to understand it better than just claiming that populist constitutions are merely semantic and overridden by political goals of the ruling parties.[32]

Therefore, the really existing populism of today should be perceived as *a chain of events within the law itself*: not only as it regards the emergence of new hybrid forms of constitutionalism in particular populist states, but also in its pan-European consequences. The prolonged existence of two openly populist governmentalities within the EU has changed EU law itself and revealed the disturbing flexibility of its current politico-legal system for accommodating non-liberal regimes. Contrary to what liberal jurisprudence might believe, the EU is not – certainly as of 2021 – built on an unconditional execution of the rule of law: lingering of the European Commission in applying systemic measures against right-wing populist EU countries[33] demonstrates that the erosion of the rule of law at the EU level is part and parcel of the problem. The presence of two hybrid regimes within the EU poisons the entire system of EU law, turning purportedly objective legal instruments into objects of political deals (as evidenced by negotiations around the so-called 'Rule of Law Conditionality Regulation'[34] in December 2020). The

30 Gábor Hálmai, 'A Coup Against Constitutional Democracy. The Case of Hungary' in Mark A. Graber, Sanford Levinson, and Mark Tushnet (eds), *Constitutional Democracy in Crisis?* (Oxford: OUP, 2018) 243–56; Théo Fournier, 'From Rhetoric to Action, a Constitutional Analysis of Populism' (2019) 20 *German Law Journal* 362, 365–74.

31 See Peteris Stučka, 'The Marxist Concept of Law' in *Selected Writings on Soviet Law and Marxism* (Armonk and London: M.E. Sharpe, 1988) 22–37.

32 Gábor Attila Tóth, 'Constitutional Markers,' 51–2.

33 Attila Ágh, 'The EU Polycrisis and Hard Populism in East-Central Europe: From the Copenhagen Dilemma to the Juncker Paradox' (2017) 13 *Politics in Central Europe* 7, 13–26; Peter Oliver, Justine Stefanelli, 'Strengthening the Rule of Law in the EU: The Council's Inaction' (2016) 54(5) *Journal of Common Market Studies* 1075.

34 Regulation 2020/2092 of the European Parliament and of the Council of 16 December 2020 on a general regime of conditionality for the protection of the Union budget, OJ L 433, 22.12.2020, 1–10.

disputes around the need of excluding Poland from the European arrest warrant mechanism due to an open assault on the independence of the judiciary epitomise this conundrum: for the sake of maintaining the principle of mutual trust, the Commission tolerates effective abuses of the judicial system by the Polish government.[35] As a result, the really existing populisms need to be seen as transformations not only within respective domestic legal systems, but within EU law as well.

The second myth makes legal scholars focus solely or mainly on particular violations of legal norms and rule of law standards. Both openly populist government of Europe – Hungary and Poland – committed a stunningly high number of sometimes flagrant violations, related to the judiciary,[36] disrespect of EU law,[37] and human rights violations.[38] Beyond any doubt these need to be recorded and analysed. But the focus on day-to-day violations of the law might make us lose the bigger picture, in which populism in power develops its own politico-legal logics. The focus on legal details is a natural tendency, especially due to the 'salami tactics' used by the populists to dismantle the rule of law: instead of venturing revolutionary transformations, they rather patiently hollow out institutions and slowly, with ample use of targeted legislation, transform domestic legal orders of their countries. Consequently, legal scholars may be easily mired in endless sequences of amendments (in the case of Hungary, even at the constitutional level). Against this myth we should, however, tend to look beyond the matrix of syllogism-based violations of the law.

Finally, the third myth produced by the clash of the above-mentioned forms of knowledge-power is "instrumentalisation" of the law by the populists. It appears as a ready-made explanation of populists' approach towards

35 John Morijn, 'Discussing Imploding Polish Judicial Independence, European Arrest Warrants and Fair Trial in Luxembourg: Silver Linings to a Grim Day?' (*Rule of Law*, 13 October 2020), https://ruleoflaw.pl/cjeu-eaw-poland/ accessed 20 October 2020.

36 *Baka v. Hungary*, App no. 20261/12 (ECHR, 27 May 2014); *Somorjai v. Hungary*, App no. 60934/13 (ECHR, 28 November 2018). See also Anna Śledzińska-Simon, 'The Rise and Fall of Judicial Self-Government in Poland: On Judicial Reform Reversing Democratic Transition' (2018) 19(7) *German Law Journal* 1839; Iustitia, *Justice under pressure—repressions as a means of attempting to take control over the judiciary and the prosecution in Poland. Years 2015–2019* https://www.iustitia.pl/images/pliki/raport2020/Raport_EN.pdf accessed 20 October 2020.

37 Przemysław Tacik, 'Poland's Defiance Against the CJEU in the Puszcza Białowieska Case (C-441/17)' in Clara Rauchegger and Anna Wallerman (eds), *The Eurosceptic Challenge: National Implementation and Interpretation of EU Law* (Oxford: Hart, 2019) 67–86; Case C-715/17, C-718/17 and C-719/17 *European Commission v Republic of Poland, Hungary and the Czech Republic*, ECLI:EU:C:2020:257.

38 See as examples: *Magyar Kétfarkú Kutya Párt v. Hungary*, App no. 201/17 (ECHR, 23 January 2020); *Szabó and Vissy v. Hungary*, App no. 37138/14 (ECHR, 12 June 2016); *Király and Dömötör v. Hungary*, App no. 10851/13 (ECHR 17 January 2017). See also Gábor Attila Tóth, 'Constitutional Markers of Authoritarianism', 54.

legality.[39] The argument is quite simple: contrary to the autotelic respect for legal norms in liberal democracy – for which the law is an overarching and unassailable framework of exercising political power – populists treat legal norms as "instruments" for their particular goals. In so doing, they twist the sense of general norms which no longer serve common and universal purposes, but more or less implicitly aim to satisfy interests of the ruling majority. Interception of constitutional courts—in which Poland gives an ominous example[40] – is a perfect embodiment of this strategy: under the mask of purportedly neutral institutions there are nothing but agents of the ruling populists who use constitutional courts to their own purposes.

Even if the idea of instrumentalisation is justified to some extent, as a generalisation it is based on a false presumption that contemporary complex and multi-level legal systems, deeply embedded in EU law and international law, may be easily subjugated to the will of the ruling majority and made "tools" in their hands. No matter how populists would like to have easy instruments to pursue their goals, the chain of counterreactions and unpredictable perturbations thus produced in the system of the law warp the idea of an "instrument." Truly, one law can be enacted as a tool, but its application will trigger response from other levels of the legal order – if not at the domestic level, it will happen from the part of the EU or the ECtHR.[41] The history of really existing populisms provides ample examples of the fact that instrumentalisation can be an ideal for populists themselves and an explanatory category for legal scholarship, but it falls short of establishing a working system of effective legal tools.

All these myths are intellectual traps that subjugate scholars into the field where the two forms of knowledge-power clash. By necessity, legal

39 See Blokker, 'Populism,' 537.

40 A good overview of the key developments in the crisis can be found in: Wojciech Sadurski, *Poland's Constitutional Breakdown* (Oxford: OUP 2019), 62–5; 'Polish Constitutional Tribunal under PiS: From an Activist Court, to a Paralysed Tribunal to a Governmental Enabler' (*Hague Journal of the Rule of Law*, vol. 11, 2019) 63–84; Sava Jankovic, 'Polish Democracy Under Threat? An Issue of Mere Politics or a Real Danger?' (2016) 9 *Baltic Journal of Law and Politics* 49; Tomasz T Koncewicz, 'The Capture of the Polish Constitutional Tribunal and Beyond: Of Institution(s), Fidelities and the Rule of Law in Flux' (2018) 43 *Review of Central and East European Law* 116.

41 This process is epitomised by the so-called "muzzle law" adopted by the Polish ruling majority in order to prevent the courts from applying a preliminary ruling of the CJEU on the illegality of the Disciplinary Chamber of the Supreme Court (Case C-624/18, C-625/18, and C-585/18 *European Commision v. Poland*, ECLI:EU:C:2019:982). See European Commission for Democracy through Law (The Venice Commission), *Poland—Urgent Joint Opinion on the amendments to the Law on organisation on the Common Courts, the Law on the Supreme Court and other Laws*, Opinion no. 977/2019, 16 January 2020 https://www.venice.coe.int/webforms/documents/?pdf=CDL-PI(2020)002-e accessed 27 October 2020.

scholarship on populism and related issues is warped by it: the very concept of "populism" – as well as his functional synonyms, such as '(neo)-authoritarianism'[42] or 'illiberalism' – traverses the scholarly domain and quilts it, to use a Lacanian concept, at the heart of political struggle. What we acutely need, however, is a critical perspective on populism that would – as much as possible – try to portray the hegemonic *episteme* in its influences rather than succumb to it.

1.4 The European Legal War

In order to grasp the relationship between populism and legality in contemporary Europe as vastly as possible, I propose to use the term 'European legal war' – a concept paraphrasing the well-known idea of the European civil war which describes both World Wars as an internal European web of conflicts. The latter term may be frowned upon for being of ambiguous pedigree, smeared with attempts to downplay the responsibility of Nazis in the infamous *Historikerstreit.*[43] Nonetheless, it has already been extricated from this questionable origin and aptly reused by Enzo Traverso.[44] As a term, it is capable of switching the perspective on European inter- or intra-state conflicts in order to address their continental or global meaning, may be weaned off from its original connotations. Its great added value consists in how it allows to reconstruct a more general line of conflict from an all-too-easy opposition between some CEE "illiberal countries" and the "liberal EU." In this sense it allows to better grasp the current map of antagonisms within the EU.

In a double essay which was finally made part of the *Homo sacer* cycle – *Stasis*[45] – Giorgio Agamben noticed a crucial paradox: the more the contemporary world is afflicted by various forms of 'the global civil war,' with terrorism being one of its symptoms,[46] the less we dispose of a proper theory of the civil war.[47] Discussing the ancient Greek views on the civil war (*stasis*) in its relations to *polis* and *oikos*, Agamben claims:

> The *stasis*—this is our hypothesis—takes place neither in the *oikos* nor in the *polis*, neither in the family nor in the city; rather, it constitutes a zone

42 Maciej Gdula, *Nowy autorytaryzm* (Warszawa: Wydawnictwo Krytyki Politycznej, 2018).
43 Ernst Nolte, *Der europäische Bürgerkrieg, 1917–1945: Nationalsozialismus und Bolschewismus* (Herbig 1997).
44 Enzo Traverso, *Fire and Blood: The European Civil War, 1914–1945* (London & New York: Verso, 2017).
45 Giorgio Agamben, *Stasis: Civil War as a Political Paradigm (Homo Sacer II, 2)* (Stanford: Stanford University Press 2015).
46 Ibid. 24.
47 Ibid. 1–2.

> of indifference between the unpolitical space of the family and the political space of the city. In transgressing this threshold, the *oikos* is politicised; conversely, the polis is 'economised', that is, it is reduced to an *oikos. This means that in the system of Greek politics civil war functions as a threshold of politicisation and depoliticisation, through which the house is exceeded in the city and the city is depoliticised in the family.*[48]

If, following Agamben's example, we understand civil war as 'a threshold of politicisation and depoliticisation' that throws two opposites into dialectical struggle, the phenomenon of right-wing populism within the EU may be interpreted *as a part of the European legal war that determines the boundaries of (de)politicisation of the law.*

This perspective allows to grasp the role of the law in the struggle between CEE populisms and "the liberal centre" that avoids the binary trap of the aforementioned two discourses. The first aims to portray the populist transformations as a somewhat barbarian onslaught on the unquestionable edifice of European legal order[49] being an effect of a peripheral "backsliding" from the otherwise unidirectional democratic development.[50] Such a perspective is founded on the vision of Kelsen-like ultimate circumscription of the political within the boundaries of the law. As if mirroring the interwar debates between Hans Kelsen and Carl Schmitt,[51] the second discourse accentuates irremovability of the political excess within the legal order.[52] Seen in this light, CEE populism is interpreted as a politically motivated rejection of the supremacy of the law. The populists' frequent invocation of "the will of the people" against "elitist" legal institutions clearly corresponds to this discourse.[53]

In a broader perspective, these two views determine camps in the European civil war. Its stake is not a victory that once and for all will define the relations between the law and the political; on the contrary, *this* permanent war is precisely the threshold between the law and the political. There is no

48 Ibid. 16.
49 András Sajó, 'The Rule of Law as Legal Despotism...', 376.
50 Gabor Hálmai, 'Transitional Constitutional Unamendability?' (2019) 21 *European Journal of Law Reform* 262.
51 Cosmin Cercel, *Towards a Jurisprudence*, 18–45.
52 See Théo Fournier, 'From Rhetoric,' 365–6.
53 According to Takis S Pappas, populism 'holds that society is split by a single overriding cleavage between the vast majority and a tiny elite, and asserts that this cleavage is unbridgeable. Populist politics, therefore, is all about social hostility and incessant conflict. In such a view, the rule of law and the protection of minority rights become secondary.' Takis S. Pappas, 'Populists in Power' (*Journal of Democracy*, vol. 30, no. 2, 2019) 71. This view, however, is marred by the tacit presumption that the rule of law can 'truly' abstract from the legal war that underlies it.

overarching framework to be established apart from it or "after" it is won: the framework of relations is nothing but a moment within this war.

The reason why it is the rule of law that condensates contemporary political disputes within the EU is to be found precisely in the question of politicisation and depoliticisation.[54] Right-wing populism today repoliticises matters hitherto shielded by the complex edifice of the European legal order, encompassing international law, European law, legal standards, and requirements as to constitutional guarantees of the rule of law. It is not an attack against the law "itself," but an attempt to actively define the threshold of politicisation which circumscribes it. In this sense, the character of the populist revolt has been determined by the almost unconditional victory of the liberal understanding of the law as an overarching framework that organises the political within its boundaries.

Therefore, legal theory has become "another scene" (in the Freudian-Derridean sense[55]) on which the European civil war is fought. Its principal stake is to be found elsewhere, in re-politicisation of the law – but theoretical debates on populism and the law is a theatre of shadows in which this war can be indirectly recognised. Crucially, it is not a war of 'models' regulating relations between law and fact; models would be here just temporary ideological tools. It is for this reason that 'illiberal democracies' of CEE have little original to offer in terms of constitutional arrangements. This war is nothing but a map of shifting goalposts that separate the legal from the political, while constitutional norms provide a bank of flagpoles erected to mark the conquered territory.

1.5 The Eastern Front: The European Legal War and the 'Other Europe'

If we adopt the concept of the European legal war, a crucial question emerges: why does the crucial front of this war run across Central-Eastern Europe? Naturally, the fight for repoliticisation or depoliticisation of the law continues elsewhere in Europe, as part of the global struggles within world capitalism. Yet in the West populist movements rarely grasp or even approach power (with the notable exception of Italy), whereas two countries of CEE have turned into openly illiberal countries, with other CEE states openly flirting with some measures dubbed as "populist," regardless of political affiliations.

54 See Gian-Giacomo Fusco and Michalis Zivanaris, 'The Neutralisation of the Political. Carl Schmitt and the Depoliticisation of Europe' (2022) 30(2) *Journal of Contemporary European Studies* 363.

55 Jacques Derrida, 'Freud and the Scene of Writing' in *Writing and Difference* (Abingdon: Routledge 2005), 246-291.

Legal scholarship on populism has found a mystifying answer to this question, in which the European legal war is ideologically reproduced by distorting it along the lines of geopolitical hegemonic tensions: 'backsliding.'[56] It looks at the history of CEE and SEE in an artificially historical perspective: the ongoing populist transformations are presented as a return to pre-liberal times. The underlying conceptuality seems simple: while Western Europe was a seat of mature liberal democracy, CEE and SEE made their attempt to build liberal institutions but failed on their way, sliding back into some kind of age-old authoritarianism or illiberalism. This answer squares well with well-known strategies of othering the East, as a seat of recurrent barbarianism only tactically covered with liberal varnish.[57]

Moreover, "backsliding" is a term built upon a grid of tacit presuppositions dating back to the years of unquestionable hegemony of neoliberalism. In the 1990s and the 2000s, the relation between CEE and SEE countries and Western standards was described in terms of socialisation to international and European norms.[58] The path seemed linear: Western Europe provided a solid framework of legal standards, based on the rule of law and human rights protection, which the Eastern European countries needed to adopt if they wanted to get away from the apparent total failure of state socialism. Their compliance with these norms could be measured as assessed, not only in scholarship, but even more importantly – by EU institutions assessing the capacity of CEE / SEE states to join the EU. It seems that at that time the academia inherited its evaluating gaze from political mechanisms. Especially

56 Pech and Scheppele, 'Illiberalism,' 4–12; Kelemen, 'Europe's Other,' 212–8; Ulrich Sedelmeier, 'Anchoring Democracy from Above? The European Union and Democratic Backsliding in Hungary and Romania after Accession' (2014) 52(1) *Journal of Common Market Studies* 105; Dimitry V. Kochenov, 'Article 7: A Commentary on a Much Talked-About "Dead" Provision' (2018) 38 *Polish Yearbook of International Law* 166; Marta Bucholc, 'Commemorative Lawmaking: Memory Frames of the Democratic Backsliding in Poland After 2015' (2019) 11 *Hague Journal on the Rule of Law* 85; Sadurski, 'Polish Constitutional Tribunal,' 64.

57 See Rafał Mańko, Martin Škop, and Markéta Štěpáníková, 'Carving out Central Europe as a Space of Legal Culture: A Way out of Peripherality?' (2016) 6(2) *Wroclaw Review of Law, Administration & Economics* 4.

58 Frank Schimmelfennig, Stefan Engert, and Heiko Knobel, *International Socialization in Europe European Organizations. Political Conditionality and Democratic Change* (Basingstoke and New York: Palgrave MacMillan 2006); Jeffrey T. Checkel, *International Institutions and Socialization in Europe* (Cambridge: Cambridge University Press, 2007); Susan Park, 'Socialisation and the Liberal Order' (2014) 51 *International Politic* 334; Quddus Z. Snyder, 'The Illiberal Trading State: Liberal Systemic Theory and the Mechanism of Socialization' (2013) 50(1) *Journal of Peace Research* 35; Judith Kelley, 'International Actors on the Domestic Scene: Membership Conditionality and Socialization by International Institutions' (2004) 58(3) *International Organizations* 428; Trine Flockhart, 'Complex Socialization: A Framework for the Study of State Socialization' (2006) 12(1) *European Journal of International Relations* 104.

political science indulged in producing theorisations of socialisation that contained factors – both domestic and international – of successful or unsuccessful compliance with liberal standards:

> the sustained compliance with liberal norms in most of the CEECs with a liberal party constellation is strongly indicative of internalization. These countries have attained high conformance levels ahead of EU or NATO accession conditionality and have maintained them across numerous elections and changes in government. This observation suggests, however, that the contribution of international institutions to internalization has been small. At best, they have helped to reinforce and stabilize a preexisting domestic consensus (which may well have formed by diffuse transnational influences during the Cold War). It is highly probable that these countries would have embarked and continued on the path of democratic consolidation in the absence of any norm promotion by international organizations, be it in the form of persuasion, social influence, or membership incentives.[59]

The socialisation paradigm (the term in itself seems derogatory towards the 'new Europe'[60]), although peculiar to political science rather than legal studies, exemplifies the type of gaze which underpins the concept of "backsliding" in the latter. Due to this entanglement, it is profoundly problematic. First, it assumes linearity of development: the existence of the only one, clear goal, from which one can backslide – which obfuscates different models of the rule of law. Second, socialisation and backsliding from it are based on the liberal hegemony of the West. What was, however, almost unquestionable in the 1990s and early 2000s, looks much crumblier today. There is no one "healthy" model of liberal democracy in Western Europe; all states are afflicted by a profound antagonism – usually ossifying into the axis "liberal"/"populist" – although to a different extent. Transposing intra-state antagonisms onto a general tension between the West and CEE/SEE is nothing but mystifying the problem. There is a deep affinity between CEE/SEE populists and their allies from Western Europe, such as *Lega*, AfD, or *Rassemblement national*. Third, socialisation is a process in which states should not be taken for ready-made totalities, but rather complex polities in which socialisation is never final and meets with tacit contestation or

59 Frank Schimmelfennig, 'Strategic Calculation and International Socialization Membership Incentives, Party Constellations, and Sustained Compliance in Central and Eastern Europe in: International Institutions and Socialization in Europe' in Checkel, *International Institutions*, 58.

60 See Rafał Mańko, *Being Central European, or some reflections on law, double peripherality and the political in times of transformation* in Tomáš Gábriš, Ján Sombati (eds.), *Central and Eastern Europe as a Double Periphery?* (Berlin: Peter Lang, 2020) 37–38.

sometimes open resistance at various levels of political and social life. The "backlash" against liberal domination is not a one-dimensional phenomenon, but the ultimate result of economic and social struggles both within each CEE/SEE society and in relation between these societies and the West. Fourth, socialisation is not a one-off process that, once successful, builds the ideal liberal democracy for ever. The common goal of development, existing still in the 2000s, was lost in the next decade. Neoliberal hegemony began to crumble in the West especially after the financial crisis in 2008, giving fuel to CEE/SEE populists. Finally, there is an effect of uncanny synergy between EU membership and strengthening of really existing populisms. In a paradoxical manner, populist governmentalities sap European resources in order to build regimes that deny liberal standards: the Hungarian "mafia state" is perhaps the best example of this strategy.[61] Even more importantly, the above-mentioned EU lingering with adopting measures that would defend the rule of law is a sign that the newly adopted liberal agenda of promoting the rule of law and EU values defined in Art. 2 TEU is structurally weak and tradeable for political compromises.

"Backsliding" does not explain one more phenomenon: why did the chief impact of populist backlash affected not the weakest links of the socialised family of CEE / SEE states – those that had trouble with adapting to liberal standards already in the 1990s, like Bulgaria – but Hungary and Poland? Both countries were regional champions of rapid transition to free market, political pluralism and liberal constitutionalism after 1989.[62] In this process adoptions of the rule of law standards was, as Jiří Přibáň once claimed, a 'ticket for a back-to-Europe journey.'[63] The rapidness of the transition in the era of the liberal consensus meant that the rule of law was adopted often hastily, with numerous legal transplants (including constitutional courts and councils of the judiciary) and the aura of unconditionality as to the choice of methods. Quite naturally, some commentators are tempted by the simplifying "regression" story, in which Central-Eastern Europe – Hungary and Poland in particular – attempted to adopt Western patterns but finally failed to do so and returned to the primacy of the political over the legal that seems to have been a trademark of socialist law.[64] Yet this story does not square with the socialisation studies from the 1990s and the 2000s, in which at least the champions of compliance with liberal norms underwent more or less irreversible transformations.

61 Balint Magyar, *Post-Communist Mafia State: The Case of Hungary* (Budapest: CEU Press, 2016).

62 Radosław Markowski, 'Creating Authoritarian Clientelism: Poland After 2015' (2019) 11 *Hague Journal on the Rule of Law* 111, 114–7.

63 Jiří Přibáň, '"From Which Rule of Law?" to "The Rule of Which Law?": Post-Communist Experiences of European Legal Integration' (2009) 1 *Hague Journal on the Rule of Law* 337.

64 Pin, 'The Transnational,' 232. See also Hálmai, 'Transitional,' 262.

As a result, the regression story is deeply problematic. There was nothing 'natural' in this backsliding: it was purposefully chosen to be an element of the agenda of populist parties and, as such, deliberately implemented. In both countries the recoil against the imposition of populist legality from judges, prosecutors, lawyers, and academia was too powerful to believe that the "backward" countries simply returned to the dim realm of legal nihilism they have supposedly always belonged to. Finally, both countries were champions of socialisation to the rule of law and human rights norms. The fact that it was these states that fell victims of populist backlash points out rather to flaws of the socialisation project itself rather than to local and temporary failures of an otherwise successful process.

Moreover, Hungary and Poland may now be European laboratories of populist governmentality, but it would be fallacious to believe that other members of the populist international, such as the French *Rassemblement national*, would not use a similar range of measures if only given a chance to implement them.[65] Countries of CEE may be "weaker links" of liberal democracy, but the fight they witness – including a fierce cultural war between progressives and reactionary conservatives – are the same battles which are fought elsewhere in Europe and in the world. It might seem easy to pigeonhole these states into the category of post-socialist flawed democracies, but this is nothing but exporting the problem which afflicts majority of contemporary democracies to "the wild East."

What is true, however, in the situation of CEE/SEE countries, is their semi-peripheral character.[66] This makes their position structurally different from Russia, which always occupied one of the key poles in every world-system. Even if this role was globally peripheral, it always maintained a direct relation with the leading economic and geopolitical hegemon (Great Britain in

65 Fournier, 'From Rhetoric,' 375–9.

66 Maria Todorova, *Imagining the Balkans* (New York: Oxford University Press, 1997); Fernand Braudel, *Civilization and Capitalism, 15th–18th century: The Structure of Everyday Life* (Berkeley: University of California Press, 1992); Immanuel Wallerstein, *The Modern World System I. Capitalist Agriculture and the Origins of the European World-Economy in the Sixteenth Century* (Berkeley: University of California Press, 1974); Daniel Chirot (ed.), *The Origins of Backwardness in Eastern Europe: Economics and Politics From the Middle Ages Until the Early Twentieth Century* (Berkeley: University of California Press, 1989); Ivan Berend, 'What is Central and Eastern Europe?' (2005) 8(4) *European Journal of Social Theory* 401; Erika Nagy and Judit Timár, 'The (Re)Production of Peripherality in Central and Eastern Europe' (2017) 24(2) *European Spatial Research and Polic* 5; Damjan Kukovec, 'Law and the Periphery' (2015) 21(3) *European Law Journal* 406; Arnulf Becker Lorca, *Mestizo International Law: A Global Intellectual History 1842–1933* (Cambridge: CUP, 2016), 200–20; José M. Magone, Brigid Laffan and Christian Schweiger (eds), *Core-periphery Relations in the European Union Power and Conflict in a Dualist Political Economy* (Abingdon: Routledge, 2018).

the 18th and 19th centuries and later the US).[67] As a result, subducting it into the sphere of influence of the liberal West could only be a short-term project. By contrast, the CEE/SEE countries remained in the semi-peripheral zone of the West for majority of their existence.[68] Only the socialist project may be read as an attempt to construct an economic and political zone that would be independent from the West. Nonetheless, during that period CEE/SEE countries were in the semi-peripheral zone of the Eastern Bloc. Therefore, 1989 marks a watershed for the region: semi-peripherality was preserved, but once again reoriented to the West. Despite constant attempts to bridge the gap, there are still palpable economic differences within the EU that separate "core" Western Europe from its semi-peripheral territories.

This makes CEE/SEE countries a special arena for the European legal war. First, the rule of law – being part of the "acceptance package" that needed to be adopted in order to join Western countries – was adopted in a long series of legal transplants. What requires stressing is that they were not significantly contested at the beginning, but preserved the potential of being undermined with a view to political goals. The following chapters of the book demonstrate that the juxtaposition of legal devices transplanted from the West and the domestic legal elites of the CEE/SEE, largely positivist in spirit and practice, produced a unique form of incontestable liberalism.[69] It was a pro-market, formalistic and somewhat narrow-minded blend of state-centred residues of the socialist legal culture coupled with liberal orthodoxy that was not well understood at its philosophical foundations, but eagerly accepted in its literal dimension.[70] If such generalisations are legitimate, one might claim that post-1989 CEE/SEE was – to a large extent – an arena of mainly literal interpretation, in which constitutional principles that could soften the brutality of pro-market transition remained unused.[71]

In this sense, the European legal war established its "Eastern front" in the early 1990s, when the rapid pro-market tradition was solidified by equally swift adoption of liberal legal standards in the aura of their unquestionability. The threshold of depoliticisation of the law was significantly increased: in lieu

67 Boris Kagarlitsky, *Empire of the Periphery. Russia and the World System*, tr. Renfrey Clarke (London & Ann Arbor, MI: Pluto Press, 2008).

68 See Rafał Mańko, 'Delimiting Central Europe as a Juridical Space: A Preliminary Exercise in Critical Legal Geography' (2019) 89 *Acta Universitatis Lodziensi – Folia Iuridica* 63; idem, 'Being Central European,' 20–9; Jan Sowa, *Fantomowe ciało króla. Peryferyjne zmagania z nowoczesną formą* (Kraków: Universitas, 2011).

69 See Adam Sulikowski, *Government of Judges and Neoliberal Ideology: The Polish Case* in Rafał Mańko, Adam Sulikowski and Cosmin Cercel (eds), *Law and Critique in Central Europe. Questioning the Past, Resisting the Present* (Oxford: Counterpress, 2016), 16–31.

70 See Ewa Łętowska, 'Bariery naszego myślenia o prawie w perspektywie integracji z Europą' (1996) 4–5 *Państwo i Prawo* 45.

71 See Adam Sulikowski, Chapter 3 in this volume.

of the fluid legality of the really existing socialism, in which the political will of the party was capable of trumping legal norms, in the 1990s the law was shrouded with the ideological veil of apolitical objectivity. Consequently, the rule of law in CEE/SEE meant something else than in Western Europe. The societies of the "new Europe" witnessed how flexible the boundary between the political and the legal might be. This, in turn, laid the groundwork for structural suspiciousness vis-à-vis liberal legal institutions. Such a perspective is significantly different from the "backsliding" story: the countries of CEE/SEE did not "backslide" on their unidirectional way to the utopia of liberal democracy, but were traversed by the front of the European legal war in which depoliticisation of the law was the main goal. The really existing populism is not, therefore, a recurrence of some accursed socialist authoritarianism;[72] it is a phenomenon that emerged in the legal battlefield dominated by the vision of unquestionability of the post-socialist liberal hegemony. Therefore, the vision of a "populist backlash" is not adequate insofar as it conveys the message of liberal neutrality that suddenly gave rise to a widespread movement of contestation. The backlash can happen only against a hegemony; but a hegemony does not appear out of itself, but is established in a battle. The really existing populism is just rekindling of the war that began to abate when liberal orthodoxy was at its peak of power.

The rise of populism and/or illiberalism in CEE/SEE should be thus seen as a continuation of the (de/re)politicisation war that afflicts contemporary Europe. The "new" EU countries may have been the weakest links in the chain of liberal hegemony, but we should not be lured: the Eastern front is not the only one. To think that the main problem of the European Union nowadays is the fight of Eastern populists against the rule of law is a kind of intellectual legal fetishism: this fight is obviously significant, yet there are two "buts." First, the war within the law is just another scene of a much more general war, which concerns anthropological visions of relations between human beings resulting in hierarchies of power, economic domination, and violence. It is a war about the possibility of equality and human self-development. By construction of different chains of equivalence,[73] it ossifies into various fronts: patriarchalism against female emancipation, authoritarian communitarianism against individualism, egalitarian inclusivism against exclusionist nationalism – all built upon the fertile mycelium of the class struggle. As a consequence, the war on the relations between the legal and the political is just a privileged scene, exposed by the importance that liberal legality attached to the law as a purportedly neutral medium of governance. In this vein, liberal legality finds its direct counterpart in a mafia state – which is deprived of any ambition to

72 Radoslaw Markowski, 'Creating Authoritarian Clientelism,' 121–5.
73 See Ernesto Laclau and Chantal Mouffe, *Hegemony and Socialist Strategy. Towards a Radical Democratic Politics* (London & New York: Verso, 2001) 127–34.

produce a long-lasting vision of statehood, but focuses on day-to-day governance through ideological struggles. The importance of the legal dimension of this war should not be underestimated, but it cannot obfuscate the fact that the "populist" societies are afflicted by the aforementioned struggles that are not properly articulated in the language of the law.

Second, the Eastern front of the European legal war should not be fetishistically treated as the main line of division in Europe. Parenthetically, such a vision squares perfectly with the ideology of Hungarian and Polish populists who eagerly exploit the West-East divide in order to present themselves as victims of unjust, hierarchical treatment. Continuing the line of military metaphors, the struggles around the rule of law in CEE/SEE are a classic proxy war, waged on a delegated territory. The EU's lingering with sanctions for Hungary and Poland give a proof for this entanglement: it seems that there are many tacit allies of CEE populists also in the West, as demonstrated in the endless process of kicking the Fidesz out of the European People's Party. Moreover, there are other contexts to this story: the use that the CJEU made of Art. 2 – elevating a norm sanctioned politically by Art. 7 TUE to the level of a judiciable rule – might not be welcome by some member states. Taking the façade of EU liberal legality for real and perceiving its conflict with CEE populisms as the main European struggle obfuscates the complexity of tensions within the EU itself.

What this dual legal fetishism obscures is the reign of technocratic postmodern capitalism that turns nation states into local managers of global governance. There is a strange line of communication between the EU – since long afflicted by what has been, rather generously, dubbed 'democratic deficit' – and the authoritarian populism of CEE. The state-centric reaffirmation of national sovereignty in the Eastern part of the EU corresponds to the long-term process of diminishing the role of communitarian institutions in favour of strong national leadership – which began already in the 2000s, with the chancellorship of Angela Merkel. Therefore, even if the trouble with the rule of law concerns countries of CEE/SEE, it reflects the underlying state-centrism of the European Union itself, well evidenced by ritual differences between the European Parliament – representing 'the European voice' – and the Council. If it had not been for the pro-national decision-making process enshrined in Art. 7 TEU, it would have probably been successfully applied earlier.

Unfortunately, this 'rule of law fetishism' has already ossified into an established stream of academic discourse.[74] It is largely of technical character,

74 See for example Daniel R Kelemen and Laurent Pech, 'The Uses and Abuses of Constitutional Pluralism: Undermining the Rule of Law in the Name of Constitutional Identity in Hungary and Poland' (2019) 21 *Cambridge Yearbook of European Legal Studies* 59; András Jakab and Dimitry Kochenov (eds), *The Enforcement of EU Law and Values. Ensuring Member States' Compliance* (Oxford: OUP 2017); Kim Lane Scheppele, Dimitry Vladimirovich

focused on the analysis of institutional and procedural measures that should be applied to CEE populisms. In its close links with EU institutions, it demonstrates a close-knit cooperation between the academia and one of the actors positing as the warring side. In this position it perpetuates the narrow vision of conflict between the EU and Hungarian and Polish populist governmentalities which abstract from the whole complexity of socio-economic background of the latter. Moreover, *it presents populism as a technical problem which may be solved with skilful use of EU law*. In this manner the European legal war is technocratically reduced to one limited front.

1.6 Conclusions

The "really existing populism" in CEE/SEE arise from the juxtaposition of universal afflictions of contemporary democracy with the local, semi-peripheral and post-socialisation states. The specificity of their regimes cannot be grasped without this interposition of contexts; otherwise, it is all-too-easy to fall into the trap of the "Eastern backwardness story." The concept of the European legal war allows for inscribing the current transformations into the long chain of fights for (de/re)politicisation that cut across the whole of Europe, but for historical and geopolitical reasons are most prominent in its Eastern part. Populism, therefore, is not a phenomenon anyhow inherent in "the new Europe": on the contrary, its elements are to be found in the West as well. In its development, it is dependent on the crumbling liberal hegemony that itself slides into sovereigntism. What seems a raw irruption of the political appears as such only against the background of the liberal vision of curbing the political by the law.

This situation poses a crucial challenge to legal scholarship. Contemporary populism in CEE/SEE should be analysed as a floating signifier which is deeply mired in ideological struggles from which the academia cannot be free. Instead, however, of active participation in the struggle between imaginary "liberal" and "illiberal" camps, legal studies may and should engage in revealing the multidimensionality of the conflicts that cut through the EU, its member states, and their societies. These conflicts tend to oscillate around the question of the rule of law not because it is inherently central to them, but because it is the scene where the struggle for redefinition of boundaries of politicisation is fought. For this reason, legal scholarship should reconsider its own position and foundations. Instead of declaring contemporary populism a particular state of exception, it should rather see it as the current chapter in the history of a long war.

Kochenov, and Barbara Grabowska-Moroz, 'EU Values Are Law, after All: Enforcing EU Values through Systemic Infringement Actions by the European Commission and the Member States of the European Union' (2020) 39 *Yearbook of European Law* 3.

Chapter 2

Against "Populism"

Critical Legal Studies and Authoritarian Politics in Central and Eastern Europe

Cosmin Cercel

2.1 Introduction

The main purpose of this chapter is to provide the conceptual groundwork for moving beyond the analysis of law and authoritarianism in Central and Eastern Europe (CEE) in terms of "populist" politics. I intend to do so by means of four distinct, albeit interconnected interventions that aim to take the stock of the limits, tensions, and ambiguities that the analysis of populism has brought about in dealing with law and politics in the past decade within CEE. Subsequently, I aim to devise a possible intellectual roadmap for escaping both the ideological mires and theoretical limitations that the debates on populism have fuelled in the field of constitutional theory during the last decade. In a first move, my intention is to approach "populism" as a failed epistemic device within the field of comparative constitutional law and to uncover its entanglement in a specific arrangement of power and knowledge that operates as a positive stopgap for grasping the social and political phenomena structurally supporting authoritarian politics in relation to law. While reflecting on the ideological, institutional, and epistemic complicities that various fields of knowledge entertain with the authoritarian turn in CEE politics, I attempt to isolate the distinct contribution that a critically informed analysis of authoritarian politics in CEE can offer to the ongoing debate, by insisting on the refusal of "populism" both as an object of study within legal studies and as a political strategy. In doing so I shall draw on historical examples of authoritarian politics drawn from CEE experience with a view of advocating a different understanding of the situation at hand through the lenses of critical legal history.

These four interventions, grounded as they are in a critical reflection on the modern legal history of Central and Eastern Europe[1] and a constant

1 Cosmin Cercel, 'Law Out of Bounds: Legal Picnolepsy, Intellectual Austerity and Romania's Legal Past' in Rafał Mańko, Cosmin S. Cercel, Adam Sulikowski (eds), *Law and Critique in Central Europe: Questioning the Past, Resisting the Present* (Oxford: Counterpress, 2016), 44–65.

DOI: 10.4324/9781032624464-3

engagement with the history of our legal present,[2] aim to open the possibility of grasping both legally and politically the extent of the unfolding politico-legal catastrophe that has engulfed our polities in the last decade.

Starting with the financial crisis of 2008, shortly followed by the Eurozone crisis of 2009, the war in Syria, the annexation of Crimea, the migrant crisis of 2015, the rise of the terrorist threat (with attacks in Paris and Brussels), Brexit, the election of Trump and culminating with COVID-19 and the war of aggression against Ukraine, the last decade has opened a new *regime of historicity*,[3] by arguably creating a rupture within the ways our societies relate to their own past.[4] The seemingly unilinear continuum of time of the end of history, that has kept the global North a relatively stable and predictable normative space, has exploded under the pressure of various crises to the point where something radically new is emerging under novel social and political conditions. *The time is out of joint.*

Such tectonic shifts within the sphere of economics, geopolitics, and international law are yet to find a specific – if at all – discursive grounding within the sphere of legal studies. To quote Mao, "there is utter chaos under heaven, the situation is excellent." Indeed, the acceleration of history we witnessed in the global North in the last decade, left many bewildered and opened a space for revisiting long-established concepts and paradigms. One would legitimately claim that there is a fundamental need to reconsider the way we have been thinking about the law and politics during the last 30 glorious years, and to reconnect with central *topoi* in social sciences and the humanities, precisely in the face of the unfolding catastrophe, if law is to keep at all any form of historical and social relevance other than being a pure articulation of power. Now would be the time for critical legal thinking.

Yet, there is perhaps very little optimism about the possibility of re-evaluating and changing the long-standing paradigms within legal and constitutional theory, even if we actually live a *critical* moment. Some of the obstacles are deeply embedded in institutional, cultural, and disciplinary presuppositions more often than not left unchallenged. Others are the remnants of long-lost battles that critical legal scholars on both sides of the Atlantic carried on before leaving the trenches for a head-on assault on the palace of legal doxa and engaging in a protracted guerrilla war with no end in sight, and no apparent strategy. Finally, some of them are purely structural and interwoven into the very historical situation that we are facing. Indeed, once the

2 Cosmin Cercel, 'The Destruction of Legal Reason: Lessons from the Past' (2019) 89 *Acta Universitatis Lodziensis – Folia Iuridica* 15; Cosmin Cercel, 'Pandemic, Exception and the Law: Notes on the Shattered Nomos of Europe' (2021) 96 *Acta Universitatis Lodziensis – Folia Iuridica* 83.

3 François Hartog, *Régimes d'historicité. Présentisme et expériences du temps* (Paris: Seuil, 2003).

4 Ibid. 208–9.

machinery of authoritarian politics – and together with it a whole apparatus of ideology and repression – was set in motion, there is very little place for critical thought, especially within a field with the institutional, social, and political history such as law. The situation is rendered even more complicated if we place all these limitations within the context of the CEE, with its particularities of *doing* law, which made this discipline and praxis to be thoroughly marked by complicities with all forms of authoritarianism during the past century just before proclaiming itself to be once again the enlightener of nations and the beacon of civilisation and democracy.[5] Yet, whatever the limitations, complicities, and failures that have marked the intellectual and institutional history of law in CEE, and, for that matter, even within the putatively established democracies of the West (or global North), the depth of the catastrophe brought about by the authoritarian turn, the politics of the COVID-19 pandemic, and, moreover, by the looming threat of a nuclear war seem in many respects unprecedented, or at least so since 1945.

If we are to find a shorthand description for the measure and depth of the changes befalling the *nomos* of Europe that would be that of a logic of the *excess*. The ideological and intellectual references that structured symbolically as a recognisable texture the fabric of the Real, is crumbling and what is left are figures of excess and abjection, from the farcical assault on the Capitol to the massacres in Bucha, and the millions of refugees fleeing invasion and atrocities. Authoritarian politics surely has something to do with it, and given the place of the law in supporting our *normative universe*, there is a glaring necessity for a critical legal gaze within the nexus of law and politics that is emerging under our eyes, arrested by the figure of the abject. In order to situate these interventions phenomenologically, I turn to Julia Kristeva, who in spite, or perhaps because of, her complex biography was able to articulate with exemplary psychoanalytical precision the operation of abjection:

> A massive, and sudden emergence of uncanniness, which, familiar as it might have been in an opaque and forgotten life, now harries me as radically separate, loathsome. Not me. Not that. But not nothing, either. A "something" that I do not recognize as a thing. A weight of meaninglessness, about which there is nothing insignificant, and which crushes me. On

5 Cosmin Cercel, *Towards a Jurisprudence of State-Communism: Law and the Failure of Revolution* (London: Routledge, 2018); Hans Petter Graver and Peter Čuroš, 'Judges under Stress: Understanding Continuity and Discontinuity of Judicial Institutions of the CEE Countries' (2021) 22 *German Law Journal* 1147; Rafał Mańko, 'Delimiting Central Europe as a Juridical Space: A Preliminary Exercise in Critical Legal Geography' (2019) 89 *Acta Universitatis Lodziensis – Folia Iiuridica* 63.

> the edge of nonexistence and hallucination, of a reality that, if I acknowledge it, annihilates me.[6]

Building symbolic and political limits is what law is about. Psychoanalysis was able to grasp this performative force of the law to institute limits,[7] be it even in the guise of mere positive law as a remnant of the law of the Father, the emblem of authority. As Lacan noted, incidentally, in relation to the institution of usufruct: 'this indeed is the essence of law, to divide up, to distribute, to pay out what is involved in enjoyment,'[8] the crux being that the law is what creates and structures a limit able to sustain and define the subject. The *affect* of abjection plays a structurally similar role: with and through it one is able to impose the limits on that which destroys the subject, the unbearable injunction of the Superego to enjoy, or the psychotic reaction to negate the Real. In Kristeva's words, 'There, abject and abjection are my safeguards. The primers of my culture.'[9] Through abjection and the all-too-human powers of horror one is able to prevent, delay, or negotiate the flux of disintegrating reality.

Marking abjection as the starting point and indeed the context that grounds my argument, is a means for getting to the core of the matter: authoritarian politics is what creates the revulsion associated with abjection. To be sure, I am not arguing for a politics affirming the *powers of horror* as a necessary condition of critical legal inquiry within the field of authoritarianism, nor do I find that the critical field might require a level of self-flagellation before the mounting authoritarianisms or an uncritical submission to the precepts of liberal democracy. Rather, I find this to be the starting point for assessing the politico-legal conundrum of what has been termed as *populism*, as well as a call for clarity, able to support a continuation of a radical ethical and political criticism of the law[10] within the unfolding catastrophe.

The affect of abjection is, in many respects, foundational to the subject: with and through it the waters are divided. Abjection is *nomotic*, law-instituting, insofar as it calls for an understanding of how one is connected to the object of horror and by this very act aims to severe those links. Not unlike anxiety, it is an encounter with the figures of the Real.[11] Within the boundaries of our legal disciplinary universe, it is about reconstructing our understanding of law, power, and authority and reflecting on the dead-ends of the project of doing law and those of criticising this praxis. In light of the

6 Julia Kristeva, *Powers of Horror: An Essay on Abjection* (New York: Columbia University Press, 1982), 2.
7 Slavoj Žižek, 'Superego by Default' (1994) 16 *Cardozo Law Review* 925.
8 Jacques Lacan, *Le séminaire. Livre XX. Encore* (Paris: Le Seuil, 1975), 10.
9 Kristeva, *Powers of Horror*, 2.
10 Costas Douzinas and Adam Gearey, *Critical Jurisprudence* (Oxford: Hart, 2005), 8–10.
11 Slavoj Žižek, *Looking Awry* (Cambridge, MA: MIT Press, 1992), 8.

abject, both law and its critique are stained, tainted,[12] as parts of the "thing" that has thrashed the frames of reality continue to remain within the body of the law. The point is not to redeem them, but at least to reintroduce a particular order within the manifold materiality of the historical debris that we encounter.

In this sense, my argument is consciously posited as a *jurisprudential* one. Insofar as legal theory is the field in which the meaning of legality is negotiated,[13] a reflection on the authoritarian turn calls for such a specific disciplinary gaze, able to reflect on and potentially reconstruct the frames through which we understand the recent onslaughts on liberal legality. In doing so, my reflection is resolutely critical, aiming to distinguish and to order the piecemeal knowledge we encounter within the field of law with regard to the present destitution of legality. Drawing on an understanding of legal theory that emphasises its status within the politics of knowledge as an agonic field of struggle in which claims over the meaning of the law are stated and competing, I defend a *critical legal theoretical* project that, while conscious and wary of disciplinary divisions, academic traditions, and discursive grammars, nonetheless questions them together with the more or less artificial boundaries of the field of law.

2.2 Psychoanalysis and the Law

I thus turn first to psychoanalysis as a primarily clinical knowledge that is able to grasp the relationship between the subject and the sphere of the symbolic.[14] This is because law is, ultimately, inscribed within the fabric of language, and regardless of what a specific tradition of vulgar positivism might have taught us, this very inscription constitutes the starting point of all legal inconsistencies. Psychoanalysis, taken here not as an ossified dogma, nor as a clinical therapeutical device, but precisely as a discourse on the speaking subject as a subject of the unconscious,[15] is a particularly powerful intellectual device apt to explore the frailties and limits of the law.

The starting point is Freud's concept of *compulsion to repeat* (*Wiederholungszwang*).[16] There is quite a clear reason for this: the last decade in law, politics, and economics was nothing but a constant series of cri-

12 Stephen Skinner, 'Tainted Law? The Italian Penal Code, Fascism and Democracy' (2011) 7 *International Journal of Law in Context* 423.

13 Anton Schütz, 'Thinking the Law With and Against Luhmann, Legendre, Agamben' (2000) 11 *Law and Critique* 107.

14 Jacques Lacan, 'La science et la vérité', in *Ecrits* (Paris: Le Seuil, 1966), 868.

15 Lacan, *Le séminaire. Livre XX. Encore*, 10.

16 Sigmund Freud, 'Remembering, Repeating and Working Through' in James Strachey (ed.) *The Standard Edition of the Complete Psychological Works of Sigmund Freud*, Vol. 12 (London: Hogarth Press, 1958 [1914]), 145–57.

ses, emergencies, and exceptional measures, yet, until very recently, the legal canon stood unchanged: law is law and nothing but law, despite the usual superficial mimicry of interdisciplinarity and the parroting regurgitation of the old distinctions between lawfulness and lawlessness. While the actual political significance of the otherwise arcane and sad life of the law might not be visible right away, its ethical numbness and intellectual scarcity do have immediate political value: the law is neutral, and lawyers are there to give form to anything. This position is only doubled by the political myopia still prevalent within various layers of our polities, starting with academia assuring us that beyond some technical flaws, the system is working in the right direction, and ending with that of the sphere of established politics sleepwalking from one disaster to another. The discourse of populism is subjected to the same logic, constantly repeating and stating the obvious,[17] suggesting that there is, perhaps, something deeper at work within this *articulation* and *thematisation* of law, power, and authority.

Writing at the dawn of World War I, Freud has discovered in his clinical analyses a curious moment within the therapy of neurosis, that was not a process of remembering, but a resistance due to repression, that hampered the recovery of the subject in overcoming the trauma. In his words, 'the patient does not *remember* anything of what he has forgotten and repressed, but acts it out. He reproduces it not as a memory, but as an action; he *repeats* it, without, of course knowing that he is repeating it.'[18] The nature of this repetition is that of a compulsion, an unconscious-driven urge to *repeat*, placing the subject in situations that re-enact the trauma, by an acting-out. While distinct from remembering, this process is closely connected to it, insofar as 'in the end we understand that this is his way of remembering'[19] that the subject experiences. To be sure, repetition is an adulterated form of remembering, as 'the patient repeats instead of remembering, and he repeats under the conditions of resistance,'[20] that is as subject to the unconscious.

The compulsion to repeat is a recurring trope in Freud's foundational texts of psychoanalysis. When analysing the uncanny (*Das Unheimliche*),[21] repetition compulsion features as one of the figures of the return of the repressed. As he writes, 'we are able to postulate the principle of a repetition-compulsion in the unconscious mind, based upon instinctual activity and probably inherent in the very nature of the instincts—a principle powerful enough to overrule the pleasure-principle, lending to certain aspects of the mind

17 Cercel, 'The Destruction of Legal Reason,' 18–9.

18 Ibid. 150.

19 Ibid.

20 Ibid. p. 151.

21 Sigmund Freud, 'The "Uncanny"' in James Stratchey (ed.) *The Standard Edition of the Complete Psychological Works of Sigmund Freud*, Vol. 17 (London: Hogarth Press, 1971 [1919]), 219–53.

their daemonic character.'[22] In *Beyond the Pleasure Principle* we encounter once again this obscure figure of repetition compulsion, when, as a resistance to the psychoanalytical intervention, the subject 'is obliged to *repeat* the repressed material as a contemporary experience instead of (...) *remembering* it as something belonging to the past.'[23] Yet repetition does not emerge only under the operation of analysis, rather it can be grasped within everyday life beyond neurosis, and arguably one could find traces within what we used to call high culture: 'what psychoanalysis reveals in the transference phenomena of neurotics can also be observed in the lives of some normal people. The impression they give is of being pursued by a malign fate or possessed by some "demonic" power.'[24] There are indeed reasons for this process, that Freud shall bring to the fore in describing the relation between repetition and another fundamental concept of psychoanalysis, namely death-drive, not without going through a lengthy and somewhat confusing exercise in metaphysical biology.

One would be tempted to connect repetition as a sign of the death-drive to the troubled context of the interwar period and reflect on its immediate cultural and political relevance, by taking into account the developments within *Civilisation and Its Discontent*,[25] and reflect on how this operates at the level of polities as an intersubjective, cultural process, by instituting the symbolic order. Incidentally, one could note the intimate relation that the compulsion to repeat entertains with the realm of law and social order insofar as, 'order is *a kind of compulsion to repeat* which, when a regulation has been laid down once and for all, decides when, where and how a thing shall be done, so that in every similar circumstance one is spared hesitation and indecision.'[26]

Accordingly, the aim is to unpack how repetition compulsion can operate as a useful device for decrypting the *errancies* of the contemporary legal mind before authoritarianism. First, repetition compulsion is a form of re-enacting a trauma by acting-out, instead of remembering it. It should be clear from the outset the connection we, as lawyers, entertain with past experiences of authoritarianism, imperialism, and crisis, in short, with a history of practices that placed the exercise of sovereign power at the core, as a power that is beyond the reach of the law, that founds it through a nothing short of traumatic act, and which seemingly recedes under the repressive function of the

22 Ibid. p. 11.

23 Sigmund Freud, 'Beyond the Pleasure Principle' in James Stratchey (ed.) *The Standard Edition of the Complete Psychological Works of Sigmund Freud*, Vol. 18 (London: Hogarth Press, 1955 [1920]), 7–64, at p. 18.

24 Ibid. p. 21.

25 Sigmund Freud, 'Civilization and Its Discontents' in James Stratchey (ed.) *The Standard Edition of the Complete Psychological Works of Sigmund Freud*, Vol. 21 (London: Hogarth Press, 1961 [1929]), 57–146.

26 Ibid. 93.

law. One could, of course, investigate this position jurisprudentially together with a long tradition we inherited from Hobbes,[27] Austin,[28] and Schmitt,[29] who would, in one way or another, give the sovereign its due in relation to the foundation of the legal order. In a more critically conscious way, one would be able to identify this particular traumatic encounter between the law and its Other together with Benjamin,[30] Derrida,[31] and Agamben,[32] by being able to point out the ghostly presence of the sovereign projecting its shadow over the legal order. Last, and perhaps in a less direct manner, this threatening presence is to be found on the background of legal formalisms starting with Kelsen[33] and ending up with Raz,[34] insofar as not only efficacy is a prerequisite of the legal order,[35] but also discretion and authority instantiate the dangerous excess of the law.[36]

However, as interesting and important as such an inquiry might be, what detains me here is the specific historically grounded trauma of the law in relation to the catastrophes of the past century. Contemporary legality, the specific *nomos* that is dissolving before our very eyes, has arguably emerged in the wake of 1945, as a part of the post-fascist consensus, in reaction of the Holocaust, the atrocities of World War II, and the authoritarianisms that enabled the catastrophe. Some distinct features of our normative universe that we still inhabit are explicitly related to the fall of what I call state communism,[37] that is the demise of the revolutionary potential inscribed and tamed by state apparatuses and by its connivence with the law and legal form. This is not to say that our legal systems in their entirety are built upon this historical trauma, rather it is to emphasise that our basic understanding of legality, that which enables us to recognise the law as valid law – our

27 Thomas Hobbes, *Leviathan* (Lerner Publishing Group, 2018 [1651]), 131.
28 John Austin, *The Province of Jurisprudence Determined* (London, John Murray, 1861 [1832]), xlvi.
29 Carl Schmitt, *Political Theology*, George Schwab transl. (Cambridge, MA: MIT Press, 1985 [1922]).
30 Walter Benjamin, 'Critique of Violence' in *Selected Writings*, Vol. 1, Marcus Bullock and Michael W. Jennings (eds) (Cambridge, MA: Harvard University Press, 1996 [1921]), 236–52.
31 Jacques Derrida, *Force de loi* (Paris: Galilée, 1994).
32 Giorgio Agamben, *Homo Sacer: Sovereign Power and Bare Life* Daniel Heller-Roazen transl. (Stanford, CA: Stanford University Press, 1998 [1995]), 18–19.
33 Hans Kelsen, *Introduction to the Problems of Legal Theory*, Bonnie Litschewski Paulson and Stanley
Paulson transl. (Oxford: Oxford University Press, 1992 [1934]), 60.
34 Joseph Raz, *The Authority of Law: Essays on Law and Morality* (Oxford University Press, 1980), 119–20.
35 Kelsen, *Introduction...*, 60.
36 Unsurprisingly for Raz there is nothing dangerous about this excess, insofar as 'all legal systems are open systems': Raz, *The Authority of Law*, 120.
37 Cercel, *Towards a Jurisprudence of State-Communism*, 99–101.

master rule – is inescapably connected to the jurisprudence and the politics of 'working through'[38] the historical catastrophe of the last World War and, to a lesser extent, to that of the fall of state communism.

However, and here lies the traumatic core of our politico-legal predicament, the *nomotic* moment of this legality has been a failed one, as if the repression that was instituted was not able to function. As David Fraser aptly observed: 'many, if not all, of the factors which created the legality of Auschwitz, continue to inhabit today's legal universe.'[39] To put it simply, the same mechanisms that were put in place to deal with the historical conundrum of the Shoah and the war, and, in a different way to Stalinism and its effects, are the very reason for the failure that we encounter today and keeps repeating itself within the jurisprudential and constitutional structures of dealing with authoritarian rule. This jurisprudential conundrum of working-through the war, that which precisely made legal theory effectively sustain a law *after Auschwitz*, and to positively close the eyes as a matter of law with regards to historical disruption, is precisely what we keep on repeating, and which constitutes the matter of the compulsion to repeat.

Let me explain this further: neither the Nuremberg nor the preceding or subsequent trials, building on the World War II cases, were able to offer a coherent jurisprudential or political theory of law, let alone an understanding of authoritarian legality. By emphasising the natural law commitment to universal principles of human life, values, and civilisation, while implicitly recognising the very positivist authority grounded in sheer military sovereign power,[40] the post-war trials, as legitimate and well-intended as they were, failed to call into question the particular Gordian knot of law in modernity: the law was not judged as such.

True, political, and moral authors of heinous crimes were judged, even judges and lawyers made the object of various forms of trials and retributions, but legality as such, its authority and complicity were never put into question insofar *as if* what we experienced in the prolonged authoritarian or fascist states of exception, the killing machine of the camps, the show trials, the great retreat, or the revolution from above, was never 'law properly so-called.'[41] Rather, we are told, and it is held as a matter of ideological legal representation, that what we have witnessed was a perversion of justice,[42]

38 Freud, 'Remembering, Repeating and Working Through', 149.
39 David Fraser, *Law after Auschwitz: Towards A Jurisprudence of the Holocaust* (Durham, NC: Carolina Academic Press, 2005), 419.
40 David Fraser, 'Evil Law, Evil Lawyers? From the Justice Case to the Torture Memos' (2012) 3 *Jurisprudence* 391, 408.
41 Austin, *The Province of Jurisprudence*, 4.
42 *U.S. v. Altstoetter et al.* (The 'Justice Case'), *Trials of War Criminals Before the Nuremberg Military Tribunals under Control Council Law No. 10*, Vol. 3 (Washington, DC: US Government Printing Office, 1951), 32 (prosecution opening statement) [Altstoetter].

an unlawful at best and certainly an illegitimate appropriation of the law to authoritarian or totalitarian ends.[43]

The complicities between the regimes of legality that permitted such judgments, were never worked through as a matter of public concern, and hardly as one of academic debate outside the sphere of legal historians or historians of authoritarianism. In the end, the trauma was complete: as an object that cannot be integrated into a symbolic structure, as an excess that punctures both scientific formalisation – that is the theory – of the law and its inner social existence. This should be read not only as a failure of lawyers in their social and institutional settings, of the legal profession with its inability to foster a proper *ethics after Auschwitz*, or after totalitarianism by rethinking its complicity to the bureaucracy of the modern Behemoth. It is not only a trauma of the jurisprudential enterprise not being able to spell out coherently the nexus between law and politics that permits a retrospective judgment in exceptional circumstances based not on imagined universal values that otherwise do not seem to prevent actual state-sanctioned, that is *lawful* killing,[44] but on a political will to punish what is reprehensible in the deeds and thought of a modernity that had gone awry.[45]

It is also the failure of political theory and of philosophy as such in its ability to render the categories through which *absolute – or for that matter – banal evil*[46] enters into the form of law as such. The question is indeed historical, insofar as we can presume or speculate on the politics supporting such a treatment of the war – either in the eyes of the Soviet Union aiming to build up a new legality, which as revolutionary as it might have pledged to be carried on the same features of modernity, or in those of the putative democracies of the West where colonialism, with its history of a-legal, or precisely *lawful* practices, still ongoing at the time of the traumatic encounter with the authoritarian Other, the *frère and semblable* of modern law turned authoritarian.

Repetition is our way of remembering the conundrum of authoritarian legality still inscribed in our understanding and practice of the law, that builds on the presupposed, yet very real, tension between law and politics at the core of the modern political and legal theories of the state. As a part of the

43 Comisia Prezidenţială pentru Analiza Dictaturii Comuniste din România [Presidential Commission for the Study of the Communist Dictatorship in Romania], *Raport Final* [Final Report] (Bucureşti: Humanitas, 2006), 406.

44 David Fraser, 'Criminal Law in Auschwitz: Positivism, Natural Law, and the Career of SS Lawyer Konrad Morgen' in Stephen Skinner (ed.), *Ideology and Criminal Law: Fascist, National Socialist and Authoritarian Regimes* (Oxford: Hart Publishing, 2019), 33–57.

45 H.L.A. Hart, 'Positivism and the Separation of Law and Morals" (1958) 71 *Harvard Law Review* 593.

46 Giorgio Agamben, *Remnants of Auschwitz: The Witness and the Archive*, Daniel Heller Roazen transl. (New York: Zone Books, 1999), 21.

basic assumptions that frame our modern legal mind, and strangely enough, even our putatively post-modern attempts of grasping the law, the default position is one of an incommensurability, a fundamental tension between law and politics. *Law* is there to contain and limit the flow of politics from its most basic forms of a distinctly intense opposition of a struggle for power,[47] to the more articulated, and arguably more rationalised (that is, *lawful*) ones of party politics within established institutional frameworks. Law is the voice of reason taming the flow of politics and limiting its dissolution into polemic. This basic presupposition, inherited from the classical theory of the state of the early 16th century, taken up by the classical theory of the 18th century and coming to full fruition within the various formalisms and positivisms of the past century, is our default legal ideological mode, one which would posit the distinction between law and politics at its core – and effectively and surreptitiously praising the capacity of law to limit the excess of the supposedly primeval conflictual tendencies nesting within the political realm.

Law's empire is always there to reassure us that the excesses of the sovereign are going to be limited. However, as much energy that lawyers and philosophers have put in instilling our faith in the law, and its ability to contain the catastrophic consequences of a full erasure of legality – if that was ever possible within the modern horizon – the fact of the matter stays that for a legal order to make sense, a level of reliance of the law on politics, has to be acknowledged. Either as a necessary constituent for legal validity, as a form of discretion, or as a historical institutional setting, as a primeval act of foundational legality, the law's empire rests on some form of sovereign power that founds and exceeds its force of formalisation. That is to say, that at some very basic level, the old critical legal studies credo that *law is politics* stays true for any form of modern legality. Surely, not everyone would acknowledge that *all law is politics*, and many on the side of formalist orthodoxy would argue, somewhat convincingly, that law contains and can contain politics. But there lies the specific traumatic core of the modern experience of the law for lawyers, the source of the melancholic attachment[48] to the legal form against all odds,[49]

Within the historical unfolding of the last century, the strategies of working through this trauma – for it is a trauma in realising that some form of sovereign power that ultimately rests on some *necropolitics*[50] is the source of validity of the legal order – were geared towards *negation*, rather than

47 Carl Schmitt, *The Concept of the Political*, George Schwab transl. (Chicago: University of Chicago Press, 1996), 26.

48 Przemysław Tacik, 'Melancholy of the Law' (2020) 33 *Law and Critique* 23, 38.

49 Cercel, *The Destruction of Legal Reason*, 17–8. Slavoj Žižek, *Tarrying with the Negative: Kant, Hegel and the Critique of Ideology* (Durham, NC: Duke University Press, 1993), 88.

50 Achille Mbembe, 'Necropolitics' (2003) 15 *Public Culture* 11, 23.

repression. The symbolic defences raised by the legal guilds and legal scholars on both sides of the Iron Curtain against the historical material of the trauma was that law had, at most, little to do with it, for what took place was a perversion of law and justice under the force of *Hitlerite* politics.[51] The law had simply vanished.[52] The equation between law and democracy – be it liberal or popular – as a sign of civilisation that had been altered by the Nazi and fascist regimes was an essential constituent of the fragile yet lasting anti-fascist consensus,[53] and later a useful instrument in the political struggles between West and East. The totalitarian thesis furthered this understanding of a fundamental opposition between *lawful* democracy and *lawless* totalitarian rule.[54]

Based on a loose and selective reading of Arendt, which downplayed exactly the historical grounding she highlighted, the conditions of possibility of totalitarianism as rooted within the emergence of mass politics within capitalism, such a clear-cut division made law a signifier of democracy, a proper insignia of civilisation that ended up by positively excluding other forms of politics as lawless, blurring the line between moral, political, and jurisprudential categories. This intellectual trajectory found its apex in the liberal triumphalism of the decades following the collapse of state communism, and became the proper ideological trope for what was to become the so-called judicialisation of politics. The time was ripe for instituting the law as the structuring element of our *law-bound societies*.

To be sure, this process did not take place only at purely intellectual level, or as a matter of a history of ideas. Rather, it was supported and driven by the social and economic transformation befalling our polities. It was also not a linear, unidimensional line of continuity, but a rather tortuous one at times traversed by tensions and inconsistencies. The inherent rationality of modern bureaucracies survived unscathed in the realm of law, be it in the common law tradition or on the continent, either in Western democracies or in actually existing socialism, just to be elevated to a fully regulatory principle of the post-communist transition[55] and ultimately of any form of transition.[56] What

51 David Fraser, '(De)Constructing the Nazi State: Criminal Organizations and the Constitutional Theory of the International Military Tribunal' (2017) 39 *Loy. L.A. Int'l & Comp. L. Rev.* 117.

52 Alexandra Mercescu, 'The Law Vanishes (Or Not): Engaging Communist Legality' (2018) 9 *Romanian Journal of Comparative Law* 449.

53 Dan Stone, *Goodbye to All That? A History of Europe since 1945* (Oxford: Oxford University Press, 2014), 15–43.

54 Hannah Arendt, *Origins of Totalitarianism* (New York: Harvest Books & Harcourt, 1985 [1951]), 462.

55 Adam Czarnota, Martin Krygier, and Wojcieh Sadurski, 'Introduction' in *Rethinking the Rule of Law after Communism*, Adam Czarnota, Martin Krygier, and Wojceh Sadurski (eds) (Budapest: Central European University Press, 2005), 1.

56 Ruti Teitel, *Transitional Justice* (Oxford: Oxford University Press, 2002), 226.

was at its core, despite ideological claims and pledges to the contrary, was law's technical ability to regulate, the inner fact that the legal norm can act as a rule, as a measure that creates a concrete order. In Agamben's words: 'the law has a regulative character and is a "rule" not because it commands and proscribes, but because it must first of all create the sphere of its own reference in real life and *make that reference regular*.'[57] As a technology of power, draped in a seemingly neutral, value-free, and a-political nature, law was able to circulate as a rule for all seasons, fostering in its own ambiguous way the circulation of capital, and ultimately social transformation.

Testimony to it stays even today in the specific role black letter law knowledge and practice has within the system of global capital.[58] The dissolution of the great narratives, that positively severed technical knowledge from its ideological ballast and effectively freed law of its humanistic pretences, coincided with the very possibility of thinking of law once again as the ultimate horizon of politics. With roots in the emerging trends of global law, comparative law, and transitional justice, and drawing on the political philosophical heritage of the last remnants of classical critical theory, a new assemblage of knowledge that we know today under the label constitutional theory or comparative constitutional law, effectively supported this view and provided the new global normativity with a somewhat coherent narrative quilting between market capitalism, political pluralism, and the rule of law. What detains me here is not a thorough intellectual genealogy of global constitutionalism or comparative constitutional law, let alone of the literature on the rule of law and populism. Rather, I am interested in pointing out how this corpus of analysis started to play core role in the strategies of the legal mind in addressing the historical and jurisprudential trauma of the possibility of *evil law*, and how it effectively entangled legal thought in a very similar process of the psychoanalytical *compulsion to repeat*.

This corpus of texts, with its origins that can be traced back to Habermas' *constitutional patriotism*,[59] and arguably to Kelsen's political writings[60] and surely the unwavering enthusiasm for a specific form of market liberalism on both sides of the Atlantic, and especially in Central and Eastern Europe, has opened the possibility for equating law and democracy, to the point where democracy itself can be reduced to being a matter of law and procedures.

57 Agamben, *Homo Sacer*, 26 (original emphasis).

58 See, Honor Brabazon (ed.) *Neoliberal Legality: Understanding the Role of Law in the Neoliberal Project* (London: Routledge, 2017).

59 Jurgen Habermas, 'Struggles for Recognition in the Democratic Constitutional State' in Charles Taylor and Amy Gutmann (eds) *Multiculturalism* (Princeton University Press, 1994), 107–48.

60 Hans Kelsen, *The Essence and Value of Democracy*, Brian Graf trans. (Lanham, MD: Rowman and Littlefield, 2013 [1929]); Hans Kelsen, 'Foundations of Democracy' (1955) 66 *Ethics* 1.

From within this intellectual horizon, once the rules are settled, the question of democracy itself becomes something that can be a matter for lawyers to foster, develop, strengthen, or support.[61] As far as we might be today from those years, the main concerns within the field around that time were indeed about endowing constitutionalism and constitutional processes with political legitimacy, with formulas such as democratic deficit calling for a rethinking of the law and democracy, in order to build a *demos*.[62] This is perhaps one of the reasons for which a long line of re-readings of Carl Schmitt has emerged, precisely on the background of the flurry of emergencies that our polities were entertaining.

2.3 Populism as a Concept and as a Phenomenon

It is within this theoretical arrangement that the *people* and *populism* emerged as objects of study within the law, and populism appeared as a particular problem for legal analysis. As Przemysław Tacik reminds us in his contribution to this book, *populism* is a limit-concept for legal studies, that was transplanted from political theory and political science with a view of explaining anomalies within constitutional projects. Now, as legitimate and useful such a concept might have been within the fields in which it emerged, and as much as it had evoked a specific relationship between political movements, political mobilisation, and the established constitutional rules affecting politics, once translated within the law it had become rather peculiar, by losing precisely its socio-political weight. Not only did such a transplant give rise to haphazard and unwarranted connections that would puzzle political scientists, but also it enabled a specific hegemony of suspicion within legal studies with regard to politics, mobilisation, and criticism of the status quo.

Since the advent of 'populism,' direct democratic processes have gained some unfathomable aura of dangerousness,[63] political mobilisation has become somewhat problematic, and indeed there is a host of literature examining the phenomenology of populism in its strategy and tactics of either fighting the law, instrumentalising it, or re-writing it.[64] The general approach

61 András Sajó and Renáta Uitz, *The Constitution of Freedom: An Introduction to Legal Constitutionalism* (Oxford University Press, 2017), 19.

62 J.H.H. Weiler, Ulrich R. Haltern, and Franz C. Mayer, 'European Democracy and its Critique' (1995) 18 *Western Politics* 4; Joseph H.H. Weiler, *The Constitution of Europe 'Do the New Clothes Have an Emperor?' and Other Essays on European Integration* (Cambridge, MA: Harvard University Press, 1999).

63 Jan-Werner Müller, *What Is Populism?* (Philadelphia: University of Pennsylvania Press, 2016), 22.

64 David Landau, 'Abusive Constitutionalism' (2013) 47 *University of California Davis Law Review* 189. Kim Lane Scheppele, 'Autocratic Legalism' (2018) 85 *University of Chicago Law Review* 545; Steven Levitsky and Daniel Ziblatt, *How Democracies Die* (New York:

is that of screening out forms of uses of the law that can have either the potential of re-writing constitutional arrangements, or that simply go against them. The problem with this approach is that it is overly narrow. It fails to account for the very framework that makes such judgments possible, and to put under scrutiny the way in which the law, especially constitutional law, itself plays an important role in facilitating *populism*.

As Saygun Gökarıksel rightly points out in his contribution, most of the phenomena associated with *populism* in CEE emerge against the failures of the so-called politics of memory[65] and the memory clashes of the last decades. The judicial themes that have pervaded historiography and memory studies, the legal frames of memory through which we are attempting to address the past and its traumas, are constitutive of the *populist moment*, insofar as the law is too rigid or blunt a mechanism for investigating the past, as much as it is for addressing political mobilisation. While there is a structural limit of the law that becomes apparent in the literature on populism and it renders the concept as a limit-one, a threshold between law and politics, we should not simply dismiss it as an *impossible concept*, or as mere ideology in the service of the status quo. As Foucault noted, the place of ideology within scientific discourse is to be found not necessarily in the substantive matter, but rather in the thematisation, in the ways in which knowledge is produced, and more specifically in the quilting points of various established discourses.[66]

Populism is the object of this knowledge that emerges at the margins of established legal discourse, at its point of juncture between political philosophy, jurisprudence, and positive constitutional law, an area where a border traffic between legal, political, and sociological concepts is traditionally taking place in what in other times was called the theory of the state. The problem is not that such a heterodoxy is not able to sustain a particularly refined analysis of the law and politics, and for sure my criticism is not that of the pretended interdisciplinarity of understanding populism. The main issue with this corpus of knowledge is that it produces populism as an object of study: if law is the technical, neutral, and a-political technology of power that can be turned into the ultimate horizon of the post-political landscape, then any of its violations, claims to restructuring, and reform are recuperated as potential threats to the existing status quo.

The depoliticisation of our societies, finds its necessary excessive supplement within the *compulsive repetition* of the ritual of identifying threats to the rule of law. This exercise is not problematic as a matter of knowledge,

Crown, 2018), 13–5; Roger Eatwell and Matthew Goodwin, *National Populism: The Revolt Against Liberal Democracy* (London: Penguin, 2018), 118–40.

65 Richard Ned Lebow, Wulf Kansteiner, and Claudio Fogu, *The Politics of Memory in Postwar Europe* (Duke University Press, 2006).

66 Michel Foucault, *L'archéologie du savoir* (Paris: Gallimard, 1969), 241.

and to be sure a great deal of useful analysis on the relationship between new political movements and the law have been offered under the label of populism during the last decade:[67] however, there is something of a mutual paranoia between the object of analysis and the subject analysing it. Populists, we are told, and not without a level of accuracy, claim to speak in the name of the *people* and disregard and disdain expert knowledge.[68] The opposite seems to be true as well: defenders of the rule of law do seem to disregard and disdain the *people*, especially when it comes to supporting the wrong political creeds. The impasse that ties them together is revealing for the compulsive nature of such an entanglement. Populists will arguably never be tamed other than by legal means, while indeed the calls for a legal struggle against populism and the democratic backsliding will take forms for a new era for militant democracy,[69] that itself is in an overt tension with the principles of the rule of law, regardless of how technical or wide they are interpreted.

On the one hand, the law is there to be protected from the corrosive forces of irrational politics, while on the other hand, the constitutional system seems to be barred by expert gamekeepers with disdain for the *people*. Now, if there is a point of conjunction between the two versions, it is the assumption that radical politics of today that might be a threat to the constitutional status quo has something to do with the people either as a matter of political rhetoric or as a form of social structure and political mobilisation. Formulated from within legal studies this analysis seems to be at least strange, insofar as for law the people as the constitutional subject, where it is presented as such, is not a socio-political reality but a legal fiction which presupposes that claims about sovereignty are being made within the confines of the constitutional system.

Pointing out that when one particular party or group makes a claim that they embody sovereignty simply misses the point: this is what politics has been since time immemorial – an attempt at defining the people. Now there might be some things particularly disturbing within recent political developments in Central and Eastern Europe as well as in Western Europe during the past ten years, but what makes them disturbing is not the means through which they make this particular claim, rather it is the content of the claim. If indeed we are witnessing a rise of right-wing authoritarianism and a forceful return of far-right ideologies globally, the point is not about the claim these

67 Mitchell Orenstein and Bojan Bugarič, 'Work, Family, Fatherland: The Political Economy of Populism in Central and Eastern Europe' *Journal of European Public Policy* (2020): 1–20; Andras L. Pap, *Democratic Decline in Hungary: Law and Society in an Illiberal Democracy* (Abingdon: Routledge, 2018).

68 Muller, *What is Populism?* 8.

69 Cristóbal Rovira Kaltwasser, 'Militant Democracy Versus Populism' in Anthoula Malkopoulou and Alexander Kirschner, *Militant Democracy and Its Critics: Populism, Parties, Extremism* (Edinburgh: Edinburgh University Press, 2019), 72–91.

movements or (once in power) regimes make about representing the people, but the very notion of the people they employ. This brings us perhaps to the core of the failure of this body of knowledge in addressing the real threat and dissolution of legality that takes place before our very eyes. By limiting itself to criticism of the means of exercising power within the conditions of liberal democracies, and this limit being necessarily structural, founded upon the very narrow frameworks through which law and legality are construed, it is not able to make any conclusive statement on the substance of the traumatic object that pervaded the spectrum of our polities.

The people have suddenly become a political subject that effectively obscures the core of its very constitutional and political meaning, that of being a legal fiction defining the part with no part within the political system.[70] Within the populist fantasy the *people* have been reduced to ethnonational phantasmatic projections. By allowing the far-right and authoritarian movements to seize the vocabulary of the people laden with symbolic weight, historical significance, and memorial importance, all carrying a specific historical luggage of struggles for democracy, extension of rights, and recognition, the current law-based discourse on populism positively legitimises illegitimate claims about the meaning of the people. At the end of the analysis, what we see emerging is the shadowy spectre of the Red-Brown alliance threatening the status quo, the very unworked through material of the trauma that liberal constitutionalism was not able to overcome in the past 30 years.

In this repetition there is also something almost dramatic, pertaining to fate, as Freud noted, and perhaps an insistence that nests within a call for a *death-drive* that pervades our frames of approaching politics.[71] As we all know from Hannah Arendt, totalitarianism is the only system with which coexistence is not possible,[72] which in itself calls for a politics of conflict. Read through these lenses the analysis of populism is not only intellectually reductive, politically misleading, and, to some extent, self-contradictory, but also politically efficient.

The flurry of studies on populism is not to be sought only within uneasy and unflattering alliances between the underfunded neoliberal academia and various political bodies, or among political creeds and class-interests tying legal scholars to the existing status quo, that might perhaps explain sociologically the success of an intellectual fashion. It is not to be sought only within the real sense of crisis that has engulfed legal studies during the last decades. To be sure, there is a lot within the realm of legal practices to be worried about the future of our democracies and that of liberal democracy as a

70 Giorgio Agamben, *Sovereign Power and Bare Life* (Stanford, CA: Stanford University Press, 1998), 178.

71 Freud, 'Civilization and Its Discontents' 118–20.

72 Arendt, *Origins of Totalitarianism*, 18.

concept, against the background of rising authoritarianism. Yet, this engagement with populism is politically efficient insofar as a discourse operates a specific friend-enemy division[73] that collapses legal, moral, and political arguments while narrowing down the possibility of an alternative. Przemysław Tacik described populism as a form of legal civil war, and rightly so insofar as what we are dealing with on both sides of the spectrum is an unrelenting problematisation of the inconsistency of the legal discourse, in which unprecedented levels of hostility have been reached with regards to the meaning of the basic laws of our polities.

As dramatic as this predicament might appear at first glance, and as accurate the diagnostic is, I believe that it can achieve its full potential only if we take into account the intellectual background that made it possible, which was that of a neutralisation of politics.[74] This state of affairs is not reducible only to neoliberalism, although it is inscribed in its ideological articulation within the context of European politics, inasmuch as it is not reducible to Europe's last post-communist *trente glorieux*. It is part of an overarching socio-economic, legal, and philosophical dispositive that has been active ever since the fall of the Berlin Wall and that relegated any substantial political mobilisation rightly or wrongly to the sphere of dangerous adventurism, political affairs to the expert knowledge of pollsters, while for all the rest, lawyers were good enough. It should be no surprise that when in the shadow of the brutal transition from state-communism to capitalism, the failures of the markets and the destructive forces of extractivism, deregulation, and austerity, new forms of political mobilisation emerged, they were to represent a return of the political as another form of the return of the repressed.[75]

The general ideological inconsistency of the so-called populist parties, the peculiar alliances between different calls of and for sovereignty, as well as the uncertain label of populism obscured the reactionary core of the driving political forces. Many on the left side of the political spectrum fell within the discursive trap, just as our reputed constitutional lawyers did, by taking for true the break with the status quo and reading in the rise of nationalism, or within all sorts of identarian demands, a crack within the neoliberal consensus. Under the conditions of a neutralisation of politics, such a return of the politics with its vociferous and existential *pathos* contrasting with the dull

73 Carl Schmitt, *The Concept of the Political* (Chicago: University of Chicago Press, 1996 [1929]), 26.

74 Gian-Giacomo Fusco and Michalis Zivanaris, 'The Neutralisation of the Political: Carl Schmitt and the Depoliticisation of Europe' (2021) 30 *Journal of Contemporary European Studies* 363.

75 Don Kalb, 'Headlines of Nation, Subtexts of Class: Working-Class Populism and the Return of the Repressed in Neoliberal Europe' in Don Kalb and Gabor Halmai, *Headlines of Nation, Subtexts of Class: Working-Class Populism and the Return of the Repressed in Neoliberal Europe* (New York: Berghahn Books, 2011), 1–37.

repetitions of financial experts and managers pontificating on the necessities of protecting the markets and not upsetting the existing arrangement while salaries were cut and living costs increased all over the continent, was perhaps all too easy to be misunderstood. Facebook and Cambridge Analytica as well as Putin's trolls were there to blur things even further. For many, this irruption of politics was as a breath of fresh air – *du possible, vite du possible ou j'éttouffe.*[76] The situation was actually bleaker than anyone imagined, and this is as true for the defendants of the rule of law as for the critical voices on some parts of the left resenting the status quo to the point that anything else might have been an opening. Limiting oneself on a criticism of the means and closing an eye to the substance of the historical process before our eyes was equally misguided.

With the benefit of hindsight we are able to see to what extent the substance was and is still the matter. The rallying call of so-called populism was in the name of the defence of state-sovereignty and ethnonationalism. Populism in action, just as "populism" in theory had very little to do with the constitutional subject of *the people* – hardly any more than any other ideology would have, or perhaps even less insofar as the rallying calls are for a very narrow understanding of the people based on exclusive notions of cultural homogeneity, sex and gender, identity, and belonging. Indeed, it should have been transparent to everyone that this was anything but a revolt of the wretched of the Earth, but was, indeed, a conservative revolution.

2.4 From Populism to Post-Fascism?

Enzo Traverso hypothesised a definitional shift from *populism* to *post-fascism* in attempting to describe the rise of contemporary authoritarianism. In his words, 'the main feature of today's post-fascism is precisely the contradictory coexistence of the inheritance of classical fascism with new elements that do not belong to this tradition.'[77] In emphasising the distance between historical fascism and the current movements, focusing on the difference within social structure, the role of the state within society, the hollowing-out of politics as a precondition for the anti-political nature of *post-fascism*, as well as the ideological inconsistency of these contemporary phenomena, the accent within this definition falls undoubtedly on the *post-* dimension: 'the historical comparisons allow us to draw analogies, but we cannot map Trump's profile onto a fascist paradigm from the interwar period. The context is simply too different.'[78]

76 Gilles Deleuze and Félix Guattari, 'Mai 68 n'a pas eu lieu' (2007 [1984]) 64 *Chimères* 23.
77 Enzo Traverso, *The New Faces of Fascism. Populism and the Far Right* (London: Verso, 2019), 32.
78 Ibid. 23.

While Traverso focuses within this instance on Trump, the argument is surely more general. In a commendable attempt to bring some further clarification by avoiding lumping together various movements under the same label, he also notes: 'Trump is as distant from classical fascism as Occupy Wall Street, the 15-M movement in Spain, the Nuit Debout movement in France are from communism in the 20th century.'[79] Before moving further there are two things that need to be retained in relation to post-fascism. First, it would be worth noting that the term was initially coined in early 2001 by Hungarian philosopher Gaspar Miklos Tamas, in a perhaps all too sweeping critique of the liberal status quo and the deeper political significance on the universality of rights in the post-communist context. It surely does not have any direct relation to the recent political developments, but foresights them with bewildering accuracy: post-fascism is the condition under which 'a break with the enlightenment tradition of citizenship as an universal entitlement (...) with its assimilation of the civic condition to the human condition.'[80] Second, as much credit can be given to Traverso for clarifying the historical distance that separates us from the interwar, I think that his assessment is somewhat too optimistic and to some extent at least silent on the continuities between historical fascism and current developments in politics.

To stay within the horizon of the American far-right, it might be of at least some anecdotical interest to recall how the Romanian fascist leader Zelea Codreanu was literally a poster-boy (or actually a T-shirt boy) for the radical fringes in Charlottesville. Historian of fascism Zeev Sternhell, in a somewhat counterintuitive move not universally shared, but with distinct accuracy, hypothesised that the birth of historical fascism was not necessarily connected to the catastrophe of World War I and with its strengthening of the executive apparatus of the state, or the general trauma and polemic hostility pervading the politics of our societies at the end of the war.[81] Rather, the main ideological tropes of fascism were already in place at the time of the takeover of Fiume and certainly at the time of the March on Rome. They developed *before* World War I in the particularly anti-political milieu of the French Third Republic, building on one hand on the dreary tensions traversing established politics and materialised in public scandals, while on the other hand on the emergence of a distinctly *a-* if not overtly *anti*-Marxist understanding of conflictual politics epitomised by the work of Georges Sorel and supported by a wide range of former socialist or anarchist circles.[82]

79 Ibid.

80 Gaspar Miklos Tamas, 'What is Post-fascism', *Open Democracy*, 13 September 2001.

81 See, e.g., Zeev Sternhell, *La droite révolutionnaire, 1885–1914. Les origines françaises du fascisme* (Paris: Seuil, 1978). Zeev Sternhell, *Neither Right nor Left: Fascist Ideology in France* (Princeton University Press, 1986).

82 Sternhell, *Neither Right nor Left*, 29.

One of the most important insights brought by Sternhell in his perhaps idiosyncratic understanding of fascism is that its crucial feature was that of a political conflict devoid of the socio-economic grounding provided by the Marxist class-struggle. Brought about by the Bernstein debate concerning the place of revolutionary action within the conditions of the emergent mass democracy that enabled workers' participation in parliamentary politics, the notion of a revolution devoid of class support, a revolution that is not grounded in socio-economic conditions, but is autonomous with regards to determinations, circulated from the left to right.[83] This political translation of one of the main features of the Marxist tradition within the various conservative and reactionary circles – from royalists to nationalists – opened up a specific type of ideological indistinction that was the initial trait of fascist movements and lingered on even at the time when fascism was in power.

One could note here that Lenin's indictment of leftism[84] was directed against attempts of the left-wing of the German communist party who emphasised a notion of support of German nationalism within the context of the Ruhr occupation. Current research on the history of fascism is more keen to unravel the hybrid nature of fascism, as a *trans-class* ideology, appealing to blood and soil as forms of ethnic political unity. Sternhell's reading of fascism is perhaps too limited to the level of the ideas and concepts that formed such a world-view. However, it is able to point out at least some parallels and continuities that we can decipher in our post-political era, moving beyond the obvious observation that one hundred years have passed since the birth of fascism.

2.5 The Refusal of Class-Struggle and the Indictment of Communism

One point to be noted is the specific disconnection between popular revolt and class-struggle that emerges as a result of a crisis within Marxism. If such a crisis had already taken place at the time of the Bernstein debate, nowadays the dissolution of Marxism within the left is more than obvious. If we consider the post-1968 shift within politics and the slow demise of *class-struggle* as a referent grounding emancipatory politics, let alone various attempts of the left to recuperate overt conservative and reactionary tropes of the political – out of which Carl Schmitt is only an epitome – we can have a better picture of the ideological crisis of our contemporary milieu.

Another point is the necessary ideological and historical connection between the refusal of *class-struggle* as a point of reference and the anti-communist

83 Ibid. 78–82.

84 Vladimir Lenin, '"Left-Wing" Communism: An Infantile Disorder' *Collected Works*, Volume 31 (Moscow: Progress Publishers, 1964), 17–118.

stand that pervades current instantiation of right-wing authoritarianism. This is less than a mere shibboleth within the discourse of the right, but very likely the historical substance that enabled the resurgence of such ideologies within the post-communist and post-fascist consensus, and deeply embedded within the practice of the law and transitional justice of the past 30 years especially within Central and Eastern Europe, where communism was decried by legal means as being a criminal regime. Whatever the failings and indeed the excesses of the communist terror and Stalinism before, during, and after World War II, the criminalisation of communism was not meant to make any historical distinctions between periods, actions, practices, and discussions of the ideological motivations of such acts. Rather, the failure of communism was perceived in itself as enough evidence for its murderous inherent character that could, later on, invalidate any claim about the democratic, emancipatory, and egalitarian thrust of socialist politics: the ideological consensus was quite clear – communism was illegitimate and anything associated with it, be it class-struggle or rational administration, smacks of totalitarianism, and is a shortcut towards a totalitarian society.[85]

Within the process, the re-writing of history – and one would say precisely constitutional history – either whitewashed or downplayed the authoritarianisms preceding the communist takeover, the institutional continuities, the social structures involved within the process, as well as the legal apparatuses that served as a basis for organising repression: in short, by fighting communist totalitarianism, most of the anti-communist analysis remained silent on the material history of both communism and totalitarianism, by failing to problematise what gave rise to the totalitarian excess in state politics. The failure of communism, followed itself by a rather inadequate way of working through the core of excess, state repression, and suppression of freedoms, is not only a feature of CEE law and politics.

The tropes of reading communism through the lens of totalitarian lawlessness have certainly spilled across the imaginary borders dividing East and West, and made a specific form of anti-communism a default ideological stand, from which any serious political engagement in questioning the core of the social formations in which we live has been constantly expunged. Against this background, economic crises, and in CEE the brutal transformation towards capitalism were not able to find any meaningful political articulation. With a number of distinct exceptions, such as Syriza and Podemos, before the rise of the France Insoumise, the central forms of opposition were inconsequential, short-lived mobilisations with very unclear political goals and ideological consistence, in many respects an embodiment of the demise of political subjectivity. Rather, the more articulated forms of political discontent operated an ideological bricolage of whatever was on the market, that is

85 Cercel, *Towards a Jurisprudence of State-Communism*, 202–5.

anti-communism, and blood and soil, in an opposition to any of the marks of the "system." Depoliticisation produced its own specific form of contender, that is a depoliticised mass that stands against the regalia of power without clear or meaningful demands.

2.6 Conclusions

The experience of the COVID-19 crisis and the rise of the antivaxx movement, with its hybrid ideology blending counter-cultural suspicion of the state, a natural law discourse glossing on the classics of liberalism, and conspiracy theories, is instructive with regards to the level of the crisis of public rationality. In a very specific sense, the Capitol insurgents and anti-Covid protesters represent exactly the phantasmatic projection of the discourse on populism: the *people* of populism *exist*. Now, this is the specific strategy that needs to be analysed and deconstructed: the *people* of the discourse of populism is just a fictional structure, whereas the social basis of the new global and diffuse discontent, is the product of the existing depoliticised order that has transformed the markets within the true *de facto* sovereigns of our polities. To put it simply, such opposition could hardly have developed otherwise than within the existing socio-economic and political conditions entertained by our vision of legality.

Attempting to analyse it with a view of criticism through the frames of populism, that is by its relation to the law of judicialised politics, cannot bring us far: it is a refusal or a cynical instrumentalisation of such a vision of politics, whose value is as good as any other. The line of continuities in theory and practice with historical authoritarian ideologies would be perhaps more helpful, yet there seems to be a specific difficulty in accepting that important parts of the populations both in CEE and in the West would overtly support such ideologies. The question is indeed embarrassing and perhaps goes to the core of our legal theoretical conundrum. How come within the Europe of human rights, of the rule of law, and democracy citizens are supporting overtly racist, protofascist, parties? Perhaps this question has to be answered not by the *virtus dormitiva* of populism, but by looking at the failures of the law to institute a democratic post-authoritarian consensus.

It is a question of looking at the politics nested within the law based on the economic, cultural, and symbolic presuppositions, the politics of the *archive* that law carries within it and that makes it not an inanimate object, a blunt instrument of power, but an ideological force that carries within its structure powerful messages about the society it de facto institutes. But in order to be able to ask such questions about how the fundamental concepts of our constitutional law are at odds with the very basic presuppositions of cosmopolitanism, and how interpretative methods – if this is the right word here – have made it possible to reinstall visions of national relativism within the understanding of rights, and, more generally, how the law keeps within it its very destitution, one would need to accept that law is politics and therefore law has to be approached critically.

I believe that the only way out of the present conundrum for legal scholars is precisely to return to an analysis of law as politics, to understand that the way in which we represent populism is just another form of politics, and as a political intervention it has to go beyond a criticism of the means and address the substantive core of the matter: *post-fascism*, as broad as it can be is a particularly useful term. Authoritarianism is perhaps another, but what should be seized upon in the use of these concepts in order to ascertain the features of the new regime of historicity opened before us, is the rupture within, the refusal of the tradition of the Enlightenment within the very structure of our legal categories.

If indeed lawyers want to turn towards a critique of the rising far-right politics in good faith, this requires an engagement with the substantive claims that so-called populists put forward and an evaluation of the role of the law within these claims. It requires first a perhaps painful yet necessary self-criticism of the very categories that constitute our basic knowledge as lawyers and the tensions we often obscure rather than overcome in our daily practice of the law. Understanding that law as a system wrought by inconsistencies, that articulates conflictual notions of being together, and conflictual imaginaries, is just the beginning of engaging in a politics of the law that takes democracy seriously. The point is, of course, not to play within the hands of the rising right, nor to take their claims for representing the *people* for holding a value of truth, but to understand and reason through theoretical and practical possibilities of instituting the *demos* through political mobilisation that aims at supporting the universalist values and promises still pledged by our constitutions.

While this may be too late for such a task, I think that there is enough political and legal creativity in redeeming the law at the same time as its politico-legal basis is rethought. For instance, there are glimpses of hope within the possibilities of rethinking not only the structure of our economic constitutions on an emancipatory basis, but also of ways of reconnecting the law with those who it is meant to protect – the *people* as that part of no-part within our polities. Equally, there is room for understanding the law as a project that can be severed from its ties of sovereign politics and open it through a *study* that would enable us to glimpse a normativity devoid of bio- – or more often – necropolitical uses. Such a utopian call is still within our reach as lawyers and especially of legal academics, if we are able to think critically about the consequences of our thought and praxis. While indeed writing academic articles or book chapters in law edited volumes is not going to advance one inch the fate of the *people*, nor offer any meaningful protection towards the rising tides of the new forces of obscurantism and reaction, it might at least be an activity that can reconnect with the utopian traditions that aimed to achieve a transformation of legality.

To be sure, this is not a call to revolution, but a plea for critical legal studies both as a method within the study of law and as a praxis of being within legal academia, by resisting dogmas, institutional pressures, and keeping alive what is worth defending within the liberal Enlightened tradition.

Chapter 3

The Polish Constitutional Court in the Grip of Neo-liberalism

Adam Sulikowski

3.1 Introduction

In 1985, the institution of judicial review of the constitutionality was introduced into the Polish legal order. At that time, this practice was held to be a significant novelty and could even be described as an important political breakthrough, within the socialist context. Such a legal political development seems to suggest that the demoliberal idea of a constitutional court did not sit comfortably within the Polish constitutional context of the past decades. While in the interwar era there had been a cautious debate on the possibility of introducing judicial oversight of constitutionality, the chances of these doctrinal intentions being implemented were severely reduced by the May Coup of 1926. Subsequently, the gradual drift towards authoritarianism culminated in the April Constitution of 1935, which introduced a presidential system with a quasi-monarchical head of state accountable only 'to God and history.' In the era of the People's Republic of Poland, the "official" position of Soviet legal science was adopted, which held that constitutional courts are an expression of the reactionary character of bourgeois societies – an illegitimate bulwark against revolution and the establishment of the real dictatorship of the proletariat.[1]

The shift in the perception of the constitutional review is tied up with the social changes that occurred in the 1970s. The increase in social welfare and the accompanying changes in lifestyle such as growing urbanisation, widespread access to medical care, culture, and media, resulted in the emergence of an increasingly important socialist middle class. In enterprises, the administration grew, the overall demand for services increased, and the importance of the so-called non-productive sector of the economy rose.[2] There were

1 Mikhail Abramovich Nudel, *Конституционный контроль в капиталистических государствах* [Constitutional Review in Capitalist States] (Moskva: Iuridicheskaia Literatura, 1968), 14–6.
2 Michał Sutowski and Maciej Gdula, 'Co nam zostało z lat 70.? [What Remains from the 1970s?], *Krytyka Polityczna* (4 June 2016), https://krytykapolityczna.pl/kraj/gdula-co-nam-zostalo-z-lat-70/ accessed 1 May 2023.

DOI: 10.4324/9781032624464-4

also significant changes in the mainstream image of the intelligentsia – in books, broadcasts, and films. In previous decades, the positive role models in speeches, films, and novels tended to be workers and peasants, while members of the intelligentsia were treated with suspicion or simply passed over in silence. Then, in the 1970s, a sudden change occurred: the discourse began to signal its unequivocal appreciation of the socialist middle class. The political justification for this revalorisation was obvious keeping in mind that the media and publishing industry were under state control. During the era of Edward Gierek, the First Secretary of the Central Committee of the PZPR (The Polish United Workers' Party), who was familiar with the West having spent a lot of time in France, the party authorities signalled that they wanted to be able to depend on the loyal part of the socialist "bourgeoisie" – the intelligentsia and professionals, thereby instilling a certain sense of responsibility for state policy. This did not, of course, mean the abolition of censorship or other forms of oppression, but it involved the promise of increased professional autonomy and improved economic status in exchange for loyalty.

Hanna Dębska, working within a Bourdesian framework, has convincingly shown that in the late 1970s the People's Republic of Poland allowed the partial autonomisation of the 'legal field' and the considerable autonomisation of the 'academic legal subfield.' The manifest aim of these endeavors was to extend the chain of legitimacy and to modernise the system.[3] The introduction of the Constitutional Court, of the Supreme Administrative Court, and of the Supreme Audit Office was intended to be a symbol of nomocratic modernisation. The discussions began in 1976 and went on for years – they were interrupted by Gierek's resignation, by a wave of strikes which culminated in the legalisation of the Solidarity opposition movement, a coup d'état led by the opponents of the 'weakening of socialism' (primarily by representatives of the army and secret services), and then the subsequent imposition of martial law. The constitutional reforms were finally carried out in 1982 and the statute regulating the powers of the Polish Constitutional Court (hereinafter also: 'PCC', or simply 'the Court') was passed in 1985.

During the first years of its functioning, the Court proved to be rather passivist and formalistic, focusing on the elimination of inconsistencies within the legal system, and on the legitimisation of reforms undertaken by the authorities. These reforms were increasingly pro-capitalist in nature insofar as free trade and private initiative policies were extended. The judges of the Court were regarded as representatives of the pro-state intelligentsia: the opposition did not generally associate them with the regime; neither were

3 Hanna Dębska, *Władza, symbol, prawo. Społeczne tworzenie Trybunału Konstytucyjnego* [Power, Symbol, Law: The Social Construction of the Constitutional Court] (Warszawa: Wydawnictwo Sejmowe, 2015) 124–7.

they criticised by the underground media. They gained the status of spokespersons of the elite and survived the revolution of 1989 without their image being tarnished. The ideological changes they operated in the field of law and jurisprudence were compatible with those being made in the mainstream political discourse. The Constitutional Court thus became a co-architect of the Polish systemic transformation and made several decisions that could be described as activist. Such a position of the Court was rendered easy by an almost universal conviction that such measures were necessary being grounded in an *opinio necessitatis*.

It is worth mentioning that, until the political forces that are now generally described under the label as "illiberal populist" emerged in an institutionalised form in the mid-2000s, the authority of the PCC was not questioned by any significant political parties. It was not until the Law and Justice Party formulated a programme for taking on the establishment and the liberal judiciary that this state of affairs changed. Interestingly, the thesis that the Polish Constitutional Court was a spokesperson of the mainstream elite is considered rather uncontroversial in contemporary professional discourse. On the descriptive level, this thesis is articulated by both the discourse of the supporters of the demoliberal *ancien regime* as well as by the currently governing populists. Where these discourses diverge is, of course, in their assessment of the role of the CT.

According to the "liberals," the constitutional judiciary is prominently a hero of the so-called systemic transformation. As such, it presents itself as a hero whose leading role has enabled unambiguous progress, manifested in the profound transformation of the socio-economic system and its legal environment – a transformation that followed an appropriate and necessary course. According to this narrative, it is largely thanks to constitutional jurisprudence that Poland can be judged as a pioneer in "departing from real socialism" and aligning itself with Western models.

In contrast, populist critics perceive the Constitutional Court as an ideological overseer that elevated the views of the elite to the status of "apolitical norms," whereas their operation was treated as a necessity. As a consequence, the Court is perceived as having limited pluralism and actual possibilities for political change infringing upon the legislative and the government, that is upon institutions endowed with the democratic legitimacy to transform the 'will of the sovereign' into binding law.

The issue of the socio-economic policies pursued by the Constitutional Court and the ideological entanglements of these policies is not widely addressed in legal theoretical analysis. If we consider the perspective of liberal discourses, this should come as no surprise. The picture they present is straightforward: the Constitutional Court acted justly, under conditions of historical necessity, and although its case-law and respective jurisprudence may not have satisfied everyone and may have impinged certain economic interests, this was necessary at the time, it had to be done, for reasons that were obvious and in no sense ideologically determined.

At the same time, the discourse of the ruling United Right does not seem to be particularly focused on the economic policies of the constitutional judiciary either. As a consequence, during the so-called 'war for the Court,' when the ruling party sought to take over the Constitutional Court and pack it with staff sympathetic to the parliamentary majority, the theme of justifying the takeover of the Court with the need to defend the social gains of the new government was increasingly popular. For instance, the slogan 'The PCC might block the Family 500 plus program' appeared in statements of politicians from the ruling coalition.[4]

As I noted elsewhere,[5] the United Right more or less consciously took over the ideas proclaimed in the 1990s by unequivocally left-wing thinkers. One of them, Jarosław Ładosz, a Marxist philosopher, who after 1989 refused to accept the transformation, due to the derogation of the competence of the Sejm to reject, by qualified majority, the decisions of the Court, asked the following question:

> What are the social reasons and real functions behind the widespread idea of establishing constitutional Courts in the constitutions of the former socialist countries, which can rule irrevocably, above parliaments, on the constitutionality of laws?

To which he formulated an interesting answer:

> What is at stake is the creation of an institution [...] which would protect the power of the famous middle class [...] in case a parliamentary majority appears willing to stop or reverse the reform [from socialism to capitalism

4 The "Family 500+" is a program of monthly benefits paid to the parents of each child, officially aimed at boosting demographics, but which, in practice, is really a social welfare policy. For examples of Law and Justice politicians threatening that the PCC could take away those benefits, see, e.g., 'Ziobro: opozycja liczyła, że TK "wysadzi w powietrze" pomysł 500 zł na dziecko' *TVPInfo* (5 December 2015), https://www.tvp.info/22937914/ziobro-opozycja-liczyla-ze-tk-wysadzi-w-powietrze-500-zl-na-dziecko, accessed 1 May 2023 (statement of Minister of Justice Zbigniew Ziobro); 'Wiceminister sprawiedliwości twierdzi, że TK mógłby zablokować ustawę 500 zł na dziecko' *TVN24* (18 December 2015) http://www.tvn24.pl/wiadomosci-z-kraju,3/trybunal-konstytucyjny-patryk-jaki-o-zmianach-w-ustawie,604022.html, accessed 1 May 2023 (statement Vice-Minister of Justice Patryk Jaki).

5 Adam Sulikowski, 'The Return of Forgotten Critique: Some Remarks on the Intellectual Sources of the Polish Populist Revolution' (2020) 45 *Review of Central and East European Law* 376.

> A.S.]. What is therefore at stake is the political police, guarding the construction of capitalism.[6]

It must be admitted, however, that this line of argument tended to appear in the discourse of supporters of right-wing parties, while it was rarely articulated openly by right-wing populist politicians, especially after they came to power (both in 2005 and then ten years later). During the 'fight with the Court,'[7] and later in the 'war over the Court'[8] the main theme was that of restraining the 'justocracy' and the interests of groups actually represented by judges. Jarosław Kaczyński, in an interview given in 2010 at the Jagiellonian University under the telling title 'Is Poland a state under the rule of law?,' argued:

> In legal theory and jurisprudence an interpretation of the rule of law was adopted that focused on the protection of acquired rights. Such an interpretation was related, I believe, both to the personnel composition of the judiciary and to the situation in the universities – practically all independent academics in the field of public law were somehow connected with the previous authorities. It is not difficult to see that such an interpretation served a certain purpose, which was to strive for the petrification of social relations, so that the beneficiaries of the previous system were not threatened with the loss of the rights they had acquired thanks to it – often on very dubious grounds'[9]

It must be acknowledged that the representatives of illiberal right-wing populism, both in Poland, Hungary, and elsewhere in post-communist Europe, rarely admit to protecting or promoting socialist solutions. As avowed right-wingers, they usually reject the 'theoretical assumptions of socialism.' Increasing social security or welfare payments are justified on the grounds of righting the wrongs done by liberals and, against internal free-market adversaries, are presented as effective methods for seducing the masses in order to

6 Jarosław Ładosz, *Sąd kasujący ustawy i dyktujący parlamentowi ich wykładnię* [A Court Annulling Statutes and Dictating Their Interpretation to Parliament], http://www.socjalizmteraz.pl/pl/Artykuly/?id=936/Ladosz__SAD_KASUJACY_USTAWY_I_DYKTUJACY_PARLAMENTOWI_ICH_WYKLADNIE, accessed 1 May 2023.

7 During the first coalition governments of the Law and Justice party, the president and the government accused the Constitutional Court of excessive interference in the legal order of the State, and of being clearly entangled in "leftist-liberal" ideology.

8 President Duda, allied with Law and Justice, refused to swear in the judges of the Constitutional Court that had been elected by the Sejm of the previous term, and then the new majority chose its own candidates for these positions.

9 Jarosław Kaczyński, 'Czy Polska jest państwem prawa? Wykład na Uniwersytecie Jagiellońskim' [Is Poland a State of Law? Lecture at the Jagiellonian University] (2010) 24 *Pressje* 222.

further the interests of the political right. The theoretical core of this procedure lies with the concept of national solidarity, which requires the building of a community under the guidance of new, truly national elites, which, however, requires the inclusion of the poor by guaranteeing them a tolerable existence.[10] Furthermore, somewhat contrary to public expectations, the constitutional courts, which have been taken over and are now controlled by right-wing populists, tend to avoid overt socio-economic issues, and do not dare to echo the slogans of anti-liberal, pro-welfare reconquest.

In this chapter, I will attempt to explore the extent to which the economic rulings of the Polish Constitutional Court were ideologically contaminated by neoliberal theories. I understand neoliberalism not only as a postulate economic ideology focused on maximum 'market liberation' – i.e., minimising the role of the state in the economy, the privatisation of public tasks, favorable tax rates for corporations, welfare cuts, limiting employees' legal protection, and moving away from the concept of the welfare state.[11] Rather, neoliberal ideology also involves the promotion of a specific mentality and ethical models – the heroes of history are entrepreneurs, active people who develop a mythical economy and contribute to global welfare by getting rich, while the anti-heroes are people who, unable to cope in a capitalist environment, 'reach out to the state' and encourage it to strengthen the processes of redistribution through political methods.

Against this background, I will focus on the period from the start of the systemic transformation (i.e., the end of the 1980s) until 2015. The year 2015 is not only the beginning of the "war over the Court," following the double electoral victory of the United Right, but also the time when the vectors in several entrenched lines of jurisprudence were 'reversed.' Even before the judges elected by the new parliamentary majority appeared in the Constitutional Court, the so-called "old judges" had started issuing rulings with unambiguously illiberal overtones that is, illiberal in the economic sense. This development indicates they were making a certain adjustment to the social mood, but at the same time it is also an admission of guilt – the CT, by changing its mind on a range of issues – such as the compliance of the banking enforcement title with the constitution, the unconstitutionality of taxing amounts lower than the subsistence minimum for personal income tax contributions, the possibility of not only employees with employment contracts to belong to trade unions, but also those employed on civil law contracts ("junk contracts") – thereby implicitly revealing the relativity and ideological entanglement of the previous solutions, which had been presented in the jurisprudence as necessary, axiologically neutral, and the only viable option.

10 Gabor Halmai, 'Illiberalism in East-Central Europe' *EUI Working Papers. LAW* 19/2005, 5.
11 David Harvey, *A Brief History of Neoliberalism* (Oxford-New York: OUP, 2005), 2ff.

In my analysis, I will necessarily rely on rather general judgments and examples from a dozen or so rulings, which I consider to be representative of a specific pattern of thinking. Of course, I am aware that in the body of rulings of the "old" Constitutional Court one can find rulings supporting social security. This is frequently pointed out today by those left-wing scholars who believe that the left should seek as many points of convergence as possible with liberals against the ruling right-wing populists.[12] Nevertheless, according to the old adage 'you will know them by their fruits,' I have to insist that, especially in the 1990s, the Constitutional Court explicitly or implicitly, by not speaking out, or by refusing to recognise the unconstitutionality of certain provisions, approved of almost all the pathological solutions that were implemented in Poland, but which could never have been introduced in the "old EU countries," in view of their excessively neoliberal character.

3.2 Hollowing Out the Social Provisions of the Constitution of 1952 that Were Still in Force After the Transformation

The attitude of the Constitutional Court is epitomised in a series of judgments from the 1990s which considered whether of a range of welfare cuts were compatible with the constitutional provisions that remained in force.[13] The rationality of these cuts was at odds with the values enshrined in the still valid provisions of the socialist Constitution. In a series of rulings, the Constitutional Court recognised the rights guaranteed by the provisions that remained in force as valid,[14] but usually refused to declare as unconstitutional any kind of limitation on the social rights acquired in the previous era. In the rulings K 13/94 and K 23/95, the Court formulated the thesis that the permissibility of 'the legislator deviating from legal solutions which are more favorable for citizens' must be regarded as typical for the welfare legislation of states undergoing political transformation. In turn, in ruling K

12 Stanisław Skarżyński, '"Trybunał zablokuje 500 plus." Kaczyński tylko straszy, brak mu argumentów ["The Constitutional Court Will Block 500 Plus:" Kaczyński is only Scaremongering, he has no Arguments] *OKO Press* (5 September 2016), https://oko.press/trybunal-zablokuje-500-plus-kaczynski-tylko-straszy/, accessed 1 May 2023; Rafał Bakalarczyk, 'Trybunał w obronie wykluczonych' [Constitutional Court Defending the Excluded] *Krytyka Polityczna* (25 December 2015), https://krytykapolityczna.pl/kraj/bakalarczyk-trybunal-w-obronie-wykluczonych/

13 Prior to the entry into force of the Constitution of 2 April 1997, the provisions of the Constitution of the People's Republic of Poland of 22 July 1952 remained in force, as they had not been repealed by later constitutional laws.

14 Witold Zakrzewski, 'Prawa i wolności obywateli Rzeczypospolitej Polskiej' [The Rights and Freedoms of the Citizens of the Republic of Poland] in Wiesław Skrzydło (ed.), *Zarys prawa konstytucyjnego* [An Outline of Constitutional Law] (Lublin–Rzeszów: Wydawnictwo UMCS, 1993), 55

21/95, the PCC stressed the need for restraint in assessing the compatibility of laws regulating social benefits with the constitutional principles of social justice and equality. These values had to be balanced by the 'socio-economic assumptions' guiding the legislator in conditions of considerable discretion, and by the requirements associated with the 'difficult budgetary situation' of the state. As a basis for the admissibility of welfare cuts, the socio-economic opportunities clause was invoked in a series of judgments from the beginning of the most free-market decade in the history of Poland – the 1990s.[15] In all these rulings the Court stressed that the principle of social justice, which was expressed directly in constitutional provisions, must, to a certain extent, give way to a 'state of overriding economic necessity,' as there exists a 'close dependence of social security on the socio-economic conditions of the country and the related possibility to collect funds for social security,' and, further, the PCC stated that the right to social security is in a 'continuous process of adjustment to social needs, but also to the financial possibilities of the state.'

At that time, hundreds of state-owned enterprises employing thousands of workers were either being declared bankrupt or being sold below value, and their new owners, who were usually foreign, made mass redundancies, while the workers who lost their jobs could count on practically no social safeguards, despite the fact that the socialist constitution, guaranteeing certain social and economic rights, was still in force. Outside the Court's windows, previously vibrant industrial centres were turning into economic deserts, with unemployment reaching 40% of those able and willing to work. At the same time, the extremely liberal labor laws made it possible for employers to reduce workers' wages without meeting any significant obstacles. In one of the judgments typical for the 1990s, the Court ruled that a change in wage laws which allowed them to deteriorate should not, in principle, take place in a democratic state ruled by law, but only 'if there is no need in a specific case to protect other constitutional values' (P 1/95 of 11 September 1995). It is not difficult to guess that the 'other constitutional values' referred to here are the requirements of the market economy.

Neither did the Constitutional Court deem the institution of the so-called 'popiwek' unconstitutional. 'Popiwek,' a tax on excessive payments of salaries and wages, was an anti-inflationary solution introduced in the 1980s into Polish labor and tax law.[16] This solution consisted of imposing a horrendous tax on the employer (ranging from 100 to 400%) on any increase

15 Such as with the judgments in cases K 7/90, K 6/91, K 14/91, K 15/91.

16 Act of February 26, 1982 on taxation of socialised economy units (consolidated text, *Journal of Laws* of 1987, No. 12, item 77, as amended), the Act of 29 December 1983 on the state fund for vocational activation (*Journal of Laws* No. 75, item 334, as amended). For more on this subject, see: Ben Slay, *The Polish Economy: Crisis, Reform and Transformation* (Princeton: Princeton University Press, 2014), 156 ff.

in salary above a certain regulated amount, unless there was a reduction in employment. As a result of gradual legislative changes, from 1991 the 'popiwek' ceased to apply to private sector companies, while it survived in the state sector until 1995. This not only resulted in a wave of redundancies in state-owned companies, but also in an exponential increase in private sector wages, while public sector wages remained unchanged. The PCC examined the 'popiwek' on its own initiative only at the end of the 1980s (the ruling Uw 4/88) and did not find it unconstitutional – it focused instead on the fact that the executive regulations implementing the act were not always consistent with the delegations authorising their issuance. Thus, until 1995, an institution that would have been almost unimaginable in the West survived in a form that unequivocally discriminated against public sector employees, while constitutional provisions were in force that explicitly guaranteed equality before the law and social justice.

A point of interest is the fact that in official political and media discourses throughout most of the transition period, many politicians and economists willingly and directly identified with neoliberalism. As the left-wing philosopher Tomasz Markiewka notes: 'In Poland, as late as in the early 1990s, Janusz Lewandowski published a book, with a foreword by Donald Tusk, entitled *Neoliberałowie wobec współczesności* (Neoliberals in the Face of Modernity), in which he praised neoliberalism. It was only when neoliberalism came to have a bad name that the people who were described as neoliberals stopped using it. The third, abridged edition of Lewandowski's 2013 book now bears a different title: *Liberalism and Modernity*.'[17] Lewandowski, who holds a Ph.D. in economics, was considered, alongside Leszek Balcerowicz, as one of the architects of the Polish transformation: in the 'crazy' 1990s he served several times as Ownership Transformation Minister – in this position he was responsible for predatory privatisation and selling off of public assets, and then, from 2010 to 2014, he was EU Commissioner for Budget and Financial Programming. Neo-liberalism was very popular in Poland, for a long time, and was largely considered 'politically neutral' thanks to its presence in the dominant media.

Balcerowicz himself, the main director of the Polish reforms (several times Minister of Finance and Deputy Prime Minister responsible for economic affairs) was also keen to acknowledge his neoliberal inspirations. He believed that democracy must be based on capitalism, and liberal democracy on liberal capitalism; he considered alternative economic approaches to neoliberalism to be mistaken and dangerous in the midst of the systemic

17 Tomasz S. Markiewka, 'Wszyscy jesteśmy neoliberałami' [We Are All Neoliberals] *Krytyka Polityczna* (18 Match 2016), https://krytykapolityczna.pl/kraj/wszyscy-jestesmy-neoliberalami-markiewka/, accessed 1 May 2023.

transformation, given the aim of 'moving away from communism.'[18] In his autobiography, written with an evident sense of pride and satisfaction with his success, Balcerowicz suggests that neoliberalism was the only available option for the Polish economy. The book was entitled *800 dni. Szok kontrolowany* (800 Days. A Controlled Shock).[19] In the second part, this liberal economist argued that the price for suppressing almost 700% inflation, and for 'healing the economy' – through 'sometimes excessively rapid privatization,' accepting a spike in unemployment and the economic decline of several hitherto highly industrialised regions – 'may only seem too high,' but the application of any other solution would have been ineffective and caused even greater damage.

As a resident of a workers' housing estate made of prefabricated blocks (the so-called 'large panels'), I had the opportunity to observe this 'controlled shock' in practice. Back in 1989, at 6 a.m., lights were still shining in the windows of all the flats and bus stops were full of people heading to the morning shift at big enterprises in Wroclaw, such as Pafawag (a railway carriage and locomotive factory), Dolmel (a turbine and engine factory), and Elwro (an electronics factory, producer of Polish computers). Two years later, at six in the morning, almost all the windows were dark, the bus stops empty. Large industrial plants were privatised and closed down (it happened that the purchaser of a state-owned enterprise, a few years after buying it, sold the land to developers after the plant had been liquidated for a price much higher than the 'privatization fee' for which he had acquired the whole enterprise).[20] Schools were forced to provide food for children on the estate. Some workers tried retraining (my father, an electrical engineer, became a bookseller and publisher), most became victims of deep pauperisation, spiraling into alcoholism and crime (several of my peers became members of organised crime groups involved in theft in Germany). The history of my housing estate is a fairly representative example of the effects of the neoliberal "shock doctrine."[21]

The neoliberal changes led to workers and farmers voting en masse for left-wing parties. As early as 1993, and so just four years after the start of the transformation, post-communist parties won a majority – a coalition was

18 Leszek Balcerowicz, 'Common Fallacies in the Debate on the Transition to a Market Economy' (1994) 9(19) *Economic Policy* 49.

19 Leszek Balcerowicz, *800 dni. Szok kontrolowany* [The 800 Days: A Controlled Shock] (Warszawa: BGW, 1992).

20 Elizabeth Dunn provides many similar examples in *Privatizing Poland: Baby Food, Big Business, and the Remaking of Labor* (Ithaca-London: Cornell University Press, 2004).

21 The Polish sociologist Jacek Tittenbrun devoted a four-volume study to the social effects of the neoliberal transformation, Jacek Tittenbrun, *Z deszczu pod rynnę: studium polskiej prywatyzacji* [From Bad to Worse: A Study of the Polish Privatisation] (Poznań: Zysk i Spółka, 2007), 4 volumes.

formed by the SLD (the official successor to the PZPR) and the PSL – the Polish People's Party (the heir to the ZSL, a licensed peasant party from a bygone era). The slogan "Komuno wróć!" (Communism, Come Back!) became very popular. However, the elite's acceptance of the path laid out by Balcerowicz meant that there was no significant pro-welfare turn in Polish politics. The elites of the post-communist parties were clearly beneficiaries of the transformation, so they were devoutly conservative when it came to economic policy.

3.3 The Bank Enforcement Title: The Neoliberal Judgment of 2005 and Its Reversal in 2015

In the 1990s, as the wealthy elite rapidly accumulated capital, the importance of the banking sector increased dramatically. Many private banks were set up, and existing banks were eagerly bought up by foreign investors interested in making quick and easy profits. In these circumstances, in order to make it easier for banks to collect debts from their customers, the "bank enforcement title" was introduced into the Polish legal system.[22] This entailed that the bank could effectively carry out enforcement against the debtor's assets without the need for court proceedings (and thus without any judicial control). The court would only grant an enforcement clause to the "title" issued by the bank, based on the debtor's statement on voluntary submission to enforcement. Despite the rather widespread opinion among lawyers that Polish banks have a competence 'unknown in civilized legal orders,'[23] the Constitutional Court, when reviewing the constitutionality of the regulations on the bank enforcement title in 2005, did not find that they violate the right to public hearing of the case by a competent, impartial, and independent court, as provided by Article 45 of the Constitution. The Court, like other Polish courts, found, in accordance with the liberal principle of *volenti non fit iniuria*, that the requirement for the debtor to make a statement on voluntary submission to enforcement sufficiently protected his interests. In practice, however, the submission of such a declaration was treated by the banks as a condition *sine qua non* for obtaining a loan. The banking enforcement title became the primary tool for enforcing bank loans, thereby severely limiting the possibilities of defending clients against abuse. A change in the line of jurisprudence occurred only in 2015, on the wave of the "pro-social" reinterpretation of many neoliberal normative acts, when it became apparent that the populist forces could, in their attacks on the "juristocracy," quite

22 Introduced by Act of 29 August 1997 – Banking Law (*Dz.U.* 140, item 939).

23 Jan Mojak, 'Bankowy tytuł egzekucyjny przeciwko spadkobiercom dłużnika' [Enforcing the Banking Enforcement Title vis-à-vis the Successors of the Debtor] (2011) 11 *Monitor Prawniczy*.

effectively argue that the existing jurisprudence was ideologically biased. The Constitutional Court then began to rule quite intensively on issues with social significance, with a simultaneous campaign by the liberal media, which tried to convey the image of the constitutional judiciary as an institution protecting not only rights important to the elite, but also rights important to the lower classes. These actions were relatively compulsive in nature, which limited their real political effectiveness.

In its judgment of 14 April 2015 (Case P 45/12), the Constitutional Court ruled that the provisions of the Banking Law introducing and regulating the institution of the bank enforcement title were unconstitutional. The judgment, however, did not concern non-compliance with Article 45 of the Constitution (the right to a court), but with Article 32 (the principle of equality before the law). Such a change in the legal basis allowed the Constitutional Court to "save face" to a certain extent, because the constitutional judges did not challenge the old ruling but stated the non-compliance with another provision 'in the face of new allegations' (interestingly, non-compliance with Article 32 had also been raised in the proceedings in 2005, as an additional argument, but had not been taken into account by the constitutional judges at that time).

It was only in 2015, when polls clearly indicated there had been a change in public sentiment and the widespread adoption of views questioning predatory capitalism, that the Court finally recognised that banks were not primarily 'subjects of public trust' (as had been argued in several previous rulings), but are instead businesses that are, by their very nature, geared towards profit maximisation. The judges concluded that profit is a factor that determines the actions of banks more than the norm of protecting the interests of their customers. Therefore, the constitutionality of the solution – according to which the basis for enforcement was what the bank had arbitrarily stated in the bank enforcement title, on the basis of its own documentation – was questioned. The Constitutional Court found that many debtors only found out about their alleged debt during the process of bailiff enforcement, when the possibilities of defense were very limited. Interestingly and characteristically, Judge-Rapporteur Teresa Liszcz, stressed in the oral reasons for the ruling, that 'banks cannot be judges in their own case.'[24] It may seem paradoxical, but this very argument had already been the basis of a motion decided in 2005. At that time, however, the Constitutional Court had not found any violation of the constitutional right to a court in the provisions of the bank enforcement title.

24 The transcript of the hearing is available at ipo.trybunal.gov.pl › ipo › dok › P_45_12_0414_15_stenogram ADO_

3.4 Judgment on the Social Minimum and Taxation

In the wave of "correcting" neoliberal lines of jurisprudence, in its ruling of 28 October 2015, Case K 21/14, the Constitutional Court ruled that the provisions of the tax law are unconstitutional, insofar as they do not provide a correction mechanism which guarantees that at least the social minimum necessary for subsistence is exempt from personal income tax. This was a decisive retreat from the line of jurisprudence stemming from decisions issued in the 1990s, the key point of which was the recognition that taxes are, first and foremost, instruments for conducting state economic policy, and that their social dimension is secondary to the primary objective of maintaining a 'healthy and competitive economy.' Justifying the 2015 judgment, Judge-Rapporteur Miroslaw Granat stated that 'the amount that is exempt from tax is not a privilege offered by the authorities to citizens (...). In the tax-free amount (...) we see a certain vision of the state and its relation to the citizen.'[25] It should be emphasised that for over a quarter of a century, throughout the 'era of transformation,' the judges of the Constitutional Court had not detected any unconstitutionality in the situation where the amount defined by the Central Statistical Office as the absolute social minimum was subject to normal personal income tax (the tax-free amount defined in the tax laws was much lower than the income that would secure the minimum subsistence level). Furthermore, the judges had no qualms about giving tax breaks to entrepreneurs operating within the so-called special economic zones (usually areas in regions particularly affected by unemployment which offer tax exemptions to encourage investors to locate businesses there), and also in contracts with large industrial concerns, for whose "investments" Poland "competed" with other countries – mainly through promises of wide-ranging tax exemptions.

The ruling in case K 21/14, which is a symbol of a much-delayed pro-social security turn, contains a subsidiary reference to the principle of the social market economy expressed in Article 20 of the Constitution, which the judges this time interpreted as being an economy governed by economic processes – but with a social orientation and sensitivity.

The change was noticeable, as the approach of the Constitutional Court to the social market economy clause had previously been rather cautious. The established line of jurisprudence had been based on the refusal to treat Article 20 as 'an independent control standard adequate for the formulation of assessments of the compatibility with the Constitution of statutory

25 'Trybunał Konstytucyjny: Kwota wolna od podatku niezgodna z konstytucją' [Constitutional Court: The Tax-Free Quota is Unconstitutional] *Gazeta Prawna* (28 October 2015), https://podatki.gazetaprawna.pl/artykuly/902021,trybunal-konstytucyjny-tk-kwota-wolna-od-podatku-niezgodna-z-konstytucja.html, accessed 1 May 2023.

regulations applicable to entrepreneurship.'[26] Without a doubt, what aroused the greatest concern among constitutional judges was not the abusive potential of 'market mechanisms' but, on the contrary, the possibility of abuse of the 'social' aspect, which had to be tempered, so that there would be no departure from the market economy. As the PCC stated in its judgment of 8 July 2008 in case K 46/07, 'the state becomes involved in entrepreneurship primarily as a regulator and guarantor of the protection of the rights of private entrepreneurs.' Leon Kieres, a professor of economic law and Court judge, in a study quite representative of the mainstream, stated that the normative (constitutional and statutory) approach to the market economy expresses, first and foremost, the principles appropriate to the postulates of economic liberalism.[27] Given the long-standing legislative and jurisprudential practice, Kieres is right, and this is despite the fact that the Polish Constitution was drafted and passed under a coalition of left-wing parties, under the post-communist SLD's majority. Kieres' view is mainly based on the understanding of the 'social market economy' in professional legal discourses and judicial decisions. Due to Poland's dependence for most of the transformation period on financing from the International Monetary Fund, which was associated with an almost ostentatious 'departure from socialism,' the constitutional principles of the economic system were indeed interpreted in a decidedly liberal way. The Constitutional Court has repeatedly emphasised the obligation of the public authorities to take initiatives of authoritative interference in the economy, but with moderation in mind, without losing sight of the intended objectives of the interference (the principle of adequacy). This adequacy is determined by the appropriateness of the interference measures adopted, entailing that the effects of their operation should be anticipated and mitigated so as not to disturb the foundations of the market economy.[28] Put more bluntly, the basic line of jurisprudence of the Constitutional Court was grounded in the assumption that state interference in the economy should be of an exceptional nature; it should be "measured" and designed in such a way that the liberal aspects of the economy are not compromised.

3.5 *Jacek Bąbka v University of Wrocław*: No Right to Free Higher Education

Constitutional judgments that are strongly neoliberal in spirit have usually passed unnoticed, without provoking political controversy. This was the case

26 Judgment of the Constitutional Court of 30 October 2001, Case K 33/00; judgment of the Constitutional Court of 19 January 2010, Case SK 35/08.

27 Leon Kieres, 'Społeczna gospodarka rynkowa w orzecznictwie Trybunału Konstytucyjnego' [Social Market Economy in the Judicial Decisions of the Constitutional Court] *Research Papers of Wrocław University of Economics*, no 372/2014, 183.

28 Ibid. 184.

with the famous ruling known as the 'the *Jacek Bąbka* case.' Bąbka was a student at the University of Wrocław (a public university financed from the state budget). He studied part-time. It is worth mentioning that full-time studies, to which students were admitted on the basis of entrance exams and now on the basis of the so-called "new *matura*" (new baccalaureate) imported from the West, are free of charge at public universities. On the other hand, since the 1990s, part-time or extramural studies require the payment of tuition fees, and the income from these fees constitutes an important part of the budgets of public universities. For many years, the number of part-time students greatly exceeded the number of full-time students, which allowed many public universities to finance infrastructural investments and pay teaching staff salaries from tuition fees.[29] This practice is common, despite Article 70 of the Constitution, which stipulates that everyone has the right to education, that education up to the age of 18 is compulsory, and that education in public educational institutions is free of charge, but the law may allow certain educational services to be provided by state higher education institutions in return for payment. Jacek Bąbka, who had been expelled from the university for not paying his tuition fees, invoked, among other things, the above-mentioned provision in the constitutional complaint which he lodged after exhausting all other means of appeal. The applicant also pointed out that the costs of his education had been covered to excess by public funds obtained by the university from the Ministry of National Education. He further submitted that the amount of the fees charged to him was discretionary and arbitrary, and that the profits derived from them were used by the university for construction investments. When supporting his allegations that specific provisions of the Constitution had been violated, the applicant pointed out that the violation of Article 32 sec. 1, which provides for equality of citizens before the law, consisted in the University distinguishing between the situation of students of state and non-state higher education institutions; in the former case the relationship was an administrative-law one, in the latter a civil-law one. This dualism results in the inferior treatment of students of state institutions, by depriving them of judicial protection in civil proceedings. Jacek Bąbka lost the case, and in its judgment of 5 October 2005 (Case SK 39/05) the Constitutional Court established a line of jurisprudence that is maintained to this day, based on the argument that part-time or extramural studies are a form of 'educational service that may be provided by public universities for payment.' This ruling completely ignored the linguistic interpretation of Article 70, but this did not generate any significant political controversy. Mainstream media and political discourses have pushed the

29 Andrzej Rozmus, 'Prywatne źródła finansowania kształcenia w szkołach wyższych – wybrane dylematy ekonomiczno-społeczne' [Private Sources of Financing of Higher Education: Selected Economic and Social Dilemmas] (2010) 6(4) *e-Finanse* 2010 59.

view that this type of funding for public universities enables their development, which would not be possible without tuition fees.[30] In addition, the development of part-time studies, being profitable for universities, makes it possible to educate people who would not otherwise have a chance to enter full-time studies.

However, many studies indicate that the problem has a class component. Students from better-off families are more often admitted to free full-time studies at public universities (in the most prestigious fields of study). They have better starting positions and outcompete their poorer peers. In the competition for higher education, poorer students are forced to choose studies that require the payment of tuition fees. As Andrzej Dryszel notes in his review of sociological research on the subject, calculations by sociologists from the Institute of Labour and Social Studies show that students from poorer families constitute a minority in tuition fee-free studies (they amount to 2%, at most), and the faculties of medicine and law at public universities are attended by 15 to 20% of students from families with average and lower income (the vast majority of them study part-time, so they have to pay for their studies).[31] Hence, there is no doubt that this line of jurisprudence developed by the Constitutional Court has deepened social inequalities in Poland.

3.6 The Right to Health: No Right, Despite a Clear Constitutional Provision

Another, similar example of restraint in granting protection is provided by the Constitutional Court's judgments concerning the right expressed in Article 68 of the Constitution ('Everyone shall have the right to have his health protected. Equal access to health care services, financed from public funds, shall be ensured by public authorities to citizens, irrespective of their material situation'). Numerous attempts have been made to derive from this provision the right to public financing of all the services necessary for individuals to maintain and recover their health. In its decision of 12 November 2003, Case Ts 11/0319, the Constitutional Court stated that Article 68 (2) of the Constitution of the Republic of Poland cannot be regarded as a source of constitutional subjective rights. This view was confirmed in the justification of the judgment of 22 July 2008, Case K 24/07. The Constitutional Court held that, despite its rather categorical linguistic wording, the constitutional provision contains only a programmatic norm, which orders the legislator to strive to ensure the best possible availability of medical services to individuals at a given moment (considering the state's financial capabilities). The

30 Ibid. 60.
31 Andrzej Dryszel, 'Student źle urodzony' [A Badly Born Student], *Tygodnik Przegląd* (29 May 2011) https://www.tygodnikprzeglad.pl/student-zle-urodzony/, accessed 1 May 2023.

increasingly inefficient public health care system is withdrawing from many spheres of activity and is being replaced by private health care services, which are available for a fee to better-off patients. It has become a normal situation that a doctor, after quickly reaching the "limits" on the admission of patients financed from public funds, confronts the patient with a dilemma: to go on the waiting list for treatment financed by the National Health Fund, i.e., the state-owned operator managing the system of financing health care (the waiting list may involve waiting several years); or to obtain the service immediately, without waiting, but for full payment.[32] Attempts to challenge the constitutionality of this state of affairs have, so far, been doomed to failure.

3.7 Conclusions

Without a doubt, in its jurisprudence over the last few decades, the Constitutional Court has strongly "softened" the pro-welfare potential of many constitutional norms, either by denying them normative character, or by giving them a content far removed from the most obvious linguistic readings, so as to limit the redistribution of public funds. One has to agree with the thesis expressed by Stuart Shields, who argues that the current right-wing populism in Poland is an obvious reaction to the neoliberalism promoted in recent decades by the political mainstream and public institutions.[33] In a sense, the revolution taking place is a Marxist revolution, albeit one that is being used instrumentally, to bring about authoritarian political reforms and to shift the ideological centre of gravity in moral issues. It cannot be denied that the ruling populist right has introduced a number of pro-welfare reforms – from the '500 plus program,' which has eliminated many pockets of poverty, to the gradual increase in the minimum wage.

In recent years, however, the political discourse of Law and Justice has been shifting strongly towards the centre. The appointment of Mateusz Morawiecki – a former board member of a large commercial bank – as Prime Minister is an overt symbol of this shift. The appointment may come as a surprise in the context of Law and Justice's anti-plutocratic rhetoric; politicians of this formation used to call bankers "banksters" – a compound of bankers and gangsters. One has to admit that after the 'war over the Court,' which was a victory for the right-wing populists, there is also no sign that neoliberal theories in jurisprudence are being dramatically abandoned. The Law and Justice packed Constitutional Court is actually quite passive and limits itself to legitimising the legislative undertakings of the government and

32 Marek Balicki, 'Problemy służby zdrowia – diagnoza i recepty' [Problems of the Health Service: Diagnosis and Solutions] (2013) 10 *Warszawskie Debaty o Polityce Społecznej* 22.

33 Stuart Shields, 'Opposing Neoliberalism? Poland's Renewed Populism and Post-Communist Transition' (2012) 33(2) *Third World Quarterly* 359.

the ruling parliamentary majority; it also recently issued a ruling restricting access to abortion, which sparked huge protests on the streets of Polish cities. The political situation in Poland is still very tense. Will the anti-liberal revolution be victorious? Will the left be able to take advantage of the change in public mood and replace the right-wing populists? Or will the rebellion be suppressed, and the consensus of the elites return? Only time will tell.

Chapter 4

Populism and the Politics of Human Rights

The Case of Poland*

Karolina Kocemba and Michał Stambulski

4.1 Introduction: The Politics of Human Rights

Reflecting on the relation between politics and human rights, French Marxist, Étienne Balibar, stated that:

> the politics of human rights is *intrinsically ambiguous*, it involves (on both sides of the ideal combination of a democratic constitution with the protection of basic rights and the implementation of new, expanded rights) the insurrectional movements linked with the invention of democracy, but also the instrumental uses of the idea of human rights to legitimize the status quo and strategies of domination.[1]

The philosopher notes that the recognition of rights results from an effective demand for them and is, therefore, mediated by the political process. The discourse of human rights has two interrelated sides: on the one hand, it is used to disrupt and transform current power relations; on the other hand, the same language can be used to legitimise the existing order. Therefore, human rights are a useful tool both for legitimisation *and* delegitimisation. In his work, Balibar often returns to Hannah Arendt's well-known argument that

* This chapter presents the outcome of research funded by the National Science Centre (*Narodowe Centrum Nauki*), Poland as part the project "Women as Subjects of Constitutional Rights in Central and Eastern Europe," (project no. UMO-2021/41/B/HS5/01421). The contributions of the authors being equal, the name ordering is purely alphabetical. This chapter draws on the results of studies partially published previously in Polish as: Karolina Kocemba and Michał Stambulski, 'Populizm a polityka praw człowieka' [Populism and the Politics of Human Rights] (2020) 31 *Studenckie Prace Prawnicze, Administratywistyczne i Ekonomiczne* 135; Karolina Kocemba and Michał Stambulski, 'Gotowanie żaby. Prawicowy konstytucjonalizm a prawa kobiet w Polsce' [Boiling the Frog: Right-wing Constitutionalism and Women's Rights in Poland] in Magdalena Grzyb and Katarzyna Sękowska-Kozłowska (eds) *Kobieta – ciąża – zarodek – dziecko. Prawne aspekty przerywania ciąży* (Kraków: Wydawnictwo Uniwersytetu Jagiellońskiego, 2023), available at SSRN: https://ssrn.com/abstract=4365933.

1 Étienne Balibar, 'On the Politics of Human Rights' (2013) 20 *Constellations* 18.

DOI: 10.4324/9781032624464-5

human rights without a network of institutions and forces dedicated to their protection are devoid of substance.[2] In this perspective it is not a coincidence that human rights are proclaimed in the 1789 Declaration of the Rights of Man and of the *Citizen*. The element of citizenship is closely linked to these rights and indicates their limits. Balibar draws our attention to the fact that, while the proclamation of the universality of rights is sometimes justified as a political strategy, universalism does not exclude historicity. Human rights, as part of the political condition of human collectivities, are subject to transformation depending on current social relations and conflicts. In this optic, political participation and human rights are closely intertwined. As critical legal philosopher Costas Douzinas noted in a similar manner:

> if the world has accepted a common humanitarian vision, have conflicts of ideology, religion, and ethnicity ceased? Obviously not. This means that human rights have no common meaning or that the term describes radically different phenomena.[3]

In other words, human rights are always political. Nevertheless, the process of determination of the scope of and demand for human rights looks different in autocratic and democratic societies. In an authoritarian society, this struggle takes the form of a fight for democracy and goes beyond the legal order – it is a strictly political struggle since, in an authoritarian legal system, there are no institutional guarantees of democratic rights that provide a real opportunity to influence or challenge the dominant power. In a democratic society, such a struggle is both political and legal. This is because, in such a system, there is a real possibility of influencing legislation and the practice of applying the law. Institutions like courts, the Ombudsman, or special committees ensure that human rights are part of the legal system of modern liberal democracies. Demanding these rights is, therefore, an argument from the realisation of what is already formally guaranteed.

Nevertheless, what does human rights politics look like in a setting of populism, and therefore a regime that is both democratically legitimate and, at the same time, abusive of power? Most scholars claim that populists usually weaken the institutions crucial for human rights protection[4] or even reject any legal limitation on their unlimited power, realising the majority's

2 Étienne Balibar, '(De)Constructing the Human as Human Institution: A Reflection on the Coherence of Hannah Arendt's Practical Philosophy' (2007) 74 *Social Research* 727.

3 Costas Douzinas, 'The Paradoxes of Human Rights' (2013) 20 *Constellations* 51.

4 Wojciech Sadurski, 'Populism and Human Rights in Poland' in Gerald L. Neuman (ed.), *Human Rights in a Time of Populism: Challenges and Responses* (Cambridge: Cambridge University Press, 2020).

will.[5] Dominant views see populism only through a negative prism, how they "destroy" human rights and not through a positive prism,[6] what rights they promote. This leads, on a conceptual level, to a blurring of the distinction between populism and authoritarianism, in which its democratic character disappears. Populism is not compatible with human rights and would thus be, at best, an instance of authoritarianism in the making. Various indexes confirm such a trajectory, and Poland may be an illustrative example. Thus, the Human Freedom Index, elaborated by the Cato Institute, indicates that after the populist Law and Justice Party took power in 2015, legal protection of individual freedom in Poland has deteriorated. In the report for 2014, the country's Freedom Index amounted to 9.18.[7] In the report covering 2020, the value dropped to 8.18.[8] At the same time, the party was able to win free parliamentary and presidential elections and thus renew its democratic mandate. This would mean that either personal freedom and its legal protection are not essential to many of the country's citizens or the relationship between human rights and populism is more complicated. In what follows, we argue for the second thesis. Our considerations lead to the conclusion that populism pursues its own human rights politics, different from liberalism, which escapes the simple democracy/authoritarianism dichotomy. The pursuit of such politics simultaneously anchors the populist regime socially and creates its symbolic and hermeneutic resources to justify the need for populist power.

4.2 Defining Populism

In 2007, Bulgarian political scientist Ivan Krastev published an article, 'The Populist Moment,' stating that we live in a time of populism.[9] Although, in the last decade, the term "populism" was frequently used in public discourse to describe current political events, it is not easy to define because of its many meanings and scopes. Nevertheless, it is possible to distinguish the main characteristics of this phenomenon. Margaret Canovan, who has followed academic disputes on defining populism, noted that in addition to relying on

5 Kenneth Roth, 'The Dangerous Rise of Populism: Global Attacks on Human Rights Values' [2017] *Journal of International Affairs* 79.

6 Although there are more emerging studies pointing to a positive dimension of populism. See Anna Śledzińska-Simon, 'Learning Lessons from the Populist Defeats: From Negative to Positive Constitutionalism' [2023] *Social & Legal Studies* https://doi.org/10.1177/09646639231167815, accessed 1 May 2023.

7 Ian Vásquez and Tanja Porčnik, 'The Human Freedom Index 2016' https://www.cato.org/sites/cato.org/files/2021-01/human-freedom-index-2016.pdf>, accessed 21 April 2023.

8 Ian Vásquez, Fred McMahon, Ryan Murphy, and Guillermina Sutter Schneider, 'The Human Freedom Index 2022' https://www.cato.org/sites/cato.org/files/2023-01/human-freedom-index-2022.pdf>, accessed 21 April 2023.

9 'The Populist Moment: The Elites vs. the People' (*Eurozine* 18 September 2007) https://www.eurozine.com/the-populist-moment, accessed 21 April 2023.

the people vs. elite relationship, historically, populism has been treated as a feature of rural societies that oppose modernisation. To organise the discussion, Canovan proposes a distinction between a sociological and a political science perspective.[10] Populism, from the sociological perspective, is considered an agrarian movement based on a socio-economic background, with progressive modernisation which affects urbanisation, open trade, industry growth, secularisation, population migration, etc. Such a movement, known as *Samoobrona*[11] ("Self-Defence") functioned in Poland in the years 1992–2012 and criticised liberal economic policies and advocated state aid for indebted farmers. From a political perspective, populism goes beyond the agrarian movement with a broader objective of community transformation. It is a group of political phenomena that refer to the idea of direct democracy, stimulate the emotional involvement of the masses, idealise the average citizen, or even escalate tensions between the elites and the citizens.[12] Such "political" populism constructs the image of "the people" in a more abstract way so that it is able to encompass and represent different, not only agrarian, interests. The shift from sociological to political populism also explains why populist movements began to be able to govern. Poland's *Samoobrona* was unable to win elections on its own and only exercised power as a coalition partner of the politically populist Law and Justice party.

What both types of populism have in common is the mechanism of their emergence, which is social or economic problems. These, in turn, lead to appeals and claims to politicians, referring to democratic ideology – the idea of the sovereignty of the people and majority rule.[13] Canovan writes of populism as an effect of the 'democratic paradox.' Democracy, as the most inclusive political system, is simultaneously opaque. Because of this disjunction between idea and practice, democracy still needs to 'bring politics closer to the people' – create a simple framework and explain who is responsible for what (or who is to blame). Thus, democracy retains its critical potential (the ability to change power) but is also open to manipulation. Populists gain support by expressing (and shaping) ordinary people's views, highlighting the masses' prevailing views, which have not been recognised by policymakers or drowned out until now.[14] Looking at the issues raised by populists (immi-

10 Margaret Canovan, 'Populizm' [Populism] in Olga Wysocka (ed.), *Populizm* [Populism] (Warszawa: Wydawnictwo Uniwersytetu Warszawskiego 2010), 56–64.

11 Ania Krok-Paszkowska, 'Samoobrona: The Polish Self-Defence Movement' in Petr Kopecky and Cas Mudde (eds), *Uncivil Society? Contentious Politics in Post-Communist Europe* (Abingdon: Routledge, 2005).

12 Margaret Canovan, 'Populizm' in Wysocka (ed.), *Populizm*, 59.

13 Margaret Canovan, 'Taking Politics to the People: Populism as the Ideology of Democracy' in Yves Mény and Yves Surel (eds), *Democracies and the Populist Challenge* (Basingstoke: Palgrave Macmillan UK, 2002).

14 Ibid.

gration, employment, religious values), we can conclude that they have been marginalised in the public sphere due to the domination of liberal values and political correctness, which populists do not care about.

For this reason, populism is sometimes seen as a threat but also as a corrective to politics that is too far away from the people.[15] The closeness to the people and the claim to represent their interests seems to be the core of populism. This is also pointed out by Jan-Werner Müller, writing in his widely commented book *What is Populism?* that:

> Populism, I suggest, is a particular moralistic imagination of politics, a way of perceiving the political world that sets a morally pure and fully unified—but, I shall argue, ultimately fictional—people against elites who are deemed corrupt or in some other way morally inferior.[16]

Therefore, this is a mechanism for viewing the political world in moral terms. At the same time, it is a zero-one moralism – either something grows out of the "good" people or is against them. There is no room for shades of grey here. Thus, an important characteristic is also populism's opposition to pluralism – populists claim that they *and only they* represent the people.[17] Based on this definition, we can also conclude that populists strive for a homogeneous society in which deviations from the norm and minorities cannot access and freely use the public sphere. Thus, "the people" is understood as the supreme sovereign, a unity, a body with a common interest and single will. This kind of approach can create the ground for nationalist movements. As Seyla Benhabib notes:

> "We, the people," is a tension-riven formula which seeks to contain the universalizing aspirations of rights claims and democratic sovereignty struggles within the confines of a historically situated collectivity. Such a collectivity has its "others" within and "without." Peoplehood is an aspiration; it is not a fact.[18]

The issue of populism thus comes down to defining "the people." With such defining comes the power to set up the boundaries of the political community. To some degree, defining "the people" and naming their expectations is at the heart of every democracy. Populism *sensu stricto* appears in the

15 Jan-Werner Müller, *What Is Populism?* (Philadelphia: University of Pennsylvania Press, 2016) 24.
16 Ibid. 40.
17 Ibid. 17.
18 Seyla Benhabib, *The Rights of Others: Aliens, Residents, and Citizens* (Cambridge: Cambridge University Press, 2004).

moment when such a definition is combined with a negative assessment of the existing political system as "tainted" or "corrupt." In a populist assessment, such a system cannot define the people's will. This justifies the need to change it. Populism is thus always transformative towards the existing order. The definition of "the people" is linked to the need to adapt institutions to the people. Such a conviction, based on moral superiority connected with the exclusive right to define the people and their needs, leads to rejecting liberal limits on power and social homogenisation. Since the populist merely embodies the morally perfect "people," it does not need limitations. The correctness of the exercise of power is guaranteed not by procedures and restrictions but by its moral resources. "Moral perfection" is presented on the background of its opposite – corruption and degeneration. In the rhetoric of populism, this role is fulfilled by elites, who are portrayed as parasitic on the hard work and purity of "the people." Populists project their enemy – "the Other," against whom it proclaims the need to mobilise. "The people" are seen as homogeneous, and therefore the scope of "the Other" tends to expand. Anyone who does not meet the criteria defined by populism for belonging to "the people" is "the Other." Therefore, the newly-improved, unifying definitions are often juxtaposed with the adjective "real" – e.g., a real patriot, a real Pole, a real mother, a real woman, a real family.

The construction of the Other opens populism to human rights. In populist logic, the Other who is not part of the community should be excluded from it. At the same time, his/her externality, the lack of ties to the community beyond the physical presence in it, incorporates the Other into human rights. Indeed, these rights were created for the Other, whose characteristic is only that of belonging to the human species, and these rights, with their natural law justification, apply independently of national legislations.[19] The Other is thus politically excluded from the community and legally incorporated into its fundamental rights.

We can see now that a populist framework is incompatible, or at least in tension, with the broader idea of human rights as a 'symbol of liberalism,'[20] with its idea of a diverse society, and with the pluralism of lifestyles in public space. Alternatively, perhaps it would be more accurate to say that the idea of human rights is based on a different political and moral imagination. The discourse of human rights was based on the assumptions of liberalism and the autonomy and rationality of the individual.[21] In this view, human

19 Costas Douzinas, *The End of Human Rights: Critical Thought at the Turn of the Century* (Oxford: Hart Publishing, 2000), 346.

20 Costas Douzinas and Conor Gearty, *The Meanings of Rights: The Philosophy and Social Theory of Human Rights* (Cambridge: Cambridge University Press, 2014), 1–12.

21 Duncan Kennedy, 'Political Ideology and Comparative Law' in Mauro Bussani and Ugo Mattei (eds), *The Cambridge Companion to Comparative Law* (Cambridge: Cambridge University Press, 2012), 39.

rights, broadly understood, are an obstacle to populism, guided by the logic of community – people. Moreover, it is a significant obstacle, opposing the homogenisation of society – any deviation from the norm or pattern is not welcome. Let us now turn to empirical examples, looking at Poland and the rule of the Law and Justice party, which embodies populism in power and its approach to human rights.

4.3 Law and Justice Party

The Law and Justice party (Polish: *Prawo i Sprawiedliwość*) was founded in 2001 by brothers Jarosław and Lech Kaczyński. Both were lawyers and members of the democratic opposition during the communist era. The party won elections and formed a coalition government in 2005–2007. The party won the elections again in 2015 and has since headed a coalition government with smaller parties and right-wing movements with the introduction of many systemic changes in the judiciary, social policies, culture and education, foreign policy, and relations with the European Union.[22] Lech Szczegóła, while examining the party discourse, concluded that it is based on an idea of 'reconstitution of Polishness.'[23] The negative assessment of the actions of the ruling elites during the systemic transition from communism to democracy leads party leaders to the need to renew community and political institutions. With this rhetoric, the communist elite made a corrupting compromise with representatives of the democratic opposition and, through the mechanism of co-optation, built a system of government based on the exclusion of civic participation in decision making and the strict control and privatisation of public resources. The concept of "corrupt" elites goes far beyond these historical terms. The party message uses a populist frame of elite vs. people division that is pragmatically adapted to the current situation. Thus, elites can mean post-transitional economic elites in one context, European political elites in another, and representatives of minorities who threaten the "traditional" model of life or "culturally" foreign immigrants in yet another. As Szczegóła states, the ideological message of Law and Justice is:

> seeking an interpretation capable of integrating the popular-social resentments accumulated during the two decades of transition, based its message on the ideas of the para-conservative reactionary milieu. Its spokespersons, creating an atmosphere of apocalyptic fears of the moral and political

22 Wojciech Sadurski, *Poland's Constitutional Breakdown* (Oxford: Oxford University Press, 2019).

23 Lech Szczegóła, *Droga do wojny kulturowej. Ideologia Dobrej Zmiany* [The Path to a Culture War: Ideology of the Good Change] (Warszawa: Elipsa, 2020).

depravity of Western civilization, are not preoccupied with developmental challenges, but with the mission of preserving identity.[24]

A constant element in the discourse of ruling party politicians is to emphasise the primacy of the collective ("the people") over the rights of individuals. It associates "the West" with destructive individualism, considering it to be a threat because the realisation of its vision leads to the disappearance of the people-community. This rhetoric is visible in statements made by Law and Justice leader Jarosław Kaczyński who often stresses the need to protect the "nature-based" "Christian civilization," which is threatened by leftist and relativist movements based on overextending the notion of individual freedom.[25] In this optic, religion, on account of its importance in the construction of identity and its historical permanence, is the cultural backbone of the Polish political community. Thus, when the rights of individuals take precedence over religion and collective identity, the political community as such disappears. Independently of each other, the critical towards the party philosopher of culture Tomasz Szkudlarek[26] and more sympathetic towards it legal theorist Lech Morawski[27] pointed out that the political thought of Law and Justice has a republican trait. According to those authors, the aim of Kaczyński's republican political project is pedagogical; what is at stake here is the transformation of Polish society and its political and legal institutions along the lines of the Law and Justice party's conservative ideology. Here we arrive again at the populist paradox: the "good" people are simultaneously already present and yet to be established. The first allows the loose restrictive institutional frames of liberal representative democracy. The second justifies the need for strong, unmediated, and direct populist policies done mainly through legal means. It also determines how rights are perceived.

The already mentioned Étienne Balibar pointed to an internal tension in the republican vision of human rights. Recognising the normatively specified role of the community vis-à-vis individuals leads to 'the people becoming a boundary for the rights of those individuals.' In such a case, the 'politics of

24 Ibid. 150.

25 TVP Info, 'Prezes PiS: Przed Polską stoi dziś problem walki ze skrajną lewicą ideologiczną'[Chairman of Law and Justice Party: Poland Is Now Facing a Struggle Against Radical Ideological Left] https://www.tvp.info/63098784/prezes-pis-jaroslaw-kaczynski-o-lewicy-ideologicznej-ukrainie, accessed 20 April 2023; Andrzej Mężyński, 'Kaczyński: Bronimy cywilizacji chrześcijańskiej w imię całej ludzkości'[Kaczyński: We Are Defending the Christian Civilisation on Behalf of Entire Humanity] https://wiadomosci.dziennik.pl/polityka/artykuly/8567153,jaroslaw-kaczynski-chrzescijanstwo-lewica-obrona.html, accessed 20 April 2023.

26 Tomasz Szkudlarek, 'Pedagogika wstydu i bezwstydna polityka' [Pedagogy of Shame and Shameless Politics] (2018) 30(1) *Forum Oświatowe* 37, 37–52.

27 Lech Morawski, 'A Critical Response' (*Verfassungsblog*) https://verfassungsblog.de/a-critical-response/, accessed 25 April 2023.

human rights becomes oriented towards an idea of the community of citizens: a *polity* which also involves *limiting* the realm of human rights.'[28] This reinforces the distinction between the private and public spheres, which is more blurred in liberalism. In each of these spheres, different rights dominate. In the private sphere, individual rights predominate and the scope of the community's power is limited here. In the public sphere, on the other hand, the rights of the community should take priority. Populist politics of rights is, therefore, about establishing this new division of public vs. private and defending the public sphere from the corrupting influence of the private sphere. Let us see how this politics is operationalised in selected areas of specific rights.

4.4 Populism and LGBT Rights

In recent history, Poland, aspiring to be a Western democracy and a part of the European community, had to conform to liberal standards after 1989, which involved ratifying international human rights treaties. For example, to gain membership in the Council of Europe, it was necessary to ratify the Convention for the Protection of Human Rights and Fundamental Freedoms.[29] During the same period, in 1993, Poland also declared to recognise the jurisdiction of the European Court of Human Rights. In Polish domestic law, the Polish Constitution prohibits discrimination for any reason in political, social, or economic life,[30] and the Labour Code prohibits discrimination in employment.[31] In a criminal trial, LGBT people can refuse to testify about the "closest person" (i.e., their partner).[32] At the same time, it is impossible to legalise same-sex relationships – Poland is one of six countries in the European Union that still does not recognise gay marriage or legal partnerships.[33]

Nevertheless, we cannot name the populist legal strategy towards the LGBT community as a simple backlash; it should be differentiated from the countries like Hungary, where the Parliament passed an "anti-gay law."[34] The Polish populist strategy focuses on small-scale, local actions and rhetoric.

28 Étienne Balibar, ibid. 21.

29 Ministerstwo Rodziny, Pracy i Polityki Społecznej, 'Europejska konwencja o ochronie praw człowieka i podstawowych wolności' [The European Convention on Human Rights and Fundamental Freedoms] https://www.gov.pl/web/rodzina/europejska-konwencja-o-ochronie-praw-czlowieka-i-podstawowych-wolnosci, accessed 10 May 2020.

30 Art. 32 of Polish Constitution 1997.

31 Art. 183a of Polish Labour Code 1974..

32 Art. 115 of Polish Criminal Code 1997.

33 In addition to Poland, these are: Bulgaria, Latvia, Lithuania, Romania, and Slovakia.

34 Laura Hood, 'EU sues Hungary Over Anti-Gay Law – What it Could Mean for LGBT Rights in Europe' https://theconversation.com/eu-sues-hungary-over-anti-gay-law-what-it-could-mean-for-lgbt-rights-in-europe-187209>, accessed 20 April 2023.

After gaining power in 2015, and during the election campaigns, the Law and Justice Party frequently raised the issue of sexual minority rights, treating public discussion of homosexuality or gender change as a threat to the political community.

The most known and controversial seem to be the words of Polish President Andrzej Duda, who, just before the presidential elections in 2020 (that he later won), stated that 'They try to convince us that LGBT is people – it is simply an ideology'.[35] He argued: 'I have respect for all people, but I will not allow children to be ideologized because this is my responsibility for Poland and Polish youth'.[36] The argument on protecting children "from the LGBT" has often been used in populist campaigns, by which we can presume that it is effective. For example, the leader of a Party, Jarosław Kaczyński, referring to the adoption of children by same-sex couples, said: 'Here we say no, especially when it comes to children, stay away from our children'.[37] He also pointed out that: 'First, the unions. What are they called? Partnerships, well, that is right, partnerships. Later, homosexual marriages, and finally, the adoption of children. That is children as an object of fun and satisfaction for certain people. Well, no. Never. Children are subjects; children must be protected, children are a great treasure, the greatest treasure of the nation.'[38]

It can be inferred from their statements that the expansion of LGBT rights allegedly constitutes a threat to children, which is the basis of a community incapable of autonomy and needs to be defended. The populists' aversion to civil unions and gay marriage and the possibility of adopting children may be due to the recognition of only one "proper," traditional family model in line with conservative Christian ideology. At the same time, in their rhetoric, the ruling populist party presents itself as the last stronghold of protection against the expansion of these community-threatening laws. Moreover, the populists' scare of the "LGBT ideology" is an aftermath and

35 Paulina Górska and Nicole Tausch, 'People or Ideology? Social Conservatism and Intergroup Contact Moderate Heterosexuals' Responses to a State-Sponsored Anti-LGBT Campaign' (2022) *Sexuality Research and Social Policy* https://doi.org/10.1007/s13178-022-00783-y.

36 Urszula Gwiazda, 'Andrzej Duda o LGBT: Próbuje się nam wmówić, że to ludzie, a to jest po prostu ideologia' [Andrzej Duda on LGBT: They Are Trying to Persuade Us that they are Humans, But This is Simply Ideology] https://www.rmf24.pl/raporty/raport-wybory-prezydenckie2020/najnowsze-fakty/news-andrzej-duda-o-lgbt-probuje-sie-nam-wmowic-ze-to-ludzie-a-to,nId,4551951#crp_state=1, accessed 20 April 2023.

37 Rzeczpospolita, 'Jarosław Kaczyński: Wara od naszych dzieci' [Jarosław Kaczyński: Stay Clear of Our Children] https://www.rp.pl/Prawo-i-Sprawiedliwosc/190319420-Jaroslaw-Kaczynski-Wara-od-naszych-dzieci.html, accessed 10 May 2020.

38 wPolityce.pl, 'Prezes PiS: Nie będzie w Polsce małżeństw homoseksualnych, nie będzie adopcji dzieci. Plan Rabieja? "Nie, nigdy nie"' [Chairman of Law and Justice: There Will Never be Homosexual Marriages in Poland, they Will Never Adopt Children] https://wpolityce.pl/polityka/463846-prezes-pis-trwa-atak-na-dzieci-my-sie-na-to-nie-zgadzamy, accessed 10 May 2020.

even a transformation of the "ani-gender ideology" panic discourse, which was described in detail by Maciej Duda.[39] He noted that by populists and even more by catholic church officials, terms such as "gender ideology," civil unions, *in vitro* conception, and equality policy were equated with each other and understood as the popularisation of same-sex marriages and sometimes even sexualisation and paedophilia. Both the notions of "gender ideology" and "LGBT ideology" have been used by populists like vessels into which they have thrown any axiologically incompatible actions and phenomena, labelling them paedophilia or sexualisation – terms that undoubtedly evoke negative connotations, after all, paedophilia is a serious offence. The scarer worked best when they said the gender or LGBT monster would attack their children. The wars with "gender" or "LGBT" are great examples of culture wars[40] and the politics of identity conducted by the Law and Justice Party. This strategy advocates the defence of Catholicism and national tradition. It promotes an anti-communist and anti-leftist stance that expressed itself in an attack on the reproductive rights of women and sexual minorities.[41]

Law and Justice's rhetoric towards the LGBT community seems to have softened after the elections, although it is still an often-commented issue, especially by the Party leader, Jarosław Kaczyński. He claims that, in Poland, there is tolerance toward LGBT people: 'There is no tradition of oppressing homosexuals.' He also asserts that 'what is being demanded of us is not tolerance because, in Poland, tolerance is full; after all, there are clubs, you all know about it.'[42] While Kaczyński makes increasingly rare statements about homosexuals, he quite often makes fun of trans people – for example, stating that: 'Of course, someone may disagree with us: one has leftist views and believes that each of us can at some point say that up to now… until an hour – now it's half past six – I was a man, and now I'm a woman. (…) One can have such views. Strange to say the least – I would examine it – but one can.' For these words, he was reprimanded by the Committee on Parliamentary Ethics.[43] Later, he said of transgender people that there's no desire to oppress

39 Maciej Duda, *Dogmat Płci: Polska Wojna z Gender* [The Dogma of Gender: Polish War Against Gender] (Wydawnictwo Naukowe Katedra, 2016) 86.

40 Culture wars – social divisions and disputes due to the different values. Cultural disputes overlap with political divisions and voters vote not according to their interests but according to the values they believe (Leszek Koczanowicz, 'Władza, seks, pieniądze. Wojny kulturowe i ich cele' [Power, Sex, Money: Culture Wars and Their Purposes] *Miesięcznik Odra*, 20 October 2020) 2)

41 Ibid.

42 Klaudia Stabach, 'Kaczyński w Częstochowie o LGBT+ i transpłciowości. "W Polsce jest pełna tolerancja"' [Kaczyński in Częstochowa on LGBT+ and Transgender Identity: In Poland There is Full Tolerance] https://noizz.pl/spoleczenstwo/cztery-najwieksze-absurdy-z-wystapienia-kaczynskiego-w-czestochowie/r2mdvqn, accessed 10 April 2023.

43 Cezary Faber, 'Jarosław Kaczyński ukarany przez Komisję Etyki Poselskiej' [Jarosław Kaczyński Punished by the Deputies' Ethics Committee] https://www.rmf24.pl/polityka/

people who have 'such disruptions,' but such people, and this phenomenon, in the quantitative sense, is very marginal, these people should receive help, but cannot dictate the world's order, which should be dictated by the mainstream with tolerance for minorities.[44]

These statements clearly show that the populists' interests and policies are only concerned with the problems of the majority, and the LGBT community is not the majority. Law and Justice politician Andrzej Sośnierz was asked to comment on Kaczyński's statement, said: 'I believe that difficult problems, other people's differences should not be the subject of such public debates as are happening on all sides of the public scene.' His statement perfectly summarises the populists' approach to LGBT people – to somehow "freeze" LGBT rights, maintain the status quo, push them into the private sphere, and not discuss it publicly. Interestingly, such a move is, at the same time, linked to a claim to the power of control over what should be publicly discussed. Identifying populist politicians with the people allows them to present themselves as the "mouth of the people."

Although the populists have not changed the state's LGBT laws, the changes – both pro- and anti-LGBT, were observed at the local level and the level of interpretations of existing laws. In February 2019, the Warsaw mayor – a politician of the largest opposition liberal party, Civic Platform – signed a declaration supporting respect for LGBT rights and announcing the inclusion of LGBT topics in sex education programmes in Warsaw schools.[45] As a reaction to this declaration, smaller local municipalities passed resolutions against "LGBT ideology," establishing so-called "LGBT-free zones." Law and Justice won the 2018 local elections, and the populist party also gained a significant advantage on municipal councils.[46] The local branches of the ruling party thus used the dualistic logic of big-city LGBT-friendly elites versus local rural communities preferring traditional lifestyles. These resolutions do not have the force of law, but they express the attitude of local government officials in the region towards LGBT people. The resolutions have included provisions expressing opposition to LGBT ideology in the public

news-jaroslaw-kaczynski-ukarany-przez-komisje-etyki-poselskiej,nId,6313954#crp_state =1, accessed 10 April 2023.

44 Wprost.pl, 'Jarosław Kaczyński o osobach LGBT. Chce pomagać tym, którym „w życiu się nie poszczęściło" [Jarosław Kaczyński On LGBT People: He Wants to Help Those 'Who Did Not Have Luck in Life'] https://www.wprost.pl/polityka/10780204/jaroslaw-kaczynski-o-osobach-lgbt-chce-pomagac-tym-ktorym-w-zyciu-sie-nie-poszczescilo.html, accessed 10 April 2023.

45 Miasto Warszawa, 'Prezydent stolicy podpisał Deklarację LGBT+' [The Mayor of Warsaw Signed the LGBT+ Declaration] https://um.warszawa.pl/-/prezydent-stolicy-podpisal-deklaracje-lgbt-, accessed 10 May 2020.

46 Państwowa Komisja Wyborcza, 'Elections 2018', https://wybory2018.pkw.gov.pl/pl/dane-w-arkuszach, accessed 24 May 2020.

sphere, opposition to sex education according to the WHO, opposition to controlling political correctness in schools, and allegiance to national and state traditions.

Interestingly, such zones covered as much as 30% of the country, primarily the southeastern part of Poland,[47] which is also the stronghold of electoral support for the Law and Justice party. It has caused widespread legal mobilisation against these resolutions – the (liberal) Ombudsman challenged them to administrative courts, which usually cancelled them.[48] The LGBT-free zones are part of a broader vision of the public sphere and public space promoted by the party with no place for LGBT people. However, the disapproval of LGBT people in the public sphere is not only a part of the political game but can also influence greater intolerance in everyday interactions.

An example of this is the case of a printer in Łódź who refused to print a poster of an LGBT organisation. The case was used as a pretext to seek to change the interpretation of the law by the Minister of Justice-Prosecutor General.[49] In the first[50] and second instances,[51] courts found the printer guilty of a misdemeanour. The courts have used a provision dating back to the 1970s punishing unjustified refusal of service, which has been used in the last years as an anti-discrimination tool. Faced with this, the Prosecutor General filed a cassation (an appeal on the point of law) challenging the second instance court's judgment. When the Supreme Court ruled that the artisan could not invoke the conscience clause and could not refuse to print,[52] the Prosecutor General challenged the provision[53] of the misdemeanour code under which the printer was found guilty before the Constitutional Court.[54] The Constitutional Court, now dominated by appointees of the ruling party,

47 Marta Ciastoch, '30 proc. Polski to strefy "wolne od LGBT". Ta mapa pokazuje, gdzie zezwala się na nienawiść' [30% of Poland are 'LGBT-free Zones': This Map Shows Where Hatred in Permitted] https://noizz.pl/lgbt/mapa-nienawisci-wobec-lgbt-30-proc-polski-to-strefy-wolne-od-lgbt-atlas-nienawisci/r3erj5p, accessed 10 May 2020.

48 Wojciech Kauczor and Jakub Skoczke, "Skutki Strategicznej Litygacji. Sprawa „stref Wolnych Od LGBT"" [Effects of Strategic Litigation: The Case of the So-Called LGBT-free Zones] (2022) SPPAiE 41, http://dx.doi.org/10.19195/1733-5779.41.5, accessed 27 April 2023.

49 Under current legislation in Poland, the Minister of Justice (a politician) is *ex lege* the Prosecutor General, i.e., head of the hierarchically organised Prosecution Service, which, of course, undermines its apolitical and independent character.

50 Judgment of the District Court in Łódź, 26 May 2017 r, Case V Ka 557/17.

51 Judgment of the District Court for Łódź-Widzew in Łódź, 31 March 2017 r, Case VII W 1640/16.

52 Supreme Court judgment of 14 June 2018, Case II KK 333/18.

53 Art. 138 of Polish Code of Petty Offences (20 May 1971): 'Whoever, engaged in the professional rendering of services, demands and collects payment for the rendering of services in excess of the applicable payment, or intentionally refuses, without justifiable cause, to render a service to which he is obligated, shall be punished by a fine.'

54 Constitutional Court judgment of 26 June 2019, Case K 16/17.

found the provision unconstitutional, arguing that it interfered 'with the freedom of the provider of services, in particular, the right to decide whether to enter into a contract, the right to express one's own opinions or act in accordance with one's conscience'.[55] In its judgment, the Constitutional Court found the punishment for refusing a service disproportionate to the freedom of economic activity. With this ruling, the LGBT community has lost one of its tools to demand its presence and respect in public spaces.

Such an attempt to exclude the visibility of LGBT people from the public sphere has far-reaching consequences. Not being present in a public space can be perceived as not having the right to be present at all. In the ILGA Europe's European ranking in 2020, 2021, and 2022 Poland ranked last (27 out of 27) in the European Union.[56] The ranking considers issues such as equality, family issues, hate speech, the legality of gender reassignment, freedom of speech, and asylum rights. Interestingly, the position in the ranking began to deteriorate in 2015, when Law and Justice came to power – as recently as 2013, Poland was in 23rd place (out of 27). Before that, there was an upward trend indicating better legal protection.[57] Although populists did not take legislative actions towards LGBT rights, an atmosphere of hostility through symbolic stigmatisation may influence restricting access to rights through interpreting laws. Also, there are no signs that under a populist government, these rights could be broadened. The populist rhetoric and actions undermining LGBT rights seem to have been driven by the casting of the LGBT community as the external Other-elites. These Other-elites have been constructed here according to need and simultaneously as (1) external to the Polish community Western, over-reaching ideology of individualism, (2) a threat to children and the traditional family model, and (3) big-city elites threatening more religious and rural communities.

4.5 Reproductive Rights and (Ab)using the Constitutional Court

Reproductive rights based on women's bodily autonomy are incompatible with the vision of corporeality presented by the Catholic Church, whose social teaching is the ideological background of Law and Justice. That is why in this sphere, much more often than against LGBT rights, party politicians took action to transform Polish law and bring it in line with the traditional vision of family and community.

55 Ibid.

56 ILGA Europe, *Rainbow Europe*, https://ilga-europe.org/rainbow-europe/, accessed 15 April 2023.

57 ILGA Europe, *Rainbow Europe 2013*, https://www.ilga-europe.org/rainboweurope/2013, accessed 15 May 2020.

First came the statutory introduction of prescription-only emergency contraception. The Health Minister, in tightening access to the so-called "morning-after pill," argued the decision was due to the abuse of these pills by teenagers,[58] even though studies indicated that minors who used emergency contraception accounted for only 2%. A law came into effect as to when doctors could invoke the so-called "conscience clause." The minister stated that as a doctor, he would not prescribe such contraception to a patient even if she had been raped – he would invoke the conscience clause.[59] Thus, access to emergency contraception - the possibility of exercising the right, has been made conditional on a doctor's acceptance and moral judgment. Protecting the moral integrity of the doctor is thus deemed more important than a woman's right to contraception, especially in rural communities, where medical services are scarce and doctors, more often than not, conservative. This provision effectively means a denial of access to emergency contraception.

The second attempt at interference with reproductive rights is the outlawing of abortion. In October 2016, the "Stop Abortion" draft, whose provisions allowed for punishing women for abortion, was submitted to Parliament. Women's reaction to the attempt to tighten the abortion law were the so-called "black protests" organised in almost all cities in Poland.[60] We can admit that, probably thanks to them, Parliament rejected the draft after the first reading. Citizens took to the streets again in March 2018 due to a parliamentary committee meeting that gave a favourable opinion to a bill banning the termination of pregnancy due to severe fetal defects. That attempt also failed. The Law and Justice party had a rule of not rejecting citizens' bills in the first reading, which was supposed to be a sign of "respect for democracy." Nevertheless, MPs did not refer to the "Save the Women" project liberalising abortion to work further – it was rejected in the first reading, even though it was a citizens' legislative initiative.[61] Every attempt

58 Magdalena Chrzczonowicz, 'Nastolatki opychają się pigułkami dzień po. Są badania, które dementują bzdurę Radziwiłła' [Teenagers Are Stuffing Themselves with Day-After Pills: There is Research Which Debunks Radziwiłł's Nonsense Claims] https://oko.press/nastolatki-opychaja-sie-pigulkami-dzien-sa-badania-ktore-dementuja-bzdure-radziwilla/, accessed 10 May 2020.

59 Martyna Kraus, 'Radziwiłł powiedział, że nie przepisałby pigułki "dzień po" nawet pacjentce zgwałconej. "Taka odmowa jest bezprawna"' [Radziwił Said that He Would not Prescribe a Day-After Pill Even to a Raped Woman] https://www.wysokieobcasy.pl/wysokie-obcasy/7,115167,21410876,radziwill-powiedzial-ze-nie-przepisalby-pigulki-dzien-po-nawet.html, accessed 10 May 2020.

60 Klementyna Suchanow, *To jest wojna. Kobiety, fundamentaliści i nowe średniowiecze* [This Is War: Women, Fundamentalists and the New Middle Ages] (Warszawa: Wydawnictwo Agora, 2020).

61 Daniel Flis, 'PiS złamał obietnicę wyborczą. Odrzucając projekt „Ratujmy Kobiety' [Law and Justice Breached Its Electoral Promise By Refusing the Proposal 'Let us Save Women']

to tighten the law on abortion has ended in protests, which does not mean that party politicians have given up trying to restrict reproductive rights; the party-controlled Constitutional Court has been used – as in the case of LGBT rights.

It is worth emphasising that positions on abortion were divided among populists – for example, Jarosław Kaczyński indicated that he would not support a bill that would completely ban abortion, as he believes the state should not cross a certain boundary.[62] On the other hand, it is not difficult to find Law and Justice MPs who would ban abortion completely. Since the populists came to power, there have been attempts to tighten the possibility of performing abortions. Minister of Justice-Prosecutor General Zbigniew Ziobro (leader of the radical "Solidarity Poland" party, in coalition with Law and Justice), as well as many other deputies of the United Right coalition, considered that the rule allowing for embryo-pathological abortion was unconstitutional.[63] At the request of a group of right-wing MPs,[64] the Constitutional Court examined legislation's constitutionality on the possibility of aborting pregnancies when prenatal testing or other medical indications point to a high probability of severe and irreversible fetal impairment or an incurable disease threatening the fetus' life.

As a result of this application, the Constitutional Court declared the premise of performing abortions due to fetal defects as unconstitutional. Thus, the restriction of women's right to terminate their pregnancies was carried out in Poland through a Constitutional Court judgment of 22 October 2020.[65] The judgment again triggered a wave of mass protests but also allowed politics to shift responsibility for such a judgment to the "constitution." The result of the judgment – restrictive abortion law – is an exception in the European Union – it is more restrictive only in Malta, where abortion is completely

https://oko.press/pis-zlamal-obietnice-wyborcza-odrzucajac-projekt-ratujmy-kobiety/>, accessed 10 May 2020.

62 Mp.pl, 'Kaczyński: Będziemy dążyli do tego, aby aborcji było dużo mniej niż obecnie' [Kaczyński: We Will Strive to Reduce the Number of Abortions Significantly] https://www.mp.pl/pacjent/ciaza/aktualnosci/151453,kaczynski-bedziemy-dazyli-do-tego-aby-aborcji-bylo-duzo-mniej-niz-obecnie >, accessed 10 May 2020.

63 Rzeczpospolita, 'Zbigniew Ziobro: aborcja niezgodna z Konstytucją' [Zbigniew Ziobro: Abortion is Unconstitutional] https://www.rp.pl/Zdrowie/305299968-Zbigniew-Ziobro-aborcja-niezgodna-z-Konstytucja.html, accessed 10 May 2020.

64 Sebastian Klauziński and Dominika Sitnicka, 'To oni chcą całkowitego zakazu aborcji. Publikujemy nazwiska posłów, którzy poparli wniosek do TK' [These People Want a Total Ban on Abortion: We Are Publishing the Names of Members of Parliament Who Supported the Request to the Constitutional Court] https://oko.press/to-oni-chca-calkowitego-zakazu-aborcji-publikujemy-nazwiska-poslow-ktorzy-poparli-wniosek-do-tk/, accessed 12 July 2021.

65 Constitutional Court Judgment of 22 October 2020, Case K 1/20.

banned by law.[66] The effect of eliminating this provision is a practical ban on abortion in Poland, as the only remaining legal causes for abortion are a threat to the woman's life and the criminal origin of the pregnancy (paedophilia, rape, incest). According to the Federation for Women and Family Planning, 1,110 legal abortions were performed in Polish hospitals in 2019, including 1,074 for embryo-pathological reasons, which means that 'as many as 98% of pregnancy terminations are performed due to the finding of severe and irreversible fetal defects.'[67]

Although the written motives of the Courts' abortion judgment do not mention its real consequences, we can presume that both judges and politicians were aware of them. After the judgment, Judge Mariusz Muszyński wrote an opinion in which he denied the accusations of exposing women to torture that appear in legal discourse by invoking the necessity of textualist argumentation:

> The Court did not negate the suffering of women or children who may find themselves in this situation. In the context of hierarchical control [i.e., constitutional review – K.K., M.S.], the Court was merely deciding questions of law in the abstract. Moreover, in the content of the examined and derogated provision, there is no confrontation of the good of the mother and child.[68]

Jarosław Kaczyński also claimed in an interview that the Court could not have decided otherwise because 'this is the constitution.' Unlike the judges, he admitted that the political motivation of the judgment was to prevent abortion on the grounds of Down's and Turner's syndromes:[69]:

> It is still permissible if the pregnancy is derived from a crime and if it threatens the life or health of the woman. It is only about Down syndrome and Turner syndrome, where the possibility of abortion has been

66 Federacja na Rzecz Kobiet i Planowania Rodziny, 'Prawa reprodukcyjne kobiet. Wybrane usługi zdrowia reprodukcyjnego w krajach Unii Europejskiej' [Womens' Reproductive Rights: Selected Reproductive Health Services in European Union Countries] https://rownosc.info/media/uploads/zdrowie_reprodukcyjne_ue.pdf, accessed 10 May 2020.

67 Federacja Kobiet i Planowania Rodziny, 'Terminacja ciąży w 2019 roku – dostępność aborcji w Polsce według najnowszych danych' [Termination of Pregnancy in 2019: Availability of Abortion in Poland According to the Most Recent Data] https://federa.org.pl/terminacja-ciazy-2019/>, accessed 12 July 2021.

68 Mariusz Muszyński, 'O skutku wyroku Trybunału w sprawie aborcji' [On the Effects of the Constitutional Court Judgment on Abortion] https://www.rp.pl/Opinie/302039901-Mariusz-Muszynski-O-skutku-wyroku-Trybunalu-w-sprawie-aborcji.html, accessed 12 July 2021.

69 Eliza Olczyk and Joanna Miziołek, 'Nie uprawiamy filozofii tylko politykę' [Let Us Not Do Philosophy But Politics] https://www.wprost.pl/kraj/10449780/jaroslaw-kaczynski-dla-wprost-kazdy-moze-zalatwic-aborcje-za-granica.html, accessed 10 June 2021.

> eliminated. (...) But I also know that there are advertisements in the press, which any moderately smart person understands and can get such an abortion abroad, cheaper or more expensive. (...) Among the possibilities of allowing abortion is a mental health wicket. This may be unacceptable to some, but it can be used. (...) In my opinion, nothing of the kind that would threaten the interests of women has happened.[70]

It is hard to say that restricting reproductive rights was one of the policy goals of the Law and Justice Party. Instead, these rights have become part of the culture wars and politics based on identity and Christian values. Agnieszka Graff and Elżbieta Korolczuk write ultraconservative actors present gender equality

> as a path to degeneration and demographic decline, a theme that occasionally takes on an explicit racist undertone. The falling fertility rates in Europe are juxtaposed against dynamic population growth among ethnic minorities and the influx of immigrants and refugees, both of which will allegedly result in the ultimate fall of the West.[71]

These actors strive for patriarchal gender norms and try to impose a Christian, traditional vision of the role of women. We cannot say the same about the Law and Justice Party – looking at their programme, we may notice their rhetoric regarding women is rather pro-equal, especially gender equality in the workplace.[72] Populists entering the culture wars and collaborating with fundamentalist and Catholic organisations had to pay their debt for electoral support, in the form of limitation of reproductive rights, through legislation and through constitutional courts.

4.6 Immigrants' and Asylum-Seekers' Rights

The rhetoric of populism, in Poland and elsewhere, often touches on immigrants and their legal status. Immigration is considered one of the fuels of populism, which is independent of whether it is a real or imagined problem for a given society.[73] This is because the immigrant is the exemplary 'Other.' His or her origin outside the community, and the limited resources

70 Ibid.

71 Agnieszka Graff and Elżbieta Korolczuk, *Anti-Gender Politics in the Populist Moment* (Taylor & Francis, 2022) 6.

72 Program Prawa i Sprawiedliwości 2019 [Programme of Law and Justice for 2019] https://pis.org.pl/files/Program_PIS_2019.pdf?fbclid=IwAR0Cw7m9L2-6jEcDWYKw3COk60PbXnufr4IzxBWTd0Eb1WeEe5W0XKBHPFU, accessed 20 April 2023.

73 Dani Rodrick, 'Why Does Globalization Fuel Populism? Economics, Culture, and the Rise of Right-Wing Populism' (2021) 13 *Annual Review of Economics* 133.

of vocalisation and asserting one's rights, allow populist politicians to instrumentally use his/her image as a threat. Thanks to this, the populist discourse gains another tool for creating constitutive dichotomies. It is no surprise that Law and Justice's politicians have frequently commented on this subject, whether during the 2015 European migrant crisis, the Belarusian-EU border crisis from 2021, and after the Russian invasion of Ukraine in 2022.

During the 2015 migration crisis, when almost 1.3 million refugees, mainly from Syria, came to Europe to seek asylum, Poland refused to participate in the refugee relocation system. Jarosław Kaczyński pointed to security and economic threats, as well as the fact that Poland was not a colonial state that participated in the exploitation of African countries.[74] Kaczyński contrasted morality with the law: although the country has committed itself to participate in the relocation scheme, it has the 'moral right to refuse.' We can see here the logic of the 'exceptio popularis' described by Rafał Mańko,[75] where the state of emergency for the populist people justifies suspending existing obligations and rights. At the same time, when this state of emergency occurs is decided by a populist politician.

This argument has been intensified in 2021 in connection with the events on the Belarusian-Polish border. After the falsification of the presidential election and the related cooling of relations between Belarus and the European Union, the government in Minsk launched operations to "flood" European countries with immigrants from the Middle East. As a result, the Polish government applied pushbacks, i.e., physical refusal of entrance and displacement of refugees to the territory of Belarus without the possibility of submitting an asylum application, which openly violates international human rights treaties. This technique has become increasingly used on other external borders of the European Union, notably in Greece or Italy, so it is hard to talk about populist or Polish specifics.[76] On the other hand, propaganda actions of support for soldiers 'defending the border'[77] or the prosecution of an actress

74 Polskie Radio, 'Jarosław Kaczyński o imigrantach: mamy pełne, moralne prawo powiedzieć nie' [Jarosław Kaczyński On Immigrants: We Have a Full Moral Right to Say No] https://www.polskieradio.pl/78/3564/Artykul/1783849,Jaroslaw-Kaczynski-o-imigrantach-mamy-pelne-moralne-prawo-powiedziec-nie, accessed 20 April 2023.

75 See Chapter 5 by Rafał Mańko in this volume.

76 UNHCR, 'News Comment: UNHCR Warns of Increasing Violence and Human Rights Violations at European Borders' https://www.unhcr.org/uk/news/news-releases/news-comment-unhcr-warns-increasing-violence-and-human-rights-violations, accessed 20 April 2023; The New Humanitarian, 'The Legal Battle to Stem the EU's Border Pushback Boom' https://www.thenewhumanitarian.org/analysis/2023/01/09/EU-pushbacks-legal-asylum, accessed 20 April 2023.

77 TVP Info, 'Koncert murem za polskim mundurem' [Concert to Support Polish Armed Forces] https://www.tvp.info/57239267/koncert-murem-za-polskim-mundurem-kto-wystapi-na-koncercie-tvn-sprawdz-nazwiska-polskich-i-zagranicznych-gwiazd-o-ktorej-i-kiedy-ogladac-na-zywo, accessed 20 April 2023.

who allegedly insulted Border Guard by criticising its participation in the pushbacks[78] were populist in nature. These events were widely commented on by government-controlled public television and constituted another element of constructing an us/stranger dichotomy. Those who did not agree to the measures were accused of treason. As President Andrzej Duda, formerly a Law and Justice MP, stated in one of his public speeches that:

> At the same time, our country was in danger. Not only the border of the Republic of Poland as such. It was not just a migration threat, it was a threat whose subtext was what we feared the most (...) that this is not a spectacular and isolated action, but part of a broader plan implemented by those who are hostile towards the Republic of Poland towards the European community. (...) We showed determination to the whole world, defending the borders of Poland, the EU, and the Schengen area. Despite various types of attacks, various fools and traitors, various irresponsible people. The Polish soldier rose to the occasion.[79]

The rhetoric of protecting the community from immigrants has not been translated into a nationwide immigration policy. The Law and Justice government did not fundamentally change immigration procedures or limit the approvals issued for permanent residence. Moreover, the rhetoric of closure and protection has changed for refugees from Ukraine after the 2022 Russian invasion. Regarding migrants from Ukraine, populists boast that Poland supports Ukraine on a military and humanitarian level – it has taken in some 3 million refugees.[80] Their rhetoric is based on references to aid and friendship.[81] To populists, Ukrainians are not so much "Other" – they do not stand out on the street, and their culture, language, and customs are similar. The difference in the treatment of Syrian and Ukrainian refugees was due to the

78 RMF FM, 'Sąd umorzył postępowanie wobec Barbary Kurdej-Szatan' [A Court Closed the Proceedings Against Barbara Kurden-Szatan] https://www.rmf24.pl/fakty/polska/news-sad-umorzyl-postepowanie-wobec-barbary-kurdej-szatan,nId,6456567#crp_state=1, accessed 20 April 2023.

79 Wprost.pl, 'Andrzej Duda: Pokazaliśmy całemu światu determinację, mimo ataków różnych durniów i zdrajców' [Andrzej Duda: We Have Shown Our Determination to the Entire Wolrd, Despite Attacks of Various Idiots and Traitors] https://www.wprost.pl/polityka/10817893/andrzej-duda-pokazalismy-calemu-swiatu-determinacje-mimo-atakow-roznych-durniow-i-zdrajcow.html, accessed 20 April 2023.

80 Maciej Duszczyk and Paweł Kaczmarczyk, 'Wojna i migracja: napływ uchodźców wojennych z Ukrainy i możliwe scenariusze na przyszłość' [War and Migration: The Influx of War Refugees from Ukraine and Possible Future Scenarios] https://www.migracje.uw.edu.pl/wp-content/uploads/2022/04/Spotlight-APRIL-2022-PL.pdf, accessed 20 April 2023.

81 Prawo i Sprawiedliwość, 'Polska wspiera i niesie pomoc Ukrainie' [Poland Supports and Helps Ukraine] https://pis.org.pl/aktualnosci/polska-wspiera-i-niesie-pomoc-ukrainie, accessed 20 April 2023.

inclusion of the latter within an imaginative community based on a commonality of race, culture, and religion. In addition, the fact of Russian aggression was combined with the historical experience of the Poles which created an additional level of understanding. This demonstrates that, given the right conditions of similarities, Polish populism is not exclusively inclusive and is able to promote inter-community solidarity.

4.7 Advancing Social Rights

Politics of human rights advanced by populist regimes is rooted in rapture from liberal political economy. After coming to power, Law and Justice introduced several social programmes that indicate a break in the previously dominant narrative that social programmes are impossible in Poland due to the indigent nature of Polish society and the associated low budget revenues and inability to finance them from the state budget. Michał Krajewski convincingly argued that social rights were displaced in the Polish constitutional liberal discourse what was 'contingent upon the specific political and intellectual climate of stimulating a free-market economy and crisis-driven austerity.'[82] The social policies were treated more as a question of economy than rights and obligations. The populist government identified this gap and broke with the austerity policy. To justify this change, the populists used the language of dignity and rights.

The flagship project of PiS and the United Right government is the "Family 500+" programme. It is a family benefit of PLN 500 (approximately 110 euros) per month, introduced in 2016 to help parents raise their children. As of 1 July 2019, this benefit is due for each child, regardless of the parent's income. Politicians of the ruling coalition present this programme as both a social policy tool and part of a policy to restore citizens' dignity. In social terms, as we can read on the website of the Ministry of Family and Social Policy, the programme primarily pursues three goals: 'It influences an increase in the number of births (the fertility rate increased from 1.29 in 2015 to 1.45 in 2017) reduces poverty, particularly among children (between 2015 and 2017, extreme poverty fell from 6.5 to 4.3 percent), and represents an investment in the family.'[83] In terms of dignity, this programme is meant to restore dignity by recognising family formation as an activity valued by the state. This is evident in this statement by Jarosław Kaczyński:

82 See more in: Michał Krajewski, 'The Constitutional Quandary of Social Rights: Questions in Times of the Polish Illiberal Turn' (2023) 21(1) *International Journal of Constitutional Law* 156.

83 Ministerstwo Rodziny, Pracy i Polityki Społecznej, 'Rodzina 500 plus' [Family 500 Plus] https://www.gov.pl/web/rodzina/rodzina-500-plus, accessed 10 May 2020.

> They attack our social policy, saying it is handouts. They do not understand what the great goals of this reform are. Poverty humiliates and takes away freedom, this is a phenomenon we have managed to reduce. Our opponents attack our social policy, worse, they attack Polish families and children. Restoring the dignity of Poles is our great goal, our opponents do not understand this goal.[84]

The programme is thus presented as "restoring dignity" to the family, which previous liberal governments failed to recognise and respect. Similarly, the former Minister of Family, Labor, and Social Policies stated, 'the family is our priority and best investment.'[85] "Children" and "family" appear very often in the statements of Law and Justice politicians, and it is to this group that most social programmes are directed. However, the concept of "families" is normative. It is worth noting that only the "real family" is protected here – initially, the 500+ programme was not directed at the first child but only the second and subsequent children. Critics have often cited the example of a single mother, who would not receive such a benefit, while people who can afford to support children, but have more than one, already does.[86]

The "Good Start" programme, introduced in 2018, is also part of such a social policy. Commonly referred to as "300 plus," this programme is paid as a school layette designed to support school children. The programme will be linked to other programmes, such as free textbooks. Introducing "Good Start," Prime Minister Mateusz Morawiecki said that it is 'an essential program to support families, as it is another element of strengthening the current government's pro-family policy' and that 'from the conversations, we are now having with Poles in many parts of the country, it shines through with great joy and satisfaction that the Law and Justice government is managing the state's public finances in such a way.'[87]

84 Telewizja Republika, 'Kaczyński: naszym wielkim celem jest przywrócenie godności Polaków!' [Kaczyński: Our Grand Goal is to Restore the Dignity of Poles!] https://telewizjarepublika.pl/kaczynski-naszym-wielkim-celem-jest-przywrocenie-godnosci-polakow,77247.html, accessed 10 May 2020.

85 Radio Maryja, 'Min. B. Borys-Szopa: rodzina jest naszym priorytetem i najlepszą inwestycją'[Minister B. Borys-Szopa: The Family is Our Priority and Our Best Investment] https://www.radiomaryja.pl/informacje/min-b-borys-szopa-rodzina-jest-naszym-priorytetem-i-najlepsza-inwestycja/, accessed 10 May 2020.

86 'Zandberg: Świadczenia społeczne, jak 500+, powinny być indeksowane' [Zandberg: Social Security Benefits, Such as 500+, Should be Indexated] *Gazeta Prawna* (7 August 2017) https://www.gazetaprawna.pl/artykuly/1207851,zandberg-swiadczenia-spoleczne-500-plus-powinny-byc-indeksowane.html, accessed 10 May 2020.

87 'Premier Mateusz Morawiecki o korzyściach programu „Dobry Start"' [Prime Minister Mateusz Morawiecki on the Benefits of the 'Good Start' Programme] https://www.premier.gov.pl/wydarzenia/aktualnosci/premier-mateusz-morawiecki-o-korzysciach-programu-dobry-start.html, accessed 10 May 2020.

Another support for "real families" was the introduction of restrictions on Sunday trading – the former prime minister said Sunday is for the family and all workers should have the privilege of spending it with their families.[88] In this matter, the Law and Justice Party acted in concert with the Episcopate of the Catholic Church, who supported a total ban on Sunday trading: 'Sunday can once again become a guarantor of emotional tranquility, as well as the building of family, religious and national community.' So, the idea was to impose the only way to spend time on Sunday. The originators of this project wrote bluntly, 'Sunday for Catholics is the Lord's day, dedicated first and foremost to God, but also to oneself and one's neighbours.'

PiS has also turned to elderly citizens, among whom it enjoys exceptionally high support.[89] They received the so-called "thirteenth pension," announced during the 2019 parliamentary election campaign – Jarosław Kaczyński announced at the time that 'there will be a thirteenth pension permanently, a quota and percentage indexation, we will try to improve the livelihood of the poorest pensioners, raise their minimum pension.'[90]

The focus on family policy is part of regional specificity. Political scientist Ivan Krastev and lawyer Stephen Holmes, in their book on the crisis of liberalism, point out that one of the reasons for the so-called illiberal democracy in Central Europe is the mass emigration from the region after joining the European Union.[91] Hence, populist social policies can be seen as a response to the demographic crisis resulting from emigration and declining fertility rates in the region's societies.

The above examples show that populism in power introduces, compared to earlier ones, rather elaborate social policies with social transfers linked to the dignity discourse. In the case of Poland, it is also linked to the discourse of valuing the family, which is derived from the social doctrine of the Catholic Church. Regardless of its ideological basis, such a policy is consistent with the concept of social human rights, particularly Article 25 (the right to an

88 Piotr Miączyński and Leszek Kostrzewski, 'Jarosław Kaczyński poparł zakaz handlu w niedzielę' [Jarosław Kaczyński Supported the Sunday Trading Ban], *Gazeta Wyborcza* (30 June 2016), https://wyborcza.biz/biznes/1,147743,20330173,kaczynski-poparl-zakaz-handlu-w-niedziele.html, accessed 10 May 2020.

89 Łukasz Lipiński, 'Jak głosowali młodzi i starsi, miasto i wieś' [How Did Young and Old People Vote, How Did Towns and Villages Vote] *Polityka* (14 October 2019) https://www.polityka.pl/tygodnikpolityka/kraj/1928140,1,jak-glosowali-mlodzi-i-starsi-miasto-i-wies.read, accessed 10 May 2020.

90 Martyna Kośka, '13. emerytura. Jarosław Kaczyński zdradził, czy będzie wypłacana w kolejnych latach' [A 13th Pension: Jarosław Kaczyński Disclosed Whether it Will Be Paid out in the Coming Years], *Money.pl* (6 September 2019) https://www.money.pl/emerytury/13-emerytura-jaroslaw-kaczynski-zdradzil-czy-bedzie-wyplacana-w-kolejnych-latach-6421691893560961a.html, accessed 10 May 2020.

91 Ivan Krastev and Stephen Holmes, *The Light that Failed* (New York: Pegasus Books, 2020) 27-33.

adequate standard of living) and Article 26 (the right to education) of the Universal Declaration of Human Rights. Moreover, social rights can be seen as one of the conditions for operationalising other rights. Only by having a minimum level of social security can one demand respect for other rights. In this respect, populism in power can be seen as an elevation of the protection provided by these rights.

According to the Central Statistical Office, 2016 saw a decrease in the extent of extreme poverty among children aged 0–17 (from 9% in 2015 to just under 6% in 2016)[92]. The Central Statistical Office also points out an overall improvement in the material situation of households in Poland. Household poverty fell from 6.5% in 2015 to 4.9% in 2016. However, in 2018, the rate rose to 5.4%[93] and decreased to 4.2% in 2021.[94] Similarly, most recent microeconomic analyses indicate that the Polish populist government is pursuing a prudent budgetary policy by boosting GDP, improving tax revenue, and reducing, at the same time, public debt and poverty.[95] It appears that, at least in the short term, populist governments can combine social spending with sustainable budgetary policies. Yet, economic commentators point out that the economic policies of the populists in Poland are not based on a coherent vision of economics, a lack of strategic vision.[96] They thus become resistant to adjustment. This also seems to be since populist social policies are treated in not only economic terms but also political and ideological terms, they create a normative vision of the family as the basis of society. The need to perpetuate their own vision of the community is as critical as the real effects of these programmes. In order to maintain ideological consistency, populists seem to accept the limited effectiveness of their social policies. By

92 GUS, 'Ubóstwo w Polsce w latach 2015-2016' [Poverty in Poalnd 2015-2016] https://stat.gov.pl/files/gfx/portalinformacyjny/pl/defaultaktualnosci/5487/1/8/1/ubostwo_w_polsce_w_latach_2015-2016.pdf, accessed 20 May 2020.

93 GUS, 'Zasięg ubóstwa ekonomicznego w 2018' [Extent of Economic Poverty in 2018] https://stat.gov.pl/files/gfx/portalinformacyjny/pl/defaultaktualnosci/5487/14/6/1/zasieg_ubostwa_ekonomicznego_w_polsce_w_2018_r.pdf, accessed 20 May 2020.

94 GUS, 'Zasięg ubóstwa ekonomicznego w 2021' [Extent of Economic Poverty in 2021] https://stat.gov.pl/files/gfx/portalinformacyjny/pl/defaultaktualnosci/5487/14/9/1/zasieg_ubostwa_ekonomicznego_w_polsce_w_2021_roku.pdf>, accessed 20 April 2023.

95 Michał Brzezinski and Katarzyna Sałach, 'Prudent Populists? The Short-Term Macroeconomic Impact of Populist Policies in Poland', *University of Warsaw Faculty of Economics Working Papers* No. 2/2023, https://www.wne.uw.edu.pl/application/files/1316/7585/5778/WNE_WP409.pdf accessed 15 September 2023.

96 Fundacja Instytut Badań Strukturalnych, '„Rodzina 500+" – ocena programu i propozycje zmian' [Family 500+ - Evaluation of the Programme and Proposals for Changes] https://ibs.org.pl/publications/rodzina-500-ocena-programu-i-propozycje-zmian/, accessed 20 May 2020; Anna Gromada, 'Rodzina 500+ jako polityka publiczna' [Family 500+ as a Public Policy], *Instytut Studiów Zaawansowanych: Seria Analizy* (February 2017) https://krytyka-polityczna.pl/file/sites/4/2017/09/Gromada_Rodzina-500.pdf>, accessed 20 May 2020.

defining their social programmes in moral terms ("dignity"), populism limits its ability to revise them.

4.8 Conclusion: Populism and a New Political Economy of Rights

Populism grapples with the opposing tendencies of political exclusion and legal inclusion of the "Other" within one community. The language of exclusion allows for the mobilisation of voters and the shaping of a collective identity and, at the same time, contradicts the liberal legal framework that populism preserves. To resolve this tension, populism makes a different redistribution of rights between the political and public and the apolitical and private. Populism political rhetoric, through its morality-based definition of a "true" member of the community, excludes from the public sphere people who, due to their sexual orientation, lifestyle, and cultural background, do not meet such a definition. At the same time, populism-in-power, due to its desire to maintain a democratic orientation and conformity to European rights standards, does not attack rights directly.[97] It may be a facade but it has real, structural consequences. This differentiates populism-in-power from authoritarian governments, where there is much more direct restriction of human rights through legislation with a simultaneous break with the inclusive language of human rights. By contrast, in the case of the Polish populist government, there is an attempt to keep up appearances through soft actions. We also see that these actions are scattered and that many actors are involved in restricting rights – central government, local government, and the Constitutional Court. The level of redistribution of power, as the ability to decide the scope of rights, is therefore also more diffuse than it is in classical authoritarian regimes.

The relationship between populism and human rights is, therefore, much more complex and cannot be reduced to a simple incompatibility thesis. We can see from the above examples that the negative attitude of populists to human rights is visible primarily at the level of public rhetoric or the instrumental use of constitutional review to reinterpret existing rights and, less often, at the level of legislative action. Populist governments restrict some of the human rights of sexual minorities, women, and immigrants. At the same time, populism-in-power strengthens social human rights by pursuing rather elaborate social policies. All citizens can use these policies, and the access criteria are not overtly ideological. How can we explain this dialectic

97 On the moderating influence of the EU on Polish and Hungarian populism see Tímea Drinóczi and Agnieszka Bień-Kacała (eds), *Illiberal Constitutionalism in Poland and Hungary: The Deterioration of Democracy, Misuse of Human Rights and Abuse of the Rule of Law* (Abingdon: Routledge, 2021).

of restriction-enhancement of rights through populism? It seems that populism is not a simple denial of human rights but an attempt to introduce a new human rights politics based on new scheme of distribution of rights. Liberal human rights politics is based on individual distribution. Equating rights to commodities, we can say that in liberal discourse, they are distributed equally – at the symbolic level – among individuals. The individual and his inherent dignity are the source and addressee of rights. The role of the state is reduced only to that of an independent distributor of these rights. Populism breaks with such an economy. The distributing subject becomes a metaphysical and unequivocally positive moral community – the nation. The embodiment of this community is the political organisation (the state), which politicians represent. In turn, rights are distributed not among individuals but among the building blocks of this community (mainly the family and rural communities).

This structural change in the economy of rights is performative. Exclusion at the level of access to the public sphere is reinforced through social transfers which can cement a new vision of the community. In other words, the longer populism remains in power and can implement its new politics of rights, the more it produces a community that conforms to its vision. Such an approach allows us to pose the question of a strategy for resisting the restriction of access to public space for marginalised groups. Such a strategy should take into account a new exclusionary-inclusive human rights policy. Merely focusing on the exclusionary aspect of populist politics may not be sufficient. A resistance strategy should recognise the inclusionary element of populism and take it to its logical conclusion concerning the public sphere. Such resistance requires developing a new vision of the political community that combines individual personal freedom with collective social rights. Since populism falls within the scope of democracy, it requires democratic and, therefore, political responses. Given the electoral sustainability of populism, creating such an answer might be the next, big task of human rights politics.

Chapter 5

Exceptio Popularis

Resisting Illiberal Legality

*Rafał Mańko**

5.1 Introduction

On 22 October 2020, the Polish Constitutional Court, dominated by the conservative appointees of the ruling Law and Justice party, issued a landmark decision outlawing embryopathological abortion (Case K 1/20),[1] the only type of abortion still legal, at the time, alongside abortion in cases of pregnancy caused by a criminal act.[2] On this occasion, the Court accomplished an important element of the illiberal[3] ruling party's religious conservative political programme, an element which – due to its general unpopularity in Polish society – was not fit for open adoption through parliamentary procedure,

* I would like to thank Cosmin Cercel and Gian-Giacomo Fusco for reading and commenting on earlier drafts of this paper. All views expressed herein reflect exclusively my personal convictions and under no circumstances ought to be ascribed to any institution or entity.

1 For a critical analysis of the legal reasoning in the case, see, e.g., Marta Bucholc, 'Abortion Law and Human Rights in Poland: The Closing of the Jurisprudential Horizon' (2022) 14 *Hague Journal on the Rule of Law* 73, 88–93.

2 Abortion on social grounds had been made illegal by a Constitutional Court judgment of 28 May 1996, Case K 26/96. For a brief overview of the evolution of Polish abortion laws after 1945, see Bucholc, 'Abortion Law,' 80–4.

3 Whereas populism may be, to an extent, a *political technique* used by Law and Justice (as exemplified by the propaganda rhetoric of 'good people' vs. 'bad elites'), the substantive core of their political ideology is best described as illiberal, conservative Christian ethnonationalism with elements of economic socialism. See, e.g., Adam Folvarčný and Lubomír Kopeček, 'Which Conservatism? The Identity of the Polish Law and Justice Party' (2020) 16(1) *Politics in Central Europe* 159, 178–82. Cf. Mirosław Michał Sadowski, 'Law and Collective Memory in the Service of Illiberalism. Through the Looking-Glass: Transformation or a Reactionary Revolution?' (2021) 18(1) *Kraków International Studies* 107. For an extensive theoretical discussion of illiberal constitutionalism, see the excellent study by Adam Sulikowski, *Postliberal Constitutionalism: The Challenge of Right-Wing Populism in Central and Eastern Europe* (Abingdon: Routledge, 2023), 66–88. On the concept of populism, as applied to Poland's right-wing ruling party, see, e.g., Michał Stambulski, 'Constitutional Populism and the Rule of Law in Poland' in Martin Krygier, Adam Czarnota, and Wojciech Sadurski (eds), *Anti-Constitutional Populism* (Cambridge: Cambridge University Press, 2022), 338–9.

DOI: 10.4324/9781032624464-6

even if the ruling party would have a sufficient majority to do so.[4] But whereas the content of the judgment, given the illiberal political background of the justices of the Constitutional Court, could have been expected,[5] what happened between the date of handing down the judgment (22 October 2020) and its delayed publication[6] three months later (27 January 2021) opens up a novel jurisprudential space. It should be noted that, in the Polish legal order, a judgment of the Constitutional Court declaring a statutory norm unconstitutional enters into force only once the operative part of that judgment is published in the official journal of the state.[7] Until then, the normative force of the judgment is suspended and the legislative act still remains in force, unaffected by the unpublished judgment. Normally, the Prime Minister – who decides when a judgment is published – does it without delay, and even without waiting for the motives of the judgment.[8] Indeed, the Constitution explicitly obliges the Prime Minister to do so 'immediately.'[9] However, first in 2015, and then in 2020, the Prime Minister used their power of publication in order to purposefully veto (in 2015) or suspend (in 2020) the legal force of the Constitutional Court's judgment.

Of course, the procedure for the publication of Constitutional Court judgments in the *Official Journal* of the Republic was conceived of as a mere formality, aimed at serving legal certainty. It can fairly be said that in Poland, the idea of publishing operative parts of Constitutional Court judgments in the *Official Journal* upon order of the Prime Minister, is a legal transfer from Western Europe; such a practice is foreseen, for instance, in § 56(3) of

4 In 2016 and 2018 attempts to outlaw embryopathological abortion via legislative enactments were blocked by mass protests, so called 'Black Protests' (Karolina Kocemba, 'Counterpublics of Polish Constitutionalism Illustrated with the Example of Women's Rights' (2019) 11(1) *Krytyka Prawa/Critique of Law* 83, 97).

5 Bucholc, 'Abortion Law,' 86.

6 *Dziennik Ustaw Rzeczypospolitej Polskiej* [Journal of Statutes of the Republic of Poland], 27 January 2021, item 175, available: https://isap.sejm.gov.pl/isap.nsf/download.xsp/WDU20210000175/O/D20210175.pdf, accessed 21 April 2023.

7 Article 190(3) of the Polish Constitution: 'A judgment of the Constitutional Tribunal shall take effect from the day of its publication, however, the Constitutional Tribunal may specify another date for the end of the binding force of a normative act. (…).'

8 In line with the Civil Law tradition, in Polish legal culture a sharp formal distinction is made between the legally binding operative part (placed at the beginning of the judgment) and the non-binding justification (motives) that follow.

9 Article 190(2) of the Polish Constitution: 'Judgments of the Constitutional Tribunal regarding matters specified in Article 188, shall be required to be *immediately published* in the official publication in which the original normative act was promulgated. If a normative act has not been promulgated, then the judgment shall be published in the Official Gazette of the Republic of Poland, Monitor Polski.' See also Article 9(1)(6) of the Publication of Normative Acts Act 2000 (*ustawa o ogłaszaniu aktów normatywnych*) which provides the publication of Constitutional Court judgments concerning the unconstitutionality of statutes.

the Austrian Constitutional Court Act 1953 which provides that the operative part (*Rechtssatz*) of a Constitutional Court judgment is published in the *Bundesgesetzblatt* upon order of the Federal Chancellor.[10] By 2015, however, in Poland the *form* of the legal transfer became unquilted from its underlying *substance*: at the time, Law and Justice still did not control the Constitutional Court and was unsatisfied with decisions of the Court finding some of its laws unconstitutional. The reaction of Prime Minister Beata Szydło was peculiar: she blatantly refused to publish three judgments of the Constitutional Court[11] claiming that they are... unconstitutional.[12] Thereby, a new level of *de facto* judicial review was added, whereby the legality of the Court's judgments is tested by the executive, which becomes – in this scenario – a "superconstitutional court,'" tasked with reviewing the constitutionality of the Constitutional Court's judgments.[13] Such a move was definitely in tune with the illiberal ideological agenda of Law and Justice which foresees the 'supremacy of politics over the law' as its 'crucial component,' even if it 'is not explicitly expressed in politicians' official statements very often,' as Adam Sulikowski notes.[14]

Whereas in the period when Law and Justice already controlled the executive and legislative powers, but not yet the top judiciary, such a creative interpretation of the constitution made sense (from a political and pragmatic point of view), the invocation of the same power vis-à-vis the Law and Justice controlled Constitutional Court – 'no longer an opponent [but] an ally'[15] of the ruling majority – is particularly perplexing. In the frank words of Mr Morawiecki, former Santander Bank executive turned conservative Prime Minister:

> Undoubtedly, the judgment of the Constitutional Court [outlawing abortion – R.M.] must be published in the *Journal of Laws*. At the same time,

10 § 56(4) Verfassungsgerichtshofgesetz 1956 (consolidated version available online at: https://www.ris.bka.gv.at/GeltendeFassung.wxe?Abfrage=Bundesnormen&Gesetzesnummer=10000245).

11 Cases: K 47/15, K 39/16, and K 44/16.

12 Wojciech Sadurski, *Poland's Constitutional Breakdown* (Oxford: Oxford University Press, 2019), 77; Stambulski, 'Constitutional Populism,' 341.

13 The legal basis for this surprising power grab was, at best, rather thin: 'The President of the Council of Ministers publishes (...) the *Journal of Laws*' – Article 21(1) of the Publication of Normative Acts Act 2000. However, some courts decided to apply the Constitutional Court's judgment even before its publication (Stambulski, 'Constitutional Populism', 341 n. 10).

14 Adam Sulikowski, *Postliberal Constitutionalism*, 114.

15 Stambulski, 'Constitutional Populism,' 342.

however, the situation of very serious social tensions demands that we analyse the proper date for this publication.[16]

Prime Minister Morawiecki clearly savours the new powers of "superconstitutional review" grabbed by his predecessor, Beata Szydło. This time, however, the use of these powers is not intended as an absolute veto, but as a moderating power: the decision when a Constitutional Court judgment shall enter into force rests not in the Court itself, but in the executive, even if both belong to the same political family. Checks and balances the illiberal way.

Thus, the period running from 22 October 2020 until 27 January 2021 was, in legal terms, the period of an unexpected suspension of legal force of the Court's controversial judgment. From a purely sociological perspective, this period was marked by mass protests of citizens – hundreds of thousands flocking to the streets, despite pandemic restrictions[17] – standing up for the right to abortion and expressing their rage with the politically motivated decision of the Court, itself considered by many lawyers as illegitimately composed and, therefore, constitutionally illegal.[18] From a political perspective, the decision of the government (which has the *legal* duty to publish Constitutional Court judgments without delay) was a reaction to the mass protests and an attempt to appease the citizens by delaying the entry into force of the judgment. Normally, the operative parts of Constitutional Court judgments are published within days from being handed down, not months.

From a juridico-theoretical perspective, which sees not only the legal form but also its political and social substance, the use of these powers by Mr Morawiecki in 2020 is very different from their use by Ms Szydło five years earlier. Blocking the publication of three Constitutional Court judgments which went against the political line of Law and Justice, Prime Minister Szydło did not, in any way, yield to public pressure. To the contrary, the popular sentiments were with the pre-2015 liberal majority still lingering at the Constitutional Court, then headed by Professor Andrzej Rzepliński, very much opposed to the incoming Law and Justice parliamentary majority. But, by 2020, the Court had already come under the unconditional control of a right-wing illiberal majority, and it ruled in line with the political expectations of that majority. Mr Morawiecki's decision to suspend the entry into

16 'Stanowisko Rady Ministrów z dnia 1 grudnia 2020 r. w przedmiocie terminu publikacji wyroku Trybunału Konstytucyjnego wsprawie o sygn. akt K 1/20' *Monitor Polski*, item 1104. Available: https://monitorpolski.gov.pl/M2020000110401.pdf, accessed 24 April 2023.

17 Bucholc, 'Abortion Law,' 86.

18 Wojciech Sadurski, *Poland's*, 64–70; Dimitry Kochenov and Barbara Grabowska-Moroz, 'Constitutional Populism versus EU law: A Much More Complex Story than You Imagined' in Krygier et al., *Anti-Constitutional*, 467.

force of the judgment was, therefore, not an act of undermining the rule of law (as was the case with Ms Szydło) in the name of supremacy of politics over the juridical,[19] but a conscious exercise of a recently created constitutional right within the framework of what had become, in the meantime, a politically uniform state (legislative, executive, and constitutional judiciary being controlled by the same political majority). This makes the unexpected[20] suspension of the Court's abortion judgment all the more interesting from a jurisprudential perspective.

For lawyers operating within the positivistic horizon of liberal legality, the purposeful and politically motivated postponement of the publication was merely a 'disgracefully open violation of the Constitution.'[21] This approach obfuscates the fact that the norm of Article 190(2) of the Constitution, and of the abrogating norm contained in the operative part of judgment K 1/20 were both during that time *effectively suspended* by the executive due to mass public protests. The popular factor – which could be described, in sociological terms, as a sudden legitimacy crisis – cannot be overlooked from any realist legal theory, lest one wishes to descend into a hopelessly Kelsenian *Himmel der Begriffe* detached from the actual life of the law in the name of a neo-Platonic hall of juridical mirrors. Rather, following Cosmin Cercel, I claim that 'any interpretation of facts is decidedly political, and any evaluation of the facts necessary for the declaration of emergency measures is political.'[22] What cannot be overlooked in this specific conjecture is that the ruling Law and Justice majority yielded to *necessity*, a concept very closely connected to the state of exception.[23]

Thus, in order to bring back theory as close as possible to the life of the juridical, this chapter advances a new juridico-political concept: *the minor state of exception*, as an attempt at theoretically conceptualising what happened not only in Poland between 22 October 2020 and 27 January 2021, but also anywhere else where the political powers decided to suspend the operation of a juridical norm in the face of a sharp legitimacy crisis. As Tormod Otter Johansen claims, '[j]urists approach the world armed with the ability to distinguish, define and conceptualise every phenomenon,' and

19 Cf. Sulikowski, *Postliberal*, 114.

20 As Marta Bucholc notes, there was 'no conceivable legal justification for the delay' of the publication, and 'the political justification seemed to be the need to await social reactions' (Bucholc, 'Abortion Law,' 87).

21 Ewa Łętowska, 'A Tragic Constitutional Court Judgment on Abortion' *Verfassungsblog* (12 November 2020), https://verfassungsblog.de/a-tragic-constitutional-court-judgment-on-abortion/

22 Cosmin Cercel, 'Pandemic, Exception and the Law: Notes on the Shattered Nomos of Europe' (2021) 96 *Acta Universitatis Lodziensis – Folia Iuridica* 83, 89.

23 Gian-Giacomo Fusco, *Form of Life: Agamben and the Destitution of Rules* (Edinburgh University Press, 2023), 38.

to order the world, they 'either use concepts already at hand or reach for new distinctions by producing new categories and typologies.'[24] The present chapter is, precisely, an attempt to produce a new concept to accommodate the reality of legal life which escapes existing categories but which, as history shows, can repeat itself.

5.2 Minor State of Exception as a New Politico-Juridical Concept

By a "minor state of exception" or "*exceptio popularis*" ('people's [state of] exception') I mean a situation in which the constituted power, under pressure from the people amounting to a *tumultus* (such as exerted through strikes or other forms of protest) suspends the operation of a certain legal norm which is the object of the people's unrest. As such, the minor state of exception is limited *ratione materiae* to only one norm of the legal system, rather than encompassing the entire legal system (or a significant chunk thereof) as the "major" state of exception does. But more importantly, the "minor" state of exception is one in which the dialectics of power and subjection are somewhat reversed: it is the people who demand the suspension or abolition of the rule, and the constituted power gives in to that popular demand. However, for some reason or another, the people do not succeed in having the norm in question completely abrogated, as it is sometimes the case.[25] Neither do the people succeed in forcibly changing the constituted power without changing the constitution (revolt), not to mention forcibly changing the constitution and acting as a new constitutive power (revolution) and exercising, until the establishment of a new constitution, sovereign dictatorship.[26] However, the minor state of exception is something more than a merely informal and "soft" practice, as it materialises itself through rendering the questioned legal norm *pro tempore* ineffective, thus producing actual legal effects, visible even through the positivistic legal lens (unless they are thoroughly deformed by the ideology of liberal legality). The minor state of exception is not just part of pure facticity, but just like necessity, it functions as a properly "juridical operator"[27] which allows to suspend the effects of the unpopular legal rule. Therefore, at times, it can play an important role in the dynamics of juridico-political struggles, keeping in mind that any 'social movement always tends

24 Tormod Otter Johansen, 'The Necessity of Legal Typologies in Crisis and Emergency' (2021) 96 *Acta Universitatis Lodziensis – Folia Iuridica* 71, 72

25 Xenia Chiaramonte, 'Social Movements and the Legal Field: Becoming-Constituent' (2019) 22(1) *Max Planck Yearbook of United Nations Law* 376, 388.

26 Carl Schmitt, *Dictatorship*, transl. by Michael Hoelzl and Graham Ward (Cambridge: Polity, 2014) 119; Cosmin Cercel, *Towards a Jurisprudence of State Communism: Law and the Failure of Revolution* (London-New York: Routledge, 2018), 68–70, 84–8, 98.

27 Fusco, *Form of Life*, 38.

to push the boundaries of the existing legality.'[28] Indeed, the minor state of exception can be a source of important gains for the people, even if temporary, or it can be used in a tactical manner by the constituted power.

By labelling the people's state of exception as "minor," I not only distinguish it from its "major" counterpart, theorised by Schmitt[29] and Agamben,[30] but I also purposefully cross-refer to "minor jurisprudence" and to "minor law." The former concept was used, probably for the first time, by Panu Minkinnen to describe the legal philosophy expressed in Franz Kafka's literature.[31] The Finnish legal theorist altered the signifier "minor literature," used by Deleuze and Guattari (1975), in order to highlight Kafka's position in the worlds of literature ("outside the realms of all major literary traditions") and of law ("an artist in the world of law"). Two years later the concept of "minor jurisprudence" was used prominently by Peter Goodrich[32] in his monograph on *Law in the Courts of Love*, devoted to feminist "courts of love" in medieval France. On this occasion, Goodrich provided a very useful definition of the concept, stating that:

> A minor jurisprudence is one which neither aspires nor pretends to be the only law or universal jurisprudence. Its referent is a law whose jurisdiction is neither jealous of other jurisdictions nor fearful of alternative disciplines. It represents the strangeness of language and so the possibilities of interpretation as also of plural forms of knowledge. A minor jurisprudence (...) is a challenge to the science of law and a threat to its monopoly of legal knowledge. It challenges the law of masters, the genre and categories of the established institution of doctrine and its artificial and paper rules.[33]

The tradition of using "minor" in legal philosophy has been recently taken up by Tormod Otter Johansen who, in an essay on *revolutionary jurisprudence* posits that even after the withering away of law some part of it – the "minor law" – would remain in place, but deposed of its present significance and role in the sanctioning of the social bond.[34] It is precisely in this discursive

28 Xenia Chiaramonte, 'The Struggle for Law: Legal Strategies, Environmental Struggles and Climate Actions in Italy' (2020) 10(4) *Oñati Socio-Legal Series* 932, 935.

29 Carl Schmitt, *Political Theology: Four Chapters on the Concept of Sovereignty*, transl. George Schwab (Chicago: University of Chicago Press, 2005).

30 Giorgio Agamben, *State of Exception*, transl. Kevin Attell (Chicago and London: University of Chicago Press, 2005).

31 Panu Minkkinen, 'The Radiance of Justice: On the Minor Jurisprudence of Franz Kafka' (1994) 3(3) *Social & Legal Studies* 349, 357–8.

32 Peter Goodrich, *Law in the Courts of Love: Literature and Other Minor Jurisprudences* (Abingdon: Routledge, 1996).

33 Goodrich, *Law*, 2.

34 Tormod Otter Johanssen, 'Minor Law: Notes Towards a Revolutionary Jurisprudence' in Cosmin Cercel, Gian-Giacomo Fusco, and Simon Lavis (eds), *States of Exception: Law, History, Theory* (Abingdon: Routledge, 2020), 76.

context that I wish to introduce the *exceptio popularis* as a minor state of exception: minor both in the sense of its lesser significance as a phenomenon (as in Johansen's "minor law"), but also minor in the sense of belonging to a minor jurisprudence and, as such, constituting a challenge to the mainstream discourse of liberal legality which, looking upon a minor state of exception, discerns only a deviation from the rule, rather than a phenomenon in its own right.

To be sure, the notion advanced here is an open challenge to liberal legality which, as Cosmin Cercel rightly observes, currently 'gives way to new politico-legal arrangements.'[35] And indeed, '[a]t the core of this process – as he notes – there is a *tension over the meaning of legality*.'[36] It is, therefore, not by chance that both the phenomenon I try to thematise appears now, in a time of transition, and that the present conjecture of the politico-juridical nomos – the 'normative universe' that 'we inhabit'[37] – lends itself to devising such a concept. In fact, it will perhaps not be too far-fetched to say that whereas we, the jurists, stay in the same place, the normative universe around us – 'the world of right and wrong, lawful and unlawful'[38] – is changing beyond recognition. In contrast to liberal legality, the approach to the notion of the exception, advanced in this paper, is distinctively Schmittian in that it is based on the assumption that 'norm and exception maintain a relationship to one another' and that it 'places more emphases on the primacy and juridical significance of the exception in making possible the normal constitution.'[39]

The concept of the people's state of exception (*exceptio popularis*) points to the concept of the people, a concept which 'always contains a more original split than the one between enemy and friend, an incessant civil war that at once divides this concept more radically than any conflict and keeps it united and constitutes it more firmly than any identity'"[40] Whereas this chapter draws inspiration from the suspension of a Constitutional Court judgment in Poland under the pressure of mass popular protests, the origins of the phenomenon of a popular state of exception can be traced back much further in history. The first historical example – the suspension of the oppressive norm of Table III allowing to bond debtors – already took place at the heart of this internal split, expressed in terms of Roman public law by the juxtaposition

35 Cosmin Cercel, 'The Destruction of Legal Reason: Lessons from the Past' (2019) 89 *Acta Universitatis Lodziensis – Folia Iuridica* 15, 21.

36 Ibid.

37 Rober Cover, *Narrative, Violence and the Law* (Ann Arbor: University of Michigan Press, 1995), 95.

38 Ibid.

39 Simon Lavis, 'The Exception of the Norm in the Third Reich: (Re)reading the Nazi Constitutional State of Exception' in Cosmin Cercel, Gian-Giacomo Fusco, and Simon Lavis (eds), *States of Exception: Law, History, Theory* (Abingdon: Routledge, 2020), 98.

40 Agamben, *State of Exception*, 31.

of the *plebs* and *populus*.[41] The *exceptio popularis* leading to the suspension, in 1971 and 1976, by the Polish government, of the 1953 decree on prices can be described in terms of the struggle between the working class, on one hand, and the bureaucratic class, on the other, the former representing the "naked life" of the toilers, the latter – the "political existence" of the Party bureaucracy.[42]

Gian-Giacomo Fusco, commenting on Agamben, notes that 'the legal and political order of the state cannot sustain the presence of its own founding agent,'[43] ultimately suggesting that the people (the *real* people, as opposed to its corresponding *fictio iuris*) is, actually, a symptom of the constitution. The symptomal irruption of the Real sovereign is precisely what is at work in the logic of the people's state of exception. And this symptomal nature of the people's demands being partly satisfied by the constituted power explains why it cannot be accounted for within the Symbolic order of formal constitutionalism.

Despite its political importance, the minor state of exception remains, until today, untheorised, probably because it is considered to be a question of *pure facticity*, not worthy of a properly juridical treatment. Given that the suspension in question is not based on any explicitly formulated legal norm, it could be assumed that the entire problem is outside the sphere of interest of jurisprudence, unless with regard to the legal consequences of the breach of the effectively suspended norm. However, jurisprudence does not object to theorising such phenomena as custom and its transition into customary law, or the opposite phenomenon of *desuetudo*. The same applies *a fortiori* to the rich theoretical literature on the state of exception, a phenomenon which cannot be fully subsumed by the system of legal norms[44] and which, undoubtedly, represents, in a certain sense, the 'negation of legal form.'[45] In its study, the 'essential task (…) is not simply to clarify whether it has a juridical nature or not, but to define the meaning, place, and modes of its relation to the law.'[46]

It is precisely such an attempt of analysing the meaning and place of *exceptio popularis* and its relation to the law (and specifically, to the legal norm it temporarily displaces) that I shall make in this present chapter. As Geoffrey Samuel notes, 'Lawyers, like scientists, do not work directly on

41 Cf. ibid. 32.

42 Cf. ibid. 30–1.

43 Gian-Giacomo Fusco, 'Ademia: Agamben and the Idea of the People' (2019) 89 *Acta Universitatis Lodziensis – Folia Iuridica* 95, 102.

44 Cf. Gian-Giacomo Fusco, 'Exception, Fiction, Performativity' in Cosmin Cercel, Gian-Giacomo Fusco, and Simon Lavis (eds), *States of Exception: Law, History, Theory* (Abingdon: Routledge, 2020).

45 Fusco, *Form of Life*, 39.

46 Agamben, *State of Exception*, 51.

reality but construct rationalized models of this reality, and it is these models that become the 'objects' of legal discourse.'[47] This is in line with law's hopeless separation from life, as a paradigmatically captured form in the act of its "application," involving *ex definitione* an attempt to bridge the gap between language and logic, on one hand, and practice, on the other.[48] The proposed concept of a people's state of exception is intended to be such a "rationalised model" of juridical reality. To ignore the reality of the *exceptio popularis* would be to go down the road of Kelsen, i.e., that of a 'theoretical attempt at preserving the status of legality outside the interplay of historical forces and political struggles.'[49] I rather contend, following Schmitt, that the popular state of exception, just like dictatorship, 'is a problem of concrete reality without ceasing to be a legal problem.'[50]

In *Signatura rerum* Agamben delivers, from historical obscurity, the ancient concept of *signatura* (signature), which goes back to Paracelsus. As Agamben explains, the 'original core of the Paracelsian episteme is the idea that all things bear a sign that manifests and reveals their invisible qualities.'[51] In order to explain the concept, Agamben gives the example of a signature *Titianus fecit* placed on a painting representing the Annunciation. Even though the

> signature merely puts the painting in relation to the name of a man, whom we know to be a famous painter (...). If this information were missing, the painting would remain completely unchanged (...). Yet the *relation introduced by the signature* is so important in our culture (...) that the reading of the cartouche radically modifies how we look at the painting in question.[52]

The essence of a *signatura* is therefore not so much an expression of the 'semiotic relation between a *signans* and a *signatum*,' but rather the operation of 'displac[ing] and mov[ing]' that relation 'into another domain, thus positioning it in a new network of pragmatic and hermeneutic relations.'[53] In other words, the signature 'does not coincide with the sign, but is what

47 Geoffrey Samuel, 'Is Law a Fiction?' in Maksymilian del Mar and William Twinning (eds), *Legal Fiction in Theory and Practice* (Springer Verlag, 2014), 74.

48 Fusco, *Form of Life*, 97–8.

49 Cosmin Cercel, '"Through a Glass, Darkly": Law, History and the Frontispiece of the Exception' in Cercel, Fusco, and Lavis (eds), *States of Exception*, 39.

50 Carl Schmitt, *Dictatorship*, transl. by Michael Hoelzl and Graham Ward (Cambridge: Polity, 2014), 118.

51 Giorgio Agamben, *The Signature of All Things: On Method*, transl. Luca D'Isanto and Kevin Attell (Brooklyn: Zone Books, 2009), 33.

52 Ibid. 40. Emphasis added.

53 Ibid.

makes the sign intelligible.'[54] Agamben argues that '[a]ll research in the human sciences – particularly in a historical context – necessarily has to do with signature.'[55] He gives the example of the notion of secularisation which 'acts within the conceptual system of modernity as a signature, which refers it back to theology.'[56] Thus, secularisation is 'a *strategic operator* that marked political concepts in order to make them refer to their theological origins.'[57]

The concept of the minor state of exception could operate precisely as a *signatura* in the sense discussed by Agamben, i.e., as a strategic operator which marks certain events – such as the deferred publication of a judgment, or the temporary suspension of a fundamental norm of state socialism – in order to refer them to the concept of the state of exception. This operation displaces what originally seems as a purely factual, "political" (as opposed to juridical) phenomenon from the hermeneutic context in which they had been placed by narratives of liberal legality, and positions them within a different network of meanings, associated with the exception.

5.3 Towards an Anatomy of the Minor State of Exception

Exceptio popularis shares many structural elements in common with the "major" or "proper" state of exception in that the legal norm in question 'is in force [*vige*] but is not applied (it has no "force" [*forza*]) and, on the other, acts that do not have the value [*valore*] of law acquire its "force."'[58] Oftentimes the suspended norm is not even "officially" (i.e., by "legal" means) suspended; its suspension is only *de facto*, but it deprives the norm in question – temporarily – of its effectiveness. It does not produce legal effects: for the time being, it is not *enforced*, even though, on a formal plane, it retains its *vigor iuris* albeit deprived of efficacy. As Gian-Giacomo Fusco notes, 'the exception produces a peculiar distortion of law's performativity since it "performs" legally a specific change in the operativity of law, according to which a set of norms and rights, while still in existence, do not have legal effects.'[59] However, we must not forget the 'dialectical paradox' at the heart of the juridical phenomenon, namely that 'the law manifests itself as force only through the negation of its commands.'[60]

The people's demands – expressed through mass demonstrations or strikes – which normally have no legal value,[61] replace with their force that of the

54 Ibid. 42.
55 Ibid. 76.
56 Ibid. 77.
57 Ibid.
58 Agamben, *State of Exception*, 38.
59 Fusco, 'Exception,' 32.
60 Fusco, *Form of Life*, 97.
61 Save for the possible criminal responsibility of the participants.

suspended norm. The *exceptio popularis* is, therefore, something like a minor *iustitium*, the latter, let us recall, being a 'standstill of the law' (*Standstill des Rechtes*),[62] a local anomie,[63] a 'generalised suspension and alteration of the legal system.'[64] However, the minor state of exception follows not from a formalised decision of the constituted power (as the Roman *senatus consultum ultimum*), but from a *de facto* suspension of the norm contested by the people. However, just as the proper state of exception 'is grounded not on facts but on a decision of what certain facts are'[65] so too the popular state of exception is the result not of the popular *tumultus*[66] but on the *decision* of the constituted power taken in light of the *tumultus*.

Whereas a "major" or "fully-fledged" state of exception of the kind envisaged by Schmitt,[67] Benjamin,[68] or Agamben[69] is concerned with a *wholesale suspension of the legal order as such* ('in its entirety' as Schmitt writes[70]), a "minor" state of exception, which is the object of the present chapter, is concerned with a *targeted suspension of a single legal norm*. However, the difference between the people's state of exception and the top-down state of exception could be somewhat smaller than one could deduce from Schmitt and Agamben. Indeed, states of exception today 'are implemented partially, discreetly and pervasively, altering the substance of the law but leaving a semblance of legality intact, often on the ground of "rhetorical" threats.'[71] States of exception have even become a 'regulated and normalised technique of government.'[72]

A minor state of exception shares with its major cousin a great deal of structural elements, especially its ambiguous relation to the law – just like the proper *Ausnahmezustand*, also the *exceptio popularis* 'cannot be circumscribed factually and made to conform to a preformed law.'[73] It openly challenges the *force de loi* which, at least since the French Revolution, denotes 'the untouchability of the law, which even the sovereign himself can neither abrogate nor modify'[74] and thereby affects the law's efficacy. Indeed, under

62 Quoted after Agamben, *State of Exception*, 45.
63 Ibid. 50–1.
64 Fusco, 'Exception,' 22.
65 Ibid. 24.
66 Cf. ibid. 23.
67 Carl Schmitt, *Political Theology: Four Chapters on the Concept of Sovereignty*, transl. George Schwab (Chicago: University of Chicago Press, 2005).
68 Walter Benjamin, 'Critique of Violence' in Walter Benjamin, *Selected Writings. Volume 1: 1913–1926*, transl. Edmund Jephcott (Cambridge, MA: Harvard University Press, 2004).
69 Agambem, *State*.
70 Schmitt, *Political Theology*, 6.
71 Fusco, 'Exception,' 17.
72 Ibid. 17.
73 Schmitt, *Political Theology*, 6.
74 Agamben, *State of Exception*, 37.

the influence of an effective *exceptio popularis*, a given norm of the legal order *temporarily loses its efficacy*: the constituted power, for a given time, ceases to apply that norm. If the norm in question is a competence norm (i.e., one which empowers a given body to enact another norm on its basis), the *exceptio popularis* can lead to the withdrawal of a norm enacted on the basis of the norm whose effectiveness is suspended within the logic of the *exceptio*. Once the *exceptio* ceases to be effective, the subordinate norms or juridical acts, based on the suspended norm, may come back to life or, as the case may be, new ones which can be enacted are acted in their place, as has been the case with the rebonding of debtors following the plebeian's victory over the Volscians, or with the reintroduction of price rises following a pacification of workers' protests in socialist Poland of the 1970s, or, finally, with the definitive entry into force of the Constitutional Court's judgment outlawing embryopathological abortion.

In Thesis VIII of his *Concept of History*, Walter Benjamin noted that

> The tradition of the oppressed classes teaches us that the "state of exception" in which we live is the rule. We must attain a conception of history that accords with this insight. Then we will clearly see that it is *our task to bring about a real state of exception*, and this will improve our position in the struggle against fascism.[75]

What is a 'real state of exception' (*wirklicher Ausnahmezustand*) in the Benjaminian sense?[76] Manuel Disegni insightfully explains that it is 'not "declared" but "brought about."'[77] Illan rua Wall adds that it 'transcends the liberal questions of declared and undeclared emergency.'[78] It is, therefore, not a "top-down" state of exception, freely decided and imposed by a sovereign ruler, but a "bottom-up" one, coming from the people and imposed *vis-à-vis* the power that is. There are good reasons to link the 'real state of exception' with 'pure' (or 'divine') violence, a concept developed in Benjamin's

75 W. Benjamin, 'On the Concept of History' in Walter Benjamin, *Selected Writings. Volume 4: 1938–1940* (Cambridge MA: Harvard University Press, 2003), 392 (emphasis added). Translation corrected after original – Walter Benjamin, 'Über den Begriff der Geschichte' (1940), available at: https://www.textlog.de/benjamin-begriff-geschichte.html, accessed 23 April 2023.

76 I leave aside here the origins of the distinction (*état de siège fictif* v. *état de siège effectif*) on which see, e.g., Agamben *State of Exception*, 3; Fusco, 'Exception,' 18–22.

77 Manuel Disegni, 'Über den Ursprung des Rechts: Eine erkenntnistheoretische Erläuterung des Disputs zwischen Carl Schmitt und Walter Benjamin um den Ausnahmezustand' (2017) 1(1) *Carl-Schmitt-Studien* 55, 63. All translations from non-English sources are mine, unless quoted from a published translation.

78 Illan rua Wall, 'The Law of Crowds' (2016) 36(3) *Legal Studies* 395, 411.

Critique of Violence,[79] and, therefore, with Sorel's concept of the general strike,[80] given that Benjamin's 'concept of divine violence shares much with the general strike, which, despite all the talk of violence, is essentially *non*-violent in outlook.'[81] A general strike or any other instance of divine – i.e., revolutionary – violence is a situation which leads to the deposition of the existing *pouvoir consituant* and the establishment of a new one.

The minor state of exception shares with the Benjaminian 'real state of exception' one important feature: it originates from the people, being a form of articulation of the people's demands. There is, however, a significant difference: the 'real state of exception' leads to the people assuming the role of the constituent power; in the case of the minor state of exception – and therein precisely lies its *minority* – the people stop short of doing so. Regardless of the reasons for the people not going further may be complex; from a strictly constitutional standpoint what matters is that the people manage to obtain a suspension of a single norm – this and nothing else.

In his 1921 essay on the *Critique of Violence*, Benjamin introduced the notion of 'pure violence' (*reine Gewalt*).[82] Pure violence, in contrast to law-making and law-preserving violence, is characterised precisely by the fact that it operates a 'deposition' (*Entsetzung*) of the law,[83] and that 'without establishing a new law.'[84] Of course, Benjaminian *reine Gewalt*, which corresponds to revolutionary violence,[85] deposes the entire law; in contrast, the *exceptio popularis* focuses only on a single norm (the limitation of the analogous concept is the same as with the state of exception, discussed above).

As Illan rua Wall notes:

> pure violence is (…) the absolute deposing that lies at the heat of "positing" but that positing must betray. The betrayal never occurs more so than

79 Walter Benjamin, 'Critique of Violence' in idem, *Selected Writings. Volume 1: 1913–1926*, transl. by Edmund Jephcott (Cambridge, MA: Harvard University Press, 2004).

80 Georges Sorel, *Reflections on Violence* (Cambridge: Cambridge University Press, 2004), 143ff.

81 Illan rua Wall, *Human Rights and Constituent Power: Without Model or Warranty* (London-New York: Routledge, 2012), 63.

82 In the English translation (Benjamin, 'Critique,' 250), the expression 'reine oder göttliche Gewalt' in the German original (Walter Benjamin, 'Zur Kritik der Gewalt' in idem, 2 *Gesammelte Schriften* [Frankfurt am Main: Suhrkamp, 1991, 200) is rendered as 'pure or divine power,' even if the Janus-faced concept of *Gewalt* is otherwise generally rendered as 'violence' throughout the translation.

83 Benjamin, 'Zur Kritik,' 2020; cf. Agamben, *State of Exception*, 53. In the English translation (Benjamin, 'Critique,' 252) 'Entsetzung' is rendered as "suspension." However, this overlooks the difference between *Aussetzung* and *Entsetzung* and is imprecise. Adam Kotsko, Agamben's translator, was therefore right to use 'depose' as a rendering of *entsetzen* (Agamben, *State of Exception*, 53).

84 Ophelia Lindemann, '"Ein Wort gegen das Recht": Walter Benjamins "Zur Kritik der Gewalt"' (2010) 43(1) *Kritische Justiz* 113, 117.

85 Cercel, *Towards a Jurisprudence*, 96.

> in the slippage from the *singularity of the deposing* to the universality of law. (...) Pure violence is singular because it is unique in each instance. It is singularity just in each instance without subsumption into law.[86]

The act of deposing[87] – *Entsetzung* – is precisely characterised by singularity and indeed the *exceptio popularis* is, at its very core, a singular act, rather than a universal one. However, in contrast to Benjaminian divine violence, the *exceptio popularis* does not depose the norm, it merely forces the constituted power to suspend it.

In the concluding words of his essay on violence/power, Benjamin notes that: 'Divine violence, which is always the insignium and seal of sacred enforcement (*heilige Vollstreckung*), but never its means, may be referred to as dominant (*die waltende*).'[88] The people, demanding the suspension of a certain legal norm, act, to an extent (limited *ratione materiae*) within the realm of divine or pure violence; in so doing, they are precisely the 'insignium and seal' of what Benjamin called 'sacred enforcement' or 'sacred execution' (*heilige Vollstreckung*), in the sense that they act as the collective sovereign, vindicating their rights nowadays inscribed in constitutional charters (which provide, as in the Polish constitutional document, that 'all power belongs to the people'). According to Lindemann, the "purity" of violence in the Benjaminian sense should be understood twofold: as liberty from any purpose and as liberty from law which it seeks to set aside (*Ent-Setzung des Rechts*) or purify itself from (*Reinigung vom Recht*).[89] Agamben explains that purity in the Benjaminian sense

> is not something that has its criterion in itself and as such must be preserved, but is always subordinate to a condition, namely, to the relationship with something external. In [Benjamin's] study on violence, this external element is the law, with respect to whose ends violence – as pure means – never refers as a means, but 'in some different way,' which ultimately corresponds with its deposition.[90]

86 Wall, *Human Rights*, 66, emphasis added.

87 In his essay on destituent power, Agamben indicates, with precision, the difference between 'constituent power, which destroys and always recreates new forms of law, without ever completely destituting it, and destituent power, which, in deposing law once and for all, immediately inaugurates a new reality' (Giorgio Agamben, 'What is a Destituent Power?' (2014) 32 *Environment and Planning D: Society and Space* 65, 71.

88 Benjamin, 'Zur Kritik,' 202. A different rendering is proposed in Benjamin, 'Critique,' 252.

89 Lindemann, 'Ein Wort,' 114.

90 Giorgio Agamben, *Karman: A Brief Treatise on Action, Guilt, and Gesture*, transl. Adam Kotsko (Stanford, CA: Stanford University Press, 2018), 81.

The people vindicating their rights by demanding the suspension of a norm are not a means (*Mittel*) of the 'sacred enforcement' precisely because '[i]f justice is the criterion of ends, legality is that of means.'[91] The act of instituting an *exceptio popularis* clearly defies legality, deposes it, depriving it of its efficacy, even if only *pro tempore*, and even if *ex auctoritate potestatis* and not *ex auctoritate populi*. The operation of the minor state of exception is, by its very definition, located outside the realm of positive legality, within which the people can exercise their power – it is an act of 'anomic violence.'[92] The legal norm which is suspended through the *exceptio popularis* becomes, in Agambenian terms, a 'mediality without end' which

> is in some way active, because in it the means shows itself as such in the very act in which it interrupts and suspends its relation to the end. Just as, in the gesticulations of a mime, the movements usually directed at a certain goal are repeated and exhibited as such – that is, as means – without there being any more connection to their presumed end and, in this way, they acquire a new and unexpected efficacy, so too does the violence that was only a means for the creation or conservation of law become capable of deposing it to the extent that it exposes and renders inoperative its relation to the purposiveness.[93]

The legal norm, subjected to the *exceptio popularis*, becomes precisely such as means without an end. It no longer serves its original (intended, usual) purpose, but becomes suspended in the normative void, inoperative and available for contemplation, but not enforceable and enforced, at least for the time being.

As Agamben summarises Schmitt's reply (in *Political Theology*) to Benjamin's *Critique of Violence*, 'there cannot be a pure violence—that is, a violence absolutely outside the law—because in the state of exception it is included in the law through its very exclusion.'[94] The act of the constituted power – be it a temporary forbearance or a withdrawal of an act based on the suspended norm – is precisely the operation of including the *exceptio popularis* within the law 'through its very exclusion.' Just as with divine (pure) violence, the *exceptio popularis* is 'removed from the dialectic between constituent power and constituted power'[95] or, to be even more precise, it is suspended between them. The people stop short of deposing the constituted

91 Benjamin, 'Critique,' 237.
92 Agamben, *State of Exception*, 54.
93 Agamben, *Karman*, 82.
94 Agamben, *State of Exception*, 54.
95 Ibid.

power and seizing it themselves as the new constituent power. *Exceptio popularis* is not a revolutionary moment.

A final aspect of comparison between *exceptio popularis* and the Benjaminian figure of *reine Gewalt* is that of the myth (*Mythos*). The term "mythos" denotes a 'word, speech, narrative' and 'it is, above all, a discursive practice, a narrative.'[96] In Lacanian terms we can identify here the tension between the Symbolic order, to which mythical violence belongs, the Real, which is the domain of pure violence. This insight has crucial consequences for understanding the nature of the *exceptio popularis* and its relationship to the legal order which belongs to the Symbolic.[97] The *exceptio* is a symptom disturbing the ideological lie of the juridico-symbolic order; it disrupts that order and cannot be symbolised within it, i.e., accounted for in terms of the Symbolic. The popular state of exception cannot be integrated into the legal order as such, in the sense of a legal norm providing for it *qua* legal institution. Nonetheless, despite being outside the realm of legality, the *exceptio popularis* impacts legality and even delineates its limits, forcing it to recede and suspend its *vigore*.

According to English legal historian, Henry Maine, a legal fiction 'conceals, or affects to conceal, the fact that a rule of law has undergone alteration, its letter remaining unchanged, its operation being modified.'[98] Under a legal fiction, '[t]he *fact* is (…) that the law has been wholly changed; the *fiction* is that it remains what it always was.'[99] Gian-Giacomo Fusco claims that the 'underlying logic of the state of exception (…) could be considered as analogous to the one of legal fiction: in both cases an alteration of the normal rule of law is the outcome of a non-objective determination of facts, while supposedly keeping the text of the law intact in its punctual suspension/modification.'[100] This observation applies equally to the minor state of exception where the suspension of the legal norm against which the people had raised a *tumultus* is covered up by the fiction that "nothing has happened." The constituted power refuses to admit openly that it suspends a norm, even if effectively this is what it does. If we agree with Fusco that 'both legal fictions and the exception are essentially illegal' but that 'this illegality (…) allows the law to preserve its integrity'[101] we could also say that, in the case of the *exceptio popularis*, the suspension of the norm allows the constituted power to maintain its place through temporary and limited concessions to

96 Lindemann, 'Zur Wort,' 114.

97 Rafał Mańko, 'Legal Form, Ideology and the Political' in Adam Sulikowski, Rafał Mańko, and Jakub Łakomy (eds.), *Legal Scholarship and the Political: In Search of a New Paradigm* (Warszawa: CH Beck, 2020), 35.

98 Henry Maine, *Ancient Law* (New York: Holt and Company, 1906), 25.

99 Ibid.

100 Fusco, 'Exception,' 28.

101 Ibid.

the people's demands in order to avoid being deposed. For Maine, legal fictions were an instrument to bring 'law in harmony with society.'[102] Whereas the popular state of exception does not, strictly speaking, bring such harmony in a durable manner, it does, to an extent, allow for more harmony in that some of the people's demands are, even if temporarily, satisfied.

As Fusco explains, the 'operative logic of legal fictions consists of the creation of specific fictitious facts that allow the law to apply to circumstances in which it could not normally be applied.'[103] The "fictitious facts" which the constituted power relies upon in order to 'save its face' despite being forced to introduce the people's state of exception can be manifold. In 1976, the Prime Minister of the Polish People's Republic fictitiously claimed that no price rises were introduced and that the announcement of the rises was merely an act of public consultation, and not a decision.[104] In the winter of 2020, the government justified the non-publication of judgment K 1/20 by relying on a fictitious norm whereby the publication of the operative part of the judgment in the *Journal of Laws* is possible only once the motives of the judgment are prepared by the Constitutional Court.[105] However, it is a notorious fact that the operative parts of judgments (which have direct legal effects upon the legislation they affect) are published long before the detailed motives of the judgment (which have persuasive and indirect legal effects) are available on the website of the Constitutional Court, not to mention their publication in the official collection of judgments. Thus, it can be said that the minor state of exception has the structure of a legal fiction.

5.4 Conclusions

Illiberal legality, advanced in Poland and Hungary in opposition to liberal legality, can become, as shown in this chapter, a fertile ground for the development of a properly critical *Verfassungslehre*.[106] The mass protests which followed the abortion judgment issued by the right-wing controlled Polish Constitutional Court forced the Prime Minister to suspend the publication of the judgment for over three months. The initial constitutional design did not foresee a power of the head of the executive (Prime Minister) to perform any kind of supervisory review of the judgments of the Constitutional Court. However, in 2015, at the height of the constitutional conflict between the illiberal majority controlling the executive and legislative powers, on the one hand, and the former liberal majority, still controlling the Constitutional

102 Maine, *Ancient Law*, 24.
103 Fusco, 'Exception,' 28.
104 Mieczysław F. Rakowski, *Dzienniki Polityczne 1976–1978* (Warszawa: Iskry, 2002), 78.
105 Morawiecki, 'Stanowisko.'
106 'Science of the constitution.'

Court, then Prime Minister Beata Szydło embarked upon a creative interpretation of her powers with regard to the publication of the *Journal of Laws*, the official journal of the Republic. Given that the Constitution explicitly links the entry into force of a Constitutional Court judgment with its physical publication in the (now digital) *Journal of Laws*, and given that the Publication of Normative Acts Act 2000 vests in the Prime Minister the power to publish the *Journal of Laws*, Prime Minister Szydło decided not to publish three judgments of the Constitutional Court (still controlled by a liberal majority) which she personally deemed unconstitutional.

This unexpected power grab emerged in a situation of *cohabitation* between the illiberal majority in the legislative and executive, on one hand, and the defeated liberals still controlling the Constitutional Court on the other. It could have been, therefore, dismissed as a temporary *excès du pouvoir* which would not repeat itself in the future.

However, illiberal legality decided to make use of this new "constitutional custom" five years later, in a very different politico-social setting. Responding to the massive popular unrest which ensued after the Constitutional Court voted to outlaw embryopathological abortion, the Prime Minister unilaterally decided to effectively suspend the Court's ruling. According to the Constitution, the power to suspend the entry into force of Constitutional Court judgments is vested in the Court itself.[107] But given the generous interpretation of Article 21 of the Publication of Normative Acts Act 2000, the Prime Minister had arrogated for themselves a power of super-judicial review of the Constitutional Court's case-law. This power came in handy in the face of massive popular unrest.

As I have argued in the present chapter, the suspension of the legal effects of the Constitutional Court's abortion judgment during the period between 22 October 2020 and 27 January 2021 amounted to no less as a deployment of a popular state of exception. The notion of a "popular" or "minor" state of exception advanced in this paper is conceived of as a conceptual metaphor, and more precisely as a device operating as the Agambenian *signatura*. *Qua* metaphor-signature, it is a notion whose main function is heuristic – it is to point to a certain different phenomenon in order to cast a new light upon the phenomenon in question. The operation effected in the paper is double: on one hand, it is diachronic in the sense of a (very preliminary) archaeological investigation of the phenomenon across legal history; on the other hand, it is synchronic in the sense of linking the minor state of exception with the conceptual framework advanced by Schmitt, Agamben, and Benjamin. By recasting the suspension of a legal norm by the constituted power, under pressure of a popular *tumultus*, into the framework of the state of exception, allows us to perceive this phenomenon not merely a question of pure facticity

107 Article 190(3) sentence 2 of the Polish Constitution.

(as liberal legality would have it), but to describe it as a politico-juridical phenomenon in its own right.

In political terms, the minor state of exception represents a concession granted to the people by the constituted power. Such a concession is temporary and revocable. The suspension of the legal norm against which the *tumultus* is directed does not mean that the norm is abrogated. Furthermore, the suspension is based on the sheer will of the constituted power which, for whatever tactical or strategic reasons, temporarily recedes before the people's demands. However, as historical examples show, the use of the *exceptio popularis* has mixed blessings for the people. The plebeians, once liberated from their debt bondage by consul Servilius, enlisted in the Roman army and won the campaign against the Volscians. However, no sooner did they come back home, the next consul revoked the popular state of exception and put back the norm of Table IV, thus throwing insolvent debtors back into bondage. In February 1971, the Polish working class won concessions from the government which revoked price rises, only to reintroduce them in June 1976. Following another wave of strikes, the government once again receded, but once again attempted to introduce price rises in 1980. This time, under the pressure of the working class the constituted power even suspended the fundamental norm of the system – the principle of the political monopoly of the communist party – only to replace the popular state of exception with a proper state of exception one-and-a-half years later, in December 1981. Similar observations can be made with regard to the suspension of Article 190(2) of the Constitution and of the legal force of the Constitutional Court's judgment of 22 October 2020. The suspension was relatively lengthy – three months – nonetheless the judgment was finally published and entered into force.

These examples of the usages of the *exceptio popularis* indicate its mixed political nature. On one hand, it represents a partial victory of the people and a symmetrical partial retreat by the constituted power, but on the other hand it is temporary and revocable, just as any state of exception. It has an emancipatory dimension, but at the same time it can be inscribed into an oppressive context if used tactically by the constituted power. We could ultimately say that the minor state of exception is like a Harlequin who serves two masters – the state power and the people, both of which operate it outside the framework of formal legal procedures – and as such it can be a double-edged sword.[108]

The deployment of the people's state of exception by the Prime Minister following the Polish Constitutional Court's judgment outlawing embryopathological abortion, creates special paradoxes given the label "populist"

108 Cf. Xenia Chiaramonte, 'The Struggle for Law: Legal Strategies, Environmental Struggles and Climate Actions in Italy' (2020) 10(4) *Oñati Socio-Legal Series* 932, 948–50.

usually ascribed to the ruling right-wing majority in Poland. On one hand, the decision of the right-wing controlled Constitutional Court, was deeply unpopular in society, and therefore, its imposition, was the very opposite of populism: the right-wing conservative elites imposed their decision upon the people. On the other hand, the suspension of the effects of that judgment by the Prime Minister in the very act of *exceptio popularis*, testified to the unstable balance of power in a culturally deeply divided society, governed by an illiberal conservative majority. The ending of the suspension of the judgment, with its official publication on 27 January 2021, dispelled hopes that illiberals in power would actually be true constitutional populists, listening to the will of the people over the heads of elites.

Chapter 6

Constitutional Signalling in Neoliberal Times

A Romanian Perspective

Alexandra Mercescu

6.1 Rethinking Society

As elsewhere in Central and Eastern Europe, Romania's transition was marked by a series of contradictions: some people were making overnight fortunes while others were becoming worse off than in the time of actually existing socialism, foreign investors were finding the country appealing for their business as Romanian workers were fleeing the country at an unprecedented rate. Undoubtedly, there was both a lot of enthusiasm and confusion as society underwent a radical transformation from a social, economic, political, ideological, and cultural standpoint: 'other values, other attitudes towards the state, the idea of authority or social and legal order, towards career, money and the reflection of "success in life", other individual and collective goals (family, firm, NGOs, party, etc.), a different courage of people to try different paths, opportunities and options.'[1]

Speaking from an economic point of view, neoliberalism came late but in a radical form to Romania.[2] The first five years of transition brought about a mixture of neoliberal and neodevelopmentalist, that is more statist, policies. Some of the ex-communists acceding to power and who held key positions in the legislature and the government 'felt that scrapping socialism altogether

1 Valentin Naumescu, *Politica Marilor Puteri în Europa Centrală și de Est* [*The Politics of the Great Powers in Central and Eastern Europe*] (Bucharest: Humanitas, 2019), 30. See also, Duncan Light and David Phinnemore (eds), *Post-communist Romania* (London: Palgrave, 2001).

2 My account of Romania's neoliberal transition relies extensively on the work of Cornel Ban, *Ruling Ideas: How Global Neoliberalism Goes Local* (Oxford: Oxford University Press, 2016). For other works, see Bogdan Murgescu, *România și Europa. Acumularea decalajelor economice (1500–2010)* [*Romania and Europe. The Build Up of Economic Gaps (1500–2010)*] (Iași: Polirom, 2010); Luminița Șoproni and Ioan Horga, 'Economic Transition in Romania: A Completed Process?' in Savvas Katsikides and Pavlos Koktsidis (eds), *Societies in Transition* (Cham: Springer, 2015); Liliana Pop, *Democratising Capitalism? The Political Economy of Post-communist Transformations in Romania, 1989-2001* (Manchester: Manchester University Press, 2006).

DOI: 10.4324/9781032624464-7

was suicidal,' as a consequence they managed to 'inflict heavy damage on liberalizing reforms and eventually dilute them.'[3] However, starting with 1996, Romania began to implement its version of shock therapy which presupposed extensive neoliberal structural reforms often going beyond international expectations: deindustrialisation, complete privatisation of the banking sector, introduction of the flat tax, pension privatisation. In a rich intellectual history, Cornel Ban shows that besides the undeniable external coercion by such international organisations like the World Bank, the IMF, and other financial institutions and the internal drive for building a competitive state, what accounts for Romania's radicalised neoliberalism had to do with the scarcely internationalised status of the economics profession. Its members seem to have drawn less on the serious economic debates of the day and more on 'international pop-academic tracts [which were] complemented by local antistate sentiment.'[4] For instance, Romanian economists insisted that tax cuts for corporations would pay for themselves despite the fact that few Western economists or the IMF took this argument at its face value. Moreover, while the World Bank, and indirectly the IMF, advocated for (partially) privatised pensions systems, the same institutions had never pleaded for a flat tax revolution in the region: 'Indeed the flat tax gained momentum not due to the IMF, but in spite of it.'[5] Similarly, corporation tax cuts were introduced not with the blessing of the EU but despite its advice.[6] That neoliberal reforms often proved appealing to both left-wing and right-wing parties is indicative of the 'Great Conflation' that occurred between democratisation and neoliberal reforms.[7] The latter ended up equated with the former mostly through the work of various "dual use" NGOs and think tanks populated by amateur economists who promoted a kind of "folk neoliberalism" – an 'ideational constriction that dwells less on the econometric modelling and universal technical languages specific to mainstream economics and more on descriptive, media-friendly and conventional public policy approaches.'[8] Surveys investigating the values of the Romanian people lend support, on the one hand, to the idea that the market economy came to be seen as synonymous with democracy. Thus, when asked what characteristics define democracy, Romanians placed "a prosperous economy" on top

3 Ibid. 76.
4 Ibid. 84.
5 Ibid. 97.
6 Ibid.
7 Ibid. 169. See also Claudiu D. Tufiş, 'Comrades or Citizens? Support for Democracy and Market Economy' in Bogdan Voicu and Mălina Voicu (eds), *The Values of Romanians: 1993-2006* (Iaşi: Institutul European, 2008), 33 '[...] external pressures have defined democracy and market economy as the two sides of the same coin.'
8 Ibid. 172.

of the list, while "taxing the rich and helping the poor" scored average.[9] Interestingly, "unemployment benefits" were also considered an essential trait of a democratic society. On the other hand, the same surveys indicate that while democracy gathered the same significant level of support from across societal sub-groups, the market economy is a much less consensual subject with differences among sub-groups depending on their income, gender, education, and residential area.[10]

Contrary to Adam Przeworski's reasonable prophecy anticipating that neoliberal reformers would be voted out of power and forced to embrace moderate policy views[11] and despite Romanians' declared attachment to redistribution as seen above, the Romanian population accepted by and large the challenges of transition, adhering thus to a vision that liberated 'market society [...] from popular demands for redistribution.'[12] Indeed, within civil society there was a sense that sacrifices must be made in order to achieve a proper 'decommunization' so much so that even 'the standard welfare institutions of Western social democracy were viewed as political pathologies whose implementation in Eastern Europe would hamper' this overarching goal.[13] The generous parental benefits are among the few more redistributive measures that went unchallenged which comes as no surprise given Romania's massive immigration and declining natality rates. Also, the mass migration of the labour force to other EU member states forced domestic politicians as well as external stakeholders to give up on their ambitions of deregulating labour.[14]

In explaining the perhaps surprising adherence of citizens to programmes which distributed 'income, opportunities and time [...] away from labour and toward capital,'[15] one must not forget that citizens lacked 'the skills of mobilizing dissent.'[16] This dovetails with findings showing that '[s]upport for the social-democratic model of market economy, (...) increase[d] significantly between 1993 and 2005. If in 1993 only 40% of the population considered that the state should be responsible for individual welfare and that income differences should be reduced, by 2005 almost two thirds of the population support these values.'[17]

9 Tufiş, 'Comrades,' 31–62.
10 Ibid.
11 Adam Przeworski, *Democracy and the Market: Political and Economic Reforms in Eastern Europe and Latin America* (Cambridge: Cambridge University Press, 1991).
12 Ban, 'Ruling Ideas,'170.
13 Ibid.
14 Ibid. 96.
15 Ibid. 66.
16 Hilary Appel and Mitchell Orenstein, *From Triumph to Crisis: Neoliberal Economic Reform in Postcommunist Countries* (Cambridge: Cambridge University Press, 2018), 115.
17 Tufiş, 'Comrades.'.

Whether the financial crisis tempered Romania's 'disembedded neoliberalism'[18] remains a matter of controversy. For Hilary Appel and Mitchell Orenstein, this is certainly the case. Specifically, the austerity measures imposed during the economic depression of 2008–2010 generated some contestation within Romanian society. People started to lose faith in the markets (a survey shows a support of almost 50% of the population for free markets as of 2006 and of only about 30% as of 2010, two years into the financial crisis).[19] Correlatively, policymakers were forced to slow down the pace of neoliberalisation. For instance, Romania did not deregulate its energy sector and decided to cancel planned increases to the contribution rate for the private pensions scheme.[20] However, according to a different narrative, by the time the financial crisis hit Romania the country's elites were already incurable radical neoliberals who duly applied the Troika's (the World Bank, the IMF, and the European Commission) requirements but who, acting in the space left to the government's discretion, took steps regarding the distribution of the ensuing costs that even the Troika itself criticised afterwards for being socially regressive. Indeed, the centre-right government of the time decided to rely almost exclusively on cuts to public expenditure.[21] Again, Ban argues, in addition to the central bank's efforts and its circle of associated academics, it was think tanks who helped to get the message across by joining the cause of economic reforms of a particular libertarian cloth to that of socially progressive issues, such as discrimination based on gender or disability and, in general, the good functioning of liberal democracy.[22] This observation in relation to the advent of neoliberalism in Romanian society upholds the thesis that 'ideological systems have an existence that is external to politics partly because they are born in spaces that may not be political.'[23]

The various ups and downs of the economic transition, the realisation that the former members of the nomenklatura acquired immense wealth at the expense of the state through the use of an extended clientelist network, and the constant exposure to the efficient yet depressing fight against corruption left the population, at the beginning of the third decade of transition, all in all favourable towards the European Union[24] but disillusioned, not so much with the idea of free markets or economic reforms as with politics *tout court* (tellingly, during protests in 2017 one of the slogans read: 'all the parties are the same dirt').

18 Ban, 'Ruling Ideas,' 66.
19 Tufiş, 'Comrades.'
20 Appel and Orenstein, *From Triumph*, 154.
21 Ban, 'Ruling ideas,' 210–20.
22 Ibid. 223.
23 Stephanie Lee Mudge, 'What Is Neoliberalism?' (2008) 6 *Socio-Economic Review* 707.
24 https://revista22.ro/actualitate-interna/peste-80-dintre-romani-cred-ca-intrarea-in-ue-a-fost-un-lucru-bun-pentru-tara-noastra, accessed 25 July 2020.

The period of austerity, under the guidance of the centre-right coalition, paved the way for the return to power of one of the major political parties in Romania and the continuator of the communist party – *Partidul Social Democrat* (PSD). With the social democrats reconquering the political stage, Romania seemed to be engaging itself, like Hungary and Poland, on the path towards illiberalism. The social democrats seemed particularly interested in weakening the fight against corruption. Under the pretext that the state became excessively punitive,[25] they engaged in several attacks against the judiciary culminating with the creation of a special section for the investigation of offences and crimes committed within the judiciary. Among other measures taken in order to intimidate the magistrates were a simplified procedure for suing them for erroneous decisions and early retirement schemes. By contrast, PSD did not appear to be particularly interested in taking a hard-line against immigration, interfering with university autonomy, disrespecting EU law, or tampering with the press, all of which we have witnessed in neighbouring countries. Indeed, Romania appears to have followed a *Sonderweg*.[26] Unlike the ruling class in Hungary and Poland, PSD could not have presented itself as a challenger of the establishment (after all, it was in power 16 years out of the 30 years of transition), never intended to bring about a conservative ideological revolution nor did it build its strength on a grassroot populist movement despite the (occasional) anti-European talk and the (more frequent) ethnonationalist discourse. Rather, in a typically opportunistic manner, the social democrats' attacks on the rule of law – considerable and dangerous – were motivated by personal and group interest (several

25 Even from before seizing power, PSD built a narrative about the existence of a "parallel state" allegedly composed of the judiciary acting in connivence with the secret services in order to decide who gets to stay in political life and who does not. Their version was a gross manipulation of a story that otherwise has a kernel of truth. For instance, constitutional law scholar Bogdan Iancu summarises thus the various critiques regarding the all too fierce fight against corruption in a contribution which otherwise highlights that the rule of law recipe concocted at the higher European level was bound to 'go native and/or develop pathologies' in Central and Eastern Europe: 'In Romania, over the past 15 years, the EU-driven need to produce anticorruption conviction quotas demonstrating success, in synergy with more 'strategic' domestic drives, has resulted in a version of "penal populism." Surveillance of all kinds spiked, with quasi-unanimous judicial approval of wiretap warrants. Perp-walks have moved high-stakes trials into the "court of public opinion", with many wiretap transcripts leaked by anticorruption prosecutors, Brazilian-style, in the friendly press. More worrisome still, protocols between apex judicial institutions with the Romanian Intelligence Service (SRI) have surfaced, including references of close collaboration on files, between the SRI and anticorruption prosecutors' (Bogdan Iancu, 'Status Quo Hegemony?: Conflicting Narratives about the "Rule of Law,"' VerfBlog, 2020/10/06, https://verfassungsblog.de/status-quo-hegemony/, DOI: 10.17176/20201006-124931-0, accessed 10 March 2021).

26 Bogdan Enache, 'Romania's "Sonderweg" to Illiberal Democracy' *The Market for Ideas*, 7–8 September 2017, http://www.themarketforideas.com/romanias-sonderweg-to-illiberal-democracy-a335/, accessed 2 September 2020.

high-profile members of PSD and other political allies had already been convicted or charged with criminal activities and therefore sought to save their skin through harassing the chief prosecutor and controlling the judiciary). As one author eloquently explains:

> the Romanian PSD has not showed any interest or capacity until now to sketch or communicate a minimally coherent ideological critique, alternative or opposite view to the Brussels-inspired agenda of the European Union like the Visegrád countries. What PSD and its allies apparently desire is simply to prevent the further democratisation of the country and, for this, it must roll back various institutional reforms, imprudently buy out public support through government largesse and, above all, reassert its control over the judiciary whose strengthened independence since Romania joined the EU in 2007 threatens in the long-run the very survival of its close-knit political elites.[27]

Whether Romanian society rests on a latent cultural bedrock of prejudices (against foreigners and religious, sexual, or ethnic minorities) that could at any time be stirred and manipulated in order to be put to problematic political use is a question open to debate.[28] Only recently, a dubious, nationalist party (AUR), which campaigned mostly online and resorted to anti-elite populist talk, made it to Parliament having obtained almost 10% of the votes. However, unlike Hungary, where populists managed to officially shape a new constitutional order[29] and Poland, whose constitutional order is *de facto* suspended,[30] Romania's liberal constitutional order continues to be in place. PSD did not seem determined to replace or dismantle the whole of the constitutional order or seriously take issue with liberal legality. Rather, it used the law in a piecemeal fashion in order to bring about reforms that would suit its members' interests. However, in so doing, it did not go as far as capturing the Constitutional Court or denying its authority.

The current government seems committed to rolling back some of the problematic measures introduced by the previous government and to preserving the pro-European status quo. Looking back at the various constitutional crises that the country has experienced in the last two decades, some

27 Ibid.

28 Naumescu, *Politica marilor*, 260.

29 See András Pap, *Democratic Decline in Hungary: Law and Society in an Illiberal Democracy* (Abingdon: Routledge, 2018).

30 See Wojciech Sadurski, *Poland's Constitutional Breakdown* (Oxford: Oxford University Press, 2019); Przemysław Tacik, 'Polish Constitutional Identity under the Illiberal Turn' in Alexandra Mercescu (ed.), *Constitutional Identities in Central and Eastern Europe* (Berlin: Peter Lang, 2020).

of which were serious enough to warrant the label 'quiet coup d'état,'[31] one can notice the inherent populist character of Romanian politics, with the country experiencing, rather inevitably, populist moments every now and then. Given Romania's ethnonationalism, there are reasons to believe that a more or less mild form of populism is a recurring feature of Romanian politics. Interestingly, present-day politics might pave the way for an apparently paradoxical type of populism, recognisable in other countries as well like Macron's France or Italy's Five Stars Movement, namely techno-populism.[32] Alliance 2020, an emerging force in the Romanian political landscape and a former part of the coalition government, attracted voters mainly by an appeal to technical mastery and the resolution to set the country straight through the best of policies, operating on the assumption that ideology matters less. Indeed, at its birth, the party sought to recruit people with no prior political background who have proven successful in their private enterprises. As such, its ideological line was unclear, with members making utterly contradictory statements. It has now become more obvious that the party will follow a neoliberal agenda which is to be presented to the public as the implementation of competent and sound decision making. In a country where the public is fed up with corrupted and failed politics it is rather easy to make the case that this technical mastery, purportedly free of any political commitments, represents the "actual" popular will.

As has been remarked, '[i]n its attempt to depoliticise the economic decision-making process and restrict the domain of democracy as a means of fostering the smooth and speedy implementation of market-based economic reforms, the Washington Consensus created the conditions for the spread of illiberal regimes characterised by widespread corruption and state failure from Latin America to Eastern Europe.'[33] In the Romanian context, nonetheless, one would be hard-pressed to draw a continuous line from neoliberalism to the present-day menace of illiberalism. Thirty years after the collapse of actually existing socialism, Romanian society feels like it has been shaped more by the whims of day-to-day politics than by any grand ideological vision (despite the resilience of neoliberalism across the political spectrum). However, this does not make the various problematic political transformations any less harmful. To the contrary, they point to the rather fragile character of Romanian democracy; only the future will tell if Romania has the capacity to steer clear of the current waves of authoritarian populism. If

31 Bojan Bugarič, 'A Crisis of Constitutional Democracy in Post-Communist Europe: "Lands In-between" Democracy and Authoritarianism' (2015) 13 *International Journal of Constitutional Law* 219, 221.

32 For an account of technopopulism, see Christopher Bickerton and Carlo Invernizzi Accetti, *Technopopulism* (Oxford: Oxford University Press, 2021).

33 Ioannis Glinavos, 'Neo-liberal Law: Unintended Consequences of Market-friendly Law Reforms' (2008) 29 *Third World Quarterly* 1086, 1093.

populism is to be understood critically, that is as 'not an attack against the law "itself", but an attempt to actively define the threshold of politicisation which circumscribes it,'[34] a turbulent clash might await Romanian society, one between techno-populists who wish to depoliticise economic and social life as much as possible, on the one hand, and, on the other, nationalist populists, who would most certainly seek to repoliticise 'matters hitherto shielded by the complex edifice of the European legal order, encompassing international law, European law, legal standards and requirements as to constitutional guarantees of the rule of law.'[35]

6.2 Rethinking Law?

With a new constitution rapidly minted in 1991, on the surface Romanian law started a new life.[36] For anyone familiarised with theories acknowledging law's cultural existence beyond its written expression it was clear, however, that the evolution of Romanian law was to be one of change within continuity. Indeed, the 'long history of understanding law as a part of the state apparatus closely connected and instrumental to political power and authority,'[37] which made authoritarianism possible, did not suddenly come to an end in the aftermath of communism. It survived both in formal institutions (consider the powers of prosecutors until the late 2000s) as well as *de facto* legal arrangements which allowed judges, prosecutors, and other legal professionals to partake in clientelist, corrupt, networks. Indeed, 'the

34 See Chapter 1 by Przemysław Tacik in this volume.

35 Ibid.

36 See, generally, Bianca Selejan-Guțan, *The Constitution of Romania* (Oxford: Hart, 2016). See also Armin von Bogdandy and Pál Sonnevend (eds), *Constitutional Crisis in the European Constitutional Area: Theory, Law and Politics in Hungary and Romania* (Oxford: Hart, 2015); Manuel Guțan, 'The Challenges of the Romanian Constitutional Tradition I: Between Ideological Transplant and Institutional Metamorphoses' (2013) 25 *Giornale di Storia Costituzionale / Journal of Constitutional History* 223; Manuel Guțan, 'The Challenges of the Romanian Constitutional Tradition II: Between Constitutional Transplant and (Failed) Cultural Engineering' (2013) 26 *Giornale di Storia Costituzionale / Journal of Constitutional History* 217; Bogdan Iancu, 'Romania – The Vagaries of International Grafts on Unsettled Constitutions' in Anneli Albi and Samo Bardutzki (eds), *The Role and Future of National Constitutions in European and Global Governance* (The Hague: T.M.C. Asser Press & Springer, 2019); Bogdan Iancu, 'Standards of "Good Governance" and Peripheral Constitutionalism: The Case of Post Accession Romania' in Giancarlo Corsi and Alberto Febbrajo (eds), *Sociology of Constitutions: A Paradoxical Perspective*, (London: Routledge, 2016) 180–97; Paul Blokker, *New Democracies in Crisis? A Comparative Constitutional Study of the Czech Republic, Hungary, Poland, Romania and Slovakia* (London: Routledge, 2013).

37 Cosmin Cercel, 'Discourse of the Master, Discourse of the University: An Archaeology of Modern Legal Education in Romania' in Michał Stambulski and Michał Pázdziora (eds), *Democracy, Legal Education and the Political* (Berlin: Peter Lang, 2023).

documents submitted to the courts by the Romanian special anticorruption prosecutors testify to the level of corruption involved in this privatisation drive.'[38] Even putting corruption to one side, the various privatisation schemes and corporate law reforms introduced post-1989 were problematic to the extent that they drew on a shallow understanding of how the previous regime worked in respect of property rights, administrative rights, and social networks of exchange and reciprocity.[39] This entertained the gap between the law in books and the law in action which already existed during communism. For instance, at the onset of transition, reformers failed to 'monitor the former socialist managers' activity during the transformation [...] [and] to address the huge agency problems that the privatisation would pose.'[40] As Liviu Damşa notes, further reforms aligned corporate law with European expectations; yet following the inflow of foreign corporate culture, 'it is highly debatable if CEE corporations became more sensitive to sustainability goals during this decade.'[41] All in all, 'privatisation shattered any remaining trust in CEE governments' capacity to pursue a common good.'[42]

The public's sentiment of lack of trust in institutions was reinforced by the fact that, in Romania, institutionalised lustration, though proposed early on by civil society representatives, remained rather limited.[43] Between 1990 and 2000, no less than ten legislative propositions were initiated that never made it into law. Another attempt to enact lustration failed in 2010 when the newly approved lustration law was declared unconstitutional on the basis of such legal principles as the presumption of innocence or the impossibility of retroactive legislation and then again, in 2012, on similar grounds.[44] Other laws, successfully passed, assumed more modest roles and never fulfilled the goal

38 Liviu Damşa, 'Sustainability and the Transformation of the Socialist Corporation into the Private Corporation' in *The Cambridge Handbook of Corporate Law, Corporate Governance and Sustainability* (Cambridge: Cambridge University Press, 2019), 313.

39 Ibid.

40 Ibid. 311.

41 Ibid. 314.

42 Ibid. 316.

43 See, generally, Lavinia Stan, *Transitional Justice in Post-Communist Romania. The Politics of Memory* (New York: Cambridge University Press, 2013); Lavinia Stan, 'Witch-hunt or Moral Rebirth?: Romanian Parliamentary Debates on Lustration' (2012) 26 *East European Politics and Societies* 274. For a comparative overview, see Cynthia Horne, 'Late Lustration Programmes in Romania and Poland: Supporting or Undermining Democratic Transitions?' (2009) 16 *Democratization* 344; Andreea Maierean, *A Comparative Study of Lustration in Central and Eastern Europe*, available at Boston University Theses and Dissertations, https://open.bu.edu/handle/2144/14123, accessed 2 April 2021.

44 See Decision of the Romanian Constitutional Court n. 820 /7 June 2010 published in the *Official Gazette* n. 420 of 23 June 2010 and Decision of the Romanian Constitutional Court n. 308/28 March 2012 published in the *Official Gazette* n. 309/9 May 2012. The European Court of Human Rights considered lustration in Romania in the case of *Naidin v. Romania*, Application n. 38162/07 from 21 October 2014.

of a comprehensive lustration process. Unofficial lustration, carried out by the executive through wild purges and sustained by both political parties and civil society through informal vetting based on rather untransparent criteria, reinforced the collective sentiment that Romanian lustration happened in a haphazard manner and that 'only personal connections and party support make or break one's career.'[45]

Specifically, this state of affairs, coupled with widespread corruption and a migration of many competent judges into more appealing opportunities offered by private practice on a new, liberal, market, left the judiciary in dismay at the start of the new regime. For instance, 'a World Bank study from the year 2001 revealed that Romanians saw levels of judicial corruption to be very high, surpassed only by a widely held perception of corruption within the customs authorities.'[46] It took the country more than two decades to build judicial capacity. Under the guidance of the EU, a series of reforms were implemented aiming for stronger accountability, merit-based selection, and independent court management.[47] For instance, the number of judicial staff increased and the salaries of magistrates tripled within a time span of six years.[48] Also, sitting judges were constantly enrolled in various training programmes and would-be judges benefited from a unitary intensive training at the National Institute of Magistracy, a public body responsible for the formation of judges and prosecutors modelled on the French *Ecole Nationale de la Magistrature*. This Institute's curriculum addresses European law and human rights to a great extent[49] so that graduates can be assumed to internalise a specific vocabulary and ethos oriented towards cosmopolitan values by the end of their traineeship.[50]

45 Stan, *Transitional Justice*,110.

46 Martin Mendelski, 'EU-Driven Judicial Reforms in Romania: A Success Story?' (2012) 28 *East European Politics* 23, 23–42.

47 Ibid.

48 Ibid.

49 Institutul National al Magistraturii, 'Strategia Institutului National al Magistraturii pentru perioada 2013–2016' [The Strategy of the National Institute of the Magistracy for 2013–2016], available at www.inm-lex.ro/fisiere/d_286/Strategia%20INM_2013_2016.pdf, accessed 2 April 2021. For instance, 'an academician in the Romanian MTA [Magistracy Training Academy] told the author [Cristina Parau] that his course centre on the jurisprudence of the supranational ECJ and ECtHR, and train pupils to emulate their activist reasoning': Cristina Parau, *Transnational Networking and Elite Self-Empowerment: The Making of the Judiciary in Contemporary Europe and Beyond* (Oxford: Oxford University Press, 2018), 264.

50 Cristina Parau finds in the existence of the National Institute of the Magistracy, alongside the absolute autonomy of the Judicial Council (*Consiliul Superior al Magistraturii*), another sign of a criticisable self-empowerment of the judiciary. According to her, 'monopoly [characteristic of the centralised MTA] is the configuration most likely to transition from education to indoctrination' and goes on to state that 'empirical evidence exists to let us infer that the MTA is indoctrinating the younger generation to think in terms of activism and supremacy

The various reforms together with an efficient fight against corruption, including judicial corruption, led to significant improvement of the judicial system. To be sure, a better judicial capacity (understood as more judges, selected on a meritocratic basis, better paid and better equipped in terms of material resources) did not immediately and entirely translate into judicial quality (understood as solutions pronounced within reasonable timespans, unitary practice, proper linguistic skills). Various obstacles on the ground such as the excessive workload of courts, the fact that the most important positions in the Constitutional Court or in the function of court president continued to be occupied by less reform-minded, senior, judges or the lack of law school reform undermined a radical transformation of the judiciary.[51] Of all the elements that prevent change, law schools and their gatekeepers are perhaps the most resilient through the formalism that they so efficiently instil in future legal professionals. Law students are taught almost exclusively black letter rule analysis and are kept at a distance from substantive, extra-legal considerations.[52]

It is possible to hypothesise that the communist regime forced many practitioners to become excessively formalistic in their reasoning so that they could avoid any involvement in the unpleasant political realm of the time.[53] After 1989, this attitude towards law would unreflexively pass on to new generations of lawyers.[54] In addition, the alleged neutrality in dealing with law matched the ambitions of many scholars to rehabilitate the legal system's image in the Western world as quickly as possible by celebrating its Roman and French heritage.[55] Also, as a reaction to what they perceived as an intrusion of politics, ideology, or economics into law, many scholars felt reluctant to go down any other interdisciplinary path in a desire to preserve the alleged purity of law as a discipline. To this day, legal scholarship is overwhelmingly doctrinal and the heritage of Critical Legal Thinking almost completely

in the making of public policy': Parau, *supra*, 263. While this assertion is plausible, it is difficult to say to what an extent such an indoctrination will actually translate into practice as long as law schools remain the bastion of hyperpositivistic thinking that they are now.

51 Mendelski, *supra*.

52 See Alexandra Mercescu, 'Redressing Romanian Legal Education (in Comparative Garments)' in Csaba Varga (ed.), *Comparative Law and Multicultural Legal Classes: Challenge or Opportunity?* (Cham: Springer, 2020), 133–56.

53 See Rafał Mańko, 'Weeds in the Garden of Justice: The Survival of Positivism in Polish Legal Culture as a Symptom/Sinthome' (2013) 7 *Pólemos – Journal of Law, Literature and Culture* 207.

54 See Zdeněk Kühn, 'Worlds Apart: Western and Central European Judicial Culture at the Onset of the European Enlargement' (2004) 52 *American Journal of Comparative Law* 531.

55 See, for instance, Paulina Święcicka, 'From Sublimation to Naturalization: Constructing Ideological Hegemony on the Shoulders of Roman Jurists' in Rafał Mańko, Cosmin Cercel, and Adam Sulikowski (eds), *Law and Critique in Central Europe: Questioning the Past, Resisting the Present* (Oxford: Counterpress, 2016).

unknown to legal academia. Romanian law schools must still travel a long way to understand that 'law cannot be approached as a matter of form, unless it is to be taken only at mere face value that is both intellectually scarce and historically problematic.'[56]

While the Constitutional and the High Court of Justice and Cassation and even lower-level courts started relying on more flexible sources of law such as broad legal principles or case-law, the fact remains that Romanian judges did not, by and large, depart from the authoritative tone so characteristic of the French legal tradition.[57] Consequently, it is a fair guess to say that whatever ideological orientation courts sustained after 1989 they did so by "squeezing" substantial ideas into consecrated categories of legal language. Elsewhere as well, the neoliberal economic transition was engaged by courts self-referentially. For instance, in a series of cases dealing with government's economic measures, the Polish Constitutional Tribunal 'primarily relied upon principles of social justice, equality, non-retroactivity, and vested rights.'[58] Similarly, the Hungarian Constitutional Court 'used various abstract and supposedly "neutral" legal concepts, such as acquired rights, purchased rights, and legal certainty, to strike down the Government's statutory measures to reform the Hungarian welfare state.'[59] The court was particularly criticised for its decision from 1995 which struck down several provisions of an austerity package bill that was supposed to reduce the increasing fiscal burden of the Hungarian welfare state.[60] Joining his own critique to Sajo's,[61] Bugarič argues that if the Hungarian government followed the advice of a leading expert on the welfare state it would have 'replace[d] social security contributions with general taxes as the source of funding for the welfare state. By constitutionalizing the insurance principle, however, the court's decision led to the opposite result.'[62] In fact, Bugarič inscribes his critique into a larger normative argument according to which 'nascent democracies

56 Cosmin Cercel, *Towards a Jurisprudence of State Communism* (London: Routledge, 2018), 203.

57 For a critical description of this 'apodictic' legal style, see Pierre Legrand, 'Perspectives du dehors sur le civilisme français' ['An Outsider's Perspective on French Civilisme'] in Nicholas Kasirer (ed.), *Le droit civil, avant tout un style? [Civil Law: A Style, Before Everything Else?]* (Montréal: Thémis, 2003), 153–83.

58 Bojan Bugarič, 'Courts as Policy-Makers: Lessons from Transition' (2001) 42 *Harvard International Law Journal* 247; Adam Sulikowski, 'Government of Judges and Neoliberal Ideology: The Polish Case' in Rafał Mańko, Cosmin Cercel, and Adam Sulikowski (eds), *Law and Critique in Central Europe: Questioning the Past, Resisting the Present* (Oxford: Counterpress, 2016), 16–27.

59 Ibid. 265.

60 Ibid.

61 Andras Sajó, 'How the Rule of Law Killed Hungarian Welfare Reform' (1996) 5 *East European Constitutional Review* 31–41.

62 Bugarič, *supra*, 266.

of Eastern Europe should not be court-centred but rather based on legislative authority.'[63]

As opposed to its Polish counterpart which decided more cases related to social and economic rights than classical political rights,[64] the Romanian Constitutional Court intervened rather rarely in the economic domain, at least not until the second decade after the fall of the old regime when it started to gain in visibility and to become a major player on the political stage. A systematic examination of the Constitutional Court's case-law (or courts in general) in relation to economic policies is missing from Romanian legal scholarship. Generally, Romanian authors confine themselves to noting that the Romanian Constitution defends a free-market economy while admitting that the language of the Constitution is susceptible of two different readings: one strongly competitional and the other predominantly social. After the constitutional revision of 2003, one can more clearly read socialism into the constitutional text. Article 1 of the Constitution declares that the Romanian state is a *social* state, a provision that one can corroborate with article 57 – the obligation of the state to provide for a decent living standard – to proclaim the socially oriented character of the state.

Otherwise, in a contribution briefly addressing the question of Romanian courts' engagement with the economy, the author remarks that in the early 1990s the Constitutional Court's judges lacked a refined understanding of how the economy works, something evidenced, for instance, by a 1995 decision in which they failed to see that a reseller can sell the merchandise at a price below that of acquisition.[65] All in all, the author concludes that as time passed by constitutional judges seem to have internalised the principles of the market economy, paying more attention today to the economic freedom of individuals.[66] Yet, the same author offers a number of examples of cases protecting the general or some specific interest against the pretensions of economic freedom,[67] thus suggesting that the story of courts unreservedly embracing neoliberalism might be more complex than at first sight or when compared to other actors, such as civil society's or politicians' unfettered versions of neoliberalism. Undoubtedly, empirical studies carefully

63 Ibid. 273.

64 Ibid. 264.

65 Dan Cărămidariu, 'Dreptul şi economia de piaţă. Un secol de căutări, derive şi neîmpliniri' ['The Law and the Market Economy: A Century of Searches, Wanderings and Unfulfillments'] in Raluca Bercea and Alexandra Mercescu (eds), *Valori, idei şi mentalităţi în drept, de la 1918 la 2018* [*Values, Ideas and Mentalities from 1918 to 2018*] (Timisoara: Editura Universităţii de Vest, 2018).

66 Ibid.

67 Judgment of the Constitutional Court n. 644/2008 (regarding taxi transport); Judgment of the Constitutional Court n. 162/2011 (regarding company law), Judgment of the Constitutional Court n. 1344/2011 (regarding gambling).

investigating the evolution of Romanian case-law in such key fields as labour law (prior and post the 2003 reform of the labour code) or corporate law would be needed to be able to assert a specific pattern regarding the relationship between neoliberalism and regular or apex courts.

More modestly, in what follows, I will sketch a tentative account of the Constitutional Court's role in securing politicians' neoliberal agendas by looking at two consequential decisions. My claim is that the Court's discourse is characterised by ambivalence towards neoliberalism.[68] One can, for sure, print the neoliberal sobriquet onto the Court's decisions. Alternatively, however, in a society in which one can even talk of "neoliberal populism," the minor concessions made by the Court to advocates of social policy can be regarded as performing an important signalling role, namely one contesting the politics of "there-is-no-alternative."

6.3 Signalling (the Other) in Constitutional Case-Law

In the aftermath of the transition to capitalism all countries of the former communist bloc

> sought to present themselves as champions of neoliberal reform and unleashed a process of "competitive signaling" to attract foreign investment. By 2007, this signaling process had fostered an exceptionally liberal business climate, with IMF data showing that Central and Eastern European states were the highest recipients of financial inflows as a proportion of GDP in the world, outcompeting developing states in Asia and Latin American by a factor of two.[69]

Contrary to expectations, Romanians did not prove reluctant to the implementation of radical neoliberal ideas. Quite the opposite, Traian Băsescu, the President who, in preparation for Romania's accession to the EU, introduced some of the most neoliberal policies, also happened to be one of the most popular politicians of post-communist Romania, surviving two impeachment procedures in referenda.[70]

68 One reason for that may be the fact that 'there is [...] a significant ambivalence in neoliberalism towards the state and politics': Rachel Turner, 'Neo-Liberal Constitutionalism: Ideology, Government and the Rule of Law' (2008) 2 *Journal of Politics and Law* 47. See also David Harvey, *A Brief History of Neoliberalism* (Oxford: Oxford University Press, 2005), 64: 'the neoliberal state may be an unstable and contradictory political form.'

69 Adam Fabry, 'Review Essay: The Rise and Fall(?) of Neoliberalism in Eastern Europe and the Former Soviet Union' (2019) 27 *Journal of Contemporary Central and Eastern Europe* 121–5.

70 For a discussion of neoliberal policies and popular/populist leaders, see Kurt Weyland, 'Neoliberal Populism in Latin America and Eastern Europe' (1999) 31 *Comparative Politics* 379.

The economic crisis put significant pressure on CEE countries. In this context, the Constitutional Court of Romania was confronted with two highly complex issues: austerity measures and the problem of foreign-currency loans. An analysis of these two legal interventions on intricate questions of economics reveals that the Court's participation in sustaining neoliberalism remains ambivalent. One avenue of interpretation would be to contend that the Court simply lacks the competence to assess such complicated extra-legal issues and that, therefore, it can hardly arrive at a coherent point of view. As has been argued, in general, 'judges cannot help but make assumptions about what motivates human behavior, how markets work, and how institutions function' and '[for these purposes] [they] [...] frequently use historical sources in ways that historians regard as scandalous, engage in bad economic analysis, rely on insupportable political science, and advance shallow if not shoddy philosophical arguments.'[71] Another interpretation, which I will pursue here, might wish to view the Court as willing to accompany its overall support for neoliberalism with specific points of critique. These might function as a reverse signalling mechanism, directed this time not at foreign investors but at society, in order to alert it to political alternatives. But before presenting the two decisions of the Court, I find an excursus on the political or ideological character of judicial decisions to be in order.

6.3.1 *A Digression on the "Political" in Law*

Following the insights offered by the Critical Legal Studies school of thought, I see "the political" as emerging in law where there is reasoned discretion, in judicial contexts this being inevitably generated by the indeterminacy of language.[72] Arbitrary discretion (as if a judge decided to flip a coin) or discretion triggered by corruption, bad-faith, or mere incompetence do not amount to political endeavours although they can and do have social and political consequences.

Consider a case between two farmers (for which there is no *a priori* social antagonism) and the law providing for no explicit allocation of rights

71 Richard H. Fallon Jr., 'Nonlegal Theory in Judicial Decision-making' (1994) 17 *Harvard Journal of Law and Public Policy* 87, 88.

72 A physician might have discretion too in the sense of a choice between two different treatments but his or her discretion is much more grounded in professional knowledge in a way a judge's discretion is not. Indeed, whereas in the first case it is the current state of medical knowledge that bestows the doctor with the possibility to choose between several medical options presumed to be equally valid, the law does not explicitly grant the judge, at least not in the civil-law world, the power to choose between ethical and political judgments whose effects are, moreover, not at all functionally equivalent. Or, to put it otherwise, '[t]he slogan "law is politics" is true enough, but we should be quite careful not to reduce it to [...] a naïve "they do whatever they please"': Steven Winter, 'Indeterminancy and Incommensurability in Constitutional Law' (1990) 78(6) *California Law Review* 1441, 1473.

between the two so that the judge's intervention is crucial for their respective faith. Let us suppose the judge must interpret the word "reasonableness" on the occasion of this dispute. He or she might decide to follow what the legal community generally prescribes in this respect but, having recently read a novel or a treatise of psychology addressing the matter, the judge now tends to view this concept in a new light that he or she deems appropriate for the case at hand. Imagine, moreover, that the judge is called to decide on a rather controversial aspect of evidence law where various judicial philosophies underpin the different options. Suppose, further, that the judge is in doubt whether to cite a piece of doctrinal writing that would shift the balance towards one of the parties. When all is said and done, after all these (micro-) decisions have been made, would we be well advised in assigning the decision an arbitrary character? I argue that we would not. As long as the interpreter mobilises *reasoned discretion*, he or she acts *politically* for he or she inevitably resorts to judgments of value which more often than not convey an entire worldview (not necessarily easily captured by the classical divide between conservatives and liberals).

Other critical legal scholars seem to embrace a narrower view of the political in that they link the inherent antagonism of a conflict to the existence of particular groups with dividing interests. For instance, in calling for a critical reading of legal decisions, Rafał Mańko argues that one has 'to read cases not only against legal texts and earlier cases, but above all against the background of conflicts they impact.'[73] 'By conflict,' he refers 'not [to] the individual conflict between litigants, which is plainly visible and hardly difficult to decipher; [... but to] proper antagonisms, i.e. collective conflicts, conflicts between classes, social groups and other collectivities.'[74] Mańko identifies several such dichotomies along the lines of which one could usefully examine legal judgments: economic antagonisms (employee vs employer, consumer vs business), symbolic antagonisms ('which are often emanations of a struggle for recognition [minority rights, women's rights]),'[75] and professional antagonisms (involving socio-professional groups such as lawyers and judges defending their interests against their peers or other authorities).

However, as soon as we cease relating social antagonisms exclusively to groups, we start realising that the conflict might very well coalesce around different sets of competing values, some of which can in fact be very abstract, disembodied categories (one can value freedom of speech over privacy, both

73 Rafał Mańko, 'Dimensions of the Political in Adjudication: A Case-Study' (2020) 92 *Acta Universitatis Lodziensis – Folia Iuridica* 5, 7. For a more detailed explanation of Mańko's critical theory of adjudication, see Rafał Mańko, 'Judicial Decision-Making, Ideology and the Political: Towards an Agonistic Theory of Adjudication' (2022) 33 *Law and Critique* 175.

74 Mańko, 'Dimensions,' 7.

75 Ibid., 11–2.

of which are values in the interest of all groups). Thus, for the political to be present even in an apparently non-political case, such as a homicide case, one does not need two groups but two sets of values regarding one of the myriad aspects of the case: in a criminal case, for instance, that could be the imperative of finding the truth versus the need to secure the defendant's rights.[76] While, as a general rule, these sets of values can be subsumed under the distinction *liberal vs conservative* (often quite clearly evidenced by a split between judges) this is not necessarily the case. Different worldviews, but not groups,[77] will vie with each other even when we might be tempted to see clear-cut groups on the two sides of the legal border such as, for instance, *consumers* vs *producers/traders*. In an insightful comparative law contribution, Yale professor and comparatist of laws James Whitman distinguishes between 'producerist' legal cultures such as France and Germany, more oriented towards protecting those involved in the production and distribution of goods and services (including workers), and 'consumerist' legal cultures such as the US (interested in ensuring for consumers easy access to markets and competitive prices).[78] Importantly for the view of the political I am operating with here, Whitman states the following:

> I will lay much emphasis on the fact that there is no single producer interest. Producerist law does not favor "the" producer interest, but *some* producer interest. When we speak of producerism, we are not speaking of any particular legal program, but of law that tends to focus on rights, interests, and most especially conflicts on the supply side. Indeed, as we shall see, the producerist worldview generally supposes that the problems of the law are very much problems of conflict between different classes of producers.[79]

Quite frequently, a case between litigant A and litigant B can be reformulated, not necessarily as a case between some collective interest represented by A and some competing collective interest represented by B but as a larger clash between value/belief X and value/belief Y criss-crossing the entire legal

76 James Whitman, 'Presumption of Innocence or Presumption of Mercy?: Weighing Two Western Modes of Justice' (2016) 94 *Texas Law Review* 933.

77 Whether we should speak of competing groups/collectivities or worldviews is ultimately a preference resting on an assumption about the extent to which politics is a question of identity politics or rather a question of preferred choices to be made from the marketplace of ideas that cannot always be readily ascribed to groups. It is true that, especially in a very polarised world like ours, specific ideas are often associated with one specific group, and that group only. Yet, looking at ideas instead of groups might have the merit of showing how one and the same idea could have an empowering or, to the contrary, a disenfranchising effect in respect of specific groups depending on context.

78 James Whitman, 'Consumerism versus Producerism: A Study in Comparative Law' (2007) 117 *Yale Law Journal* 340.

79 Ibid.

field, which, depending on the cultural context and the factual background of the case, can incidentally lead either to the victory of A or to that of B. An abortion case, for instance, can obviously be read as opposing women to the state. Consequently, it can be useful to align the possible results of the case 'on an axis extended from the maximisation of interests of group A to the maximisation of the interests of group B.'[80] However, given that not all women think alike (indeed, one can also find conservative women who are clearly opposed to abortion) the case could and should probably be framed at a more abstract level as opposing distinct views about the philosophical question of knowing, for instance, when life begins. Or, to quote again from Whitman:

> [C]onsumers and producers are not two different classes of persons. All productive members of society in a modern economy have both of these identities: we are all both "consumers" and "producers". When a worker works, he is a producer; when he shops, he is a consumer. Correspondingly, the choice between emphasizing consumer rights and emphasizing producer rights is not a choice between favoring "the" economic class of consumers and favoring "the" economic class of producers. It is a choice about which of these two identities we will regard as deserving protection by law. It is a value choice about whether we think that the citizen's interests in his guise as "consumer" are more fundamental than his interests in his guise as "producer", or vice versa.[81]

Irrespective of the view of the political – broader or narrower – one wishes to embrace, it is certain that judicial decisions can and should be scrutinised in other terms than the habitual doctrinal ones so as to reveal the various societal, philosophical, economic, ideological, and cultural clashes that undergird their legal surface. In what follows I propose to unveil 'the political' of two judgments of the Constitutional Court of Romania. My reading of the two decisions follows roughly the 'research protocol' proposed by Mańko with a view to exposing the 'radical contingency of the juridical' and thus alerting us to the alternatives that remained silent in that particular context.[82]

80 Mańko, 'Judicial Decision-Making,' 188.

81 Whitman, 'Consumerism.'

82 Mańko, 'Judicial Decision-Making,' 190. As this author suggests, I focus, although not necessarily in this order, on the antagonism at stake, the legal materials employed by the judges, the interpretative alternatives that failed to carry the day, the court's choice, its relation to ideology (in particular, here, neoliberalism), and the legal techniques possibly supporting the losing party/group/worldview.

6.3.2 Austerity Measures: 'I am afraid we will all be responsible ...'

In 2010, Romania ran the risk of a balance-of-payments crisis. Previous policies created a 'macroeconomic toxic brew through a combination of neoliberal tax policies, clientelist public sector employment, and the replacement of redistributive social safety nets with ad hoc pension and wage increases right before the elections.'[83] While prior to the crisis all countries in the region experienced important growth rates and flows of foreign direct investment, most of them went through severe economic constriction during 2009–2010, far worse than other developing countries in Asia or Latin America.[84] In this context, Romania had no other choice in trying to overcome the economic hardship than to resort to international funding, which was to be conditioned by a series of austerity measures. Consequently, after negotiations with the European Commission, the World Bank, and the IMF, the Romanian Parliament enacted Law n. 118/2010 regarding Measures Necessary to Restore Budgetary Balance by which it diminished public sector salaries by 25% and pensions and other social security benefits, such as unemployment, parental leave benefits, and child allowances by 15%. The High Court of Cassation and Justice (*Înalta Curte de Casaţie şi Justiţie*) challenged the law before the Constitutional Court arguing that the measures infringed on fundamental rights without respecting the constitutional criteria for being legitimate restrictions. In particular, it was claimed that Parliaments' interference was disproportionate and constituted a threat to judicial independence since they covered magistrates' salaries as well. The Court upheld all cuts except for pensions reduction.[85]

In deciding that the salaries of public servants could be diminished, the Court framed the conflict before it in typical legal language as one between *fundamental rights* (to work), on the one hand, and *national security* – a general public interest that, according to Art. 53 of the Romanian constitution, could justify restrictions of the former – on the other. Thus, the Court had to determine whether these specific austerity measures were necessary in a democratic society, proportionate to the goal being sought, and applied in a non-discriminatory manner. Invoking an analysis of the European Commission with regard to the economic status of the country and reports by the World Bank and IMF, the Court retained that the economic crisis was menacing the economic stability of the country and therefore its national security. In its examination of the measure's necessary character, the Court quoted the Government's motivation: '*if these actions are not implemented until June*

83 Ban, 'Ruling Ideas,' 211.

84 Appel and Oppenstein, *supra*, 144.

85 Judgment of the Constitutional Court n. 872/2010 published in the *Official Journal* n. 433 from 28 June 2010.

2010 or do not lead to early consolidation, additional actions will be implemented to increase budget revenues, including measures of tax increases.' This argument, on which the Court relied, betrays that the choice was not between securing a fundamental right and protecting national security but between one manner of protecting national security and a different manner of achieving the same purpose. Reading between the lines of the decision allows one to reframe the conflict ideologically as one between *salary cuts* and *tax increases*. Indeed, salary cuts appear necessary only as long as tax increases are off the table. In deciding to uphold the salary cuts, the Court avoided the discussion of whether other measures could have fulfilled the same goal of budgetary reduction. Thus, it also failed to assess, comparatively, the impact that the various competing measures would have had on society. The proportional character was asserted in one single paragraph as apodictically as was the necessary character: '*As regards the proportionality of the situation which led to the restriction, the Court notes that there is a link of proportionality between the means used (25% reduction of the amount of the salary / allowance / balance) and the legitimate aim pursued (reducing budget expenditures / rebalancing the state budget) and that there is a fair balance between the requirements of general interest of the community and the protection of fundamental rights of the individual.*' Its analysis of the non-discrimination requirement is equally authoritative: '*[t]he Court also notes that the criticized legislative measure is being applied in a non-discriminatory manner, in the sense that the 25% reduction applies to all categories of public employees in the same amount and manner.*' One can easily see that the Court examined discrimination from within the perspective of the public sector only (whether the measure was applied uniformly to all sub-groups of this sector) and failed to consider whether the measure would be discriminatory because it placed the burden of austerity only on a certain part of society, namely on the public and not on the private sector as well.

It is no doubt that redressing the economy was in the general interest of society. Yet, there was no single answer as to how this purpose could be efficiently achieved. Moreover, different options meant a different redistribution of the burden of solidarity across society and therefore presupposed a political decision. As such, the Constitutional Court did more than just rubberstamp an allegedly technical solution. It chose, together with the Government, one possibility to the detriment of another, which was not without critique. Indeed, '[t]his "flat tax"-style spending cut was so harsh that IMF managing director Dominique Strauss Kahn flew to Bucharest and delivered a speech in the Romanian parliament asking for cuts that shifted a greater part of the burden onto those more able to pay.'[86] In an interview, the President of the Court adopted a surprisingly realist position and seemed to

86 Ban, 'Ruling Ideas,' 185.

let the public know that the Court acted on grounds of opportunity, in good faith, hoping that the implementation of the wage cuts will yield the expected economic results: 'This is also a question that politicians and lawyers alike must ask themselves: if the person [the Government] called to take action knows what they are doing, if the measures they take lead to results, or we torment the people, we are affecting their fundamental rights – and we accept this damage because we have a constitutional justification – the result that will be obtained in the end, if it is not the way out of the crisis, I am afraid we will all be responsible.'[87]

Feeling perhaps that cutting pensions in addition to salaries and thus affecting a segment of the population which is especially vulnerable amounts to an excessive political move, the Court decided not to play along with the Government on this question. Consequently, it "found" (etymologically, one should recall, "to find" is "to invent") a legal argumentation based on the idea of acquired rights and legitimate expectations. First, the Court decided to differentiate between a salary and a pension (one is oriented towards the future, the other is based on past contributions). Second, it made the right to pension into an absolute right by declaring that the derogations inscribed in Art. 53 of the Constitution do not apply to it (although the text of the Constitution does not provide for such an exception). Third, it quoted foreign constitutional and international case-law in support of its decision in the typical unreflective manner such materials often get cited in courts.[88] And yet, despite all the seemingly reassuring legal schemes of reasoning, discretion was, of course, not eliminated being contained in the very act of forging these intellectual "crutches."

This is also proven by the Court's treatment of the other forms of social protection. In declaring the pensions cut unconstitutional the Court founded its argument on Art. 47 ('living standard') by granting pensions a special status and refusing to discuss them in terms of property. Or, as has been pointed out, 'the exclusive reliance on the "living standard" guarantee of Art. 47 fails somewhat to explain the complete denial of protection to other rights enumerated in that article and affected by the austerity measures (maternity, unemployment benefits, etc.).'[89]

As such, since it implied choices and imagination, the Court's declaration of unconstitutionality in respect of pensions is no less political than its declaration of constitutionality in respect of wages and other social allowances.

87 https://www.capital.ro/augustin-zegrean-ccr-va-trebui-sa-raspundem-cu-totii-daca-masurile-de-austeritate-nu-vor-duc.html, accessed 2 September 2020.

88 For a critique of the use of foreign law in courts, see Ganesh Sitaraman, 'The Use and Abuse of Foreign Law in Constitutional Interpretation' (2009) 32 *Harvard Journal of Law and Public Policy* 653, 677; Pierre Legrand, 'Proof of Foreign Law in US Courts: A Critique of Epistemic Hubris' (2013) 8 *Journal of Comparative Law* 343.

89 Iancu, 'Romania,' 1077.

The difference resides in the outcome. Whereas in the latter case, the Court chose the Government's choice, in the former case it implicitly chose to force the Government to change its choice by considering other measures for attaining the same objective. As a matter of fact, immediately after the Court's decision the Government announced an increase in VAT to compensate for their inability to cut public expenses as predicted. Thus, the Court's intervention partially rearranged the burden of economic solidarity. Moreover, symbolically, it suggested that some measures which were presented by the Government as a result of expert knowledge should not be taken for granted and that alternatives can be envisaged. In a society which became accustomed to paying respect to the Constitutional Court's decisions, often seen as "true," the fact that politicians lost a fight, if only partially, was of huge significance. It signalled that they can and should be challenged, that while democracy might be the only game in town, economic ideas other than those promoted by the establishment are up for grabs and can be negotiated.

Incidentally, another ruling of the Court pronounced on the same day regarding special pensions (i.e., pensions of Members of Parliament, members of the military and diplomatic services, the judiciary, prison system, police) can be regarded as embodying what Mańko calls the 'symbolic antagonism [...] concern[ing] specific professional groups.'[90] Thus, the Court upheld all cuts but those concerning the pensions of judges, prosecutors, and law clerks of the Constitutional Court as these were considered immune to state interference in preservation of the principle of judicial independence. This decision appears inconsistent with the previous ruling which did not shield judges' salaries from interference. Moreover, upon reflection, the Court could have set the principle of judicial independence against the equally valuable principle *nemo iudex in causa sua*. By failing to do so, the Court produced a decision which, rather visibly, operated in terms of (preferred) concrete groups (and their interests).

6.3.3 Consumer Credits: 'Our solution is diversified, divided – two admissions, two rejections. You could say it was a kind of Solomonic judgment, but it wasn't like that at all'[91]

In the aftermath of the economic crisis, even as economies started recovering, countries in Eastern Europe had to face the problem of household defaults generated by the fact that a high proportion of mortgage loans were denominated in foreign currencies, like the euro and the Swiss franc (given

90 Mańko, 'Dimensions,' 12.

91 https://www.qmagazine.ro/valer-dorneanu-legea-darii-in-plata-partial-neconstitutionala/, accessed 3 May 2020.

their attractive lower interest rates), at a time when local currencies severely depreciated. This situation rendered credits much more expensive than initially anticipated by consumers. For instance, it is estimated that in Latvia, Romania, and Ukraine the rate of mortgage loans in foreign currencies came close to 90% and the increase in the cost on a monthly basis represented almost 20%.[92] In this context, the Romanian Parliament adopted two laws meant to provide equitable relief for over-indebted consumers, a reform pioneered by the Orbán government in Hungary and later considered by Poland as well. As was argued, the adoption of such 'populist economic policies in the heartland of neoliberal reform in Central and Eastern Europe represented a symbolic step back from the competitive signaling that had characterized earlier periods of transition.'[93] From the very start, it became clear that such legislation would pit banks against consumers and would trigger fierce reactions either of contestation or support depending on the faction one happened to side with. It was unsurprising then that both laws were soon challenged before the Constitutional Court. This time, the Court was called to assess legislation that was, arguably, as equally intrusive as the one implementing austerity but that, for all intents and purposes, found itself at the socialist end of the economic and political spectrum in its intention to protect individuals (consumers) against big business (banks).

Thus, Law n. 77/2016 provided for the possibility of borrowers in a mortgage loan to liberate themselves from their debt by transferring, to the bank, the property of the secured real estate if exceptional circumstances intervening during the execution of the contract rendered the contract excessively expensive for them (thereafter referred to as *transfer in lieu of payment*). The formulation of the law was, it must be said, generous towards credit consumers, as it did not make any distinction between those borrowers who were unable and those who were unwilling to pay, nor between those who up until the intervention of exceptional circumstance acted in good-faith or, to the contrary, in bad-faith. Everyone seemed to be authorised *ope legis* to retreat from an otherwise binding contract much to the dismay of bankers who warned that such *largesse d'esprit* would bring about a 'perfect storm' in the banking system.[94]

The Court decided that such imprecise provisions, to the extent that they failed to make the necessary legal distinctions and automatically applied to all categories of debtors who qualified for the procedure of transfer in lieu of payment, violated the rule of law, the constitutional text regarding the right to a fair trial, and the constitutional provisions protecting the access to justice. As a consequence, the Court could have easily pronounced the

92 Appel and Orenstein, ibid. 143.
93 Ibid. 169.
94 https://www.arb.ro/mesaj-arb-privind-legea-darii-plata/, accessed 3 May 2023.

unconstitutionality of the law. Indeed, it could have decided (without too much difficulty) that it is for the legislator to correct the law and for lawyers and legal scholars to come up with legal solutions redressing the problem of disbalanced credit contracts. And yet, manifestly, the Court wanted to save the law at least in part. Therefore, it concluded that it remains constitutional as long as it is interpreted to mean that it shall be the courts to decide on the consumers' faith, case-by-case, not only on the basis of the law under examination itself but also by reference to a traditional civil law institution (*impreviziunea*, in approximate English translation: hardship or in Latin: *rebus sic stantibus*) of which the law was considered a specific application (to the domain of credit contracts). Thus, like in the austerity package case, the Court stood for compromise and positioned itself mid-way between the antagonistic interests of the main stakeholders.

One year later, in 2017, discussing the constitutionality of the law converting Swiss francs mortgage loans into Romanian lei at a favorable, historical rate, the Court took a firmer stance and declared it unconstitutional altogether (essentially on grounds of a legal technicality having to do with the principle of bicameralism). Nonetheless, it proceeded with clear indications on what is to be done. Thus, the problem of over-indebtedness stemming from these burdening contracts was to be resolved on a case-by-case basis by regular courts which were to apply the same civil law mechanism retained for the case of mortgage loans. Again, the Court proposed a trade-off which was identified as such by the National Bank Governor who also qualified the decision as 'correct.'[95] The President of the Court himself hinted to compromise only to dismiss the claim that this is what the Court sought to obtain: 'Our solution is diversified, divided – two admissions, two rejections. You could say it was a kind of Solomonic judgment, but it wasn't like that at all.'[96]

Two examples, taken moreover from constitutional adjudication only, are certainly of limited value in understanding the full complexity of the role of the judiciary in Romania's neoliberal transition. Still, being a response to exceptional circumstances, they shed some light on courts' frame of mind in respect of difficult political choices with a broad societal impact. At each time, when it scrutinised neoliberal policies as when it discussed social measures, the Court supported the Government, yet it did so with a caveat meant to temper what would have appeared for many critiques as the radicality of the Government's decisions. Or to frame this more theoretically, at each time, there was something there for the other (party). Also, in both cases, the Court strived, in a more or less convincing manner, to present its decisions as the necessary outcome of legal technique alone. Even so, its decisions never

95 https://incont.stirileprotv.ro/credite-si-economii/curtea-constitutionala-s-ar-putea-pronunta-marti-pe-legea-conversiei-creditelor-in-franci-elvetieni.html, accessed 2 September 2020.

96 See reference above, note 90.

ceased to be political, from the way they were produced (expressing one choice between multiple interpretative possibilities) to the consequences they subsequently generated.

In fact, a look at the actual consequences allows one to make a further, important, point, namely that a Constitutional Court's decision will have an "afterlife" in regular courts whose path does not necessarily coincide, ideologically speaking, with its point of departure (for that matter, constitutional case-law has an afterlife in the future practice of the Constitutional Court itself as well since new decisions often qualify the meaning of previous ones in ways that can be seen as novel). Therefore, from the point of view of its societal impact it makes little sense to proclaim for good a decision to be "neoliberal" or "socially progressive" as long as its practical operation might turn out to be the opposite. It is to say, with Jacques Derrida, that '[a] thousand possibilities will always remain open even as one understands something of that sentence which makes sense.'[97]

Specifically, in the Romanian context, while the Court's willingness to save a law – the transfer in lieu of payment – that in many (specifically legal) respects was flawed betrays a pro-consumer preference, it is far from clear whether its afterlife follows the same pattern. Left to the discretion of ordinary courts, the matter could have been resolved, if the judges were to follow the concise indications of the Constitutional Court, in at least three ways which allocate the distribution of the economic hardship differently (thus placing the burden entirely on the bank, the consumer, or somewhere in-between).[98] According to some commentators,[99] ordinary courts have in practice 'perverted' the spirit of the law and have gone to great lengths to 'neutralize' it by giving gain of cause to consumers in only a few cases.[100] This, in turn, triggered a political reaction with consumer associations and other activists lobbying for a more constraining legislative framework which finally led to a modification of the law in May 2020.[101] Based on the

97 Jacques Derrida, *Limited Inc.*, (ed. by Elisabeth Weber, Paris: Galilée, 1992), 122.

98 Lucian Bercea, 'Riscul valutar, impreviziunea și conversia creditelor în valută' 10 April 2017, https://www.juridice.ro/essentials/1116/riscul-valutar-impreviziunea-si-conversia-creditelor-in-valuta#_ftn74, accessed 10 September 2020.

99 https://www.bursa.ro/gheorghe-piperea-scopul-legii-darii-in-plata-pervertit-de-nenumarate-exceptii-de-neconstitutionalitate-42408532, accessed 2 September 2020.

100 This is in line with judges' attitudes towards "hardship" (*rebus sic stantibus*) in other jurisdictions: Bercea, *supra*; Marco Torsello, '"All Roads Lead to Rome": The Multiple Grounds Under Italian Law to Challenge a Contract Due to Supervening Changes of Circumstances' in Başakş Başoğlu, *The Effects of Financial Crises on the Binding Force of Contracts – Renegotiation, Rescission or Revision* (Berlin: Springer, 2016), 168; Edward Purnell, 'Hardship and Contract Modification: Framing Ex Ante Expectations and Making Contract Adjustments Using Discounted Cash Flow Techniques' (2016) 20 *Korea University Law Review* 39.

101 Law n. 52/2020 published in the *Official Journal* n. 386 from 13 May 2020.

(absolute) presumptions that the new law institutes, it became easier for a consumer to prove that they find themselves in a situation which legally constitutes hardship and that, therefore, their contract with the bank would be in need of recalibration. Nonetheless, it is very unlikely that the story of consumer credit ends here: more *traces* shall be added.[102] To start with, one can expect the constitutionality of this law to be challenged as well.

Inspired by European law (Directive 2014/17/EU of the European Parliament and of the Council of 4 February 2014 on credit agreements for consumers relating to residential immovable property), the movement to protect consumers through the legislation examined here (other than that which had to be transposed by virtue of the directives) has taken on the form of a *local* struggle, a back and forth between more liberal and more social interventions.[103] Up until now, the Court appeared reserved in steering the wheel in one particular direction. A harsh critique could infer that the Court has not done enough for the goal of social justice, denouncing the 'dominant understanding that poverty is a problem to be addressed through policy and advocacy, not through structural changes in legal thought.'[104] However, a more indulgent interpreter would appreciate the Court's minimal gesture of signalling that multiple directions are possible.

6.4 With the Help of the Legal Form (or Instead of Conclusion)

'Although based in economics, neoliberalism's framework is disseminated and legitimated by the legal discourse.'[105] In Romania, it was the proximity of neoliberal reforms to democracy and the rule of law talk, in politics as in civil society, that facilitated the large acceptance of the former.[106] The Constitutional Court, for its part, used law's formalism to uphold these reforms. Yet, as evidenced by the two case-studies here explored, on at least two crucial occasions, both triggered by so-called market failures, the same legal formalism was employed to "signal" that other political options could have been legitimately pursued. In a country where the rhetoric of "there

102 I allude here to Derrida's concept of *trace*: Jacques Derrida, *Parages* (2nd edn, Paris: Galilée, 2003) 118–9.

103 Note that in both cases we are talking about state's *intervention*. Indeed, '[w]hat the neoliberal position advances is not a claim of "market against state" or even simply a push for "more market, less state", but rather a call for a particular kind of state'; 'neoliberalism can never be a "hands-off" antiregulatory doctrine as classical liberalism purported to be': David Singh Grewal and Jedediah Purdy, 'Introduction: Law and Neoliberalism' (2014) 77 *Law and Contemporary Problems* 1.

104 Corinne Blalock, 'Neoliberalism and the Crisis of Legal Theory' (2014) 77 *Law and Contemporary Problems* 71, 77.

105 Ibid. 103.

106 Ban, 'Ruling Ideas'.

is no alternative" prevailed long into the transition period such a signalling might be of certain value for the cause of social justice no matter the temporary impact of the Court's case-law. Given its ambivalence, it is safe to say that the Court posed as the typical neutral arbiter working with the law. Upon reflection though, we are reminded, once more, that '[t]he law, as a minimum, is about interpreting texts'[107] and that texts can be made to speak ideologically. As we have seen with these two examples, proportionality tests are open-ended enough to invite the interpreter to inject ideological preferences in the meaning of the law. In countries of the CEE region, which have not known an established practice of constitutional adjudication,[108] this might translate into a particular hollowness of the legal form (at least in the sense in which courts are ill-equipped, or in any case less well-equipped or well-trained than their Western counterparts, to conceal their decisionism in language that would appear as substance-laden). However, this should not lead us to conclude that Constitutional Courts are failed transplants.

First, the notion of failure in relation to legal transfers is in and of itself quite problematic. Declaring a transplant failed or, by contrast, successful presupposes a reference to the original – to which the copy is being compared – in a context in which the two operate under different societal circumstances. One should therefore not expect that a legal transfer behaves identically to its source.[109] If a comparison premised on the idea of authenticity is held to be the reference by which the transfer is judged, then one could argue that any legal transfer is *always already* a *failed* legal transfer.

Second, assuming that success is not a matter of conformity to some original but is to be assessed internally (i.e., how effective the functioning of a given borrowed institution has come to be in that particular society) one should be clear about what the institution seeks to achieve in the first place. Despite the many views on the reach of constitutional review, scholars generally agree that constitutional courts serve the purpose of providing society with a supplementary check on power. However, it would be a fallacy to conclude to the failure of constitutional review in the particular context of the CEE region because this check on power turns out itself to be an act of power. To do so would mean to suggest that in other places, especially in the 'donor' systems, constitutional review can somehow miraculously accomplish a total submission of politics within the realm of law. Such a theoretical

107 Costas Douzinas, 'Law and Justice in Postmodernity' in Steven Connor (ed.), *The Cambridge Companion to Postmodernism* (Cambridge: Cambridge University Press, 2004), 200.

108 In Romania centralised constitutional review by a specialised court was not part of the constitutional tradition. As early as 1911, Romania's Supreme Court had developed judicial review by striking down a Parliament's statute despite the fact that the 1866 Constitution did not vest such powers in the court.

109 Pierre Legrand, 'The Impossibility of "Legal Transplants"' (1997) 4 *Maastricht Journal of European and Comparative Law* 111.

position would ultimately amount to upholding the 'liberal vision of curbing the political by the law'[110] and to ideologically offer grist to the mill of the 'Eastern backwardness story.'[111]

Of course, the many constitutional or apex courts have different styles of reasoning with some going to great lengths in order to cloak the political in legal jargon, others less so (after all, the tone of the French highest courts or of the European Court of Justice is notoriously magisterial).[112] In any case, all decisions 'have some textual basis (whether real, imagined, sincere, or tactical).'[113] But this changes nothing to the fact of their discretion and the corresponding emptiness of the legal form. Thus, the two important judgments of the Constitutional Court of Romania hardly depart from standard legal reasoning (as such, their language is at once both inclusive and exclusive). Ideologically however, they reveal how indecisive the Court was when faced with complicated topics of economic policy, so much so that it tried to deliver a message palatable, in part at least, to actors of all political hues. This mixed attitude should not be confused with neutrality. These were instances when the decision itself (which, generally, is one, trenchant, categorical, unilateral) mirrored, and thus exposed more visibly, the 'structural undecidability of the juridical.'[114]

The specific role of ordinary courts in Romania's neoliberal transformation remains to be assessed by further research. Meanwhile, the recent challenges to liberal legality, much less programmatic than in Hungary and Poland, cannot be directly linked to the uncritical embrace of neoliberalism and remain largely connected to one topic in particular, namely the fight against corruption, which many politicians would want to see enfeebled. Radical nationalist-populist parties stay on the margins of the political scene for the time being. Yet mainstream parties seem more and more determined to embrace bits of populist discourse if this is what it takes to put them in power (after all, all of the traditional parties have been labelled by scholars at some point or another as populist, which only shows that '[p]opulism is cyclic, it never goes away for good'[115]). The kind of opportunist populism

110 Tacik, *supra*.
111 Ibid. See also Peter Cserne, 'Discourses on Judicial Formalism in Central and Eastern Europe: Symptom of an Inferiority Complex?' (2020) 28(6) *European Review* 880.
112 See Mitchel de S.-O.-l'E. Lasser, *Judicial Deliberations* (Oxford: Oxford University Press, 2004), 103–238. Lasser shows that 'behind the apparent formalism, a vibrant—though well hidden—discursive sphere exists within the French civil judicial system': ibid. 15.
113 Ibid. 315.
114 Mańko, 'Judicial Decision-Making,' 189.
115 Robert Adam, *Două veacuri de populism românesc* [Two Centuries of Romanian Populism] (Bucureşti: Humanitas, 2018), 287.

Romania has been witnessing every now and again,[116] coupled with the frustrations of large parts of the population such as migrant workers and their families,[117] the continued presence of clientelist networks for the management of everyday life[118] and the crumbling of the liberal order in the region and beyond, makes the country into an unlikely candidate for 'fail[ing] better'[119] in the face of current illiberal trends.

116 Silvia Suteu, 'The Populist Turn in Central and Eastern Europe: Is Deliberative Democracy Part of the Solution?' (2019) 15 *European Constitutional Law Review* 488.

117 Bruno Meeus, 'Welfare Through Migrant Work: What If the Romanian "Safety Valve" Closes?' (2013) 13 *Southeast European and Black Sea Studies* 175.

118 Romania is not mentioned in John Keane's recent book *The New Despotism* (Cambridge, MA: Harvard University Press, 2020) and rightly so given that many of the elements highly problematic in countries such as China, Singapore, or Russia are absent from Romanian politics. Nonetheless, his description of state capitalism as based on clientelist networks sounds sadly familiar in many respects to a Romanian readership as well.

119 Samuel Beckett, *Worstward Ho* in *Nohow On* (Grove Press 1996 [1983]), 99.

Chapter 7

'Law Is Not Politics'

The Role of the Liberal View on Law in the Rise of "New Populism"*

Mátyás Bencze

7.1 Introduction

At the time of the political transition, around 1990, Hungary, in terms of Western-type democratisation, was one of the role-models of ex-Socialist Central and Eastern European (hereinafter: CEE) countries. Until 2010, democratic and rule of law institutions had been seemingly solid and the opposition parties had realistic chances to take over political power in free and fair elections. After 2010, when the right-wing Fidesz party defeated the then governing Socialist party in the general election and took political power, the situation changed surprisingly fast.

The speed and smoothness of the profound political and legal changes has made Hungary a special case among CEE countries. That is why a deeper, country-specific scrutiny is needed in order to find the causes of democratic decline in this region. In this chapter, I examine the factors which made Hungary the forerunner of neo-authoritarian populism ('new populism')[1] among CEE countries. I believe neo-authoritarian populism or 'new populism' is a more accurate label for the Hungarian political developments than referring to it simply as 'populism.'

This is partly because political populism has many forms and not all of them are necessarily anti-democratic.[2] Besides this, although the Hungarian government uses anti-elitist rhetoric (for example, the fight against the EU-elite)[3] which is a characteristic of "classic" populist politics, it is also carrying out a campaign against homeless and Roma people as well as against

* This publication is part of the DEMOS project and has received funding from the European Union's Horizon 2020 research and innovation programme under grant agreement No. 822590. Any dissemination of results here presented reflects only the authors' views.

1 See András L. Pap, *Democratic Decline in Hungary: Law and Society in an Illiberal Democracy* (Routledge 2018), 2–3.

2 See David van Reybrouck, *Pleidooi voor populisme* [Plea for Populism] (Querido, 2008).

3 For the latest development see 'Orbán: Hungarian, Polish Forces "Repelled International Attack of Liberal Brigades"' (*Hungary Today*, 24 July 2020) <https://hungarytoday.hu/orban-govt-eur-3-bn-funding-brussels-summit-eu/>, accessed 20 July 2020.

DOI: 10.4324/9781032624464-8

migrants and refugees who certainly do not belong to the elites of any society.[4] Moreover, the ruling party publicly supports certain national and foreign entrepreneurs who are part of the economic elite.[5] Nonetheless, the Fidesz government uses anti-pluralistic rhetoric, stating that they and only they can represent the interests of the Hungarian people which is a typical populist communication strategy.[6] As Pap characterises the cherry-picking nature of Hungarian new populism:

> [it] is hollow in the sense that there are no positive, alternative grand narrative constructions. Playing on the criticism and rejection of the current discourses, political and policy regimes seem[s] to suffice. This shallowness and emptiness are the unique and engaging features of the (potentially exportable) Hungarian model of illiberal democracy and, as I argue, of new populism.[7]

Considering these peculiarities of the current Hungarian (and other CEE) governmental politics, it seems to be reasonable to distinguish it from the classic form of populism.

The story of the neo-authoritarian turn in Hungary is commonly told as a story where the focus is on the populist tide,[8] or on the weakness of democratic traditions and Rule of Law institutions.[9] Without denying that these factors have played a significant role in the democratic decline, I focus on

4 See Keno Verseck, 'Hungary's Homeless Ban: When Poverty Becomes a Crime' (*Deutsche Welle*, 15 October 2018) <https://www.dw.com/en/hungarys-homeless-ban-when-poverty-becomes-a-crime/a-45900111>, accessed 18 July 2020; Péter Cseresnyés, 'Gov't Finds Court Ruling on School Segregation of Romas "Unfortunate", Refuses to Pay Compensation' (*Hungary Today*, 20 January 2020) <https://hungarytoday.hu/govt-finds-court-ruling-on-school-segregation-of-romas-unfortunate-refuses-to-pay-compensation/>, accessed 18 July 2020; Lydia Gall, 'Hungary's Xenophobic Anti-Migrant Campaign' (*Human Rights Watch*, 13 September 2016) <https://www.hrw.org/news/2016/09/13/hungarys-xenophobic-anti-migrant-campaign#>, accessed 18 July 2020.

5 Neil Buckley and Andrew Byrne, 'Viktor Orban's Oligarchs: A New Elite Emerges in Hungary' (*Financial Times*, 21 December 2017) <https://www.ft.com/content/ecf6fb4e-d900-11e7-a039-c64b1c09b482>, accessed 18 July 2020.

6 Jan-Werner Müller, *What Is Populism?* (University of Pennsylvania Press, 2016).

7 Pap (n 2) 2–3

8 Gábor Halmai, 'Populism, Authoritarianism and Constitutionalism' (2019) 20 *GLJ* 296; Jens Becker, 'The Rise of Right-Wing Populism in Hungary' (2010) 13 *Journal for Labour and Social Affairs in Eastern Europe* 29. Michael Stolarski and Michael Malcolm Stolarski, 'Persistent Populism: Uncovering the Reasons behind Hungary's Powerful Populist Parties' (2019) CMC Senior Theses 2188 <https://scholarship.claremont.edu/cmc_theses/2188>, accessed 16 July 2020.

9 Bojan Bugarič, 'The Rule of Law Derailed: Lessons from the Post-Communist World' (2015) 7 *HJRL* 175. For the criticism of this kind of approach, see Przemysław Tacik, chapter 1 in this volume.

an element of the puzzle which has remained mostly unreflected in studies discussing the authoritarian turn in Hungary. This element is the liberal view on law which, from the change of the political regime (1989/90) until 2010, has been predominant among social-democrats and liberals. My hypothesis is that this liberal view included an illusion regarding the nature of law (and politics) which had a fatal consequence in terms of the timely recognition of the signs of the neo-authoritarian offence by the political right-wing in Hungary.[10]

7.2 The Formation of Liberal Legal Thinking in Hungary

The appearance of modern, liberal legal thinking in Hungary dates back to the last few decades of the 19th century, when the country – as a part of the Austro-Hungarian Monarchy – went through a social, economic, and political change from feudalism to capitalism (embourgeoisement, industrialisation, urbanisation, general economic growth). Several new laws of great importance (the Act on Commercial Activity, the Criminal Code, the Act on Civil Court Procedure, etc.) were adapted which established the legal framework of the capitalist political system serving the interests of the ruling aristocratic and bourgeois classes.[11] Equality before the law was also an achievement of that period.

The functioning of the capitalist economic and political system required the state bureaucracy and court system to work consistently, in a predictable manner (legal certainty). State officials and judges had to be professionals who were subjected to the law and their acts had to comply with the standards of legality. One might say that a "bureaucratic" type of legal thinking

10 Further critical analyses should also take account of the neo-liberal economic policy after the regime change which prevented members of the working classes from rising to the level of "middle class," and thus making those people susceptible to populist demagoguery. See Zoltán Pogátsa, 'The State of Capitalism and the Rise of the Right in the 1930s and Today: Hungary as a Case Study' in Jeremy Rayner, Susan Falls, George Souvlis, and Taylor Nelms (eds), *Back to the '30s? Recurring Crises of Capitalism, Liberalism, and Democracy* (Palgrave Macmillan, 2020); Márk Áron Éber, 'Class Structure of "Hungarian Society" in the Modern World-System' (2019) STRG Working Papers <http://polhist.hu/wp-content/uploads/2019/01/2019_1_STRG-Working-Papers.pdf>, accessed 20 July 2020. It would also be worthwhile to consider the professionalism of the political machinery run by Fidesz. The governmental party functions rather as a multinational business enterprise than as an ideology-driven political party. See János Vencel Téglás, 'A Fidesz reflexív politikai profizmusa: a politika és a politikatudomány határdiskurzusa' [The Reflective Political Professionalism of Fidesz: On the Border of Political and Political-Scientific Discourses] in Márton Szabó (ed.), *Fideszvalóság: Diszkurzív politikatudományi értelmezések* (L' Harmattan, 2006), not to mention the necessity of studying the consequences of recent Russian and Chinese influence on the CEE region ("autocracy-export").

11 See Ivan T. Berend and György Ránki, *Hungary, a Century of Economic Development* (Barnes and Noble Books, 1974).

was established at that time, which is manifested in an accurate and professional application of the existing law rather than in the formation of a real constraint on powerful political actors (a formalist understanding of Rule of Law).[12] It was also the time when a common belief was formed that legal practice is a highly professional activity which should be kept separate from politics. Nonetheless, the new political system was far more democratic than the previous (feudalistic) one, and the peaceful economic and social development from 1867 to 1914 left positive impressions in the social and legal memory as 'Belle Époque'.

After World War I, the Austro-Hungarian Monarchy was dismembered and Hungary became a sovereign country. Due to the shock of the defeat (the territory of Hungary was reduced to one-third of its original size), and later, because of the Great Economic Depression, Hungary gradually drifted towards an authoritarian political regime. As a consequence of this process Hungary fell back from the level of democracy and the Rule of Law it had already achieved as a member of the Monarchy.[13]

The parliamentary majority actively used the law to maintain its power. Due to the anti-Semitic character of the regime, Jewish people were stripped of some of their rights from the very beginning of the interwar period.[14] Critics of the prevailing political system had to face criminal charges, which had been unusual before World War I, and 80% of the electorate had to vote by open ballot in the parliamentary elections. The ideology of the governmental parties was based on nationalism and Christianity.[15] Some characterise this era as 'feudal-capitalism.'[16]

It is quite symptomatic that the mainstream discourse in public law scholarship revolved around the questions of "legal continuity" after the dethronement of the Habsburg emperor and the legitimacy of the new constitutional order (regency), while constitutional scholars dedicated much less

12 Gábor Máthé, 'A magyar burzsoá igazságszolgáltatási szervezet kialakulása. 1867–1875' [The Formation of the Hungarian Bourgeois Justice System. 1867–1875] (Akadémiai Kiadó, 1982), 17–26; Kálmán Kulcsár, 'Jogalkotás és jogrendszer' [Legislation and Legal System] in István Kollega Tarsoly (ed.) *Magyarország a XX. században* (Babits Kiadó, 1996–2000) 444–55.

13 Kulcsár (n 13) 468

14 Moshe Y. Herczl, *Christianity and the Holocaust of Hungarian Jewry* (NYU Press, 1993), 79–169.

15 Sean Lambert, *The Horthy Era (1920–1944)* <https://theorangefiles.hu/the-horthy-era-1920-1944-long/>, accessed 17 April 2021.

16 Pál Gervai and László Trautmann, 'A neoliberális "kapitalizmus" fogalom megszűnése' [The Disappearance of the Term "Neoliberal Capitalism"] (2013) 8 *Közgazdaság* 15 <http://unipub.lib.uni-corvinus.hu/1180/1/kg_2013n1_08.pdf>, accessed 17 April 2021.

effort to exploring the violation of the rights of exploited classes and ethnic minorities.[17]

By the end of World War II, Hungary (which even then was still an ally of Nazi Germany) was under the military control of the Soviet Union which started to convert the country into a socialist state. Socialist Hungary declared the "unity of branches of political powers" and "democratic centralism." In the 1950s, state organs (including courts) operated under strict and direct political control, leaving very little room for adjudication based on the Rule of Law; this strengthened, at the same time, the bureaucratic approach to the application of law.[18] After the defeat of the Hungarian Uprising by the Soviet army in 1956, the returning Communist Party used the law and the justice system to punish the leaders and supporters of the Uprising and to deter citizens from further resistance.[19]

As a legal theoretical reflection of the political situation, Imre Szabó – the leading Marxist legal philosopher during the socialist era – wrote in 1960 that "proletarian law" (as opposed to "bourgeois law") need not to hide its class-character and need not pretend to be neutral, either. Hence, in his theory, "socialist normativism" requires a reduction of the interpretive activity of judges to a grammatical and logical interpretation of laws – because the application of other methods would lead to the distortion of the original intention of legislation manifested in the text of the law.[20]

From the beginning of the 1960s the Communist party changed the strategy it employed to preserve its power and gave up open oppression. Consequently, a new period began in Hungary, often called the "soft dictatorship." The main characteristic of this period (which ended in 1989) was a certain duality. At the level of the 'legal complex' this meant that the official ideology (Marxism) remained unchanged until the late 1980s (though its influence gradually weakened), but legal practice and legal scholarship converged to their Western counterparts.

The direct political control of courts gradually disappeared; however, the bureaucratic mentality of judges did not change. Judges were generally

17 Gábor Schweitzer, 'Közjogi provizórium, jogfolytonosság, új közjogi irány: Az 1919/1920-1944 közötti magyarországi alkotmányjog-tudomány vázlata (II. rész)' [Provisionality in the Constitutional Order, Legal Continuity, New Public Law Direction: Outline of the Public Law Scholarship in Hungary Between 1919/1920 and 1944] (2014) 7 *Közjogi Szemle* 9–20

18 Attila Horváth, 'A magyar bírósági szervezet története a szovjet típusú diktatúra idején (1945–1990)' [The History of the Hungarian Judicial Administration in the Time of the Soviet-Type Dictatorship (1945–1990)] (2017) *Jogtörténeti Szemle* 128

19 Miklós Dorsch, '1956: 60 Years Ago, Hungary Rose Against Communism' <https://visegradpost.com/en/2016/10/22/1956-60-years-ago-hungary-rose-against-communism/>, accessed 16 April 2021.

20 Imre Szabó, *A jogszabályok értelmezése* [Interpretation of the Law] (Közgazdasági és Jogi Könyvkiadó, 1960).

conceived of as state officials and apolitical civil servants.[21] It was relatively easy to maintain this self-image, because judges did not have to adjudicate in politically sensitive cases. The government handled its critics outside the courts (for example, it forced them to leave the country).[22] Following from this, the instrumental approach to law which preserved and strengthened the formalist legal attitude of the pre-World War II era, remained the dominant view among legal practitioners.[23]

In the field of jurisprudence even Imre Szabó himself abandoned the theory of socialist normativism, and, in his book published in 1971, he argued that the law already exists in a 'preformed' manner in the 'relationships of production of the society' and thus it is actually not the product of the Will of the Legislator.[24] Others also challenged the idea of the politically-bound law. Kálmán Kulcsár, as a legal sociologist, examined the "law in action" in Hungary (searching for norms that actually govern the behaviour of the people) and warned of the limits of intentionally created law.[25] András Sajó, and later Béla Pokol, emphasised the relative autonomy of law against the political institutions of the society. In their theory it is the doctrinal (dogmatic) layer of the legal system which guarantees the consistency of the law, and it is the professional legal practitioners as well as legal scholars (and not the politicians) who have the relevant knowledge for the maintenance and development of the complex system of legal concepts and principles.[26]

The idea of the autonomy of law was widely conceived of as a progressive one in the 1980s. It was obvious that the socialist economic and political system was not competitive enough on the international stage. The obvious difference in the quality of life and in the state of political liberties in the East and the West discredited Marxist political philosophy. Thus, the concept of the class-struggle dynamic as the driving force of change in the legal system had become obsolete as well.

In the last phase of the process of democratisation (from 1988) the official Marxist ideology lost its position as the "official theory," which resulted in a general feeling of liberation from the political usurpation of law. The hope

21 Zoltán Fleck, *Jogszolgáltató mechanizmusok az államszocializmusban* [Judicial Mechanisms in the Era of State-Socialism] (Napvilág, 2001), 104.

22 András Sajó, 'New Legalism in East Central Europe: Law as an Instrument of Social Transformation' (1990) 17 *J. Law Soc* 329, 333

23 Ibid. 332, 340–1

24 Imre Szabó, *A jogelmélet alapjai* [Foundations of the Theory of Law] (Akadémiai Kiadó, 1971).

25 Kámán Kulcsár, *A jogfejlődés sajátosságai: a jog mint eszköz* [The Characteristics of Development of Law: The Law as Instrument] (Akadémiai Kiadó, 1983).

26 András Sajó, *Kritikai értekezés a jogtudományról* [Critical Treatise on Legal Doctrinal Scholarship] (Akadémiai Kiadó, 1983); Béla Pokol, 'Law as Professional System of Institutions' (1990) 21 *Rechtsttheorie* 335.

was that the law could be a purely professional activity, free from any external pressure. This picture of legal activity was in line with the self-understanding of legal practitioners who became quite apolitical in the decades of the soft dictatorship. Under these circumstances it is understandable that most of the lawyers and legal scholars engaged (though in an unreflected way) with the concept of an autonomous legal system.

The most significant and most influential representative of this approach was Béla Pokol who established his social-theory based on a biological analogy borrowed from the German sociologist Niklas Luhmann. According to Luhmann, society consists of autonomous sub-systems guided by their binary codes, and the by-products of their autonomous operations make the whole society a functioning system (just as in the case of the human body where the independently operating organs make the body a living person). In the Luhmannian theory the 'organs' of society are the different communicative sub-systems such as the economy, science, law, politics, religion, etc. These subsystems are guided by their binary codes such as profitability/non-profitability (economy), true/false (science), legal/illegal (law), government/opposition (politics), transcendent/immanent (religion), etc.[27] Béla Pokol modified the original Luhmannian theory by reducing the scope of the communicative sub-systems to the communication by professionals of a certain sub-system (businessmen, scientists, legal practitioners, professional politicians, etc.). Other communications carried out by 'ordinary people' constitute part of everyday life ('Lebenswelt'). This theory can be considered the theoretical reflection of the social change of the modern era, where the division of work and professional specialisation has spread in an unprecedented manner across Western societies.[28]

This theoretical model of society had two implications which are relevant for us. On the one hand it suggests that society only functions well if the sub-systems operate autonomously, that is as independently from each other as possible.[29] The professionals of each sub-system are obliged to follow the binary code of that particular sub-system, regardless of its impact on other sub-systems. This approach creates a sharp boundary between the realm of the "political" and the "legal." Both spheres have their own different norms (binary codes) and members of the sub-systems act accordingly. This theory met with a positive reception among lawyers who wanted to rebuild a legal

27 Niklas Luhmann, *Social Systems* (John Bednarz, Jr. with Dirk Baecker trans., Stanford University Press, 1995).

28 Béla Pokol, *A professzionális intézményrendszerek elmélete* [Theory of the Professional Systems of Institutions] (Felsőoktatási Koordinációs Iroda, 1991).

29 It must be noted that Pokol somehow blurred the line between descriptive and normative theories. He explicitly stated that his scientific approach is free from evaluation, but the whole theory still suggests that the model he established represents a progression towards the 'right' direction ("social modernization").

system for the new republic which was free from political interference. On the other hand, in Pokol's social theory there was no room left for class interest. Society was divided into sub-systems ('professional systems of institutions' as he called it) and the world of everyday life, neglecting (the existence of) classes and interest-groups. The driving force of social progression, therefore, is not the conflict of interests between groups and classes, but the gradual realisation of the inner logic (binary code) of the professional systems of institutions. This idea was also acceptable for the Hungarian legal practitioners who did not want to see the law and its application as the arena of contest between classes.

7.3 Beliefs and Realities During the Democratic Era – The Case of the Hungarian Constitutional Court

Pokol's theory fitted well with the atmosphere of the political transition, where the liberation of the law from the captivity of (socialist) politics was welcomed. Thus, it was natural that in the transition period (1989/90) the reconstruction of the legal system was guided by the principle of Rule of Law – an idea which is the reflection of the theory of an autonomous legal system.

Although some authors warned of the dangers of a combination of the instrumental and bureaucratic 'Eastern' approach to law with autonomous legal institutions,[30] at the time when "the End of History" was declared it seemed perfectly normal to reframe the economic, political, and legal order in accordance with the neoliberal "Washington Consensus." That meant the transplantation of Western-type legal institutions such as a constitutional court, administrative courts, an ombudsman, an independent State Audit office, and civil laws with a high degree of conformity to the market.[31] This transformation was, on the one hand, encouraged by the Western economic and political elite, and, on the other hand, was welcomed by the technocrat leaders of the former political regime who experienced the crisis of the state-socialist economic system.[32]

The democratic institutional change was based on the idea that legal institutions can have an effective control on the existing government and can prevent it from exercising political power in an arbitrary fashion. The widely received approach to law as a "professional system of institutions" strengthened the common belief that the actors of legal institutions mostly

30 The same institutions can operate differently in CEE countries than in Western Europe and thus, old, anti-democratic structures can manage to survive; see Sajó (n 23) 337.

31 Bugarič (n 10) 178–9; Sajó (n 23) 335

32 Zoltán Barotányi, 'Nem fasiszta életet' ['Non-Fascist Life' – interview with Gáspár Miklós Tamás] *Magyar Narancs* (Budapest, 9 July 2020).

act according to their professional standards and can set aside their prejudices, political preferences, and interests during their professional activity.

The newly established legal institutions, especially the Hungarian Constitutional Court, (hereinafter: HCC) have maintained this belief. László Sólyom, the first chief justice of the HCC said in an interview that the court treated the constitution as an ideology-free, neutral legal text.[33] Another member of the HCC declared that politics 'fell into the trap of the law' by its institutionalised judicial review of acts of parliament, and only the constitutional court is competent to determine the basic principles of any branch of the law by relying on the 'inner value system of the constitution.'[34]

The fact that some of the most respected Hungarian legal scholars were appointed as constitutional justices led to the high reputation of the HCC. The argumentations of their decisions were highly sophisticated and they used the elevated language of constitutional legal dogmatics, which increased their reputation in the eyes of the lay audience.

Of course, many legal professionals were fully aware of the fact that the law is not mathematics and there are cases where judges can deliver decisions which even contradict each other and which they can provide with equally rational justifications. The indeterminacy of the law, without any doubt, was a challenge to the formalist understanding of the Rule of Law doctrine.

The liberal answer to this challenge was that it is not the personal convictions, or class-interest, of the judge that play a pivotal role in the decision making in "hard cases'" but the "political morality" of the given society which serves as a basis for decisions where the law is "uncertain" (and not "indeterminate").[35] By political morality they meant a certain conception of political justice which justifies the prevailing political institutions and the legal order in a given political community (thus it differs from the morality of the majority of a given political community).[36] The task of the judge is to find these justifying principles and to decide accordingly. In that way s/he can find the "right answer" to any legal question.[37]

33 Gábor Attila Tóth, 'A "nehéz eseteknél" a bíró erkölcsi felfogása jut szerephez' [When it Comes to "Hard Cases" the Moral Views of the Judge Plays a Crucial Role – interview with László Sólyom] (2006) 1 *Fundamentum* 31. It was the HCC itself which declared, in one of its landmark decisions, that 'legal certainty supported by objective and formal principles has priority over the always partial and subjective justice' (Decision 11/1992 (III. 5.)).

34 András Szabó, 'Alkotmány és büntetőjog' [Constitution and Criminal Law] (1999) 54 *Jogtudományi Közlöny* 165, 169–70.

35 For the crucial difference between "uncertain" and "indeterminate" see Ronald Dworkin, *A Matter of Principle* (Harvard University Press, 1985), 119–45.

36 For example, behind the general suffrage of modern democracies one can find the justifying principles of equality.

37 This is the famous Dworkinian approach to adjudication and judicial interpretation, cf. Ronald Dworkin, *Law's Empire* (Fontana, 1986), 225–58.

During the time of the liberal consensus, the idea that the conception of justice can be different in cases involving different social groups and classes was forgotten. Similarly, the fact that there is no guarantee that judges are free from political prejudice or from other interests did not feature in mainstream legal scholarly thinking. The predominant view in the legal literature was that constitutional judges, although they can have political preferences, are far from serving the interests of a given political party.[38]

The jurisprudence of the HCC had a certain "'national flavor." In the first several years of its first term the HCC followed a classic liberal agenda in some symbolic cases (the abolishment of the death penalty, and freedom of the press and freedom of speech cases)[39] which represented the minimal liberal requirements against the surviving elements of the former, dictatorial system. However, after that the HCC gradually engaged in political fights – mostly on the side of right-wing political parties,[40] especially after 1994, when the Hungarian Socialist Party (in coalition with a liberal left-wing party, the Alliance of Free Democrats) came to power. From that time the HCC ruled against them in almost all cases of great political significance. In some decisions a Christian-conservative ideological commitment of the HCC was detectable, but sometimes it served exclusively the current political interests of right-wing political forces. My hypothesis to be tested is that the political bias of the court originated not from any direct or personal interest in the triumph of right-wing parties, but from the fact that the identity of the majority of the first cohort of jurists elected to the HCC was determined by their antipathy towards the Socialist era, and the Hungarian Socialist Party was commonly deemed to be the heir of the former political regime.[41]

38 Mauro Zamboni, '"Markers" vs. "Makers": Are Constitutional Courts Legal or Political Actors?' in Suzanne Comtois and Kars Jan de Graaf (eds), *On Judicial and Quasi-Judicial Independence* (Eleven International publishing, 2013); János Kis, *Constitutional Democracy* (CEU Press, 2003), 286; Péter Paczolay, 'A "politikus" Alkotmánybíróság' [The "political" Constitutional Court] *Népszabadság* (Budapest, 30 October 1995), 10.

39 Kis (n 39) 249–77; Gábor Halmai, 'The Hungarian Approach of Constitutional Review' in Wojciech Sadurski (ed.), *Constitutional Justice: East and West* (Kluwer Law International, 2002), 189–212.

40 Mátyás Bencze, 'Díszítőelem, álcázóháló vagy tartóoszlop? A büntetőbírói gyakorlat és az alkotmány' [Ornament, Camouflage Net or Pillar? The Practice of Criminal Courts and the Constitution] (2007) 11 *Fundamentum* 5, 8–9. As János Kis characterised – euphemistically – this process, the right protective practice of the court 'has lost its momentum' since 1992. See Kis (n 39) 278–84.

41 Ex-chief justice László Sólyom in 2005, as already head of state, refused to award Gyula Horn, a former Socialist prime minister (between 1994 and 1998), declaring that Horn's role in the 1956 revolution was not reconcilable with the 'values of the constitution.' See Gábor Attila Tóth, 'Chief Justice Sólyom and the Paradox of "Revolution Under the Rule of Law"' (Academia.edu), 18–9 <https://www.academia.edu/38227555/Chief_Justice_S%C3%B3lyom_and_the_paradox_of_revolution_under_the_rule_of_law_>, accessed 30 July 2020

The ideology-driven Christian-conservative attitude was reflected in a series of decisions abusing human rights, and instead of deploying their emancipatory force, the HCC used these rights to repress the liberty of social minorities ("Others").[42] Other important decisions of the court can be explained, as I have previously mentioned, by the political bias of justices. The practice of the HCC serves as evidence for Costas Douzinas' thesis that, in the case of human rights courts, the political affiliation of judges matters more in the results of their decision making than the case law of the court itself.[43] As a series of decisions of the HCC proves, it is the "political" and not the "legal" which finally determined the content of human rights and constitutional principles.[44]

As an example of the above, the HCC found a law (adopted by the right-wing parliamentary majority) constitutional in 1991 that made it possible for banks to increase the interest rate of home loans retroactively (in order to preserve the economic stability of the country). Two years later (also during the governing of right-wing parties), the court delivered another judgment affirming a law which reduced the rise in pensions – the HCC was not particularly sensitive to the social rights of the citizens in this decision either. However, four years later the court (still with the same justices), under a left-wing government, decided along a different line and struck down many elements of the austerity measures introduced in order to avoid the financial and economic collapse of the country. By doing so, it curbed the restrictions on the scope of some social benefits for families. As critics pointed it out, some arguments of the court were surprisingly weak.[45] It is telling that chief justice Sólyom, right after the parliamentary adoption of the Bill on Economic Stabilization, said that in the event of an initiation of a constitutional review

42 Gábor Attila Tóth, 'Unequal Protection: Historical Churches and Roma People in the Hungarian Constitutional Jurisprudence' (2010) 51 *Acta Juridica Hungarica* 122, 122–35; Gábor Attila Tóth, *Túl a szövegen [Beyond the Text]* (Osiris, 2009), 82–3; Tamás Győrfi, 'Üzenet az elefántcsonytoronyból' [Message from the Ivory Tower] (2005) 9 *Fundamentum* 73.

43 Costas Douzinas, *The End of Human Rights. Critical Legal Thought at the Turn of the Century* (Hart, 2000), 120.

44 For criticism, see Mátyás Bencze, 'Kié a túlhatalom?' [Who is Over-Empowered?] (2006) 10 *Fundamentum* 94; Bundula István, '"Tényleg veszélyes precedens"' [Really Dangerous Precedent – interview with Gábor Halmai] (*Magyar Narancs*, 5 July 2007 <https://magyarnarancs.hu/belpol/tenyleg_veszelyes_precedens_halmai_gabor_alkotmanyjogasz_az_ovb_elnokhelyettese-67339>, accessed 31 July 2020.

45 Tamás Győrfi, 'Politika a jog fogságában: az alkotmánybíráskodás következményei' [Politics as a Captive of Law: The Consequences of Constitutional Review] in Miklós Szabó (ed.), *Elsadások a jogelmélet köréből* (Bíbor Kiadó, 1996) 137–42; András Sajó, 'A materiális természetjog árvái, avagy hogyen védi Alkotmánybíróságunk az elesetteket?' [Orphans of the Material Natural Law: How Does our Constitutional Court Protect the Poor?] (1996) 43 *Magyar Jog* 205; Kis (n 39) 295–302.

of the Act by the opposition parties, the court would delay its vacation time in order to work on this task.[46] The Hungarian liberal philosopher, János Kis, considered the court's newly acquired social sensitivity ('welfare-turn') to be the reflection of the modernised and family-centered Christian-conservative ideology of the majority of constitutional judges.[47] However, in 2004 (in the period of a left-wing government) the court's social sensitivity "evaporated" and it did not hesitate to annul a governmental decree which ordered a reduction in the price of certain medicines.[48]

The legal argumentation was also problematic in another infamous decision of the court which allowed the holding of a referendum (the so-called "social-referendum") initiated by the Fidesz party. The questions in the referendum affected the annual budget – a subject which was *expressis verbis* extracted from the scope of referenda by the constitution itself.[49] The political debate between the social-liberal head of state and the conservative government in the early 1990s was decided in favour of the government by the HCC, the decision of which narrowed the competence of the head of state (by interpretation of the constitution *in abstracto*). However, in the second half of the 2000s, where the conservative head of state came into conflict with the social-liberal prime minister, the court restricted the competence of the latter.[50] The criticism of the direction of the adjudication was only sporadic between 1990 and 2000. Most legal scholars and politicians believed in the "separation of law and politics" doctrine, neglecting the realities of judicial activity. Constitutional law scholars analysed, evaluated, and sometimes criticised the decisions of the HCC, mostly from a dogmatic point of view, and avoided asking fundamental questions of the legitimacy and political nature of constitutional adjudication.[51]

Nonetheless, there were some attempts in the legal literature to shed light on the political character of constitutional adjudication. It is not a coincidence, that it was Béla Pokol, the main promoter of the separation of law and politics, who, in 1993, warned of the danger of the activism of the court, an attitude based on the moral interpretation of abstract constitutional rights and principles. In his opinion, the activist adjudication of the court,

46 Kis (n 39) 316.

47 Kis (n 39) 294–5.

48 <https://fdlaw.hu/publications/life_sciences_pharmaceuticals/Pharmaceutical%20Law%20Update%20November%202004.pdf>

49 Nóra Chronowski and Miklós Kocsis, 'Az OVB és az AB (több mint hétszer) a népszavazásról' [The National Election Committee and the Constitutional Court on the Referendum (More than Seven Times)] (2007) 62 *Jogtudományi Közlöny* 371, 378–9.

50 Tóth (n 42) 18.

51 The situation was very similar to the Polish case where, as Sulikowski wrote, the Constitutional Tribunal had no 'natural enemy.' See Adam Sulikowski, chapter 3 in this volume.

by annulling the acts of legislation, can hollow out parliamentary democracy.[52] As his criticism was not based on a thorough scrutiny of the jurisprudence of the court, it was mostly ignored by the professional and scholarly community.

A constitutional scholar, Gábor Halmai, in a comprehensive study on the first nine years of the HCC made an unspecified remark, that László Sólyom, 'had not been always able to resist the temptation of doing politics.'[53] Another serious liberal critic defended the court from the accusation that it follows a political agenda.[54] There was only one constitutional law scholar, Zoltán Szente, who firmly criticised the political motivation of the court in the case of the economic stability decisions taken in 1995.[55]

As for the practice of the HCC, these criticisms proved to be ineffective, as the court – due to its rights-protecting landmark decisions in the early 1990s – acquired indisputable authority as the ultimate defender of rights and the Rule of Law among the members of Hungary's intellectual elite. Besides this, there were several decisions made by the HCC which went against the interests of the first Fidesz-led government between 1998 and 2002 (nonetheless, these judgments did not significantly limit the government's room for manoeuver).[56] That is why leading intellectuals who also had political influence maintained the common belief that the HCC is a politically neutral body which decides cases in line with constitutional law standards and the case-law of the tribunal. In that intellectual and political climate politicians strictly refrained from openly criticising any decision of the court. One can add that Socialist politicians, perhaps in order to avoid the accusation of a re-establishment of the *ancien régime*, were extremely careful when it came to the independence of legal institutions.[57] Moreover, the acceptance level of the HCC among the citizens was very high,[58] which is why criticising the HCC, even if the criticism was well-founded, could easily have resulted in a loss of popularity.

52 Béla Pokol, 'A törvényhozás alkotmányossága' [Constitutionality of the Legislation] (1993) 34 *Világosság* 41.

53 Gábor Halmai, 'Az aktivizmus vége?' [End of Activism?] (1999) 3 *Fundamentum* 24.

54 Kis (n 39) 286–95.

55 Zoltán Szente, 'Ki ellenőrzi az Alkotmánybíróságot?' [Who Guards the Constitutional Court?] *Népszabadság* (Budapest 16 October 1995), 11.

56 'Az Alkotmánybíróság a politikában' [The Constitutional Court in Politics] (*Political Capital*, 28 May 2004) <https://www.politicalcapital.hu/kereses.php?article_read=1&article_id=1196>, accessed 1 August 2020.

57 For example, the socialist-led parliament guaranteed the organisational independence of the Hungarian courts by the introduction of full judicial self-governance.

58 'A magyarok negyede szerint a politika diktál a bíróknak' [One Quarter of Hungarians Think That Politicians Influence the Result of Judicial Decisions] (*Origo.hu*, 20 September 2005) <https://www.origo.hu/itthon/20050919amagyarok.html>, accessed 1 August 2020.

The belief in the neutrality of the court was in accordance with the social theory analysed above, a crucial element of which was the thesis of the autonomy of law. Thus, a common conviction prevailed among socialist and liberal politicians and their intellectual supporters until 2010 that adjudication and any legal decision making are strictly legal-professional (and not political) activities. Legal decision making belongs to the sphere of educated and disciplined practitioners who are in charge of running the legal system. Even if political bias is sometimes detectable, it is only an accidental error in the system and not a natural part of legal practice.

7.4 The Fatal Consequences of Liberal Beliefs

The liberal illusion that there is an overlapping consensus among political parties on the value of constitutional democracy was the dominant opinion among democrats.[59] It seemed that there was no risk of an authoritarian comeback, and they did not need to fight for a strengthening of liberal democracy. Chantal Mouffe's observation that liberals, due to their rational and individualistic approach, tend to see politics as the field of rational debates and consensus instead of a struggle between social groups driven by collective identities,[60] applied to Hungarian liberals too.

Following from this, many social-liberals, ignoring the actual political and social condition of Hungary, forced left-wing governments to implement a Western-type progressive agenda (extending LBGTQ+ rights, drug liberalisation, introducing quotas for women, etc.).[61] Right-wing parties, by deploying populist demagoguery, could turn these progressive efforts against liberals, stating that 'deviant' minorities are much more important for the social-liberal parties than the interests of 'ordinary' Hungarian people.[62] It was also an illusion then that our Western-type institutions were strong enough to

59 Even around 2010, when the Schmittian 'friend/enemy' politics of Fidesz was obvious to many, two distinguished Hungarian liberal constitutional theorists wrote that '[a]s one political regime, a Soviet-type dictatorship, was fully replaced by another, liberal democracy, the destructive logic of friend and enemy well known from the history of revolutions – purges, proscriptions, massive denial of rights and terror – was fully avoided [in Hungary].' Zoltán Miklósi and Andrew Arató, 'Constitution Making and Transitional Politics in Hungary, 1989–1998' in Laurel E. Miller (ed.), *Framing the State in Times of Transition* (U.S. Institute of Peace, 2010), 350.

60 Chantal Mouffe, *On the Political* (Routledge, 2005), 8–13.

61 Mátyás Bencze, 'Minden héten háború' [Any Given Sunday] (2019) 23 *Fundamentum* 55, 58.

62 For the latest example of a governmental attack against a liberal agenda see Ábrahám Vass, 'Gov't to End "Prison Business" by Suspending Payment of Compensations for Poor Living Conditions' (*Hungary Today*, 16 January 2020) <https://hungarytoday.hu/govt-prison-business-suspend-compensation-poor-conditions/>, accessed 4 August 2020.

protect the rights of the citizens and the Rule of Law against a government tempted by authoritarianism.[63,64]

These views on the law and politics contributed to the democratic decline. Social liberals were always ready for compromise when it came to the appointment of candidates to constitutional judgeship or other important legal-institutional positions. Therefore, it could happen that the social-liberal parliamentary majority between 1994 and 1998 voluntarily limited its powers while holding a two-thirds majority. It established a parliamentary committee, in which parliamentary factions could delegate one MP, and the committee had the exclusively right to select candidates for constitutional judges.[65] This is why during that parliamentary term the fragmented right-wing opposition parties had four delegates in the committee, while governmental parties had only two MPs.

Right-wing politicians recognised the significant role the law plays in politics and also the political character of the legal practice. They could "use" the HCC in order to achieve their political goals by the "judicialization" of a part of the political conflict. The neutral, highly formalised legal language of the judgments of the court could hide the political motivation behind the text, and the authority of the court could legitimise the political efforts of the winning party by the authority of the court.[66] That is why the Fidesz party always made serious efforts to choose candidates whose political attitude was in line with its interests. They did it in a clever way, seeking conservative candidates who had a high professional reputation and had no direct relation with Fidesz. For example, between 2002 and 2010, the social-liberal coalition accepted the constitutional judge-candidates proposed by right-wing parties (and the re-election of constitutional judges who had previously voted

63 Zoltán Fleck, 'Majd az intézmények megvédik jogainkat?' [Will the Institutions Protect our Rights?] (*Élet és Irodalom*, 14 April 2006) <https://www.es.hu/cikk/2006-04-17/fleck-zoltan/majd-az-intezmenyek-megvedik-jogainkat.html>, accessed 2 August 2020; Bugarič (n 13) 190–3.

64 Because of the lack of a "healthy sense of danger" liberal-democrat thinkers, and other opinion-leaders, were the harshest critics of the social-liberal governments, paving the way for their political competitors to win the general election in 2010 by a two-thirds majority. For the credo of this highly critical attitude see Sándor Révész, 'Baráti? Tűz!' [Friendly? Fire!] (*HVG*, 5 November 2019) <https://hvg.hu/itthon/20191105_Revesz_Barati_Tuz>. According to Cas Mudde, this mentality of democrat intellectuals stemmed from their anti-political attitude acquired during socialism. Cas Mudde, 'In the Name of the Peasantry, the Proletariat, and the People: Populism in Eastern Europe' in Cas Mudde (ed.), *Democracies and Populist Challenge* (Palgrave Macmillan, 2002), 225–7.

65 Erdős Csaba, 'Az Alkotmánybíróság kontrollmechanizmusának változásai' [Changes in the Control Mechanism of the Constitutional Court] in Gábor Kecskés (ed.) *Doktori műhelytanulmányok* (Széchenyi István Egyetem Állam- és Jogtudományi Doktori Iskola, 2013), 137–41.

66 András Sajó already warned of this danger in 1990. Sajó (n 23) 338–9, 342.

against them in politically significant cases). This decision greatly contributed to the formation of a constitutional tribunal with a clear conservative majority. In 2007, the HCC proved its conservative political preference when it allowed the initiation of the demagogic "social-referendum" which, at least partly, led to the fatal weakening of the left-wing coalition.

The underestimation of the impact of legal institutes on the political field also resulted in the appointment of the new prosecutor general in 2006, when the left-wing governing parties elected a person who, in 2010, authorised criminal investigations against governmental politicians a few months before the general election. These criminal procedures – which in 2010 were suggesting that all left-wing politicians were corrupt – turned a large part of the public against the socialist and liberal parties. Years later, when these cases had already lost their political significance, criminal courts acquitted the vast majority of the defendants (or the cases were terminated at an earlier phase of the criminal procedure).[67]

It is also worth mentioning the story of the ex-chief justice László Sólyom, who despite the fact that his conservative political views were well-known, was elected as the head of state by the social-liberal majority parliament, (most of the liberal MPs of the social-liberal coalition did not vote, which is why Sólyom, supported by right-wing parties, triumphed over the socialist candidate).[68] Liberal MPs did not see that event as a political tragedy, because they believed that Sólyom was committed to the defence of human rights and the Rule of Law, and would exercise his political and legal power in a balanced way. Notwithstanding these expectations Sólyom, as head of state, used both his legal competence (by vetoing several politically significant parliamentary acts) and his symbolic power (as head of state he made speeches against the social-liberal government) in a marked confrontation with the left-wing government.[69]

These three examples illustrate that social-liberal governments did not take the political character of legal institutions seriously. It seems that they believed in the neutrality and objectivity of the application of law. One might

67 Erika Pálmai, 'Szinte teljes kudarc az "elszámoltatás", Orbán erre az esetre csúnya jövőt jósolt' [The "Accounting" is Almost a Complete Fiasco – Orbán Predicted a Nasty Future for that Case] (*HVG*, 18 December 2016) <https://www.fecsego.eu/2016/12/18/szinte-teljes-kudarc-az-elszamoltatas-orban-erre-az-esetre-csunya-jovot-josolt/>, accessed 3 August 2020.

68 '2005-ös köztársaságielnök-választás Magyarországon' [The Election of the Head of State in Hungary in 2005] <https://hu.wikipedia.org/wiki/2005-%C3%B6s_k%C3%B6zt%C3%A1rsas%C3%A1gieln%C3%B6k-v%C3%A1laszt%C3%A1s_Magyarorsz%C3%A1gon>, accessed 3 August 2020.

69 Molnár Benedek, 'A határig el kellett mennem – Interjú Sólyom Lászlóval – II. rész' [I Had to Push it to the Limits – interview with László Sóloym – 2nd part] (*Ars Boni*, 9 December 2013) <https://arsboni.hu/solyom_interjureszlet_2/>, accessed 3 August 2020.

formulate that their driving idea was "law is law and only law" instead of saying: "law is politics."

Of course, this is not to say that the political mistakes the leftist parties made in personnel policy are direct consequences of their liberal view on law and politics; however, it does seem plausible that the liberal thought on the nature of law made them less vigilant to the risks of their decisions. It was the political right-wing which has been fully aware of the true nature of legal institutions and the new Fidesz-led government appointed a new head of state and prosecutor general as well as changing the members of the HCC as soon as this was possible. Although the majority of these actors had a conservative political preference, they were autonomous thinkers, thus dangerous to the neo-authoritarian political agenda. The current head of state and the prosecutor general were former Fidesz party members who had proved their loyalty to the party many times before they were appointed to these apex positions. In a few years the parliament, where Fidesz has had a supermajority, packed the HCC, filling it with lawyers who no longer decide against the government (only in a very few, politically insignificant cases, thus pretending that constitutional review is alive in Hungary).[70] Moreover, to be on the safe side, Fidesz drastically reduced the HCC's competence (by abolishing the *actio popularis* against laws and by extracting financial laws from the scope of constitutional review).[71] These steps were presented by theoreticians of Fidesz as the triumph of "political constitutionalism" over "legal constitutionalism."[72]

One of the characteristic features of the above-outlined (and many other) governmental actions is that all of them have been executed in a legally

70 Gábor Halmai, 'In memoriam magyar alkotmánybíráskodás. A pártos alkotmánybíróság első éve' [In Memoriam Constitutional Review. The First Year of the Partisan Constitutional Court] (2014) 18 *Fundamentum* 36.

71 Gábor Halmai, 'Dismantling Constitutional Review in Hungary' [2019] *Rivista di Diritti Comparati* 31. It is only the ordinary courts which so far have been able to resist the neo-authoritarian pressure. However, there have been tendencies in the past decade that some judges decide cases in a way that pleases the populace and in line with the political agenda of the Fidesz-led government. See Mátyás Bencze 'Explaining Judicial Populism in Hungary – a Legal Realist Approach' [2020] *Iuris Dictio* 83. Paradoxically, the formalist legal argumentation which is common in CEE legal systems, facilitates judges following a hidden political agenda. Formalist legal arguments can generate the illusion of the professionalism of their reasoning among the audience even if there is no logical connection between the arguments and the merit of the decision. See Zdeněk Kühn, 'Worlds Apart: Western and Central European Judicial Culture at the onset of European Enlargement' (2004) 52 *Am. J. Comp. Law* 531, 566.

72 Ágnes Kovács, 'Fényevők? A hazai alkotmányelmélet esete a politikai konstitucionalizmussal' [Living on Light? The Case of Domestic Constitutional Theory with the Political Constitutionalism] (2015) 19 *Fundamentum* 19.

impeccable manner.[73] The parliament always adopted the laws which created the necessary legal framework for their political actions. A legal community that was socialised to internalise the formalist understanding of law could not have the conceptual apparatus to criticise the legality of neo-authoritarian endeavours. Critical legal studies, discredited due to its Marxist roots, could have had the potential to reveal the political character of these legal steps, as well as the politics of legal decision makers, before 2010 when it might not have been too late.

7.5 Conclusion

In the course of modernisation in Hungary, legal thinking was based on the assumption that legal practice is a neutral professional activity where the focus is on formal legality and not on the idea that the state is subject to the law. After the socialist period the dominant liberal view, popular among Hungarian democrats, strengthened the myth of the objectivity and neutrality of the law and legal practice, which was a natural reaction to the state-centred socialist approach to law. The dominance of this view made left-wing parties and their supporters unable to see the deeply political nature of legal decision making.[74] This blind spot has led to several political mistakes: they did not take into consideration the political preferences of the individuals they elected to several crucial legal positions (constitutional justice, prosecutor general). These ill-chosen political steps later took their toll and led to the fatal weakening of democratic political parties because the right-wing parties, who broke the unwritten rules of constitutional democracies (while they observed the "letter of the law"), could utilise their realist view of the legal practice.

73 Kim Lane Scheppele, 'Constitutional Coups and Judicial Review: How Transnational Institutions Can Strengthen Peak Courts at Times of Crisis (With Special Reference to Hungary)' (2014) 23 *Transnat'l L. & Contemp. Probs* 51.

74 See also Tacik, chapter 1 in this volume.

Chapter 8

Who Stands in The Mirror and Who Stares Back

Traditions of Populism in Slovakia

Peter Čuroš

8.1 Introduction

As a living dead, the spectre of populism, haunting Central and Eastern Europe (CEE),[1] was supposed to be buried and overcome by the rise of liberal constitutionalism. However, society has brought the spectre back. According to Max Weber, a period of charismatic authority occurs when a community bestows on an individual or a body the magical aura of charisma.[2] Carl Schmitt sees such a period as a revival of the sovereign.[3] Using the Lacanian metaphor of the reflection, a society in crisis, filled with anxieties of unstable times ahead, sees its reflection in the mirror as an object that does not possess all these anxieties.[4] Often, a figure or collective body shows the way out of this crisis, be it an economic, cultural, or identity crisis.

I claim that the current politics of populism in the CEE region are the effect, not the cause, of crisis, because the demand for populism is already rooted in popular sentiments, and populist politics are just a reflection of the state of society. The atmosphere in CEE societies is welcoming to politicians who are ready to answer this call: a populist leader is called to recreate the signifying chain, a never ending line of signifiers, that establishes a quest for society to reach. However, this quest must be anchored with the goals. Liberal constitutionalism, teamed up with capitalism, could provide a signifying chain based on constant consumption and progress. However, it did not provide enough opportunities for filling the desire for everybody, and this led to the feeling of economic precarity instead of security for many. The

1 See Rafał Mańko, Przemysław Tacik, and Cosmin Cercel, 'Introduction: Law, Populism, and the Political in Semi-Peripheral Central and Eastern Europe,' in this volume.

2 Max Weber, *On Charisma and Institution Building* (Chicago IL: University of Chicago Press, 1968).

3 Carl Schmitt, *Political Theology: Four Chapters on the Concept of Sovereignty* (University of Chicago Press, 2021).

4 Jacques Lacan, 'The Mirror Stage as Formative of the Function of the I as Revealed in Psychoanalytic Experience,' *Reading French Psychoanalysis* (Abingdon: Routledge, 2010).

DOI: 10.4324/9781032624464-9

transition to imported institutions that are stable in the western democracies after 1989 has been destined to fail, as the expectations of what the ordinary person desired have been different than what the liberal democracy delivered.

The disappointment of the masses has been transferred towards elites, who failed in governing, as "subjects supposed to have known." The elites were assigned to govern and provide "justice for all" and when the expected outcomes did not arrive, the elites were to blame, perceived as despicable and corrupt. When the call of disappointment is answered, the populist strategy of politics starts, and once the wheel of populism is put in motion, it is hard to stop it, until later catharsis of the society, that starts the cycle again – starting with remorse for atrocities committed and creating rules that will govern to the same decline of stepping out of the rules to solve another crisis.

A shift towards populism is nowadays perceived as "democratic backsliding."[5] The term originates in the biblical apostasy: it is the very same concept that originally represented an act of falling away from the faith. However, it was not pure faith that was affected. This fall meant a decline of trust in the righteousness of the authority. That the authority is powerful as it claims to be. This process starts from doubting authority's power and ends in doubting the existence of the authority itself. A similar phenomenon is hidden in the term today. It is about falling away from the faith in a liberal constitutional democracy, its elites, and the rules which maintain it. Furthermore, the very term "backsliding" denies the notion of liberalism that the way of history is a straightforward way of progress, whereby liberal democracy was perceived as the final stage of history.[6] If there is no way further, and liberal democracy deteriorates, then the explanation must necessarily be – the society "slides back." Is it necessary, though, to change the view on the process of history? Is not the shift experienced in CEE just a way forward in Hegelian dialectics? Every systemic change targets the lack of the system.[7] The contradictions that occur between philosophy and reality are the roots of that change. Is the current "backsliding" just a way forward attacking the contradictions within the existing ideology of liberal capitalism?

8.2 Alienation as the Crisis

It is nothing new to say that a crisis is rooted in some kind of alienation. What philosophically would be called alienation could be, in an economic perspective, seen as decline or in politics as corruption. In other words, being

5 See more on backsliding in Laurent Pech and Kim Lane Scheppele, 'Illiberalism Within: Rule of Law Backsliding in the EU' (2017) 19 *Cambridge Yearbook of European Legal Studies* 3.

6 Francis Fukuyama, *The End of History and the Last Man* (New York: Simon and Schuster, 2006).

7 M. De Kesel, 'Act Without Denial: Slavoj Žižek on Totalitarianism, Revolution and Political Act' (2004) 56 *Studies in East European Thought* 299, at 318.

alienated in the broadest sense is not fulfilling the "socially constructed as natural" goal. The problem of alienation in philosophy has been handled as a gradual separation of subject and object. For Hegel, history begins at the stage of an absolute spirit defined by the totality of subject and object.[8] In the second stage, subject and object become detached. There is the material world without consciousness and consciousness with limited access to the material world. That is the moment of alienation. The alienation might be overcome when the consciousness becomes in complete control of its subjectivity within objective conditions. Then subject and object will become united again. We are looking for the totality of the subject and object not only through individual life but, according to Hegel, through the whole existence of humankind.

On the other hand, young Karl Marx understood alienation as capitalism's consequence on the individual. He recognised four types of alienation: 1) from self, 2) from work, 3) from nature 4) from others.[9] The individual is alienated from itself because of creating a process of value for ourselves.[10] It serves as an instrument – a cog in the machine for the profit of others. It is alienated from others because instead of seeing other members of society as fellows, it sees them as competition.[11] It is alienated from work of lack of ownership over the product of work.[12] Finally, it is alienated from nature because it perceives nature as a source of material which goal is exploitation.[13] All in all, the individual feels alienated and does not feel at home in the world. The subject will unify with an object in the community, where its position will become fully embedded. Misinterpreting Marxism and the 20th century's totalitarian regimes made frantic attempts to fight that "alienation," break that resistance, and reconcile man with his "true" sociability.[14]

In Lacan's theory, alienation is the essential quality of the subject. The subject emerges via stages of psychological ontogenesis. In the Real, the subject is in unity with an object. It is only via the acquisition of language when the individual starts to understand the object as detached from the subject. The Symbolic and Imaginary registers form the individual's perception of reality as opposed to the Real register. The reality is a fiction that protects from the yawning chasm of the Real. The Real is the abyss of meaning. The Imaginary and Symbolic registers cover the Real and give meaning to the

8 Georg Wilhelm Friedrich Hegel, *The Phenomenology of Spirit*, transl. A.V. Miller (Oxford: Clarendon Press, 1979), 58.
9 Karl Marx and Friedrich Engels, *The Economic and Philosophic Manuscripts of 1844 and the Communist Manifesto* (Amherst NY: Prometheus Books, 2009), 69.
10 Ibid. 77.
11 Ibid. 80.
12 Ibid. 71.
13 Ibid. 76.
14 De Kesel, 'Act Without Denial,' 315.

objects. Outside Imaginary and Symbolic, the meaning does not exist. We are only dealing with an "unreal," "virtual," and "symbolic" world, a world "castrated" from the real.[15] After being covered by Imaginary and Symbolic register, what persists from the Real is the lack and desire resulting from this lack. It is a lack of unity with an object. According to Lacan, alienation is embedded in the fact that the subject defined by desire cannot know and control its object of desire – *objet petit a.*[16] The signs signifying the object of desire are only attached to other signs, and there is no possibility to attain the ultimate object of desire. The individual is doomed to be the subject of signifiers. In Lacan, there is no emancipatory way out of being subjected. Behind every signifier, another signifier awaits. The desire is a remainder unity, every subject once experienced, and it will jump from signifier to signifier without being satisfied by an encounter with the Real.

While Marx deems alienation as the price for modern life, in Lacan, alienation is not a symptom only of modern life but of every social life. Alienation, or this feeling of not being how it is supposed to be, is inevitable. Subjects are alienated from the unity with the world the moment they enter the language. Since that moment, the process of alienation will only be stronger, as the consciousness finds out that signifiers are only attached to other signifiers and are not attached to the signifieds. Every individual is stuck in the loop of chasing signifiers. However, the problem appears imminent when the chain of signifiers breaks. At that moment, the individual becomes aware of their alienation, and it becomes unbearable, especially when confronted with social expectations of what it is supposed to be and do, but the social reality does not allow it to be or do so.

The feeling of alienation, the condition of the broken chain of signification, or in other words, the feeling of being stuck, establishes crisis. A crisis is a state defined by stagnation.[17] It is a moment in which the old mode of thinking or action cannot be followed anymore because the problem faced is not capable of being solved by the current modus operandi. The crisis in liberal capitalism is based on the fact that while some part of the population feels less alienated as they can connect their chain of signification to consumption or professional development, a large group within society does not have the conditions to do so. Their signifying chain is stuck. While the ideological fantasy[18] of liberal capitalism encourages them to chain with consumption and progress, the very actuality of their lives does not offer instruments to fulfill

15 Ibid., 301.

16 The ultimate object of desire is an object, which the Other – the system, the ideology, the society, etc. – has originally locked out in order to keep desire going. Ibid., 324.

17 See more on the concept of crisis in R. Koselleck and M. W. Richter, 'Crisis' (2006) 67 *Journal of the History of Ideas* 357.

18 Ideological fantasy is the deepest framework of belief that structures how subjects and political community comes to terms with what exceeds its norms and boundaries.

this goal. Therefore they feel alienated. They cannot connect to the reality that is presented to them.

The desire is still present, and it waits for new incentives towards signification. Every individual has that insatiable lack that is defined by desire. It is the desire for unity, unity with objective conditions. However, with entering the language, the subject's desire for unity with objective conditions was blocked by the otherness – the language itself. After this moment, the subject's desire will follow signifiers within language that represent fulfillment. Instead of the jouissance of primordial unity with an object, in the Symbolic and Imaginary, the subject perceives jouissance when following the object of desire provided by the big Other. Whatever we do, we remain ensnared within a virtual world of signifiers.[19]

The subject's desire is to be seen as complete, in social conditions – to be what is expected from the individual to be. The object that desire follows is constructed by the symbolic order – big Other. The discourse of the Other creates the object which the subject desires.[20] The big Other is in the language itself, the language that constitutes the subject. The language that speaks through the subject, where the subject is a passive element. It thinks, speaks, and behaves only within the structure created by the language. It is a subject constituted by the language.

The big Other is the trans-subjective gaze: 'A twofold mediation is at work: who I am is not simply mediated by a second, but by what this second hypothesizes about me via a third.'[21] It represents not merely what the group members think of the individual but what group members think other group members think of the individual. The big Other is the domain of the unconscious. It is a symbolic figure in front of whom the subject maintains appearances. It is non-present third in every dialogue, which determines the ego and the desire. Therefore, the desire of the subject is nothing else other than the reflection of the desire of the Other. The awareness of the empty signifiers is sliding on the signifiers from unconscious to conscious. However, the chain of the signifiers is neverending, and there are always other signifiers behind the unconscious curve.

8.3 Ideology

The chain of signification is a metonymic line of signifiers that the subjects misrecognise as standing for signified objects. Every once in a while, there is

19 De Kesel, 'Act Without Denial,' 302.

20 Jacques Lacan, *Seminar XX, On Feminine Sexuality: The Limits of Love and Knowledge, 1972–1973* (New York: Norton, 1999), 142.

21 D. Hook, 'Towards a Lacanian Group Psychology: The Prisoner's Dilemma and the Trans-Subjective' (2013) 43 *Journal for the Theory of Social Behaviour* 115, 119.

a metaphor within the metonymic chain. This metaphor is a manifestation of the object of desire. In the metaphor, we still cannot reach the object of desire. However, at least for a while, we can see it. This metaphor is called a quilting point or *point de capiton*. The movement of the signifier is a movement of desire. The quilting point or anchoring point is the part of the chain where signifier and signified seem to be knotted together. Hence, there is no constant slippage of signified under signifier:[22] '*The result of the paternal metaphor is to tie a specific meaning to particular words without regard to an absolute referent.*'[23] The quilting point is when the signifier within the Symbolic order seems to be attached to the signified.[24] It seems that a quilting point is a place where the Symbolic and the Real are connected. It is a point at which a short circuit stops the indefinite sliding of signifiers between a signifier and its signified. It is a task for ideological fantasy to establish quilting points. To make the ideology work properly, the signifier in the imaginary must be materialised and sent away to make the signifying chain continue after the desire moves to another signifier. The subject is then always in the process of becoming.

Subjects are unconscious of the what is the *objet petit a*. It is hidden behind the neverending line of signifiers. In politics, subjects transfer the desire to the strong political figure, just like the big Other, because "the Other is supposed to know." In other words: "we do not know, but you figure it out what we want." And populism responds. It aspires to give people identities that liberal constitutionalism refused to. It will establish quilting points that determine their position in the world and make them worthy of the gaze of the big Other. To do so, the populist has to convince those who ask to be convinced with ideological fantasy.

In the liberal system, from its nature, the ideology is not built on some strong central source, and it misses quilting points. It is the burden of the individual to slide on the signifiers of desire. Basically, in liberal democracy, there is no material body that stipulates the values and what should be considered the goal for the individual to attain. This space is left for sources of ideology different than the state. In capitalist economies, therefore, desire is often led by consumption. However, what to do, when the individual cannot afford to consume? It is led towards connecting signifiers of consumption. However, in reality, it becomes stuck in this chain.

What the populist politician does in such a moment of crisis of signification is that it changes the appearance of the big Other. Changing the rhetoric

22 Jacques Lacan, *The Seminar of Jacques Lacan, Book 3: The Psychoses 1955–1956* (New York: Norton, 1993), 167.

23 Bruce Fink, *A Clinical Introduction to Lacanian Psychoanalysis: Theory and Technique* (Cambridge, MA: Harvard University Press, 1999).

24 Slavoj Žižek, *The Sublime Object of Ideology* (London: Verso, 2008), 112.

of public discourse changes the quilting points within signifying chain to which the subject can relate. In other words, this shift changes what the big Other expects from the subject, and in this new framework of quilting points, it gives subjects the opportunity of being worth of big Other's gaze. It gives them a refurbished object of desire that will make their current stuck desire move. We need a slippery world of signifiers, and subjects are desperate to get it on track.[25]

Two contemporary approaches to ideology are: first, announcing the end of ideology, that the capitalist liberal democratic constitutionalism is the best system that will not be overcome. The second one wants to reassert the pertinence of ideology as liberal capitalism does not put its values under critique.[26] The former mistreats ideology as some propaganda that it is an influence of the state to fool the subject and make the population subjected to power by this ruse. However, such a view leaves out a lot of the influences that determine the subject. The influence of the state institutions is only one of many. Not even totalitarian states at the peak of their existence could eliminate other sources of influence on the subject. If the state occupies the whole symbolical order, then it is possible to talk about the state as the only source of ideology. On the other hand, we can see a competition of various sources that create the ideology that constitutes the subject. A state is one of them. And in some periods, it is becoming stronger source than in other periods.

Ideologies are political discourses whose primary function is not to make correct theoretical statements about political reality but to orient subjects toward the shared reality. The ideology that is perceived as the "natural way how things are" is essential for social life. The subjects must be convinced that the regime, how it is, is the best possible and therefore natural. And therefore, unconscious of the inherent flaws and artificiality. The regime must provide the subject with a complete narrative of the identity within the system. Every successful regime must create its narrative around a sublime object that is impossible to grasp but covers everything as a master signifier. It is an object that every political regime uses as a reason to transgress any other duty or sacrifice its own life for the sake of this object.

8.4 Who Stands in the Mirror and Who Stares Back

A demand for populism is like an immunity reaction of the society when a crisis of signification happens. Populism itself is a symptom of alienation from the meaning within the society. In the fight to overcome this alienation, populism provides the solution to stepping in the law as an autonomous

25 De Kesel, 'Act Without Denial,' 302.

26 Joseph Glynos, 'The Grip of Ideology: A Lacanian Approach to the Theory of Ideology' (2001) 6 *Journal of Political Ideologies* 191, 192.

system and changing the rules. It is a strategy of changing the quilting points of ideological fantasy in favour of those who cannot relate with the current ideology. The way how to do so is to step outside the rules and create an exception. It means to diminish the law as an autonomous system and maintain the exception.[27]

The rise of populist and a lack of liberal ideology echoes in what Böckenforde claimed 45 years ago, that 'the liberal (secularized state lives by prerequisites which it cannot guarantee itself. This is the great adventure it has undertaken for freedom's sake.' The demand for a populist approach is directly connected with dissatisfaction with a myth of liberalism. The representative of the rules of liberalism is an autonomous system of law. This system of rules to which creation and interpretation only elites have access reminds Marx's notion of the superstructure that maintains the control of elites over masses or that 'legal constitutionalism fall short, reducing the constitution to an elite instrument, especially in countries with weak civil societies and weak political party systems.'[28]

Legal autonomy is studied as the extent to which the law constitutes a closed system with an internal dynamic, as a self-referential system.[29] Kelsen's "Pure Theory of Law" is a well-known example. Legal autonomy is also understood as a normative ideal of independent legal institutions within liberal political theories on the rule of law or the Rechtsstaat. The concept of an autonomous law is a crucial concept of liberal constitutionalism, as a system of rules that can govern a community without external interference. It is a very centre of the idea of the rule of law. It is a social theory that makes sense of the circularity of legal authority – that it is a law that decides what is to count as law.

The people in a crisis require their representatives to step outside the rules. Solving the crisis requires not being bound by the rules that led to it. Judicial constitutionalism must be averted, as nothing should constrain "the will of the (pure) people."[30] The populist, if willing to fulfill the call from the electorate, must therefore get rid of courts, or better, amend the professional per-

27 Carl Schmitt, *Political Theology: Four Chapters on the Concept of Sovereignty* (Cambridge, MA: MIT Press, 1985).

28 Wojciech Sadurski, 'Transitional Constitutionalism: Simplistic and Fancy Theories' in Adam Czarnota, Martin Krygier, and Wojciech Sadurski (eds), *Rethinking the Rule of Law after Communism* (Budapest: CEU Press, 2005), 23.

29 On legal autonomy see, e.g., Gunter Teubner, *Law as an Autopoietic System* (Oxford-Cambridge: Blackwell Publishers, 1993); Niklas Luhman, *Law as a Social System* (Oxford: Oxford University Press, 2004).

30 See more on critique of judicial constitutionalism, Cas Mudde and Cristobal Rovira Kaltwasser, 'Exclusionary vs. Inclusionary Populism: Comparing Contemporary Europe and Latin America' (2013) 48 *Government and Opposition* 147, and Mudde and Rovira Kaltwasser, *Populism: A Very Short Introduction* (Oxford: Oxford University Press, 2017), 81.

sonnel to secure a favourable outcome of the control of stepping out of rules. To change the ideology, the populist leader must get rid of the element that guards ideology and status quo by nature of the profession. The judiciary is the litmus paper of the appearance of populism because it is its first target.

In Central and Eastern Europe, it is visible that populism is back if it has ever left. The first symptom of populism on the rise is the step against the judiciary. We could hear this quite recently in Hungary how the populist speech called to abandon the concept of judicial independence when the Speaker of the Parliament László Kövér announced that '150 years ago the question was whether the Hungarian state wants to guarantee the independence of the judges. Today the question is whether the Hungarian judges want to ensure the independence of the state.'[31] Similarly, we could witness in Poland when Justice Minister Zbigniew Ziobro said: 'The judiciary had 25 years to purify itself and conduct reforms. And they have done nothing, so they lost their opportunity. Today the democratically elected politicians need to change it. Repair of the judicial system is the most important issue for which the voters elected us.'[32] Finally, in Slovakia, parliament proposed control over the judiciary:

> Taking into account the fact that the judicial status, respectively the judiciary as such does not enjoy public trust to the extent that it would guarantee the general acceptability of the judiciary as a guarantor not only of legality but also of justice and of judges as professional and moral authorities, the judiciary itself must take real responsibility for this situation.[33]

When a systemic change is on the horizon, the government of rules, or the rule of law, must be limited in favour of exception. When doing so, the first target is judicial independence. Judicial independence is the golden calf of liberal constitutionalism. It serves liberal constitutionalism as the Lacanian *objet petit a*, which is impossible to attain, as there will always be another way to amend and improve it. For liberal constitutionalism, the legal system to be effective, it must be trusted by the subjects of law, on the grounds of fairness. In the society claiming that equality in the eyes of the law, it is essential to provide that the arbiter deciding upon the conflict of the parties

31 E. S. Balogh, 'Soon Enough, Hungarian Judicial Independence Will Exist Only in History Books,' *Hungarian Spectrum* (24 April 2019) <https://hungarianspectrum.org/2019/04/24/soon-enough-hungarian-judicial-independence-will-exist-only-in-history-books/>, accessed 11 October 2021.

32 'Zbigniew Ziobro: Nie cofnę się w walce o sprawiedliwość' [I will not turn back in the fight for justice], <https://perma.cc/E4T9-PNYR>, accessed 11 October 2021.

33 Explanatory Report to the Constitutional Act No. 161/2014 Coll. 'Proposal' <https://www.nrsr.sk/web/Dynamic/DocumentPreview.aspx?DocID=397222>, accessed 10 October 2021.

is impartial. In such an ideological fantasy, subjects must believe that no one stands above the law. The arbiter will stay impartial and will uphold the rule of law. The system of law will maintain autonomy without any need for intervention from outside. All the limitations for any political actor willing to influence the arbiter are the instruments of judicial independence.[34] To sum up, in liberal constitutionalism, the administration and the parliament accept to be under judicial control, either of the administrative or constitutional judiciary.

Populism, on the other hand, builds its popularity on the capacity to enter the rules and application of the rules when perceived as unjust. To deliver promises given, populists need support or at least ignorance from the courts. Political power represented by the parliaments and administration needs to have control over the judiciary. Such control ensures that the courts will not turn down their policies, leading to the shift of quilting points within ideology. In other words, a systemic change. This seems to be quite an "evergreen" move in the CEE region following the Austro-Hungaian Empire, through democratic and socialist Czechoslovakia, until nowadays. Short periods of liberal constitutionalism change for long periods of the strong sovereign, whose typical move is to change the judiciary's position within the system. Now we have a look closer at the strategies of the populists after World War II.

8.5 A Tradition of Populism in Slovakia and Interference into Judicial Independence

Not long after the coup of the Communist Party in Czechoslovakia, the judiciary lost its independence and changed its position in the structure of power. It was a natural step when the ideology needed to be changed quickly. Nothing can stand in the way of the shift of the quilting points. The new Minister of Justice, Alexej Čepička,[35] announced the need 'to remodel the judiciary into a weapon ... put it in service of working people.'[36] From the branch of power, which was supposed to control the executive power and decide on disputes and breaches of law, it became a branch furthering the

34 John A. Ferejohn, Pasquale Pasquino, 'The Countermajoritarian Opportunity' (2010) 13 *University of Pennsylviania Journal of Constitutional Law* 353.

35 Alexej Čepička – Minister of Justice of Czechoslovakia 25 February 1948 to 25 April 1950, from 1950–1956 Minister of National Defense, after 1956 was dismissed from political and Party positions due to his political activities in previous years. In 1963 expelled from the Communist Party for 'major part in organizing political trials against Communists in the personality cult period.'

36 J. Vorel et al., 'Československá justice v letech 1948–1953 v dokumentech II' (2003) 8 *Sešity úřadu dokumentace a vyšetřování zločinu komunismu* 360.

goals of the Party that represented the interest of the whole community. Such a shift happened in several steps and various ways.

With the emergence of new tasks of the regime, the judiciary also got a new role – 'to help to re-educate our man.' The reports delivered from the criminal trials were supposed to be 'detailed and convincing, representing the professional level and real democracy of our people's judiciary.'[37] Trials labelled "political" were supposed to be 'evidence of the existence of anti-state powers and ought to highlight the class struggle that is going on. The trials were supposed to demask the real nature of the anti-state elements and reveal their motivation to their criminal activity, elucidate the connection to imperialists – their employers.'[38]

The role of the law changed into an instrument of the interest of the working class. The methods of delivering justice also needed amends. Giving the sovereign the power to mediate the outcomes of the proceeding "telephone justice" system enabled control of the decisions before they were delivered. Decisions on politically sensitive cases were handled by "collective work" – the meetings of political deputies with deputies of courts and the prosecution. The institute of the "Security Committee," which consisted of five members who became known as the "Security Five,"[39] was essential in subordinating the judiciary. The performance of judges was put to the limelight as well. Czechoslovak judge Otto Ulč, who had personal experience with the judiciary in the 1950s and who emigrated to West Germany and later to the US, writes about the quotas that all the judges had to meet and how 'the entire spectrum of judicial activities was translated into norms, specifying the hours and even minutes required for execution.'[40]

Aside from the Ministry's direct interference, several indirect instruments were used by the Communist Party to affect judicial decisions. One of the steps toward acquiring complete obedience to the justice system was to put it under the prosecutor's office's control. It provided the Ministry an opportunity to use the prosecutor's office as an extended hand in guiding the court toward preferred decision making.[41] This was also why the judiciary's purges were not that imminent and visible, as the change within the personnel in the prosecutor's office.

This personnel issue was solved early after February 1948. It was not in the Party's interest to rely on judges and prosecutors loyal to the previous

37 Ibid.
38 Ibid.
39 Political committee coordinating cooperation of security forces in the region and regional Party organisations.
40 Otto Ulč, *The Judge in a Communist State: A View from Within* (Athens OH: Ohio University Press, 1972), 42–8.
41 SÚA [State Central Archive], f. ÚV KSČ [collection Central Committee of Communist Party of Czechoslovakia], Security Committee, vol.. I, unit. T 4474/56.

political regime, but it seemed impossible to replace them all. After World War II, the personnel situation was already difficult when the Czechoslovak judiciary was missing half of its pre-war judges.[42] The State Secretary at the Justice Ministry commented on the situation: 'old bourgeoise court organization, laws on the judiciary from bourgeoise era and the vast majority of judges and prosecutors politically confused, part of them even hostile to our regime.'

Because of the lack of politically loyal and reliable judges, extraordinary law schools were established after February 1948. The goal was to solve the problem of the lack of personnel and secure political control over the courts. Therefore, the initial purge was not as dramatic as expected,[43] as the modification of personnel took longer than in the 1950s.[44] Furthermore, the Party did not aim to purge but secure a strong control of the judiciary. Therefore, the graduates of the so-called Law School of Working Class[45] were mostly filling the positions of prosecutors or presidents of the courts.[46] The "Law school of Working Class" consisted of the ex-proletarians, the only group with power and political importance. It was known as 'the mill to convert carefully selected proletarians with no prior advanced education into "lawyers" in less than one year.'[47] These graduates gradually took most of the positions of political significance, mainly within the Ministry of Justice, the Supreme Court, and in the prosecutor's office.[48] 'By the end of the 1950s, eighteen out of nineteen Regional Prosecutors came from PŠP…in the case of the chairs of the nineteen Regional Courts, there was no exception.'[49]

Moreover, since 1957 the tenured positions of judges were abolished, and elections were installed to select new judges. This step helped to finalise the personnel change and confirm the subordination of the judiciary to political influence. Political bodies elected judges, including the National Assembly or

42 See O. Motejl, 'Soudnictví a jeho sprava' in Michal Bobek et al. (eds), *Komunistické právo v Československu* (2009), 814; Zdenek Kühn, 'Socialisticka justice' in Bobek et al. (eds), *Komunisticke*, 825.

43 Zdeněk. Kühn, in 'Socialisticka justice' mentions that 10% left the judiciary at this point, In the statement of Karel Klos, State Secretary of the Ministry of Justice between 1948 and 1952, there is the same number – approximately 10% of the judges. SÚA, f. ÚV KSČ, Piller Committee, (1. dubna 1963), uncategorised.

44 Ulč, *The Judge*, 16.

45 Vorel et al., 'Československá Justice,' 156.

46 Report on Courses of the Law School of Working Class and Re-Location Of The Cadres Within Judiciary (August 5 1950), SÚA, f. ÚV KSČ, Ústřední dělnická škola, a. j. 38.

47 Ulč, *The Judge*, 9.

48 Ibid.,.47.

49 Ibid., 9.

local party committees,[50] and were nominated by the National Front.[51] First, in 1957,[52] the tenure was three years, then extended to four years in 1964,[53] and finally set at ten years in 1969.[54] The short-term and recurring "retention elections" allowed political bodies to clear the judiciary of judges who did not conform to the Party's expectations and maintain control over personnel within the judiciary.

The discontinuity with the previous political regime is apparent. The latter period despised its predecessor. Therefore in the initial years of the regime, a revolutionary approach towards law prevailed. The explanatory document on the criminal code adopted in 1950 is explicit in this matter: 'The role of the criminal code is to contribute to the degradation of the reaction effectively, and it must serve as a sharp knife of the working people against all enemies.'[55] The position of the sovereign – the Communist Party, strengthened and the judiciary causally became what is expected from the judiciary in an authoritarian system – an 'executive mechanism of political bodies and state security.'[56] Such a system seems, from the point of view of liberal constitutionalism, like standing upside-down. No separation of power, judicial independence, or legal certainty is necessary when the strong sovereign can decide on the exception anytime. This Party's definition of fundamental rights is explicit in its exceptional character: 'Fundamental rights are by the socialist state stipulated, and in the Constitution is written an option that allows every citizen to choose the ways and limits of their behavior and to use the benefits of the system in the personal or public interest.'[57] The rights apply to everybody, under the condition that the socialist state recognises them as legitimate. The judge does not interpret what an individual's rights encompass but rather guess what the sovereign would prefer.

50 Act on election of judges §§ 2-5, 36/1957 Coll.
51 During the communist era in Czechoslovakia (1948–1989), the National Front was the vehicle for control of all political and social activity by the Communist Party of Czechoslovakia. These elections were just confirmation of Party candidates.
52 Act. no. 36/1957 Coll. § 2. (election of the judges for the period of three years), Act. No. 36/1964 Coll. Par. 39 (for four years),
53 Act. No. 36/1964 Coll. § 39 (for four years).
54 Act no. 156/1969 Coll. § 40 (prolonged the period to ten years).
55 Explanatory document on Criminal Code no. 86/1950 Coll. NS RČS 1948–1954, Press 160, Part no. 4, https://psp.cz/eknih/1948ns/tisky/t0160_04.htm, accessed 5 February 2021.
56 Piller Committee, SÚA, f. ÚV KSČ, k. 19.
57 David L'vovich Zlatopol'skiĭ and Stanislav Zdobinský, *Světová socialistická soustava a státní výstavba v evropských socialistických zemích socialisticka soustava a statni vystavba v evropskych socialistickych zemich* (Praha: Orbis, 1977), 293.

8.6 After 1989 – Is the Sovereign Gone or Just Hiding?

After the turmoil in 1989, populism took a different direction. It led to the revolution from state socialism to liberal constitutionalism but strongly competed with nationalism and authoritarianism, without any inherent value that it would lean-to. All of these three directions were capitalist in economics and right-wing in politics. It became apparent that the newborn system would be built on the principles and values missing in the previous system. It became Hegel's antithesis. While to Communist Party system was built on a strong position of the central power of the state, after the revolution was the central government so weak that the country became a hostage in the hands of powerful groups, whose leaders were often in prison before 1989, however not as dissidents, but primarily petty criminals. While the Communist Party held back the nationalism within the non-existent federacy, the outburst of nationalism after 1989 became one of the main reasons for Czechoslovakia's dissolution. Moreover, while the desire for consumption was limited before 1989, it became the object of desire in the new regime. Slovakia struggled between these three directions from the dissolution of federacy with Czechia until the election in 1998. After the 1998 election, when Vladimír Mečiar was defeated, liberal constitutionalism started its quest in Slovakia. A little bit later than in Hungary, Poland, and Czechia, the accession processes to NATO and the EU accelerated the democratic transition, and Slovakia entered both NATO and the EU together with its neighbours.

Now, let us have a look, how it affected the perception of the law's autonomy. Between 1998 and 2005, Slovakia implemented substantive reforms to strengthen judicial independence, which became a central focus of the EU after adopting the EU Copenhagen Criteria.[58] As the EU claimed to be built on a willingness to share values,[59] the candidate countries had to meet specific requirements before they could join. Slovakia worked enthusiastically to achieve an independent judiciary to fulfill the accession criteria. Deciding for the Rule of Law and implementing all required checks and balances was an attempt to join the western countries in their common effort towards creating a law as autonomous system, that could be more trustworthy, as it would be able to function independently on the politics in power.

Regarding legal autonomy, Slovakia adopted all the required institutional frameworks and adhered to all the significant international recommendations designed to safeguard judicial independence. The critical powers in the

58 Cristina E. Parau, *The Drive for Judicial Supremacy* (Berlin: Springer, 2012), 619.

59 Article 2 of the Treaty on European Union: 'The Union is founded on the values of respect for human dignity, freedom, democracy, equality, the rule of law and respect for human rights, including the rights of persons belonging to minorities. These values are common to the Member States in a society in which pluralism, non-discrimination, tolerance, justice, solidarity and equality between women and men prevail.'

management of judicial affairs were given to the newly established Judicial Council of the Slovak Republic (JCSR), and the powers of other branches were reduced. Political pressure on the courts was formally hindered. The judiciary's independence was reinforced at all formal stages of a judge's career: selection, appointment, relocation, promotion and advancement, training, performance appraisal, and disciplinary responsibility. The concept of judicial independence has been nuclear for the Slovak discourse.

Even though the regulatory framework for securing judicial independence has been formally fulfilled, the perceptions of the judiciary held by Slovak citizens have not followed with increased trust. Public perception of independence and inappropriate interference are also measured regularly. Regarding the subjective independence of the judiciary, the Slovak judiciary has continually ranked worst or second-worst among European countries in major surveys measuring public trust in the judiciary, the perceived independence of judges, and other aspects integral to the functioning of a fair judiciary in Europe. The justice system, particularly the judiciary, has faced continual low levels of trust from the public, as reflected in these surveys. According to the 2020 Eurobarometer survey results, 64% of the public ranked the justice system's independence as bad, while 26% ranked it good.[60]

The strong sovereign never disappeared from the judiciary when it became apparent that the strong figure of the President of the Supreme Court and the Chair of the JCSR has been since the beginning a political choice. The position of judicial elites was, to some extent, still dependent on political allies. The election of the President of the Supreme Court in 2009 was a merger of political and judicial power, during which the Judicial Council elected Harabin as incumbent Minister of Justice. The joint position of the presidency of the Supreme Court and Chair of the Judicial Council was strengthened by Harabin himself as Minister of Justice. The election in 2014 was also influenced by political actors who decided to end the reign of Harabin and elected his former ally but current rival Daniela Švecová.[61] It was apparent that moving the competence to elect the President of the Supreme Court from the National Assembly to the Judicial Council did not abolish the influence of political power on the selection of leading figures within the judiciary. The political leaders kept interested in who was elected to the chief justice, and they still got involved informally in the selection process.[62]

60 'Eurobarometer – Public Opinion in the European Union' <https://europa.eu/eurobarometer/screen/home>, accessed 31 October 2021.

61 David Kosař and Samuel Spáč, 'Post-Communist Chief Justices in Slovakia: From Transmission Belts to Semi-Autonomous Actors?' (2021) 13 *Hague Journal on the Rule of Law* 107, 127. On reasons of Harabin's toxicity and loss of political support see Tomáš Ľalík, 'Tracing Constitutional Changes in Slovakia between 2008–2016' (2017) 58 *Hungarian Journal of Legal Studies* 117, 133.

62 Ibid. Kosař and Spáč, 'Post-Communist,' 127.

The President of the Supreme Court was an extended hand of rulling politicians for affairs in the judiciary all that time. Especially in Harabin's tenure, he enforced obedience from the judges by disciplinary proceedings, financial bonuses, and anti-discrimination lawsuits.[63] With a strategy of carrots and sticks, he subordinated the judiciary to himself and the wishes of those who had power over him. Here comes the paradoxical situation. Despite the strong political preference to join the EU values, it is evident that the preference for the strong sovereign never ceased in various political camps in Slovak society. Within populist politicians and their supporters and among the guardians of the rule of law – judges and the liberal voters. Judges used this power vacuum within the judiciary and created a system based on the strong figure for their interest. The whole system around the infamous former President of the Supreme Court and Justice Minister Stefan Harabin was at one time supported by the vast majority of judges. Harabin's strategy was very much about creating the state of exception within the judiciary. The two camps based on Schmittian distinction of friend and enemy have existed within the judiciary ever since. Interestingly, liberal voters and liberal politicians, who supported the separation of power and judicial independence, asked for a strong sovereign in the political office who would pacify Harabin and dissolve the power centers within the judiciary. However, this wish came true not from the liberal politicians but Harabin's former ally, Robert Fico, and his Party SMER-SD.

8.7 2014 – The Sovereign Is Back

When the relationship of the ruling Party SMER-SD and Harabin deteriorated, the political sovereign became visible again. What was done "under the veil of public ignorance" when Harabin was a loyal friend to Robert Fico must have been done directly after their hegemonic break-up. Despite many hidden interferences in the judiciary,[64] the first openly hostile step towards

63 Furthermore, re-establishment of judicial candidates. This was largely appreciated among the judges, as it gave courts – and its presidents and judicial boards – much more control over the selection of their new colleagues. In 2012, as many as one in five judges had at least one family member working in the judiciary. Moreover, by temporary assignments of judges from courts to the Ministry of Justice, where they participated in the preparation of judicial policies. See Samuel Spáč, Katarína Šipulová, and Marína Urbániková, 'Capturing the Judiciary from Inside: The Story of Judicial Self-Governance in Slovakia' (2018) 19 *German Law Journal* 1741, 1751.

64 The Minister of Justice had strong control over the court presidents, with the power to appoint and remove them at her own discretion. Data gathered since 1998 show that all the ministers of justice used their competence to remove and appoint court presidents extensively. All ministers of justice claimed they acted to depoliticise the judiciary, but all of them wanted to fight politicisation with their candidates as court presidents. Ján Čarnogurský (1998–2002) replaced 30% of district court presidents (DCP) and 50% of regional court

judiciary to earn the political points related to the low public trust in the judiciary came from the Fico's party SMER-SD that was able to create a government on their own in 2012–2016. The initial move was the Constitutional amendment of 2014.

In 2014, the National Assembly passed a Constitutional Act as a direct amendment of the constitution containing the vetting procedure for new judges and control mechanisms for sitting judges.[65] The legislator concluded that suspicions surrounding the judiciary needed to be addressed, and social developments in Slovakia needed to be considered on the constitutional level. Based on the explanatory report, the amendment had the goal of improving the judiciary's functioning, efficacy, and quality by limiting the immunity of judges and removing the need for the consent of the CCSR[66] to prosecute judges. After this change, judges retained immunity for decision making – functional immunity. Furthermore, the amendment extended the competence of the JCSR and separated the position of the Chair of the JCSR from that of the Chief Justice.[67] The most controversial part of amendment 161/2014 was the transitional provision on preconditions of judicial abilities, which included the termination of the office of a judge appointed before 1 July 2014, as a legal consequence of non-fulfillment of the preconditions.[68] Based on the amendment, the preconditions for judicial abilities guarantee that judges will perform their function correctly. The Judicial Council was supposed to decide whether requirements were met to allow the candidate or judge to exercise the judicial office independently. This decision was based on documents obtained from a body performing the protection of classified information.[69] In practice, the information included private and family life, prior work experience, and social contacts.[70]

The former Chairwoman of the Judicial Council filed a complaint to the CCSR and challenged, inter alia, the retroactive part on the judges who have already been appointed. Based on the argumentation on retroactive results towards sitting judges, the CCSR suspended these provisions in decision no. PL. ÚS 21/2014. Consequently, there was no vetting procedure against sitting

presidents (RCP). Daniel Lipsic (2002–2006), 28% of DCP and 12.5% of RCP, Stefan Harabin 57% of DCP and 50% of RCP, Lucia Zitnanska (2010–2012) 48% of DCP and 75% of RCP, and Tomas Borec 48% of DCP and 62.5% of RCP.

65 Constitutional Act no. 161/2014 Coll.

66 It was a precondition, the judge could have been convicted only with the consent of the Constitutional Court.

67 As before the amendment was the Chair of the Judicial Council and the President of the Supreme Court connected.

68 The Slovak Constitution, art. 154d, par. 3.

69 Ibid. art. 154d, par. 1.

70 Tomáš Ľalík, 'Tracing Constitutional Changes in Slovakia between 2008–2016' (2017) 58 *Hungarian Journal of Legal Studies* 117, 132.

judges based on this amendment of the constitution, and the vetting process has been applied only toward new candidates. According to the explanatory report, the National Assembly intended to create better conditions for judicial independence.[71] The CCSR had the opposite understanding of this amendment.[72] The Constitutional Court stated that the constitution does not explicitly regulate the amenability of some of its articles, as other countries' constitutions do.[73] Nevertheless, the constitution is value-oriented, while the importance of some constitutional values is also fundamental to the constitution and the state itself. This is undoubtedly related to the possibility of intervention in these values, which are ultimately the immutable parts or material core of the constitution. Constitutional laws may also conflict with the material core of the constitution.[74]

Because the constitution does not contain explicit provisions concerning unamendable articles, the material core of the constitution is an implicit concept, the scope of which is determined by the case law of the CCSR.[75] The CCSR concluded that the independence of the judiciary and the related independence of judges must also be considered as principles inherent in the rule of law.[76] Independence does not mean that judges cannot be controlled, but this control must be balanced and proportionate.[77] The method of con-

71 Explanatory report to the Constitutional Act 161/2014 Coll.

72 PL. ÚS 21/2014, 30.1.2019, For detailed analysis, See Marek Domin, 'A Part of the Constitution Is Unconstitutional, the Slovak Constitutional Court Has Ruled' (*Verfassungsblog*) <https://verfassungsblog.de/a-part-of-the-constitution-is-unconstitutional-the-slovak-constitutional-court-has-ruled/>, accessed 9 June 2021

73 For example Art. 79 § 3 of the German Basic Law, Constitution of Norway, Article 121, Constitution of Portugal, Article 288.

74 Decision of the CCSR no. PL. ÚS 21/2014 par.88. CCSR argued that Art. 124 of the Constitution, according to which the Constitutional Court is an independent judicial body for the protection of constitutionality. If, in the event of a violation of the material core of the constitution, even by a constitutional norm, the Constitutional Court did not intervene, it would cease to fulfill the role of a body for the protection of constitutionality. To the oath of a judge of the Constitutional Court, whose task is, among other things, to protect the principles of the rule of law. However, dissenting opinions use the oath as the argument against the competence of the CCSR to decide on constitutional acts.

75 Two fundamental decisions of the previous years appeared in argumentation. First, the judgment of the CCSR PL. ÚS 7/2017 (the so-called Mečiar's amnesty), in which the Constitutional Court stated that the material core of the Constitution is formed by the principles of a democratic and rule of law, which do not have definite content and are constantly evolving. Any intervention in the material core of the Constitution must be assessed separately. It relies also on the judgment of the CCSR PL. ÚS 17/08 (Special Court), in which the CCSR emphasised the unconstitutionality of the law, according to which the security check of judges was to be performed by an executive body that is not bound by a legal procedure meeting the requirements of a fair trial, because it also obtained information in a classified manner and from various sources.

76 Principle of the rule of law in Article 1(1) of the Slovak Constitution.

77 Decision of the CCSR no. PL. ÚS 21/2014, par. 116.

trol introduced by the legislation in question did not meet those criteria, for the sensitive information obtained by the National Security Authority (NSA) could be misused to influence judges and the decision-making activities of the courts. At present, standard methods of controlling the activities of judges (disciplinary, civil, and criminal liability) exist but must be used properly.[78] The decision PL US 21/2014 is controversial because it went further than previous attempts of constitutional courts in other European countries when deciding over the compliance of constitutional acts with the constitution itself on substantial grounds, not procedural.[79]

The move of parliament towards the limitation of the autonomy of law that happened in 2014 and was decided as unconstitutional in 2019 did continue in 2020. Despite the change of the government. The CCSR strengthened the rigidity of the constitution with its decision that not everything included in the constitution falls within the amending competence of the political majority. The answer from the National Assembly came after the close of the seventh term. After the election of 2020, the new majority decided to play the ball that was now in their possession. After the "Threema scandal" in 2019 and 2020,[80] one of the new government's priorities was to fight corruption, including that of the judiciary.

The Ministry of Justice prepared a proposal for significant constitutional reform focused on the judiciary. The proposal was ambitious and broad, and its planned constitutional amendment was to be extensive. The President of the CCSR communicated his disapproval when 'This is an essential intervention in the constitution. Please reconsider if it is necessary...this proposal is absolutely unacceptable.'[81] Some parts of the amendment appeared as genuine attempts to raise the judiciary's efficacy and balance accountability with independence, while others recalled the attacks in Poland and Hungary. This step also earned a reaction from the CCJE.[82] The amendment called for a reform of the composition and powers of the Judicial Council, Adjustment

78 Decision of the CCSR no. PL. ÚS 21/2014, par. 138.

79 See Verfassungsgerichtshof (VfGH) (Constitutional Court), Nov. 11, 2001, Erkenntnisse und Beschlüsse des Verfassungsgerichtshofes [VFSLG] No. 16.327/2001 (Austria); Ukrainian Constitutional Court Decision no. 1-45/2010 (30 September 2010); Constitutional Court of Hungary, Decision 45/2012 (XII.29); Constitutional Court of the Czech Republic, Decision Pl. ÚS 27/09: Constitutional Act on Shortening the Term of Office of the Chamber of Deputies.

80 See Michal Ovádek, 'Deep Rot in Slovakia' *Verfassungsblog* (15 October 2019) <https://verfassungsblog.de/deep-rot-in-slovakia/>, accessed 3 May 2023.

81 V. Prušová, 'Ústavný súd zrejme príde o kompetenciu, ktorú si sám privlastnil. Koalícia reaguje na kontroverzné rozhodnutie z minulosti' (*Denník N*, 24 November 2020) <https://dennikn.sk/2156633/ustavny-sud-ma-prist-o-kompetenciu-ktoru-si-sam-privlastnil-koalicia-reaguje-na-kontroverzne-rozhodnutie-z-minulosti/>, accessed 3 May 2023.

82 'The CCJE Publishes an Opinion about the New Provisions Relating to the Judicial Council of Slovakia' (*Consultative Council of European Judges*) <https://www.coe.int/en/web/ccje

of Proceedings Before the Constitutional Court and Prevention of Decisions on the Compliance of Constitutional Acts with the Constitution, Immunity of Judges, and Creating the Supreme Administrative Court of the Slovak Republic and a new court map.

8.8 Conclusions

In all the Visegrad countries, we can observe a visible shift towards a "strong sovereign."[83] The tradition of populism in Slovakia and the CEE region in general, has been following the same scenario. Once it became clear that the liberal ideology has failed to provide signifying opportunities to a certain amount of people, the need for a strong sovereign appeared. In order to change the quilting points of the ideological fantasy, guards of the institutions of liberal constitutionalism had to be weakened. The reason is simple, the change of quilting points is systemic. The priority of the position of the judges within liberal constitutionalism is to maintain the status quo, to keep reproducing the rule of law, a system based on the autonomous processes of the law, that does not need any interference from the outside. The populism that was summoned by the disappointment from the liberal constitutionalism has always the goal of the subordination of guards of the system. A look on the interference in the judiciary of last 70 years shows that this period is mainly characterised by a strong sovereign rather than autonomous law. Even when it seemed that the sovereign was gone, the sovereign was there all the time, even though some refused to see it. It seems to be encoded in the atmosphere of Central and Eastern Europe, echoes that call for the figures who will establish the exception.

/news/-/asset_publisher/8Wd6RJfyNLaO/content/the-ccje-publishes-an-opinion-about-the-new-provisions-relating-to-the-judicial-council-of-slovakia>, accessed 3 May 2023.

83 Fryderyk Zoll and Leah Wortham, 'Judicial Independence and Accountability: Withstanding Political Stress in Poland' (2018) 42 *Fordham International Law Journal* 875; Laurent Pech, Patryk Wachowiec, and Dariusz Mazur, 'Poland's Rule of Law Breakdown: A Five-Year Assessment of EU's (in) Action' (2021) 13 *Hague Journal on the Rule of Law* 1; Wojciech Sadurski, 'How Democracy Dies (in Poland): A Case Study of Anti-Constitutional Populist Backsliding' [2018] *Revista Forumul Judecatorilor* 104; Anna Śledzińska-Simon, 'The Rise and Fall of Judicial Self-Government in Poland: On Judicial Reform Reversing Democratic Transition' (2018) 19 *German Law Journal* 1839; Katalin Kovács and Kim Lane Scheppele, 'The Fragility of an Independent Judiciary: Lessons from Hungary and Poland—And the European Union' (2018) 51 *Communist and Post-Communist Studies* 189.

Chapter 9

Judicialising Communism

Transitional Justice and Nationalist Populism in the Uneven Time-Space of Eastern Europe

Saygun Gökarıksel

9.1 Introduction

While the invocation of law to address past crimes or wrongdoing is not a novelty, the fall of state communism in Eastern Europe in 1989–1991 has attributed law a special location. The field of "transitional justice" has emerged to reckon with military dictatorships and apartheid and authoritarian regimes in Africa, Asia, Latin America, and Eastern Europe through diverse legal measures including criminal prosecutions, purges, and quasi-judicial truth commissions and memory institutions.[1] Informed by post–Cold War liberal cosmopolitan imaginary, these measures, as often noted, are deployed in order to come to terms with the past and facilitate the transition to a peaceful, stable, liberal-democracy, and capitalism.[2]

Transitional justice has recently been subjected to trenchant criticism, and rightly so. These critiques have taken issue with transitional justice's Eurocentric and teleological assumptions about the endpoint of transition as Western liberal-democracy, its top-down and state-centered focus that shuns local and grassroots initiatives and vocabularies of justice, and its elision and even reproduction of historical structures of power and inequality including colonial, heteropatriarchal, and capitalist relations of race, gender, and class.[3] The historical course of transitional justice in post-socialist Eastern

1 Paige Arthur, 'How "Transitions" Reshaped Human Rights: A Conceptual History of Transitional Justice' (2009) 31 *Human Rights Quarterly* 321; Ruti Teitel, *Transitional Justice* (New York-Oxford: OUP, 2000).

2 Costas Douzinas, 'Theses on Law, History and Time' (2006) 7 *Melbourne Journal of International Law* 13; Pierre Hazan, *Judging War, Judging History: Behind Truth and Reconciliation* (Stanford: Stanford University Press, 2010); Robert Meister, *After Evil: A Politics of Human Rights* (New York: Columbia University Press, 2010).

3 See, e.g., Zinaida Miller, 'Effects of Invisibility: In Search of the "Economic" in Transitional Justice' (2008) 2(3) *International Journal of Transitional Justice* 266; Alexander Hinton, *The Justice Facade: Trials of Transition in Cambodia* (Oxford: OUP, 2018); Rosalind Shaw and Lars Waldorf (eds), *Localizing Transitional Justice Interventions and Priorities after Mass Violence* (Stanford: Stanford University Press, 2010); David Scott, *Omens of Adversity:*

DOI: 10.4324/9781032624464-10

Europe shows well what is at stake in those critiques. But it also highlights the following paradox that is rarely attended by the critical scholarship on transitional justice: how is it that transitional justice measures that are supposed to promote liberal democracy might turn into a useful instrument of nationalist populist groups to articulate their authoritarian sovereignty politics of security and purification, as in Hungary and Poland? What might such nationalist appropriation of transitional justice reveal about the general relationship between law, politics, and populism at this current historical conjuncture, which is usually characterised as the crisis of liberal democracy and neoliberal capitalism, and the rise of authoritarian populism and fascism or post-fascism?[4]

Legal scholars commonly address these questions within the thriving genre of "populism studies." These studies tend to take Western liberal legal ideology as their norm, against which they consider populist legality and transitional justice as either pathological aberration or exception. Przemysław Tacik, in his essay in this volume, suggests that populism as a social-historical phenomenon can be usefully understood as an 'eruption of the political in the de-politicized liberal environment,' calling into question the boundaries of the legal and the political posited by liberal legalism. In liberal politics, observes Tacik, the concept of populism mainly functions to highlight 'how law is mired in politics' and how politics becomes 'excessive' in the legal domain, undermining the rule of law's alleged political neutrality and objectivity. To the populist challenge, liberal scholars and pundits in Eastern Europe, similar to those in the West, often respond with alarming views. They describe populism as resulting from Eastern Europe's "underdeveloped" legal culture, its low appreciation of liberal values, or the moral-psychological disorder caused by the democratic transition of the 1990s. Populism, in those accounts, appears mainly as the "regression" or "backslide" of democracy into some authoritarian past, that is, the communist past, which haunts the present like a "curse."[5] Moreover, when populist governments present their

---

Tragedy, Time, Memory, Justice (Duke University Press, 2014); Mahmood Mamdani, *Neither Settler nor Native: The Making and Unmaking of Permanent Minorities* (Cambridge: Harvard University Press, 2020); Joan W. Scott, *On the Judgment of History* (New York: Columbia University Press, 2020).

4 Wendy Brown, *In the Ruins of Neoliberalism: The Rise of Antidemocratic Politics in the West* (New York: Columbia University Press, 2019); Jeremy Rayner (ed.), *Back to the 30s? Recurring Crises of Capitalism, Liberalism, and Democracy* (London: Palgrave Macmillan, 2020); Enzo Traverso, *The New Faces of Fascism: Populism and the Far Right* (London: Verso, 2019).

5 For an overview of the legal approaches to populism in Eastern Europe, especially in Poland, see Michał Krotoszyński, 'Transitional Justice and the Constitutional Crisis: The Case of Poland (2015–2019)' [2019] 3 *Journal of the Polish Section of IVR* 22; Przemysław Tacik, 'A New Popular Front, or, on the Role of Critical Jurisprudence under Neo-Authoritarianism in Central-Eastern Europe' (2019) 89 *Acta Universitatis Lodziensis. Folia Iuridica* 31;

rule as a way of settling accounts with the communist past and rectifying the failures of liberal reckoning, those scholars often consider it as merely a political instrumentalisation of transitional justice to discredit their opponents.[6] However, these approaches not only largely fail to address the broader legal, ideological, and political economic conditions that make transitional justice instrumental in the first place, but by uncritically employing Western liberal norms, they also tend to downplay and even obscure the law's *constitutive* relation to politics and power, which led to, in this context, disregarding, if not exonerating the complicity of liberal legal ideology and capitalist order with the rise of nationalist populism. The longstanding uneven legal and political relations of power between and within the West and East fade into the background, figuring merely as a register of Eastern Europe's backwardness, its historical destiny.

Here, I want to engage these discussions of law, politics, and history by focusing on the conditions of transitional justice, specifically, the judicialisation of communism that prepares the ideological and material ground for the rise of nationalist populism in Eastern Europe. The judicial treatment of communism as an immoral, criminal system and ideology is certainly not specific to Eastern Europe. Nor is it a novelty to the global post–Cold War moment. Yet, inscribed within the clamour of the liberal celebrations of the "end of history" and the death of communism and articulated within the ideology of capitalist nation-state making, this post-socialist judicialisation of communism in Eastern Europe expresses a distinct historicity and legal-institutional force.

First, that judicialisation reduces the entire pluralist and agonistic history of communist practice and ideological formation to the historical form of Soviet state communism and in that, to the violence and crimes perpetrated in its name.[7] By identifying communism with the death of Soviet state communism, this judicialisation aims to seal off the history and future of communism as a finished past. Yet, post-socialist judicialisation not only

Wojciech Sadurski, *Poland's Constitutional Breakdown* (Oxford: OUP, 2019); Ivan Krastev and Stephen Holmes, *The Light that Failed: A Reckoning* (London: Penguin, 2020); Irena Grudzińska-Gross, 'The Backsliding' (2014) 28(4) *East European Politics and Societies and Cultures* 664.

6 See, for instance, Adam Michnik, *The Trouble with History: Morality, Revolution, and Counterrevolution* (Connecticut: Yale University Press, 2014) and, for an overview of transitional justice arguments in Eastern Europe, see Nadya Nedelsky and Lavinia Stan (eds), *Post-Communist Transitional Justice: Lessons from Twenty-Five Years of Experience* (Cambridge: Cambridge University Press, 2015).

7 For a good overview of how the history of communism is today judicialised, see Daniel Bensaïd, *Köstebek ve Lokomotif: Tarih, Devrim ve Strateji Üzerine Denemeler* (İstanbul: Yazın Yayıncılık, 2006); Costas Douzinas and Slavoj Žižek (eds), *The Idea of Communism* (London: Verso, 2010), and Enzo Traverso, *The New Faces of Fascism: Populism and the Far Right* (London: Verso, 2009).

deals with the past, the legacies of bygone communism embodied by some "tainted" people and institutions in the present onto which capital's violence is displaced (blaming "red deposits" for capitalist inequality), but it also seeks to act upon the future.[8] It aims to *prevent* the spectres or new incarnations of communism in their motley and fleeting forms, which are currently described, for instance, by conservative nationalists in Poland as totalitarian "gender ideology," "LGBT ideology," anti-fascists, and vegetarians or by liberal groups as "right-wing Bolsheviks" or uncivilised *homo Sovieticus*.[9] To this end, this judicialisation of communism has worked as part of the general, expansive security mechanism that was introduced to the post-socialist constitutional order during the process of accession to the European Union. In that, liberal legal ideological hegemony, I argue, is complicit with not only the judicialisation of communism, but also the broader legal and material conditions that have given way to the nationalist populist rule by law. Thus, before uncritically embracing the defence of post-socialist liberalism, one needs to reckon with the ways in which it has contributed to the current political moment beyond the genre of its 'unfortunate failures.'[10]

In what follows, I will first unpack what I mean by judicialisation and highlight the transnational dimension of the judicialisation of communism at the "end of history." I will then briefly track the articulation of this judicialisation in Eastern Europe, first, in the making of liberal constitutional order and transitional justice, then, in the establishment of truth commissions and national memory institutions after 1989.[11] The chapter argues that the post-socialist judicialisation, which is ideologically legitimated in the liberal constitutional order and harnessed by the liberal politics of security and transitional justice, entrenches and widely disseminates a nationalist, moralistic, and amorphous anti-communism. In doing so, this judicialisation of communism not only disables the popularisation, if not the articulation of an effective anti-capitalist critique of structural inequalities by associating it with "communist crimes," but this mode of judicialisation also contributes to the flourishing of nationalist populist groups that radicalise and transform the already existing liberal security mechanisms to criminalise and repress their opponents as the new incarnations of communism. If part of what populism does is to insert the question of the political at the heart of liberal legal order, this chapter then offers insight into the *kind* of politics nationalist populists

8 Tacik, 'A New.'

9 See Gökarıksel, 'Antifascist' for the discussion of historical forms of anti-communism in Eastern Europe and *Praktyka Teoretyczna*'s special issue on anti-communism, especially, Łukasz Moll (2019), 'Erasure of the Common: From Polish Anti-Communism to Universal Anti-Capitalism.' *Praktyka Teoretyczna* 1 (31): 118–45.

10 Krastev and Holmes, *The Light*.

11 While my primary focus is on the legal and political processes in Poland, most of the tendencies tracked here would apply to the region, especially in Visegrad countries.

seek to articulate through transitional justice institutions and practices; how they aim to redraw the boundaries of political community in contemporary Eastern Europe.

9.2 Populism and the Judicialisation of Social Relations

The constitutive relationship between law and politics is by now a well-established assumption of critical legal approaches. Challenging the instrumentalist and narrow legalist conceptions of law, those approaches have detailed the ways in which legal institutions, ideologies, and practices have shaped and been shaped by the social-historical processes of capitalism, colonialism, and heteropatriarchy, as well as social struggles such as class struggles, feminist struggles, and anti-colonial liberation movements.[12] The liberal legalist identification of law with political neutrality has been challenged by those social struggles, but also by right-wing populist groups which 'repoliticize matters hitherto shielded by the complex edifice of the European legal order.'[13] As often noted, this populist repoliticisation typically involved de-institutionalisation, personalisation, and moralisation of public political life through Manichean division of society into enemy camps and through antagonistic memory work.[14] In his recent work, Wojciech Sadurski, for instance, usefully analysed the legal battles waged by the current Polish government to hollow out and capture the legal institutions through piecemeal measures.[15] In this chapter, I focus on one particular dimension of this whole story, namely, the judicialisation process and its relation to transitional justice and nationalist populism in post–Cold War Eastern Europe.

The post–Cold War, which was inaugurated with the hasty proclamations of the death of communism and liberalism as the final stage of human history, had been accompanied by the increasing judicialisation of politics, history, and memory. In the 1990s, in the South, more than a hundred constitutions were made and the rule of law became the main *lingua franca* in international relations.[16] In Pierre Hazan's terms, the new 'judicial diplomacy'

12 See, e.g., Anthony Anghie, *Imperialism, Sovereignty and the Making of International Law* (Cambridge: Cambridge University Press, 2005); Wendy Brown and Janet Halley (eds), *Left Legalism/Left Critique* (Durham: Duke University Press, 2002); Matthew Stone, Illan rua Wall, and Costas Douzinas, *New Critical Legal Thinking: Law and the Political* (London: Routledge, 2012).

13 Tacik, 'A New.'

14 See, for instance, Jan-Werner Müller, *What is Populism?* (Pennsylvania: University of Pennsylvania Press, 2016) on populism and Charles Forsdick, James Mark, and Eva Spišiaková, 'Introduction. From Populism to Decolonisation: How We Remember in the Twenty-First Century' [2020] 1 *Modern Languages Open* 1, on memory and populism.

15 Sadurski, *Poland's*.

16 Jean Comaroff and John Comaroff, *Theory from the South or, How Euro-America is Evolving toward Africa* (London: Paradigm, 2012).

was born that assumed the task of economic development, peace-making, reconciliation, and judging history and war through, for instance, international criminal courts.[17] This judicialisation was not only a matter of the liberal institutional understanding of separation of powers, that is, the rising domination of the judiciary over the legislative and executive powers; but it also involved the increasingly popular invocation of the 'moral and performative force of the law to compel transformation, to produce incontestable evidence, to set right from wrong' and 'to offer a more authoritative, inclusive account of bygone times,' as Jean and John Comaroff put it.[18] As such, judicialisation extended well beyond the narrowly circumscribed legal-institutional domains such as courts and specific legal procedures.

Here, I draw on this broad understanding of judicialisation. Seen this way, the judicialisation of communism refers to a particular set of practices that produce and reproduce the judicial form in their treatment of communism as a historical past and ideology. What does this judicial form consist of? Carlo Ginzburg's reflections on law offer a promising departure point.[19] The judicial approach to history, in his view, could be well delineated in the historiography of the French Revolution and modern positivist history writing more generally. By reconstructing the past on the basis of individual actors and events, the judicial approach to history aimed to establish causal connections and determine guilt as though in a court of law. The question of individual motivation, "who are you?" and "why you did it?," was central to its reasoning and examination that came to intensively focus on the criminal personality, what Michel Foucault called the 'dangerous individuals,' against which 'society must be defended.' The judicial form of truth, above all, concerned the inner truth of the person, around which legal, psychiatric, sociological, and criminological discourses proliferated and became institutionalised.[20]

Moreover, this preoccupation with individual actors and events reinforced a binarised victim or plaintiff and perpetrator approach to the past. Thereby, this judicial approach restricted remarkably the object and scope of scientific research and the understanding of evidence. The impersonal structures of power or imagined events that could not be traced to individual actors or be ascertained through "material evidence" would be left outside the understanding of the past. Thus, it failed to address the long-term historical processes and dynamics of social struggles and popular movements

17 Pierre Hazan, *Judging War, Judging History: Behind Truth and Reconciliation* (Stanford: Stanford University Press, 2010), 45–6.

18 Comaroff and Comaroff, *Theory*, 141.

19 Carlo Ginzburg, 'Checking the Evidence: The Judge and the Historian' (1991) 18(1) *CriticalInquiry* 79.

20 Michel Foucault, 'Truth and Juridical Forms' (1996) 2(3) *Social Identities* 327; idem, *Society Must Be Defended* (New York: Picador, 2003).

that produced the conditions of individual actions and events.[21] Further, the legal positivism of modern state law informed the historical understanding of evidence and the language of communication. The judicial approach to history held that evidence reflected reality as it was, offering unmediated or transparent access to the world. The formalist abstraction of modern law, which aimed to transcend particular actions and make them intelligible and equivalent through its general categories, contributed to the entrenchment of this judicial approach. As I discuss below, national memory institutions established in Eastern Europe largely drew on the judicial approach to history and memory.

How might we think of populism with this judicialisation of history and social relations? Pierre Rosanvallon's work, *Counter-Democracy* is useful, in this respect.[22] Basing his study on the history of the French Revolution and nation-state formation, Rosanvallon showed that modern democracy did not only produce representative institutions and forms of government to address popular sovereignty, but also comprised what he called 'counter-democratic' practices. The revolutionary process gave way to the proliferation of popular practices of judgment, where people claimed to act as the judge, alongside the practices of public denunciation and oversight of the government. The public tribunal of opinion, the interpellation of the people as a judge, has been a fundamental part of the exercise of democratic popular sovereignty. Many social struggles, certainly class struggles waged against the owners of capital, invoked the people as judges and aspired to popularise their judgment in public political life.

Yet, contemporary populist movements, claimed Rosanvallon, appropriated these democratic people-as-judge practices and took them to 'pathological' and extremely punitive directions. The 'enlightened' tribunal of public opinion then turned into a 'theater of cruelty,' where vindictive punishments passed on against different kinds of 'others': foreigners, sexual minorities, religious minorities, and corrupt elites, all of which are pitted against the 'pure' and self-righteous people.[23] The Manichean approach to society became central to these populist judicial practices and representation of the people. While Rosanvallon mainly had in mind right-wing populist groups and his view of populism as pathology, in my view, does not offer much analytic insight, his works helps understand the way judicial practices might work in nationalist populist movements and rules beyond the formal-legal domain of the judiciary. The post-socialist judicialisation of communism, especially when it is driven by nationalist populist groups, employs a range

21 Ginzburg, 'Checking.'

22 Pierre Rosanvallon, *Counter-Democracy Politics in an Age of Distrust* (Cambridge: CUP, 2008).

23 Ibid. 272.

of informal judicial practices that seek to redraw the boundaries of public political life.

9.3 Judicialising Communism at the "End of History"

The post-socialist judicialisation of communism is articulated at a particular post–Cold War conjuncture, marked by the global ascendancy of neoliberal capitalism, human rights, and transitional justice, as well as the increasing fragmentation of memory and grand historical narratives and the rise of particularistic and ethno-national identity politics, based on competitive victimhood.[24] Communism as an ideology and historical past took its share. It became a prosaic object of criminal prosecution and judgment, if not in the actual court of law, then in the public tribunal of opinion and cultural courtrooms such as anti-communist museums and memory sites that called for the 'Nuremberg of communism.'[25]

Post–Cold War anti-communism and historical revisionism mainly recycled the Cold War anti-communist ideas of communism as evil totalitarian regime of extreme violence and dangerous ideological fanaticism. These discussions set the ideological framework, which had important consequences for the legal-moral ideology of transitional justice in Eastern Europe. Of particular importance here is the landmark "historian's debate" sparked by the conservative historian Ernst Nolte's historical revisionism in West Germany in the late 1980s. Communists, argued Nolte, long masked their crimes by using anti-fascism and presenting themselves as the liberators of the Jewish people. Instead, Nolte claimed that the Nazi genocide of the Jews was, first and foremost, a response to the violence of Soviet communism, which had preceded it. Enzo Traverso offered a useful insight into the political stakes of Nolte's revisionism:

> For Nolte, Auschwitz was a 'copy' of an 'Asiatic' barbarism originally introduced to Europe by the Bolsheviks. ... As the first totalitarian regime to adopt a politics of terror and of 'class extermination' from the onset of

24 For a useful overview of memory studies from a historical perspective, see Nikolay Koposov, *Memory Laws, Memory Wars: The Politics of the Past in Europe and Russia* (Cambridge: Cambridge University Press, 2017); Cristian Cercel, 'Whither Politics, Whither Memory?' (2020) 1 *Modern Languages Open* 18; Charles Forsdick, James Mark, and Eva Spišiaková, 'Introduction. From Populism to Decolonisation: How We Remember in the Twenty-First Century' (2020) 1 *Modern Languages Open*,1; Małgorzata Pakier and Joanna Wawrzyniak (eds), *Memory and Change in Europe: Eastern Perspectives* (New York: Berghahn, 2015).

25 Kristen Ghodsee, *Red Hangover: Legacies of Twentieth-Century Communism* (Durham, NC: Duke University Press, 2017); Gal Kirn, *Partisan Ruptures: Self-Management, Market Reform and the Specter of Socialist Yugoslavia* (London: Pluto Press, 2019); Maya Nadkarni, *Remains of Socialism: Memory and the Futures of the Past in Postsocialist Hungary* (Ithaca: Cornell University Press, 2020).

> Russian civil war, Bolshevism acted on the German mind as both a 'frightful image' (*Schreckbild*) and a 'model' (*Vorbild*). Thus, Nazi genocide and criminal practices could be explained as an 'exacerbated' reaction to a threat of annihilation embodied by Russian Bolshevism.[26]

The 'barbaric' Bolshevik violence, argued Nolte, was so fearsome and traumatic for Germans that it led them to perpetrate the Holocaust and wage a racist, capitalist, colonial war against the peoples of Eastern Europe. By shifting the attention towards Soviet communism and highlighting its Eastern "barbarism," Nolte and scholars following him mitigated and even exculpated the German responsibility for Nazi violence and anti-Semitism and aspired to recover the wounded national dignity of Germans. While their arguments paved the way for Holocaust denial, they also implied that many Jewish people were indeed responsible for their own deaths, because they had been communists or aligned with them.[27]

Ernst Nolte's reactionary, conservative view was at the time strongly challenged by intellectuals such as Jürgen Habermas and Saul Friedlander for mystifying and whitewashing Nazi violence and promoting national victimhood politics that exonerated Germans. But the end of state communism in 1989–1991 brought popularity to this anti-communist revisionism. Ex-Maoist Stephane Courtois' edited volume *The Black Book of Communism: Crimes, Terror, Repression* that came out in France in 1997 was perhaps the most blatant expression of that revisionism.[28] Through a careless and inflated body count, which was even disputed by some of the contributors of the book such as Nicolas Werth, Courtois 'blackwashed' the history of communism, to use Kristen Ghodsee's term,[29] and equated communism with Nazism as a violent, criminal totalitarian ideology. In his account, communism was basically destined to be a criminal totalitarian phenomenon and its historical ruptures and the dilemmas of its actors had no importance. Nor was there any need to make a distinction between Stalin and the communist victims of Stalinism, between bureaucratic state regimes and revolutionary movements, and between structures of oppression and social egalitarian policies. International communist struggles and anti-colonial liberation movements, waged in the Third World within the horizon of communism, was all but another instance of communist crime and violence. In this way, such an approach, in effect,

26 Enzo Traverso, 'The New Anti-Communism: Rereading the Twentieth Century' in Mike Haynes and Jim Wolfreys (eds), *History and Revolution: Refuting Revisionism* (London: Verso, 2007), 140.

27 Ibid.

28 Stephane Courtois (ed.), *The Black Book of Communism: Crimes, Terror, Repression* (Cambridge, MA: Harvard University Press, 1999).

29 Ghodsee, *Red Hangover*.

discarded the entire history of political desires, translations, and creolisations of the October revolution and Marxism beyond.[30]

This teleological and judicial approach to communism gained wide prominence and institutional force in post–Cold War Europe, promoted by national and European memory laws and policies. It constituted a part of the legal-moral ideology of reckoning with the communist past. Let me emphasise that this historical revisionism and judicial approach was *not* first invented in the West and then exported to the East as historical research agenda or as a particular legal form. The Cold War exchanges between West European intellectuals and parties and the "dissidents" from the Eastern bloc, especially from the USSR, Poland, and Czechoslovakia from 1968 onwards, had been formative. Those dissidents, for instance, Adam Michnik from Poland, acted as the authentic witness of communist repression and sought to create international publicity for the opposition at home by invoking international human rights and recycling the Cold War totalitarianism paradigm that emphasised the oppressive nature of Soviet communism.[31] The language of totalitarianism, as Abbot Glaeson (1997) analysed it at length, was never value-free and always implied strong normative judgments that typically took Western liberal-democracy as its norm, against which it judged other illiberal regimes as violent, inefficient, and authoritarian.[32] After 1989, totalitarianism frameworks made a comeback in full force to Eastern Europe, institutionalised as part of transitional justice and nation-state ideology that aspired to 'return to Europe,' that is, 'normality.'[33] Below, I briefly reconstruct the legal space of post-socialist transformations in which such a judicial approach to communism/transitional justice was articulated and attached to a security mechanism that was introduced as part of the Europeanisation process.

30 Fadi Bardawil, *Revolution and Disenchantment: Arab Marxism and the Binds of Emancipation* (Durham, NC: Duke University Press, 2020); Rossen Djagalov, *From Internationalism to Postcolonialism: Literature and Cinema Between the Second and the Third Worlds* (Montreal: McGill-Queen's University Press, 2020); Jane Anna Gordon and Drucilla Cornell (eds), *Creolizing Rosa Luxemburg* (London: Rowman & Littlefield, 2021).

31 Robert Brier 'Adam Michnik's Understanding of Totalitarianism and the West-European Left: A Historical and Transnational Approach to Dissident Political Thought' (2011) 25(2) *East European Politics and Societies* 197.

32 Abbott Gleason, *Totalitarianism: The Inner History of the Cold War* (Oxford: Oxford University Press, 1997).

33 Cosmin Cercel, *Towards A Jurisprudence of State Communism: Law and the Failure of Revolution* (London and New York: Routledge, 2018); Zhivka Valiavicharska, 'How the Concept of Totalitarianism Appeared in Late Socialist Bulgaria: The Birth and Life of Zheliu Zhelev's Book *Fascism*' (2014) 15(2) *Kritika* 303.

9.4 Defending Democracy through Transitional Justice

Both this return to Europe and transitional justice faced a number of challenges and contradictions that largely arose out of the simultaneous introduction of neoliberalisation and electoral democracy, the problems which are also observed in different Southern peripheries of world capitalism including post-apartheid South Africa and postcolonial India.[34] The longstanding uneven legal, political, and economic relations asserted themselves with great force in post-1989 Eastern Europe.[35] The ruling classes' proclamation of freedom and equality for all encountered the social-material realities of privilege and private property, which not only reproduced already existing inequalities but also created new ones. The meaning of freedom and equality was reconceived in the changing legal architecture under the new conditions of neoliberalisation and democratisation. The dominant liberal legal and political elite came to associate freedom with privatised entrepreneurial freedom that saw the citizen chiefly as property-owner, while they recast equality largely as formal legal equality, 'equality before the law.' Overall, the legal-institutional arrangements expressed the tensions resulting from the legacy of Cold War ideological division of rights, the process of "Europeanisation" (harmonisation of laws and standards), and the persistence of past legal traditions including socialist law's "hyper-positivism."[36]

The post-socialist judicialisation of rights manifested itself in privileging judiciable civil and political rights through courts over social rights that demanded public provision, as the constitution-making process in Poland glaringly showed.[37] This judicialisation corresponded to the shift in the material basis of citizenship/belonging, which involved neoliberal restructuring of the economy through massive and opaque privatisation of state-owned companies, public cuts, and outsourcing of social services to private agencies. The judicialisation aimed not only to facilitate neoliberalisation and "catch up with the West," but also to entrench and secure the emergent

34 Partha Chatterjee, *Lineages of Political Society: Studies in Postscolonial Democracy* (New York: Columbia University Press, 2011); Comaroff and Comaroff, *Theory*.

35 József Böröcz 'Dual Dependency and Property Vacuum: Social Change on the State Socialist Semiperiphery' (1992) 21(1) *Theory and Society* 77; Manuela Boatca, 'Semiperipheries in the World-System: Reflecting Eastern European and Latin American Experiences' (2006) 12(2) *Journal of World-Systems Research* 321; Rafał Mańko, 'Being Central European, or Some Reflections on Law, Double Peripherality and the Political in Times of Transformation' in Tomáš Gábriš and Ján Sombati (eds), *Central and Eastern Europe as a Double Periphery?* (Berlin: Peter Lang, 2020).

36 Rafał Mańko, 'Weeds in the Gardens of Justice? The Survival of Hyperpositivism in Polish Legal Culture as a Symptom/Sinthome' (2013) 7(2) *Pólemos: Journal of Law, Literature and Culture* 207.

37 Ewa Łętowska, 'A Constitution of Possibilities' (1997) 6 *East European Constitutional Review* 76.

capitalist democratic order against its dangers, past and present, such as the potentially rebellious dislocated and dispossessed working people. As part of it, the Polish state, like other states in the region, quickly ratified the European Convention for the Protection of Human Rights and Fundamental Freedoms in early 1993 and adopted legal procedures to protect individual rights against their possible violation by elected governments.[38] Overall, the constitutional courts in Eastern Europe, especially in Poland, Hungary, and the Czech Republic, were hailed as the "guardians" of the emergent legal and political economic order. They were to contain and arbitrate over the social antagonisms of post-socialist transformations.[39]

The ethos of postwar Western European constitutionalism had a crucial impact on post-socialist legal transformations.[40] It not only reinforced the judicial activism of constitutional courts, but also introduced an expansive security mechanism into the legal field, particularly under the doctrine of 'militant democracy' (*streitbare Demokratie*).[41] This doctrine, which was entrenched during the European accession process, informed the ideological vision of the transition justice process.

The Germanic idea of "militant democracy" was first coined in 1937 by Karl Loewenstein shortly after the Nazi takeover of the Weimar Republic, to articulate the vulnerability of liberal-democracy against fascism and defend it through exceptional or emergency legal measures, bans, and purges.[42] As such, militant democracy articulated the well-known paradox of defending democracy through anti-democratic means and, thereby, pointed to the authoritarian dimension of liberalism.[43] Many postwar West European states integrated militant democracy into their constitutional framework, using it

38 Jacek Kurczewski and Barry Sullivan, 'The Bill of Rights and the Emerging Democracies' (2002) 65(2) *Law and Contemporary Problems* 251.

39 Adam Sulikowski, 'Government of Judges and Neoliberal Ideology: The Polish Case' in Rafał Mańko, Cosmin Cercel, and Adam Sulikowski (eds), *Law and Critique in Central Europe Questioning the Past, Resisting the Present* (Oxford: Counterpress, 2016); Adam Czarnota et al. (eds), *Rethinking the Rule of Law After Communism* (Budapest: Central European University Press, 2005).

40 Mark Brzeziński, *The Struggle for Constitutionalism in Poland* (New York: Palgrave Macmillan, 2000); Wojciech Sadurski, 'Postcommunist Charters of Rights in Europe and the US Bill of Rights' (2002) 65(2) *Law and Contemporary Problems* 223.

41 Uladziaslau Belavusau, *Freedom of Speech: Importing European and US Constitutional Models in Transitional Democracies* (London: Routledge, 2013); Patrick Macklem, 'Guarding the Perimeter: Militant Democracy and Religious Freedom in Europe' [2012] *Constellations* 575.

42 Carlo Invernizzi Accetti and Ian Zuckerman. 'What's Wrong with Militant Democracy?' (2017) 65 *Political Studies* 182; Michael Wilkinson, 'Authoritarian Liberalism in Europe: A Common Critique of Neoliberalism and Ordoliberalism' (2017) 45(7–8) *Critical Sociology* 1023.

43 Giovanni Capoccia, 'Militant Democracy: The Institutional Bases of DemocraticSelf-Preservation.' (2017) 9 *The Annual Review of Law and Social Science* 207–26.

as a security measure against the "communist threat" at home and from the East. Jan-Werner Müller observed that the European integration project partly fed on this authoritarian impulse for security and distrust of popular democratic sovereignty and social struggles. The integration involved the delegation of powers to 'unelected domestic institutions and to supranational bodies, in order to "lock in" liberal-democratic arrangements and prevent any backsliding towards authoritarianism.'.[44]

In the 1990s, East European countries, in particular, the Czech Republic, Hungary, and Poland, quickly incorporated the European treaties and conventions to "lock in" their precarious transition to liberal-democratic capitalism. The special resolution (No. 1096) adopted in June 1996 by the European Parliamentary Assembly of the Council of Europe, provided an important guideline (soft-law) for post-socialist candidate countries about the 'measures to dismantle the heritage of former communist totalitarian systems' and build democracy in a 'civilized' and 'humane' manner.[45] 'The goals of this transition process are clear,' the resolution noted; it was 'to create pluralist democracies, based on the rule of law and respect for human rights and diversity.' However, 'to re-establish a civilized, liberal state' posed many challenges that arose out of the legacy of 'former communist totalitarian systems': 'the militarization of civilian institutions, bureaucratization, monopolization, and overregulation,' as well as former totalitarian subjects' 'collectivism,' 'conformism,' and 'blind obedience.' To deal with these problems, the resolution proposed the well-known recipe of liberal-democratisation: 'the separation of powers, freedom of the media, protection of private property, and the development of civil society,' which included the elimination of totalitarian dispositions such as the fear of responsibility and disrespect for diversity, intolerance, and racism. If necessary, this dismantling of totalitarian heritage could employ exceptional measures in accordance with the 'general principles of law recognized by civilized nations.'

The European resolution offered a useful insight into how the communist past was thoroughly contrasted with almost every aspect of democratisation and capitalist transformation. Deregulation of the economy, protection of private property, transformation of the state, development of civil society, and production of new liberal subjectivity were integral to post-socialist transitional justice processes like lustration, the screening and banning of the secret agents of the communist-era security service from public life. But lustration, the resolution stated, also performed a crucial security function, formulated with a goal to 'protect the newly emerged democracy.' In fact, the language of security, accompanied by the frequent invocations of the

44 Jan-Werner Müller, 'Beyond Militant Democracy?' (2012) 73 *New Left Review* 39, 43–4.
45 See Parliamentary Assembly of the Council of Europe, Resolution 1096, 'Measures to Dismantle the Heritage of Former Communist Totalitarian Systems' (1996).

rule of law and human rights, pervaded the entire resolution. It was central to the moral-legal ideology of transitional justice that aimed to establish and protect the "humane" and "civilized" world of liberal-democratic capitalism in Eastern Europe.

However, this liberal security mechanism gave ample room for anti-communist nationalist groups to instrumentalise and radicalise transitional justice, as the history of Polish lustration showed.[46] Conceived initially as a relatively moderate, liberal legal measure in 1997, the Polish lustration gradually turned into a weapon of nationalist populist "moral revolution" by the mid-2000s when right-wing groups came to dominate the institution of lustration. Lustration has become part of the highly contentious legal-political battles waged by right-wing groups and intensively so since the Law and Justice party came to power in 2015. The current "constitutional crisis" driven by the right-wing populist government extensively used transitional justice measures such as the cleansing of names associated with communism from public space, non-binding anti-communist parliamentary resolutions, and the sweeping conduct of lustration.[47] As in Hungary, the Polish government targeted the judiciary, especially the Constitutional Court and the Supreme Court, which the populist government presented as polluted with corrupt 'red judges.' By using different means of publicity, it claimed to finish the reckoning with the communist past, which the previous liberal governments supposedly treated too leniently.[48]

Memory laws and quasi-judicial institutions have been among the transitional justice measures to criminalise communism and regulate its memory.[49] Like lustration, memory laws draw on the militant democracy doctrine in its aim to protect democracy by legislating on the past[50] and raise a similar paradox, which Nikolay Koposov expressed well: how is it that those legislations on the past, which were initially formulated in Western Europe in the 1980s

46 For a good overview of the lustration laws in Eastern Europe, see Alexander Mayer-Rieckh and Pablo de Greiff, *Justice as Prevention: Vetting Public Employees in Transitional Societies* (New York: SSRC, 2007).

47 Krotoszyński, op.cit.; Anna Wójcik, 'Reckoning with the Communist Past in Poland Thirty Years After the Regime Change in the Light of the European Convention on Human Rights' (2019) 39 *Polish Yearbook of International Law* 135.

48 Krotoszyński, op.cit.

49 There are a number of agents and processes involved in the production of the memory of communism such as the commodification process and depoliticised nostalgia market, see, e.g., Maria Todorova and Zsuzsa Gille (eds), *Post-Communist Nostalgia* (New York-Oxford: Berghahn, 2010). Here, my focus is on the state-run national institutions and legislations that aim to judicialise communism often by using the terms of criminal justice.

50 Uladzislau Belavusau and Alexandra Gliszczyńska-Grabias, 'Introduction. Memory Laws: Mapping a New Subject in Comparative Law and Transitional Justice' in Uladzislau Belavusau and Alexandra Gliszczyńska-Grabias. (eds), *Law and Memory: Towards Legal Governance of History* (Cambridge: Cambridge University Press, 2017), 9.

to institute a liberal cosmopolitan Holocaust-memory that challenges self-congratulatory nationalist narratives, has become transformed into weapons of nationalist populist regimes to propagate exclusionary and antagonistic memory?[51] To explore this question, I will now turn to the making of those quasi-judicial memory institutions and laws.

9.5 Nationalising and Criminalising the Memory of Communism

Two types of institutions emerged in Eastern Europe to nationalise and judicialise the communist past: the state-run institutes of national memory, as in Poland, the Czech Republic, Slovakia, and Lithuania, and history commissions, as in Romania, Lithuania, Estonia, and Latvia, both of which were largely conceived during the European Union accession of these countries to secure their Western identity.[52] Similar to the aforementioned European resolution, these institutions presented communism as a 'bleak criminal inversion' of liberal-democracy.[53] To take one example, the Presidential Commission established in Romania in 2006, during the conservative anti-communist government, vividly expressed the image of communism painted by such institutions:

> The Communist regime was of a criminal nature, in the sense that it instigated, ordered and committed crimes against humanity. It was a regime, which looked to reduce the population to the condition of slaves, exploiting them pitilessly under the pretext of creating a utopian, egalitarian and free society. ... The Communist regime was an *anti-modern* one which merely *simulated* modernity . . . it was a regime of *foreign occupation* which liquidated the Romanian elite and its institutions of democracy, its market economy and private property. All this was *annihilated* for forty-five years, a false turn on the path of true modernization . . . it was a giant step *backwards*, which led us to chronic poverty, the isolation of the country, the wasting of human and material resources, the alienation of the individual and the destruction of our traditions and national culture.[54]

The report offered a lucid view on how anti-communist history and memory politics reconstructed the former regime. The communist regime was not just anti-modern, criminal, and destructive of national culture, but was also a

51 Koposov, *Memory Laws*.
52 See James Mark, *Unfinished Revolution: Making Sense of Communism in East-Central Europe* (New Haven, CT: Yale University Press, 2011) for an insightful discussion of national memory institutions in Eastern Europe from a comparative historical perspective.
53 Mark, *Unfinished*.
54 Quoted after Mark, *Unfinished*, 40, emphasis added.

diversion from the natural course of history, which was identified with the path of Western capitalist democracy. It was a 'giant step backwards.'[55] This widely shared view of communism among the dominant classes in post-1989 Eastern Europe indeed resonated very well with the revisionist works of Ernst Nolte and Stephane Courtois that we discussed earlier.

In Poland, it is the Institute of National Remembrance – the Prosecution of the Crimes against the Polish Nation – that emerged as the major agent of post-socialist official memory politics. Unlike the German Gauck authority, which mainly guarded the communist-era security archives and supervised their public access, or the Czech Institute of the Study of Totalitarian Regimes, which was mandated to conduct historical research on the Nazi occupation and the communist rule in the country, the Polish Institute of National Remembrance (thereafter, IPN) was a giant organisation that performed a number of archival, pedagogical, research, and prosecutorial functions. It ran the security archive which contained files from the Nazi occupation and the communist-era secret services, conducted and published historical research, performed lustration since 2006, organised out-reach pedagogical and cultural activities, and hosted the state prosecutorial office that investigated "Nazi crimes" and "communist crimes." It was the first institution of this kind in the region and served as a model for other institutions, for instance, in Slovakia and Lithuania.

The IPN was established in 1998, two years after the aforementioned European resolution, at a crucial moment of nation-state making shaped by the process of Poland's accession to NATO and the European Union. The 1998 legal act on the IPN prohibited the denial of Nazi and Communist 'crimes perpetrated against persons of Polish nationality and Polish citizens of other ... nationalities' and was followed by a number of similar Eastern European enactments.[56] The IPN was tasked both to preserve the memory of victims and the 'Polish Nation's struggles with occupants, Nazism and Communism,' and to 'prosecute crimes against peace, mankind and war crimes.' Like the aforementioned Romanian commission, the IPN associated

55 See Florin Poenaru, '"Tismăneanu Report" as Autobiography. History Writing at the End of (Soviet) Modernity' (2011) 56(2) *Sociologia* 19 and Ovidiu Țichindeleanu, 'Towards a Critical Theory of Postcommunism? Beyond Anticommunism in Romania' (2010) 159 *Radical Philosophy* 26 for a perceptive discussion of the Romanian commission's construction of communism and its politics of time, memory, and history.

56 Nikolay Koposov, 'Populism and Memory: Legislation of the Past in Poland, Ukraine, and Russia' (2022) 36(1) *East European Politics and Societies* 272. Koposov observes that the 1998 legal act of the IPN attempted to 'downplay the importance of the Holocaust and present the Poles rather than the Jews as Hitler's main victims. The law passed over in silence the participation of Poles in the Holocaust.' (2021, 7). 'While several countries (e.g., Bulgaria, Romania, Slovakia, Slovenia, and Croatia) criminalized the denial of crimes against humanity in accordance with the EU model,' writes Koposov, 'others have followed the Polish example by prohibiting the denial of both communist and Nazi crimes.' (ibid., 9)

communism with crimes and endorsed a judicial approach to the past. By framing together the post-1939 Nazi occupation and postwar communist regime as foreign occupations, the IPN's vision of history not only fuelled national victimhood sentiments, but also channelled the discussion of "collaboration" to the one with the communist state, marginalising the history of Polish anti-Semitism and collaboration with the Nazi forces. Moreover, with the recently renewed act on the IPN in 2016, the temporal scope of the institution extended to the October Revolution of 1917, which allowed for a more thorough criminalisation of the history of socialist and communist movements in Poland.

But the IPN's judicial approach to the communist past and ideology cannot be reduced to its formal prosecutorial investigations, which did not produce much effect in terms of actual prosecution, or to lustration that associated communism with the secret police and its treacherous agents. Through public activities and historical research, the IPN sought to adjudicate communism through cultural and media tribunals such as the controversial exhibition of the faces of the security officers that it organised in entire Poland in 2006–2007.[57] It attempted to change the names of the streets and public squares associated with communism as part of the de-communisation process, and rename them with the new patrons of history. It redistributed new names, titles, and sensibilities to remake the everyday public space. In short, the institution aspired to cement the post-socialist anti-communist hegemony in the field of memory and history writing. With its positivistic approach that claimed political neutrality and scientific objectivity, the IPN treated the police archives as a transparent repository of facts to be unearthed. It aimed at uncovering the hidden events and filling in the blanks of history.[58] In other words, the IPN judicialises history and memory of the past not only in the kind of knowledge it produced, but also in the very positivist and state-centred methodology it pursued, which recalls Carlo Ginzburg's discussion of the judicial approach to history.[59]

57 Saygun Gökarıksel, 'Facing History: Sovereignty and the Spectacles of Justice and Violence in Poland's Capitalist Democracy' (2019) 61(1) *Comparative Studies in Society and History* 111.

58 See Saygun Gökarıksel, 'Antifascist Strategy Today: Lineages of Anticommunism and "Militant Democracy" in Eastern Europe' in Jeremy Rayner (ed.), *Back to the 30s? Recurring Crises of Capitalism, Liberalism, and Democracy* (London: Palgrave-Macmillan, 2020) for a more detailed discussion of the IPN's historical and methodological approach to the police archives.

59 However, the irony is that both the IPN's mode of research and its national vision and legal-institutional design could be partly traced back to the communist-era – see Dariusz Stola, 'Poland's Institute of National Remembrance: A Ministry of Memory?' in A. Miller and M. Lipman (eds), *The Convolutions of Historican Politics* (Budapest: Central European University Press, 2012).

The judicialisation of communism becomes even more poignant when we consider the IPN's, and other such memory institutions', preoccupation with the concept of "communist crime." Widely used in Eastern Europe, this concept is constructed on the model of "Nazi crime" and the Holocaust memory to nationalise the memory of communism on the sanctity of victimhood and sacrifice. Many Polish conservative intellectuals have welcomed the concept of communist crime, which would make the suffering of the Polish nation and other former Soviet bloc countries more visible and respectful in the international arena. But the category did not stick easily, at least not in Poland. It was criticised for its lack of precision, especially the forms of violence it aimed to address. Like in other Eastern European countries, for instance, Romania, the category of communist crime was used vaguely and included a wide variety of actions ranging from political repression, persecution, to man-made famine and disastrous economic policy.[60]

The category of communist crime performed both a pragmatic and ideological function. In fact, many of those acts, such as the fabrication of false documents and homicide covered by the category, were already punishable under the criminal code of the communist state in Poland. The main problem was their enforcement and the statute of limitations regarding ordinary crimes. By redefining them as communist crime and treating them like war crimes and crimes against humanity, post-socialist state authorities aimed to overcome the statute of limitations and prosecute those acts 30, or in some cases such as homicide, 40 years after the end of state communism. In practice, many of those crimes, especially those committed during the Stalinist period, were difficult to prosecute due to the evidentiary problems related to the passing of time, for instance, problems in finding witness.[61]

But the most important function of the category of communist crime was arguably ideological. The category enabled political authorities to legally identify communism with criminal acts and transcend the particular time and history of communism into an abstract, timeless zone of universal crimes. By proclaiming to prosecute those crimes which long enjoyed de facto impunity, the authorities, especially right-wing groups, attempted to accumulate political and moral authority in the post-socialist era. Further, by modelling communist crime on Nazi crime, they sought to capitalise on the moral authority of the semi-sacred status of the Holocaust in post–Cold War Euro-America. Across Eastern Europe, the governments built a number of memory sites,

60 Mark, *Unfinished*, Gökarıksel, 'Facing.'

61 For a brief overview of the concept of communist crime and the challenges of prosecuting those crimes in Poland, see Maria Wilczek, 'Poland Removes Statute of Limitations on Communist Crimes' *Notes from Poland* (20 July 2020), available https://notesfrompoland.com/2020/07/20/poland-lifts-statute-of-limitations-on-communist-crimes/, accessed 2 May 2023.

parks, and museums such as the Museum of Terror in Budapest by drawing on and at times mimicking the Holocaust memory sites and museums.[62] In this way, they sought to make their national victimhood more credible in the era of Holocaust-centred, competitive memory.[63]

The concept of "victims of communism," which is the flip side of "communist crime," also posed important problems, in that it expressed the tensions marking what Enzo Traverso called the 'age of victims'[64] That concept defined people mainly with respect to their victimisation by the communist regime, irrespective of their specific political identities, acts, and struggles.[65] Which meant, in practice, rehabilitating radical nationalist and fascist groups as victims of communism and conflating them with communists and non-communist leftists who were also victimised by the communist states. By embracing the logic of liberal legalism, this category abstracted and de-politicised the different histories of struggle and paved the way to the resurgence of radical nationalist groups, which invoked historical anti-communist symbols and ideas. Moreover, the obsession with national victimhood and innocence led to the making of a number of memory laws, which criminalised or repressed public discussion on crucial issues such as the Polish involvement in anti-Jewish violence during and after World War II. Such memory laws aimed to put the nation on the pedestal of victimhood and exonerate it from responsibility and, thereby, endangered the democratic freedoms of expression, speech, and scholarly research.[66] By denouncing other (often neighbouring) countries' historical narratives as misleading or criminal, those laws also fuelled competitive memory politics in the international arena.

The European Union, the USA, and Russia contributed remarkably to the legal institutionalisation of nationalist competitive memory politics. Eastern European countries' search for recognition for victimhood was deeply embedded in the longstanding uneven material and ideological relations between and within the West and East, specifically, those countries' peripheral and semi-peripheral condition. At a moment when the Holocaust memory and the language of Nazi crime became a global currency of suffering, displacing

62 Ghodsee, *Red Hangover*, Mark, *Unfinished*, Nadkarni, *Remains*.

63 Hazan, *Judging*, Michael Rothberg, *Multidirectional Memory: Remembering the Holocaust in the Age of Decolonization* (Stanford: Stanford University Press. 2009).

64 Enzo Traverso, *Left-Wing Melancholia: Marxism, History, and Memory* (New York: Columbia University Press, 2016).

65 Marc, *Unfinished*.

66 Uladzislau Belavusau and Aleksandra Gliszczyńska-Grabias. *Law and Memory: Towards Legal Governance of History* (Cambridge: Cambridge University Press, 2017). Lustration laws can also be seen as memory laws. Nikolay Kaposov, discussed in the case of the Polish 2006 lustration act, which also aimed to prohibit the 'Slander of the Polish People': 'Anyone who publicly imputes to the Polish people participation in, organization of, or responsibility for communist or Nazi crimes shall be subject to the penalty of imprisonment for up to 3 years'. (2021, 10).

other memories of violence such as colonial violence in Algeria, Eastern European states used it to assert their moral and political credibility before the West in the hierarchy and competitive marketplace of victimhood.[67] They highlighted their sacrifice for European civilisation by pointing to the barbarity of eastern totalitarian Soviet communism and to their belonging to the West, even to the extent of "defending white Europe" against dangerous immigrants.[68]

One key moment at the European level of memory politics was 3 June 2008 when a group of right-wing Eastern European politicians and intellectuals came together in the Czech Parliament and signed the Prague Declaration on European Conscience and Communism. The signatories stated that the 'millions of victims of Communism and their families are entitled to enjoy justice, sympathy, understanding and recognition for their sufferings in the same way as the victims of Nazism have been morally and politically recognized' and that there must be an 'all-European understanding... that many crimes committed in the name of Communism should be assessed as crimes against humanity... in the same way Nazi crimes were assessed by the Nuremberg Tribunal'.[69] As Kristen Ghodsee observed, between 2008 and 2013, partly to manage social discontent against the financial crisis and ensure Eurozone stability in Spain and Greece, European leaders instituted many of the recommendations of the Prague Declaration, which involved declaring officially 'The European Day of Remembrance for Victims of Stalinism and Nazism' and organising a transnational consortium of research institutes and foundations including conservative think-tanks in the USA. This transnational consortium raised money for anti-communist memory work, which eventually reinforced conservative nationalist agendas in Eastern Europe. The moral equivalence of Nazism and communism as twin totalitarianisms was not new, but was now officially sanctioned in the international sphere and equipped with financial and logistical means to propagate a revisionist, judicial approach to communism. This judicial approach then served to rehabilitate fascism and the Holocaust complicity of many nationalist groups in Southeastern and Eastern Europe as victims of communism.[70]

The memory politics and laws also highlighted the uneven relations within and between Eastern European countries. The "mnemonic triangle"

67 Comaroff and Comaroff, op.cit., Hazan, *Unfinished*, Rothberg, op.cit.

68 "Defending white Europe" has been one of the well-known slogans of radical nationalists in the "Independence Day" march in Poland.

69 Quoted in Ghodsee op.cit., 2017, 133.

70 See Kirn, *Partisan*, Jana Tsoneva, 'Never Forget What the Fascists Did,' *Jacobin* (October 2019), https://jacobin.com/2019/10/bulgaria-fascism-nazism-anticommunism-historical-memory accessed 2 May 2023; Jelena Subotić, 'The Appropriation of Holocaust Memory in Post-Communist Eastern Europe' (2020) 1 *Modern Languages Open* 1 for a discussion of this dynamic.

of Poland-Russia-Ukraine illustrates the "conflictive constellations" arising out of those uneven relations.[71] All these states in the first quarter of the 21st century came to be governed by authoritarian nationalist governments that were keen to wage memory wars through particular kinds of legislation on the past. In the last years of the USSR and during much of the 1990s, state authorities openly promoted memory laws that condemned Soviet state violence.[72] Yet, especially with Putin's leadership in early 2000s, the form of memory laws shifted from a relatively more liberal approach to aggressive nationalist and neo-imperial memory policy. In this nationalist politics of history, the history of Soviet communism came to be reinterpreted as the glorious history of the Russian nation, symbolised by military victories. In this respect, the history policy revived the Stalinist cult of the "Great Patriotic War" to monumentalise the Russian sacrifice and victory over fascism, which it used in the international arena against, for instance, anti-Russian Ukrainian nationalist groups to denounce them as fascist. In turn, those groups, after coming to power in post-Maidan Ukraine, initiated a series of de-communisation acts in 2015, which made it illegal to publicly defame the memory of groups that fought for national independence including the Ukrainian Insurgent Army (UPA), known to have collaborated with the Nazis against the Soviets and performed the ethnic cleansing of Polish people in Volhynia and Eastern Galicia during the 1940s. This memory policy became part of a heated memory war between Ukraine and Poland, which culminated in the controversial memory law the Polish populist government drafted in 2018 to denounce the crimes of Ukrainian nationalist groups including the UPA. The Polish memory laws also engaged the Russian history policy through de-communisation acts that involved the removal of "totalitarian" symbols and monuments from public spaces.

In brief, in many Eastern European countries, memory laws have become instruments of authoritarian populist groups to promote nationalist mobilisation. These laws, Nikolay Koposov argued, often 'whitewash their countries' history' and 'shift the blame for historical injustices to other countries (the 1998 Polish, the 2000 Czech, the 2010 Lithuanian, the June 2010 Hungarian, and the 2014 Latvian statutes) and, in some cases, openly protect the memory of the perpetrators of crimes against humanity (the 2005 Turkish, the 2014 Russian, the 2015 Ukrainian, the 2006 and the 2018 Polish enactments)'.[73] But the point is not that memory laws have taken this shape due to some innate Eastern deficiency or authoritarianism,

71 See Félix Krawatzek and George Soroka. 'Circulation, Conditions, Claims: Examining the Politics of Historical Memory in Eastern Europe' (2022) 36(1) *East European Politics and Societies and Cultures* 198.

72 Koposov, 'Populism and Memory.'

73 Ibid.

or as a natural outcome of their history of "totalitarianism." These memory laws, and transitional justice politics in general, have been articulated within the highly uneven time-space of Eastern Europe under the dominance of Russia and Western Europe. The asymmetrical legal, military, and political economic relations offered substantial material and symbolic ground for right-wing populist groups to espouse their sovereigntist vision of justice and history, which they typically pitted against the West, or against Moscow and Brussels and their domestic allies. These attempts have fed on, and reinforced, a highly judicialised, exclusionary and antagonistic understanding of memory and identity, which adversely affects democratic life in those countries and beyond.

9.6 Conclusion

This chapter has explored the way the judicialisation of communism through transitional justice measures, including lustration and memory institutions, contributed to the expanding force of nationalist populist movements and governments in Eastern Europe. This judicial approach to communism took different forms and worked through multiple areas. Liberal legal ideology and constitutional order, especially with its anti-communist security mechanism articulated within the historical doctrine of militant democracy, has been complicit with this judicialisation of communism as a dead and criminal past and ideology. This security drive, in turn, helped nationalist populist and far-right groups gain political ground and wage a counter-hegemonic struggle against liberal and left-wing groups. The Europeanisation process and the soft-law guidelines for transitional justice prepared by European bodies contributed significantly to the legal-institutional entrenchment of such liberal anti-communist politics of security and, more generally, twin totalitarianism thesis that morally equated Nazism and communism. In other words, it is partly the post-socialist liberal and neoliberal institutions and constellations of power that led to the current so-called "backslide" or "regression" of democracy. Thus, one could better understand the dynamics of nationalist populism not simply as "anomaly" or "pathology" of actually existing liberal-democracy, but the radicalisation and expansion of its certain features including anti-democratic and anti-communist security drives ingrained in it.

Moreover, anti-communist memory laws, policies, and institutions have an important role in the consolidation of nationalist populism. By legitimising and reinforcing the victimhood agenda, based on national innocence and exoneration of guilt, these memory practices gave way to essentialist, exclusionary, self-righteous identity politics, which right-wing populist groups fuel as part of their nationalist politics of sovereignty and security. The historical and material realities of uneven relations between the West and East and within the East feed these kinds of sovereignty aspirations that work through both legal and extra-legal practices. The post-socialist judicialisation of communism, I have suggested, is not only about the communist past, but about the material and immaterial spectres of communism – 'communism to come', to use Jacques Derrida's formulation. The ahistorical and reified approach to the history of communism nourishes that spectral quality. That is part of the reason why "anti-communism after communism" could still exert such power after three decades and is able to be mobilised by nationalist conservatives to denounce vegetarians, environmentalists, LGBTQ activists, and ongoing social protests in Poland led by young women about their social and civil rights such as reproductive freedoms as neo-Bolsheviks, radical leftists, fascist leftism, and so on. Emptied of its social-historical content, communism became a general name to interpellate what is alien and dangerous in the post-socialist national, capitalist heteronormative ideological order.

Last but not least, such a judicial approach to communism as a finished, criminal past and ideology disables the articulation and popularisation of anti-capitalist critique of the structural contradictions of post-socialist neoliberalisation in the peripheral time-space of Eastern Europe. It displaces the understanding of capital's violence or "capitalist crimes" by blaming it on the spectres of communism ("red capitalists") or the legacies of the communist past. This discussion of judicialisation of communism is not a mere scholastic exercise. It has practical political stakes in it, one of which concerns the making of a popular left movement with a critical understanding of the history of socialism and communism in Eastern Europe and beyond, with its historical ruptures, dilemmas, struggles, and tragic actions of the actors and states that claimed to embody its name. As in every hegemonic formation, post-socialist anti-communist hegemony is also fragile, filled with tensions and contestations waged from different sides. Some statutes could not be dismantled, as the right-wing government attempted and some street names could not be renamed, but above all, anti-fascist and anti-capitalist politics find increasingly more popular ground, as the bleak realities of post-socialist transformation become more pronounced. This new formation requires a critical, socially embedded, and constitutive understanding of the relationship between law, history, and politics.

Chapter 10

Russian Conservatism and Populism

Between the Legal and the Political*

Mikhail Antonov

10.1 Introduction: Conservatism and Its Causes

In recent years one can observe how a number of countries of Central and Eastern Europe (CEE)[1] attempt to construct their identities through questioning their relation to the West,[2] underlining their disagreements with certain points on the EU's political agenda. In a broader context, Russia also seeks to assert its identity through opposing itself to the West and, in recent years, even challenging the world order established after the Cold War.[3] When Poland, Hungary, and some other countries raise objections against the distribution of migrants and other controversial decisions of the EU-authorities, this reveals certain similarities with the objectives pursued by Russia when it challenges the principles proclaimed by the CoE and other European organisations in which Russia is a member.[4] The present paper will argue that these similarities in attitudes towards the West in Russia and in the CEE are not a pure coincidence. Their strategy of resistance through identarian and conservative narratives might have deeper roots in the common socialist history

* The present chapter was prepared during my fellowship at the Institute of Eastern European and Comparative Law of the University of Cologne (2019–2020) with the financial support of the Alexander von Humboldt Foundation.

1 Here, this term covers all the ex-Warsaw bloc countries, except Russia and other ex-URSS countries.

2 Here, "the West" geographically more or less coincides with Western Europe within the EU borders before the 2004 and subsequent enlargements. Another meaning of "the West" implies associating certain ideological messages and political institutions (e.g., liberalism and democracy) with this notion. See, e.g., Guerman Diligensky and Sergei Chugrov, 'The West in Russian Mentality' (2000), at https://www.nato.int/acad/fellow/98-00/diliguenski.pdf, accessed 3 May 2023.

3 Elias Götz and Camille-Renaud Merlen, 'Russia and the Question of World Order' (2019) 20(2) *European Politics and Society* 133.

4 Robert Sata and Ireneusz Pawel Karolewski, 'Caesarean Politics in Hungary and Poland' (2020) 36(2) *East European Politics* 206.

DOI: 10.4324/9781032624464-11

of the CEE countries and also be grounded in their actual discontent with the peripheral positions they have in European institutions.[5]

Expressions of this discontent in Russia and in the CEE region coincide, at least in one dimension – the use of conservative arguments such as protection of national sovereignty and cultural identity, or defence of traditional values or Christian civilisation. Such conservative resistance has an observable impact on the legal development of these countries: a number of repressive laws against minorities adopted and practiced in these countries in recent years can be quoted as an example, as well as the laws that are allegedly aimed at curbing democratic institutions.[6] This conservative backlash introduces the perceivable tension between these legal systems and the supranational European law (the law of the CoE or/and EU law respectively) to which these systems are theoretically subordinated.[7]

Such repressive laws often rely on public opinion which, in the CEE region and in Russia, is remarkably less tolerant towards various minorities as in the West.[8] It might appear as a self-evident strategy to the governments in this region to rely on public opinion in order to instrumentalise its xenophobic and homophobic attitudes for maintenance of their legitimacy, especially in the situation when this legitimacy suffers from criticism from the European institutions and pro-European politicians and intellectuals. Unsurprisingly, this instrumentalisation preys on opposing the particularism of national cultures to what is taken today as principles of common European legal culture.[9] This instrumentalisation creates another pole around which the conservative resistance rotates – the anti-globalism which is articulated in the harsh rhetoric of Russian authorities against the West or in milder conservative

5 Ivan Krastev and Stephen Holmes, 'Explaining Eastern Europe: Imitation and Its Discontents' (2018) 29(3) *Journal of Democracy* 117.

6 E.g., Alina Polyakova et al., 'The Anatomy of Illiberal States: Assessing and Responding to Democratic Decline in Turkey and Central Europe' (2019), at https://www.brookings.edu/wp-content/uploads/2019/02/illiberal-states-web.pdf.

7 Normative grounds, conditions, and extent of this subordination of national legal systems to European law are not unfrequently contested both in legal scholarship and in political debates.

8 Sociological polls seem to confirm this. E.g., the October 2018 poll by the Pew Research Center showed that East-Europeans are almost twice less tolerant than West-Europeans: 'Eastern and Western Europeans Differ on Importance of Religion, Views of Minorities, and Key Social Issues', at https://www.pewforum.org/2018/10/29/eastern-and-western-europeans-differ-on-importance-of-religion-views-of-minorities-and-key-social-issues/.

9 Stephanie Law, 'From Multiple Legal Cultures to One Legal Culture? Thinking About Culture, Tradition and Identity in European Private Law Development' (2015) 31 *Utrecht Journal of International and European Law* 68.

narratives in the Visegrad countries against usurpation of political power by the European courts and other institutions.[10]

This twofold (conservative and anti-globalist) resistance reveals the paradox common to it. On the one hand, all these countries all claim to belong to the Western legal culture (sometimes, with certain civilisational reservations, as Russia) and, on the other, they tend to interpret the general principles of this culture (such as judicial independence, democracy, or antidiscrimination)[11] in ways that are incompatible with how they are interpreted nowadays by European courts and in the prevailing legal scholarship.[12] This attitude reveals the contradictory wish to be a part of Western civilisation and, at the same time, to stress their otherness from this civilisation. The conundrum can be explained by the differences between the real West, with its actual policies and institutions, and the imaginary West which is construed in various conservative, nativist narratives.

The strategies employed to deal with this conundrum also unveil some striking parallels. They often build on criticism of the so-called post-Christian culture in the real West supposedly detached from national cultures and their religious roots that characterise the imaginary West. It comes as no surprise that this resistance draws inspiration from conservative ideologies and that it is not unfrequently supported by the historical religious denominations (Catholicism and Orthodoxy). This support is often perceptible in public discourses about "normal families," about legal containment of LGBT and other movements incompatible with the religious dogma, and sometimes has decisive importance. For their part, working in tandem with illiberal governments in these and other aspects, the historical churches give their sympathetic consideration or prefer to keep silence about the governmental efforts to curb political opposition – this latter not unfrequently being pro-Western and anti-conservative.

In the political sphere, this tension reveals itself in the ways the friend-enemy distinction is framed in public discourse and is reflected in the law. In

10 Katharina Bluhm and Mihai Varga, 'Conservative Developmental Statism in East Central Europe and Russia' (2020) 25(4) *New Political Economy* 642; Robert Csehi and Edit Zgut, 'We Won't let Brussels Dictate Us: Eurosceptic Populism in Hungary and Poland' (2020) 22(1) *European Politics and Society* 53.

11 There are many varieties in which these principles are formulated. See, e.g., Armin Cuyvers, 'General Principles of EU Law' in Armin Cuyvers et al. (eds), *East African Community Law: Institutional, Substantive and Comparative EU Aspects* (Brill, 2017), 217–22.

12 Here, we do not discuss the adequacy of the interpretations given by European courts and institutions to such principles as rule of law, and the proportionality of the resistance to these interpretations in the Visegrad countries. See, e.g., Dimitry Kochenov and Petra Bárd, 'Rule of Law Crisis in the New Member States of the EU: The Pitfalls of Overemphasizing Enforcement', 1 *Reconnect Working Papers* (2018), at https://reconnect-europe.eu/wp-content/uploads/2018/07/RECONNECT-KochenovBard-WP_27072018b.pdf, accessed 3 May 2023.

Russian political discourse, the West is usually not portrayed as an unequivocal enemy on the main axis of the political: quite often in the narratives both of the governments and churches, the West is paradoxically placed on both sides of this axis – seen as "enemy" because supporting post-Christian values and as the cradle of the Christian civilisation which implies placing the West among "friends."[13] This attitude also reminds of the manner in which the West is perceived and evaluated by sundry conservators from the CEE region.[14]

In the legal sphere, this ambiguity is underscored by the fact that constitutions, basic laws, and ratified treaties usually target the achievement of common European values (e.g., the 1993 Russian Constitution) but statutory or case law sometimes introduces important exceptions into this targeting, making it dependent on the discretion of policymakers. The paradoxicality of this situation is that both Russia and the "disobedient" Visegrad countries prefer to maintain this contradiction in their law and to exploit the symbolic value of this contradiction in their relations with the West (bargaining better deals) and in their internal policies (demonstrating to the population their allegiance to the Western legal culture and, at the same time, their resoluteness to defend the national interest and local specificity).[15] This is only one of the sequences of the more general identarian paradox mentioned above – identifying itself with the imaginary West by declaring its otherness towards the real West.

This inconsistency can be also explained in terms of the notorious dualism of Russian law observed by some Western pundits:[16] two de facto parallel legal orders that coexist as "normal law" and "law of exception," the latter being defined ad hoc with references to political objectives. Elements of such dualism can also be found, albeit to a lesser extent, in the legal cultures of CEE countries – as a legacy of their previous Soviet period of their history. This ambiguity reveals (or rather seeks to hide) the tension which exists in many legal orders between rule and exception, between the legal and the political. Albeit the rule-exception tension is analytically independent from

13 Boris Groys, 'Russia and the West: The Quest for Russian National Identity' (1992) 43(3) *Studies in Soviet Thought* 185; Rosalind Marsh, 'The Nature of Russia's Identity: The Theme of "Russia and the West" in Post-Soviet Culture' (2007) 35(3) *Nationalities Papers* 555.

14 Katharina Bluhm and Mihai Varga (eds), *New Conservatives in Russia and East Central Europe* (Abingdon: Routledge, 2019).

15 Marianna Muravyeva, 'Conservative Jurisprudence and the Russian State' (2017) 69(8) *Europe-Asia Studies* 1145; Timea Drinóczi and Agnieszka Bień-Kacała, 'Illiberal Constitutionalism: The Case of Hungary and Poland' (2019) 20(8) *German Law Journal* 1140.

16 See about the Western perception of Russian nihilism and its drawbacks: Kathryn Hendley, 'Varieties of Legal Dualism: Making Sense of the Role of Law in Contemporary Russia' (2011) 29(2) *Wisconsin International Law Journal* 232.

the friend-enemy distinction, but in practice these two distinctions often work together.[17] The ubiquitous references to sovereignty in the case law of the Russian Constitutional Court can be cited as one of the examples of this coupling – these references usually rely on understanding sovereign power as the power of definition of "enemies" of the Russian state. In a broader perspective, this Schmittean dialectic also lies at the foundation of discourses about constitutional identity in the Visegrad countries.[18]

Although partisans of nativism would argue that their countries resisted Western globalism from time immemorial, in reality these tensions are not eternal and are likely to have pragmatic reasons in the current political situation. Some scholars reasonably explain the ambivalent attitude of the CEE countries towards the West as a sign of the dissatisfaction with the peripheral position of their countries.[19] The perceived "moral imperialism" of the European courts and institutions which impose principles and patterns stemming from German or French jurisprudence and scholarship in a top-down manner, only nurtures this ambivalence.[20] Once having concentrated political power in their hands, political leaders may feel the insentive to resist this top-down treatment. Declaring such resistance can help them, at the same time, to mobilise political and other elites and to flatter popular mind-sets which are often incapable of resisting the temptation of grand narratives about their nation and its uniqueness.[21]

To use Francis Bacon's figure of speech, these nativist narratives can successfully function as *idola specus* – they place national legal orders into larger interpretative frameworks where key interpretations are derived from the local "political theology" and, with this, turn out to be incompatible with the supranational law and its interpretations by supranational courts and institutions. Naturally, other *idola* mentioned by Bacon only contribute to this "nativisation" of the legal discourse and reinforce its dependence on the political. This does not necessarily mean that such movements are orchestrated from the Kremlin – a more plausible explanation might be the similarity of the historical past and pragmatic reasons of the moment.

17 Marie Goupy, 'The State of Exception Theory of Carl Schmitt and the Ambivalent Criticism of Liberalism' (2018) 28 *Zeitschrift für Politikwissenschaft* 395.

18 Aliaksei Kazharski, 'The End of "Central Europe"? The Rise of the Radical Right and the Contestation of Identities in Slovakia and the Visegrad Four' (2018) 23(4) *Geopolitics* 754.

19 E.g., Tanja A. Börzel and Julia Langbein, 'Core-Periphery Disparities in Europe: Is there a Link between Political and Economic Divergence?' (2019) 45(2) *West European Politics* 941.

20 Dagmar Rita Myslinska, 'Not Quite Right: Representations of Eastern Europeans in ECJ Discourse' (2020) 34 *International Journal of Politics, Culture, and Society* 271.

21 This kind of superimposition of certain dominant legal cultures is per se an important source of problems and not only for the countries considered as (partly) authoritarian.

It comes as no surprise that identarian narratives are widely utilised as efficient tools for consolidating political power and maintaining legitimacy. As will be shown in this paper, in Russia these narratives are gradually incorporated into constitutional law either directly (through legal amendments) or indirectly (through case law). As a result of this incorporation, the Russian political leadership incapsulated itself from the criticism of the ECtHR and other supranational bodies and, at the same time, gained popular support in sociological polls.[22] From a purely pragmatic perspective, political leaders in other countries can consider this Russian policy as a worthy example and be inclined to follow similar strategies in bargaining with the West and in maintaining their own legitimacy inside the country.[23]

These narratives can not only help authorities to mobilise elites and the wider population, but also to make the people more law-obedient, "demystifying" the law from the sublime ideals and conceptions (such as human rights) understandable only to narrow circles of intelligentsia. If legal narratives are made thereby more understandable to the population, this can bring into popular mindsets more thrust into the law and, therefore, make this law more efficient. With this fact one can see how populism can work in law: changing the law (or its interpretations) in accordance with popular mistrust towards minorities in order to demonstrate that the government 'hears the voice of the people' and makes the laws that are 'wanted by the people' and not by hostile forces from outside.[24] Here, the representation of "enemy" might play its role again: the need for legitimation suggests that the authorities would attempt to make the population more loyal both to the rulers and to the legal commands emanating from them.

10.2 The Legal and the Political in Identarian Discourses

The divide between friends and enemies plays an important role in defining exceptions from law and the sovereign power that is enabled to such exceptions.[25] With this, the friend-enemy distinction penetrates in legal discourse: such was the contrast between capitalist and socialist law in legal theory or the distinction between the "law of civilised nations" and the law of other

22 Sociological polls demonstrate that public opinion usually supports restrictive laws against minorities and the exceptionalist rhetoric of the authorities. E.g., 'A Closer Look at How Religious Restrictions Have Risen Around the World', at https://www.pewforum.org/2019/07/15/a-closer-look-at-how-religious-restrictions-have-risen-around-the-world/.

23 Melissa Hooper and Grigory Frolov, 'Russia's bad example' (February 2016), at https://www.humanrightsfirst.org/sites/default/files/Russias_Bad_Example.pdf.

24 Bojan Bugarič, 'The Two Faces of Populism: Between Authoritarian and Democratic Populism' (2019) 20(3) *German Law Journal* 390.

25 Bruno Gulli, 'The Sovereign Exception: Notes on Schmitt's Word that Sovereign is He Who Decides on the Exception' (2009) 1(1) *Glossator* 23.

(implicitly uncivilised) nations in international law of the past, such is the basic division between Western and non-Western legal systems in comparative law today.

This divide is often articulated, or at least implied, in identarian discourses and, thereby, frame them into the larger picture of the political. It is far from being unusual that human beings identify themselves not only with their country or culture, but also with their law, their political system, and so on. This identification implies what Fukuyama called *isothymia* – the demand to be respected on an equal basis with other peoples that drives demands for equal recognition, which are unlikely to ever be completely fulfilled.[26] These demands can be effectively utilised for political mobilisation by those who argue that the declared equality within the EU or the CoE does not correspond to the reality in which the decision-making power is shared between several economically prosperous countries, while other countries are pushed on the periphery.[27]

The friend-enemy distinction frequently repeats, with some nuances, the key philosophical differentiation between "correct" (natural, reasonable, etc.) and "incorrect" law, which is therefore sometimes classified as *Unrecht*. Once, many Sovietologists refused to consider Soviet law as "law" because of the drawbacks incompatible with how the ideal of the rule of law is understood in the West. Even today, certain experts continue to speculate whether Russian law is "law." In the same way, particular statutory laws (e.g., the controversial Polish laws about judicial nominations) can be challenged as to their legal nature – whether they are compatible with the core of "law" as this latter is defined by European courts and institutions.

Challenging positively impeccable laws (in terms of procedure and form) can result in blurring the topography of the legal (mixing it up with the political), on the one hand, and in mobilisation of the population and elites around what is "our" law and, probably, also what "our" political system is and around those who defend them, on the other. This criticism of the acting law would normally follow the friend-enemy distinction – not only at the national level, as this distinction is formulated in official narratives, but also at the supranational (European) level where the same processes of differentiation of "our" law and "their" (authoritarian, dictatorial, repressive, etc.) law are taking place from various ideological standpoints. Differentiation between "our" and "their" law (in its various forms) can be seen as one of

26 Francis Fukuyama, *Identity: Contemporary Identity Politics and the Struggle for Recognition* (London, Profile Books, 2018).

27 Andrés Santana, Piotr Zagórski, and José Rama, 'At Odds with Europe: Explaining Populist Radical Right Voting in Central and Eastern Europe' (2020) 36(2) *East European Politics* 288.

the developments of the friend-enemy divide, instrumentalised in the legal discourse.[28]

The divide between the socialist and capitalist worlds provided the framework for identarian discourses in the USSR and in the CEE countries during the Soviet period. After this period was over, the post-Soviet countries (with some notable exceptions such as Belarus) attempted to identify themselves as parts of Western civilisation, putting the West on the axis of "friends." The "enemy" side of this divide was filled by the actors of their own history and by the Soviet Union as the occupation power.[29] Gradually, the CEE countries placed Russia on the axis of enemies both as a successor of the USSR and as a continuator of its imperial policies. On the other end of the axis stood the West and its institutions which counteracted the Soviet (and then Russian) threat and thereby were "friends" protecting these countries.

Amazingly, Russia in its first post-Soviet years also followed this pattern. There were quite practical reasons for Yeltsin's disfavour to the Soviet past: communists and many traditionalists were in the camp of his antagonists, so that the government pragmatically chose to frame Russian political identity into Western patterns. At this time, Russian leaders seriously considered adherence to NATO and other Western organisations, to become a part of the "big Europe from Lisbon to Vladivostok." The liberal values enshrined in the 1993 Constitution reflected this illusion, albeit it soon became clear that the West was not about to stop its eastward expansion or to accept Russia in its structures.

Yeltsin attempted to go as far as to outlawing communist ideology, as it was made in almost all the CEE countries, but was stopped by the Constitutional Court. As the Court argued in the 1992 milestone CPSU (the Communist Party of Soviet Union) case, there can be no limitation on political opinions and convictions in a democratic state, so that the communist ideology cannot be outlawed. Based on this argumentation, the RF Constitutional Court partly invalidated Yeltsin's decree on disbanding the CPSU and excluded responsibility of the CPSU for the past.[30] This ruling meant that, different to many other countries of the ex-Warsaw bloc, Russia was not to reconsider its past and was resolute in abstaining from naming and shaming those who were guilty of atrocities commited by the Soviet regime.[31] Symptomatically, the 1991 Law dealing with the rehabilitation of

28 Eric J. Mitnick, 'Law, Cognition, and Identity', (2007) 67(3) *Louisiana Law Review* 823.

29 Helga A. Welsh, 'Dealing with the Communist Past: Central and East European Experiences after 1990' (1996) 48(3) *Europe-Asia Studies* 413.

30 Judgment of the RF Constitutional Court No.9-П of 30 November 1992.

31 Jane Henderson, 'Making a Drama out of a Crisis: The Russian Constitutional Court and the Case of the Communist Party of the Soviet Union', 19:3 *King's College Law Journal* (2008), 489–506.

victims of the Soviet regime[32] did not condemn the Soviet ideology as such, but condemned in general totalitarian practices to punish people because of political and religious convictions (Preamble). For time time being, Russia remained at the midway of its transition.

In the post-Yeltsin years, Russia slowly changed its attitude and ceased to unequivocally place the West on the "friend axis" of the political. This brought a cleavage between vectors of political development of Russia and the CEE countries. At the same time, Russian political leadership refrained from unambiguously placing the West on the axis of enemies. The main objective of Putin's government in this aspect was to maintain the status quo and to prevent the Western powers from interfering with Russia's internal affairs. When, in the mid-2000s, Putin consolidated the power in his hands and Russia decided to actively contain NATO, the EU, and other Western organisations in their continued *Drang nach Osten.*[33]

Putin's 2007 "Munich speech" signalled that Russia had recovered from the turbulent years of transition, has the power to step in against the West's suspected misuses of international law, and to challenge its ideological narratives. The ensuing 2008 war in Georgia confirmed Putin's plans to challenge the post-Soviet system of international relations, at least in Europe. To resist Western "moral and legal imperialism," Russia chose the role of a protector of the established order (based on sovereignty and the supremacy of domestic law) and traditional values (those rooted in religious traditions).[34] This role of a supporter of moderate conservatism was not then claimed by the other big powers, so that Russia could profit from its new ideological stance to recruit followers both domestically and abroad. Instead of the expensive Soviet model of requiting friendly regimes by giving credits and writing them off for recognition of the communist ideology, Russia counteracted US military and political operations by positioning itself as a protector of the status quo, trying to create a bloc of similarly-minded regimes.[35]

In the 2000s, such anti-Western attitudes would hardly be thinkable in the CEE countries. The frustration with neoliberalism in the economy and ultraliberalism in the law increasingly spurred malcontents in this region in the early 2010s; this suggested to some politicians to collect political dividends

32 Law of the Russian Federation (18.10.1991, No.1761-1) 'On Rehabilitation of Victims of Political Repressions.'

33 Nicolai Petro, 'How the West Lost Russia: Explaining the Conservative Turn in Russian Foreign Policy' (2018) 3(3) *Russian Politics* 305.

34 Vincent Keating and Katarzyna Kaczmarska, 'Conservative Soft Power: Liberal Soft Power Bias and the "Hidden" attraction of Russia' (2019) 22(1) *Journal of International Relations and Development* 1.

35 Glenn Diesen, 'Russia as an International Conservative Power: The Rise of the Right-Wing Populists and their Affinity towards Russia' (2020) 28(2) *Journal of Contemporary European Studies* 182.

from this frustration. In the mid-2010s, Russia's relative success in containment of the West in Georgia, Ukraine, or Syria, on the one hand, and perceptible rifts in the Western block after the 2015 migration crisis and the 2016 election of Donald Trump, on the other, created the impression that such a strategy could eventually bring more legitimacy inside the country and a more privileged position within European institutions. It was at that time that a number of political leaders (such as Viktor Orbán) actively started to defy the EU policies and institutions, implying that they go aloof from the true principles of the Christian civilisation of Europe.[36]

These processes in Russia and in the Visegrad countries had at least one aspect in common. All these countries seemed to be unhappy with the place attributed to them in the European systems of political decision making. This frustration can be intertwined into a right-wing political programme of what is actually happening. But there seems to be no necessary analytical connection: dissatisfaction with the subordinated position of their country in the regional political system may as well prompt left-wing movements to stick to the traditionalist agenda.[37] This frustration relies on the assumption that the CEE countries underwent geopolitical modernisation under the influence of the West and abandoned the communist past to confirm their belonging to Western civilisation, which gave the West the ground to consider them as backward: despite the solemn declarations of the Western powers, the newcomers (the post-Soviet countries) are "unjustly" placed into a peripheral position and feel that they have the moral right to struggle for its recognition as an "equal power" from the West.

This malcontent with the peripheral position of these countries is expressed through conservative rhetoric. In Russia, this rise of conservatism took place at the beginning of the 2000s and, thereafter, could also be observed in so-called velvet dictatorships in the CEE region.[38] In public discourse, the change of perspective became more visible – the local and national were situated on the positive side, while the global and the universal were not unfrequently seen as negative signposts of cosmopolitism and as harbingers of a catastrophe.[39] The friend-enemy divide became even more blurred in the perspectives

36 Aron Buzogány and Mihai Varga 'The Ideational Foundations of the Illiberal Backlash in Central and Eastern Europe: the Case of Hungary' (2018) 25(6) *Review of International Political Economy* 811.

37 This is the case in Russia where the RF Communist Party, the second party at the Russian Parliament, stands on even more nationalist and exceptionalist positions than the ruling party (the United Russia). If such exceptionalism and nationalism is compatible with Marxism is another question which is not the subject matter of this paper.

38 Atilla Ágh, 'Increasing Eupopulism as the Megatrend in East-Central Europe: From Façade Democracies to Velvet Dictatorships' (2016) 5 *Baltic Journal of Political Science* 21.

39 Attila Melegh, *On the East-West Slope: Globalization, Nationalism, Racism and Discourses on Central and Eastern Europe* (Budapest: Central European University Press, 2006).

of traditional values and religious ethics. Given this dimension of the political, it is not surprising that some contemporary conservative diatribes about preservation of "true European values" or defence of Christian civilisation sound similarly in Russia and in the CEE countries and lead to similar ideological conclusions.[40]

This agenda has as strong a performative potential as any conservative programme that asserts a systematic preference for practice over theory.[41] In this sense, Huntington correctly suggested that conservatism is not an ideology, but rather a relational method of thinking aimed at defending the status quo.[42] Conservatism might be the best vehicle for such protection of the status quo – different traditions are all worth of being preserved, none of them (e.g., those promoted by the most powerful countries) may pretend to be superior over the other ones. With this, conservatism turns out to be a powerful anti-globalist vehicle that prioritises national sovereignty as a cornerstone of any true legal order. As far as every nation (people) is embedded in its culture, imposition of universal values would endanger both the nation and its culture, unless these universal values are themselves grown out of different cultural traditions unified by a common religious belief. Below, we will show how this conservative argument was applied in the case law of the Russian Constitutional Court.

Russia is a part of Western civilisation but Russia's principal adversary lies in the West – this ambiguity was central for Russian intellectual history. The contradictory attitude towards the West persistently appeared in medieval narratives about Russia as the sole protector of the true Christianity (the Third Rome) to Slavophile musings about Russian people's messianic role in world history (the Holy Rus') or to the Marxist-Leninist dogma according to which it belongs to Soviet Russia to put an end to injustice in the world and to change it for the better. The real incentives for these endeavours were, analogously to contemporary exceptionalist discourses, connected with Russia's malcontent with its peripheral role in Europe and its longing for equal standing with other European powers.[43] However, the West as a whole

40 Fedor Stanzhevskiy and Dmitry Goncharko, 'Pluralism and Conflict: The Debate about Russian Values and Politics of Identity' (2019) 13(2) *Journal of Nationalism, Memory and Language Politics* 251. There is an implicit consensus in the Western media and among political analysts to qualify these conservative narratives as populism. There seems to be no good reason for this word usage: these narratives shall be considered for what they are – expressions of conservative ideologies. Another question is what stands behind utilisation of these ideologies and how they are employed in practice.

41 Michael Oakeshott, *Rationalism in Politics and Other Essays* (London: Methuen, 1962).

42 Samuel Huntington, 'Conservatism as Ideology' (1957) 51(2) *American Political Science Review* 454.

43 Richard Sakwa, 'Greater Russia: Is Moscow out to Subvert the West?' (2020) 58 *International Politics* 334.

has never been portraited as an "enemy."[44] Europe is the point of attraction for Russia, it is an integral part of Russia's identity which separates it from the Orient[45] and makes it a part of Christian civilisation. It is with Europe that most Russians identify their culture.[46] This popular perception is echoed in political narratives from the 19th century until now.

A full identification is impossible too: let alone that Russia geographically also belongs to Asia, it is also politically exempt from participation in the key European alliances (such as the EU or NATO), perceiving both as targeted against Russia's interests. To blame "enemies" and to look for "friends" in the West – this Russian emotional reaction had become proverbial as early as the 18th century and pushed sundry Russian politicians and intellectuals to show off Russia's real or imaginary otherness, *samobytnost*.[47] This response is not uniquely Russian – Turkey's attitude towards the West today is also largely shaped by a similar emotional frustration; Germany similarly fought for its recognition as a peer among the lead European powers (England and France) in the 19th century.· It is likely that this frustration is also shared by such "disobedient" members of the EU as Hungary and Poland, although they do not go as far Russia and Turkey in asserting their "otherness."

Russia's inconsistency in this respect is that, asserting its otherness from the West, it seeks to become a full member of Western civilisation. Self-identification as an alter-ego of the West seems to be a deadlock for Russia: cleaned from the Western elements, Russian identity would hang in the air or remain a game of imagination – as it was the case of the Slavophile and other romanticised constructions in the 19th century.[48] In the course of Peter the Great's westernisation reforms at the beginning of the 18th century, hardly any sphere of social life remained unchanged: Russia exported culture, bureaucracy, law, and many other elements of Western civilisation, followed its development and sometimes even pretended to take the lead of it: e.g., Russia's role in the Holy Alliance or the 1917 Bolshevik Revolution. This latter ideologically consisted in exporting socialist ideals from the West

44 Peter Duncan, 'Contemporary Russian Identity between East and West' (2005) 48(1) *Historical Journal* 277.

45 In Russian political narratives one can hardly find such identification, also the majority of Russian intellectuals (including such nativists as Slavophiles, Byzantinists, or Soilers) looked at Russia as a part of Europe, with only few exceptions such as Lev Gumilev who identified Russia as a geopolitical whereabout between the West and the Great Desert in the East.

46 Irina Semenenko, 'The Quest for Identity. Russian Public Opinion on Europe and the European Union and the National Identity Agenda' (2013) 14(1) *Perspectives on European Politics and Society* 102; Irina Souch, *Popular Tropes of Identity in Contemporary Russian Television and Film* (New York: Bloomsbury Academic, 2019).

47 Teodor Shanin, *The Roots of Otherness: Russia's Turn of Century* (New Haven, CT: Yale University Press, 1986), in volume 2.

48 Andrzej Walicki, *The Slavophile Controversy: History of a Conservative Utopia in Nineteenth-Century Russian Thought* (Oxford: OUP, 1975).

and implementing them before they were carried out in other parts of the European continent.[49]

Contemporary Russia's frustration at being excluded from the Western political and military structures is nothing new if seen in the context of Russia's historical struggle for recognition as one of the Western powers. This struggle had started long before Peter the Great's reforms which paradigmatically symbolised it. Because the West's reluctance (real or imaginary) to accept Russia's claims to a full-fledged membership in European structures, Russia seeks to identify itself as "the other Europe" standing for conservative values.[50] In this dimension, Russian political behaviour today does not radically differ from how Russia acted in the 19th century.

Nor can Russian law be detached from the Western legal tradition. A short glimpse confirms that Russian law is based on Western principles, is shaped according to Western patterns, is unthinkable without the Western legal technique. Without the Western content and forms, Russian law would be empty. Not unfrequently statutes are simply copied, or at least are drafted with reference to Western "best practices." Even the most "original" parts of the legislation aimed at defining Russian constitutional identity are taken from the constitutional law of Germany and other European countries – similarly, in the 19th century, Slavophiles and Vladimir Soloviev passionately wrote about Russia's otherness, basing their ruminations on the ideas of the Germans Hegel or Schelling.

10.3 Instrumentalising the Historical Past

Another common issue that connects Russia with the CEE countries is how to deal with the communist past. This past is not easily reconcilable with the precedent "organic" development based on religion, private property, monarchy, and rural culture common to most of the population before 1917 or, respectively, 1945. In Russia, these cornerstones of the previous social order were ousted by urbanisation, atheism, "popular democracy," industrialisation, and other hallmarks of the Soviet époque. Narratives of some Russian conservators and religious leaders suggest that they would welcome a return to the preindustrial past significantly impregned by religion. But this does not seem to be a feasible solution, and the golden age of the pre-1917 Russian Empire is unattainable.

Russian attitudes in the early 1990s to Soviet history were similar to those of the CEE countries – the 1917 Bolshevik Revolution and the Soviet past were seen rather negatively, with the glorification of the Imperial (pre-1917)

49 Nicolas Berdyaev, *The* Russian Idea (New York: Macmillan, 1942).
50 Richard Pipes, *Russian Conservatism and its Critics: A Study in Political Culture* (New Haven: Yale University Press, 2005).

legacy.[51] Condemning its Soviet past in a wholesale manner in the 1990s, Russia quite quickly felt itself "defrauded," in the sense that this was exploited by the West for asserting Russia's backwardness. The military campaigns in Iraq, Yugoslavia, or Libya, the creeping expansion of NATO and other signals demonstrated that Russia's voice is not likely to be heard in decision-making processes. The Soviet past seemed to be among the reasons for being pushed to the political periphery as a backward country.[52]

A solution to this intellectual and emotional conundrum was found in Russia during the rise of authoritarianism in the 2000s, when the leadership started to widely employ the conservative rhetoric for attacking the liberal façade which allegedly hides the real, supposedly unfair, Western mechanism of decision making.[53] The requirement to defend a country's sovereignty and cultural specificity, to maintain political and social stability, to deal with complicated issues of the past unsurprisingly mandated the need in a strong state (the "vertical of power" in Russian political vocabulary) directed by an authoritarian leader. In its turn, this vertical of power shall be sheltered from unnecessary perturbations and shall, as far as possible, secure continuity. These ideological messages relied on historical examples (Russia's past was mostly the history of autocracy, *samoderzhavie*).[54]

It comes as no wonder that similar situation of "unjustly bereft" of the factual power may provoke similar ideological responses against the neoliberalism and globalism that are often associated with political ambitions of the dominating Western countries.[55] In this perspective, Russia and the CEE countries faced similar, although not identical, challenges on their trajectories of the post-communist transition.[56] Initially, the main objective of this transition was to get rid of the Soviet past, but the key consequence turned out to be that the CEE countries, before the end of this transition

51 In the narratives of the 1990s the Bolshevik Revolution and the ensuing Soviet rule was generally represented as a national tragedy, as an interruption of normal development of Russia (Alexei I. Miller, 'The Russian Revolution of 1917: History, Memory, and Politics' *Russia in Global Affairs* (26 February 2018), available at https://eng.globalaffairs.ru/articles/the-russian-revolution-of-1917-history-memory-and-politics/ accessed 15 September 2023). The membership of Russia in the USSR was, in this perspective, considered as a kind of occupation, as an encroachment on Russia's sovereignty, so that the first Russian foundational act was the 1990 Declaration of Independence (12 June 1990).

52 Whether this reaction was adequate or based on false perception, goes beyond the scope of this paper.

53 Mikhail Antonov, 'Law and Memory Politics in Russia' (2019) 65(4) *Osteuroparecht* 410.

54 Paul Robinson, *Russian Conservatism* (Ithaca: Cornell University Press, 2019).

55 Laure Neumayer and Georges Mink, 'Introduction' in Georges Mink and Laure Neumayer (eds), *History, Memory and Politics in East Central Europe. Memory Games* (New York: Palgrave Macmillan, 2013), 1–20.

56 Nikolay Koposov, *Memory Laws, Memory Wars: The Politics of the Past in Europe and Russia* (Cambridge: Cambridge University Press, 2018).

period, were doomed to remain on the periphery of the European political system. The rising exceptionalism translates the problem of self-identification and expresses the disagreement with the European political order that was formed in the aftermath of the Cold War.

The attitude towards Soviet history is also brought into question in Russian political discourse, especially in what concerns modelling the friend-enemy axis in line with certain ideological interpretations of World War II.[57] In some CEE countries one can observe comparable nostalgia of the Soviet past – in political narratives, certain past achievements (especially in the social sphere) are represented as laudable, while the neoliberal reforms inspired by the West that took place in the post-communist period are criticised in the perspective of their social consequences. This leads to further problematisation of the friend-enemy distinction.[58]

These narratives of the contemporary Russian leaders are nothing new against the backdrop of intellectual history which emphasised both Russia's inclusiveness into Western civilisation and its specificity that would justify the political autocracy. In the 19th century, the catch-phrase "Orthodoxy, Autocracy and Nationality" outlined this strategy of exceptionalism and indicated at its milestones.[59] This national specificity is putatively formed through religiosity of the population, which requires justification of the political by the religion: 'every Russian *muzhik* believes in God and tsar,' and justifies the linkage of Russian people and religion to autocracy. The reinterpretation of the old Russian discourse that was undertaken in the mid-2010s, seeks to "update," in the collective mind, the narratives about Russia's vocation to protect the true religion and to do away with injustice in the world. Using the old musters of ideological narratives about Russia's exceptional vocation in world history (to fight against evil in the form of false religions or class domination), the new identarian discourse of Russian authorities apparently seeks to revitalise the century-old narrative and to promote, thereby, the national self-identification of Russians around the friend-enemy axis.[60]

57 Serguei Oushakine, 'Remembering in Public: On the Affective Management of History' (2013) 1 *Ab Imperio* 269.

58 Igor Torbakov, 'History, Memory and National Identity: Understanding Politics of History and Memory Wars in Post-Soviet Lands' (2011) 19(3) *Demokratizatsiya: The Journal of Post-Soviet Democratization* 209; Ewa Stańczyk, 'Caught between Germany and Russia: Memory and National Identity in Poland's Right-Wing Media Post-2004' (2013) 91(2) *Slavonic and East European Review* 289.

59 Sean Cannady and Paul Kubicek, 'Nationalism and Legitimation for Authoritarianism: A Comparison of Nicholas I and Vladimir Putin' (2014) 5(1) *Journal of Eurasian Studies* 1.

60 Marlene Laruelle, 'Russia as an Anti-Liberal European Civilisation' in Pål Kolstø and Helge Blakkisrud (eds), *The New Russian Nationalism: Imperialism, Ethnicity and Authoritarianism 2000–2015* (Edinburgh: Edinburgh University Press, 2016), 275–97.

The expected conclusion in this identarian discourse is the theory that for maintenance of the social order and for preservation of "national specificity" one needs a strong state which would keep the laws of the country under control, defending them from the decaying effect of liberal decadence (LGBT rights, disappearance of national sovereignty, etc.), or of "propaganda of Nazism" (in which a considerable number of the post-Soviet countries are accused).[61] This memory politics contributed to further elaboration of the friend-enemy distinction both in Russia and in the CEE countries.

10.4 Identity Through Law and Law Through Identity

The examples given above are intended to demonstrate how conservative identarian narratives can serve the Russian authorities in framing the political and the legal. At the same time, these narratives are emotionally close to many Russians and their symbolic power seems to be stronger than that of the liberal values enshrined in the Constitution. This suggests to utilise these narratives as tools to maintain legitimacy.[62]

For several years the political leadership of Russia was undecided how such utilisation was in the framework of Russian law. Adopting a new constitution would be a too risky enterprise, but how otherwise to underscore that Russia disagrees with the liberal values imposed on it in the early 1990s when the country was too weak and unready to resist the Western "moral colonisation" after Russia's defeat in the Cold War? The recipe was soon found – to create a parallel interpretative field where the liberal texts would acquire their "correct" meanings. This new constellation can be described in terms of "real" and "formal" law or "law in action" and "law in books" – the situation where there is a considerable discrepancy between the law as it is enacted and the law as it is applied, is well known in other legal orders and thoroughly described by legal realists and sociologists on many occasions.

The leading role in this reinterpretation was assigned to the Russian Constitutional Court. Its jurisprudence is often criticised as sham-constitutionalism – the Court always remains a medium of political will. This policy is perfectly compatible with the second main feature of Russian law (the first one is hard positivism) – decisionism. The frequent use of the sovereignty argument by the Constitutional Court reflects this feature and the intrinsic fusion of the legal and the political in Russian law.

61 Deborah Larson and Aleksei Shevchenko, 'Russia Says No: Power, Status, and Emotions in Foreign Policy', (2014) 47(3) *Communist and Post-Communist Studies* 269.

62 Lev I. Jakobson, Boris Rudnik, and Stefan Toepler, 'From Liberal to Conservative: Shifting Cultural Policy Regimes in Post-Soviet Russia' (2018) 24(3) *International Journal of Cultural Policy* 297.

One of the main irritating factors for the new Russian conservative policies was the rise of supranational law with its claims to global or regional universality – these claims are most patently reflected in the narratives about human rights and common European values. Such pretended universality is often criticised as a justification of neocolonialism, and is opposed by the contrary tendencies of domestic law which underscores the national specificity and requires a particular treatment for itself. In the public narratives of Putin, Orbán, and some other East-European political leaders, this serves as one of the catalysts of the frustration with the peripheral position of their countries, which was described above. The authority of the ECtHR to pronounce about the national law of CoE countries became the *casus belli* in the ideological conflict between Russia and the West in recent years.

Russia did not fail to profit from this theoretical and political ambiguity of the power of the ECtHR and pour water on its mill of conservative ideology. In the cases of *Markin*,[63] *Anchugov*,[64] or *Yukos*,[65] Russia was not the first European country to contest this power of the ECtHR, albeit this contestation was particular. Remarkable in this reaction of Russia was that Russia deliberately defied the ECtHR, instead of trying to find a common ground for dealing with specific questions revealed by the ECtHR. The *Anchugov and Gladkov* case is symptomatic: after the RF Constitutional Court ruled out the possibility to execute in Russia the ECtHR judgment because of its purported unconstitutionality, the CoE established that this judgment was de facto executed by Russia. Apparently, it was rather a case of "principled resistance," without any factual need to discard the ECtHR judgment.[66]

In these and other cases, the RF Constitutional Court has reinterpreted the conception of human rights so that, in fact, it excluded its application in a number of sensitive high-profile cases. According to this reinterpretation, in a conflict between individual rights and the collective interests, the former shall be defeated as is well illustrated in the series of cases concerning Yukos and, personally, Mikhail Khodorkovsky. To defend this reinterpretation, the Constitutional Court chose to deny the universality of human rights,

63 ECtHR Judgment *Markin v. Russia* (Grand Chamber) (22 March 2012) Application No.30078/06; RF Constitutional Court Ruling (6 December 2013) No.27-P.

64 ECtHR Judgment *Anchugov and Gladkov v. Russia* (4 July 2013) applications No.11157/04 and 15162/05; Ruling of the RF Constitutional Court (19 April 2016) No.12-P in a case about execution of the ECtHR Judgment in *Anchugov and Gladkov v. Russia.*

65 ECtHR Judgment *Yukos v. Russia* (31 July 2014) Application No.14902/04; RF Constitutional Court Ruling (19 January 2017) No.1-P.

66 Vladislav Starzhenetskiy, 'The Execution of ECtHR Judgments and the "Right to Object" of the Russian Constitutional Court' in M. Breuer (ed.), *Principled Resistance to ECtHR Judgments – a New Paradigm?* (Berlin: Springer, 2019), 245–74.

arguing that national states have the power to make exceptions with a view to national interest and justice as it is understood in the society.[67]

It is also interesting to notice another communitarian argument that crept into the Yukos judgments of the RF Constitutional Court. Even if it is wrong from the formally legal standpoint to deprive an owner of his assets (the individual injustice), this deprivation can be justified in terms of the public good (the collective justice) – oligarch's wealth to be utilised for supporting the poor and underprivileged people. This "socialist" reason was, in fact, the *ratio decidendi* in the RF Constitutional Court's decision that the ECtHR judgment cannot be executed in Russia.

The "civilisational argument" is inevitably utilised for referring to the specific legal culture and traditions of Russia that, presumably, differ from Western ones. This mantra is repeated in all the cases which the Russian Constitutional Court and the Russian political authorities employ when they seek to affront the ECtHR and the liberal values behind its judgments. If international-law norms and their interpretations contravene so-called traditional (or constitutional) values, judges may give preference to national law in which these values are embodied or, even better, turn to the foundational narratives relying on the idea of organic development[68] or, in terms of public law, on a "living constitution."

Employing this set of arguments, the RF Constitutional Court extended its scope of competences, de facto assuming an ideological function. Albeit, any state ideology is interdicted by Art. 13 of the RF Constitution, the Court does not hesitate to proclaim certain ideas or views to be congruent with Russian constitutional values what, taken from the other side, implies that different opinions and views are contrary to these values and shall have no legal protection, even if set out in the legislation. An array of cases on the protection of minorities demonstrate the extent to which this approach is embedded in Russian case law.[69]

This and many other facts prompt us to think that challenging the power of the ECtHR and other European supranational institutions is a part of

67 Bill Bowring, 'Politics and Pragmatism: The Constitutional Court of the Russian Federation and Its 20 Years of Engagement with the European Convention on Human Rights' (2018) 1(1) *East European Yearbook on Human Rights* 5.

68 See the manifesto of this Kremlin's ideology 'National Identity and the Future of Russia' *Valdai Discussion Club Report* (February 2014), available at <http://vid-1.rian.ru/ig/valdai/Identity_eng.pdf>.

69 Mikhail Antonov, 'Balancing Religious Freedoms: Some Examples from the Practice of the RF Constitutional Court' in Piotr Szymaniec (ed.), *The Principle of Proportionality and the Protection of Fundamental Rights in the European States* (Wroclłw: Wydawnictwo Państwowej Wyższej Szkoły Zawodowej im. Angelusa Silesiusa, 2017), 259–68; ibid., 'Religion, Sexual Minorities, and the Rule of Law in Russia' (2019) 7(2) *Journal of Law, Religion and State* 152.

Russia's broader strategy to undermine the "Europe of values" and to bring it back to the system of pragmatic alliances based on the realist understanding of international law and on legal formalism – it is the force and not the values that decide *ultima ratio* about definition of rights and obligations for the states and, indirectly, about limits of rights conferred to citizens.[70]

The 2020 Amendments to the Russian Constitution confirmed this trend towards conservative interpretation of the Constitution without changing its literal meaning – the main provisions (basic rights and principles in chapters 1 and 2) remained intact, but different mentions that were brought into other parts of the Constitution (e.g., mentioning "belief to God" as one of the foundations of Russian federalism or the definition of marriage as a heterosexual union) create a specific interpretative framework for these rights and principles. Also, the Amendments fixed the right not to execute decisions of foreign and suprastatutory courts if they are considered to be incompatible with the Constitution, albeit the priority of international law remained untouched in Art. 15 of the Constitution and Russia does not denounce its obligations connected with the participation in the CoE.

10.5 Conclusion: Populism at the Crossroads between the Legal and the Political

Putin's regime is utterly susceptible to its ratings in sociological polls and does its best to keep up these ratings. But the reason of this concern is not about winning next elections (these have rather a ceremonial meaning) – these ratings are important for the internal rivalry between different groups in the ruling elite. A considerable decrease in popularity might trigger changes in the political elite and redistribution of political power between groups of interest.

On many occasions Russian political leaders underscored that they are free from the drawbacks of democracy – they do not need to flatter the people and their goal is not to win elections. This comes as no surprise – these drawbacks are really inapplicable to non-democratic political systems. This "managed democracy" secures the full control of the political elites over the public sphere, so that maintaining political power does not depend on winning elections. The system of transit of power works differently here as compared with democratic systems. One of the consequences of this difference is that the political rulers do not need to attract voters by promising to stand by the people and to implement what is likely to be approved by the population. This is one of the well-known advantages of autocracy already noted by Plato and reiterated by sundry conservators. Another consequence

70 Arcady Ostrovsky, *The Invention of Russia: The Journey from Gorbachev's Freedom to Putin's War* (Atlantic Books, 2016).

is that political leaders do not attract voters by assuring them that they stand together with the people against the elites – in the Russian situation it would make no sense, as the governing party belongs to the political elite. In this sense, populism in Russian law and politics can mean, rather, other phenomena as compared with law and politics in the classical Western democracies.[71]

At the same time, to achieve long-standing objectives (to get rid of corruption, to secure sustainable economic growth, etc.), Russia needs a well-functioning legal system – this is something that is repeatedly asserted by the political leadership and seems to be taken seriously by it. One of the evident ways to improve the legal system (along with other, more difficult ways which would require structural reforms and the corresponding political changes, or would be too expensive) is to connect the law with the *Lebenswelt* of ordinary people, to make the law more comprehensible and more valuable to them, thereby securing their law-abiding behaviour.

In this consists one of the main applications of the conservative legal policies of Putin's regime – to connect the law with such narratives and ideals that are supported by public opinion. If this opinion is hostile towards minorities, if it can be flattered by references to the "glorious national past" or to "Russia's historical mission" (whatever both may be), if it can be mobilised by portraying the West or other imaginary entities as antagonistic (against whom Russia shall protect its sovereignty) on the main axis of the political (friend/enemy), these narratives can be helpful propaganda tools. This is the crossroads where the legal and the political can utilise populism for obtaining the pragmatic objectives of the government – in this sense, a number of scholars in recent years started to speak about "constitutional populism."[72]

In the broadest meaning of the term "populism," it shows how ideological narratives are used to gain public approval for laws, by appealing to the prevailing 'morality of law' (in the terms of Lon Fuller, but not necessarily coinciding with how he described this morality). Politicians not only use attractive slogans and narratives to mobilise voters for elections, but also after elections they seek to uphold their legitimacy and win popular approval for the laws they introduce. Most of the governments seek support to their policies from their *populus*, so that "populism" technically can be applied to them and not only to a number of political regimes marginalised in the Western political discourse and media.

71 Some commentators find that populism in Eastern and Central Europe is focused on economic nationalism and the revival of authoritarian traditions, and has other important differences from Western populism (e.g., László Andor, 'Against a General Theory of Populism: The Case of East-Central Europe' (2020) 55(1) *Intereconomics* 21).

72 Paul Blokker, 'Populism as a Constitutional Project' (2019) 17(2) *International Journal of Constitutional Law* 536.

As a matter of fact, the pejorative use of this term implies criticism of antiliberal political narratives. Trump, Putin, Orbán, or Erdoğan would be qualified as populists because they rely on conservative narratives with which they seek to win elections, or to maintain their power, or to mobilise the population behind their programmes. However, from the analytical point of view, there are no convincing arguments why utilisation of liberal narratives for the same purposes (acquisition and maintenance of political power, mobilisation of the population behind certain programmes) cannot be qualified as "populism" too.[73]

Differences in mindsets and in cultural patterns may explain the fact that sociological polls usually confirm the popularity of the legislation against sexual, religious, or other minorities in Russia and elsewhere in the CEE region. Those who stand against these mindsets would need to consider how it works on their rankings and votes: the last presidential election in Poland in 2020 demonstrated the force of conservative ideology which mobilised the voters behind the unpopular candidate because he chastised the 'gay propaganda' of his rival.[74] Employing such illiberal narratives is a legitimate tool of political struggle, albeit they might be at odds with national constitutional law or with the European law.[75]

The present paper demonstrates possible uses of populism in law: how ideological messages can be utilised to make the population more receptive of the law and thereby encourage lawful behaviour, reinforcing legitimacy. There can be, naturally, other meanings of populism and other implications of the phrase "law and populism" – e.g., for examining how governments use their lawmaking competences to influence public opinion, or how they try to secure the upper hand in elections by using the law, how conservative politicians use legislation and courts in their fight against liberal ideologies, etc. Examination of "populism in law" in this sense would mean: how this identarian discourse is employed to mobilise the masses and to make them more law-abiding and more susceptible to the ideologies that stand behind the law.

73 In the present paper we will not address the debates about the definition of populism.

74 Philipp Ayoub, 'Attacking LGBT Life Helped the Right-Wing Polish President Win Reelection – Barely' *The Washington Post* (21 July 2020), at https://www.washingtonpost.com/politics/2020/07/21/attacking-lgbt-life-helped-right-wing-polish-president-win-reelection-barely/, accessed 3 May 2023.

75 Martin Krygier, 'The Challenge of Institutionalisation: Post-Communist "Transitions", Populism, and the Rule of Law' (2019) 15(3) *European Constitutional Law Review* 544.

Conclusions

Post-communism, Neoliberalism, and Populism in the Semi-Periphery*

Adam Sulikowski and Rafał Mańko

Formulating the conclusions of a volume written by many authors with different assumptions, views, and styles of academic writing is not an easy matter. The chapters of the book, despite the fact that they all deal with similar topics and fit into a specific plan, remain "autonomous" works of their authors. Paraphrasing them would effectively mean, if Jacques Derrida is right, rewriting them. Therefore, in our concluding remarks, we will not summarise or conclude individual chapters of the book, but will focus on highlighting the issues that turned out to be crucial for us.

In Foucault's theory of discourse, what is external and what is internal is in an irremovable clinch. Discourse produces reality, but at the same time it is determined by the material. Eastern Europe was clearly created by discourse.[1] As noted by Larry Wolff, this discourse was shaped by the luminaries of the Enlightenment, who recognised the West as the civilisational core and saw the periphery in the East.[2] The fact that Königsberg, where Immanuel Kant wrote his famous 'Beantwortung der Frage: Was ist Aufklärung?' being further east than Prague, Warsaw, or Budapest did not matter. No one had any doubts that Kant and his works were created in the circle of Western civilisation. At the same time, the discourse that created Eastern Europe was strongly entangled in the relations of politics and power on very different levels. This may be evidenced by the attitude in the West to the Hungarian anti–Habsburg uprising of Rákóczi. In Western countries, the Magyars were perceived either as noble freedom fighters or as uncouth barbarians – depending on what kind of relations the country had with Austria. What is more,

* All views expressed in this chapter are entirely personal and do not purport to present the position of any institution.

1 Michel Foucault, *The Archaeology of Knowledge and The Discourse on Language* (New York: Pantheon Books, 1972), 38.

2 Larry Wolff, *Inventing Eastern Europe: The Map of Civilization on the Mind of the Enlightenment* (Stanford: Stanford University Press, 1994).

DOI: 10.4324/9781032624464-12

in France, Enlightenment thinkers approached the system of the largest state in Eastern Europe – the disintegrating Polish-Lithuanian Commonwealth – in extremely different ways. Rousseau admired this system while Voltaire deeply criticised it. In general, however, Eastern Europe appeared to the inhabitants of Western countries as wild, dark, mysterious lands inhabited by half-barbaric peoples, descended from Asian tribes. Undoubtedly, however, what is material also contributed to the formation of the specificity of Eastern Europe. Already in the late Middle Ages, the arable land owned by the peasants was rapidly shrinking east of the river Elbe.[3] In the 15th century, a manorial economy based on serfdom developed in Eastern Europe,[4] a fact that Immanuel Wallerstein linked theoretically with the birth of the capitalist world-system.[5] From the point of view of the capitalist core, the region of Eastern Europe has become permanently different. When Enlightenment discourses identified the Age of Lights as the culmination of history, reactions in Eastern Europe varied. In Russia, the rulers tried to force the elite to modernise (famously cutting the beards of the boyars). In Poland, a relatively small group of nobility supported by the Warsaw bourgeoisie led, as a result of a partial coup d'état in May 1791, to the adoption of the first modern constitution in Europe, which preceded the revolutionary French Constitution by several months. The history and content of the Constitution of May 3[6] well illustrates the specificity of the region. Polish radicals read French books and identified themselves as the Left, and yet they formulated views contradictory in some aspects to the postulates of French radicals – they demanded the centralisation of power in the hands of the monarch. What is more, they did not formulate demands for the freedom of all people, the abolition of peasant serfdom, and they wanted to grant only limited political rights to the "third estate." On the other hand, the extremely conservative Targowica Confederation, organised against the May Constitution, presented itself as the main defender of freedom and was compared by many uninformed observers in the West to French and American revolutionaries.[7] The above example shows that ideological conflicts in Eastern Europe were usually mirrors of Western ones, but they took a specific form, sometimes difficult to

3 Jerzy Topolski, 'Continuity and Discontinuity in the Development of the Feudal System in Eastern Europe (Xth to XVIIth Centuries)' (1981) 10(2) *Journal of European Economics* 373.
4 Jerzy Topolski, 'The Manorial-Serf Economy in Central and Eastern Europe in the 16th and 17th Centuries' (1974) 48 *Agricultural History* 341.
5 Immanuel Wallerstein, *The Modern World-System. Capitalist Agriculture and the Origin of the European World Economy in the Sixteenth Century* (New York-San Francisco-London: Academic Press, 1977).
6 See, e.g., Marian Hillar, 'The Polish Constitution of May 3, 1791: Myth and Reality' (1992) 37(2) *The Polish Review* 185.
7 Adam Sulikowski, *Postliberal Constitutionalism: The Challenge of Right-Wing Populism in Central and Eastern Europe* (Abingdon: Routledge, 2023), 8.

understand in the West. As Przemysław Tacik notes in Chapter 1, this is still the case today. Contemporary disputes over the rule of law and identity conflicts are part of the processes present in the West, but at the same time there remain far-reaching differences between what is going on in the centre and periphery.[8]

The differences between East and West are particularly concerned with issues of freedom. As indicated above, the conservative nobility in the region saw a threat to freedom in granting political rights to the townspeople and in abolishing the serfdom of the peasants. Moreover, modernisation and the related emancipation took place in our part of the continent in the conditions of colonisation "enslavement" and the subordination of local traditions to the policies of Western empires. Even more strange is that the slogan of liberation was carried on its banners by the Soviet army, which, implementing distorted Western ideas of Marxism, introduced long-term authoritarian rule in the region. Not only Marxism, but also fascism was different here than in the West. This makes both the universalism of Western research categories and paradigms (also in relation to populism) and the assumption of the omnipresence of the Enlightenment a mistake, as pointed out in Chapter 2 by Cosmin Cercel. The author calls for courage in questioning popular categories and for the broadest possible consideration of local entanglements in research on a part of the continent that has been different from the West for centuries.

The wave of revolution in the region that began in 1989 resulted in the rejection of actually existing socialism in the region. This system was commonly considered as a form of enslavement, despite the fact that it brought unprecedented emancipation of the lower social classes and introduced universal access to free education and health care. However, the "liberation" from Marxism resulted in the dominance of neoliberalism, which brought real oppression to a large part of society. Neoliberalism in the context of changes in Central and Eastern Europe should be understood broadly: not only as a postulative economic ideology focused on maximum "market liberation" – i.e., minimising the role of the state in the economy, the privatisation of public tasks, favourable tax rates for corporations, welfare cuts, limiting employees' legal protection, and moving away from the concept of the welfare state.[9] Neoliberal ideology also involves the promotion of a specific mentality and ethical models – the heroes of history are entrepreneurs, active people who develop a mythical economy and contribute to global welfare by getting rich, while the anti-heroes are people who, unable to cope in a capitalist environment, "reach out to the state" and encouraging it to strengthen the processes of redistribution through political methods. In

8 See Chapter 1 by Przemysław Tacik in this volume.
9 David Harvey, *A Brief History of Neoliberalism.* (Oxford-New York: Oxford University Press, 2005), 2ff.

matters of political decision making, neoliberalism is decidedly undemocratic.[10] In decision-making processes related to economics, i.e., in practice in almost all political issues, the voice of an expert based on "objective laws of economics" must have priority.

The career of neoliberalism in CEE can be described as strange. On the wave of democratisation, the ideology supported by a relatively small percentage of society became hegemonic. In the early 1990s, Polish sociologist and constitutionalist Piotr Winczorek was astonished to state that with the relatively strong intensity of populist tendencies in the society and in some political groups, the values inherent in populism marked their presence in the content of the law rather poorly. Moreover, despite the lack of liberal traditions in the region, the axiology preferred by the law was clearly liberal in nature. Although the sense of democratisation was widespread, law-making was not based on the realisation of social preferences. On the contrary, it was legislative processes that shaped society's axiological preferences.[11]

The neoliberal bias concerned not only economic policy and legislation, but also judicial decisions. Moreover, the case-law sometimes went much further than legislation. More cautious researchers write in this context about judicial activism,[12] while those more radical indicate that the concept of juristocracy should be used.[13] It was not infrequently that the courts formulated their decisions based on a very controversial understanding of the law, sometimes even *contra legem*.[14] Numerous studies show that the case-law of the highest courts in the matters of social rights, usury restrictions, labour relations, and limitation of claims were much more neoliberal than the linguistic wording of the provisions and justifications of legislative drafts.[15] As Alexandra Mercescu points out with regard to Romania, liberal excesses were fostered by the narrative moulding together of the rule of law, legal form and neoliberal ideology, whereby formalism provided a pretext and camouflage for controversial decisions.[16] The liberal approach to the law as a neutral means of agreeing upon an objectified consensus around key

10 Sulikowski, *Postliberal Constitutionalism*, 74.

11 Piotr Winczorek, 'Uwagi o aksjologicznych aspektach działalności legislacyjnej w dziedzinie prawa publicznego w Polsce' [Some remarks on the axiological aspects of legislative activity in the area of public law in Poland] (1994) 56(4) *Ruch Prawniczy, Ekonomiczny i Socjologiczny* 53.

12 Wojciech Sadurski, *Rights Before Courts: A Study of Constitutional Courts in Postcommunist States of Central and Eastern Europe* (New York and London: Springer, 2005), 62.

13 Béla Pokol, *The Juristocratic State: Its Victory and the Possibility of Taming* (Budapest: Dialog Campus, 2017), 85.

14 Adam Sulikowski, 'Government of Judges and Neoliberal Ideology: The Polish Case' in Mańko et al., *Law and Critique in Central Europe*, 22–3.

15 See Chapter 3 by Adam Sulikowski and 7 by Mátyás Bencze, in this volume.

16 See Chapter 6 by Alexandra Mercescu, in this volume.

political issues not only made it possible to mask the ideological bias of judicial decisions, but also became the cause of a populist reaction. As Mátyás Bencze writes in his chapter, activism and mistakes in filling key positions in the judiciary made it very easy for the illiberals to take control of the state in Hungary.[17] Undoubtedly, the sense of a lack of justice and real alienation of the majority of society in terms of influence on politics and economy was a factor influencing the crisis of demoliberalism in Central and Eastern Europe. Some social groups have turned hope for change towards authoritarianism. As noted by Peter Čuroš, writing in the context of Slovakia, the specificity of our region also lies in the fact that authoritarianism is capable of generating in society a much deeper illusion of participation than liberalism was able to create.[18]

Illiberal populists won successive elections promising to reduce the neoliberal bias of politics and law. According to some authors, the implementation of the populist agenda has contributed to a wider inclusion of the problems of the lower classes in mainstream political discussions.[19] The informal revolution initiated by Orbán and Kaczyński is even interpreted as the necessary completion of the systemic transformation started in 1989 – after the phase of liberalisation and building the legal foundations of constitutionalism, there is democratisation combined with a wider inclusion of the interests of the popular masses into official politics.[20] Undoubtedly, Polish "conservative revolutionaries" refer to the narratives typical of all populism about including the people in decision-making processes and the fight against elites for a more just rule.[21] Nevertheless, there is little evidence of broader social inclusion in both Hungarian and Polish policies. There has been a decisive centralisation of state management. The critical reaction of *Solidarna Polska* (one of the parties forming the illiberal populist coalition in Poland) to the presidential bill on justices of the peace can be presented as an example of the anti-democratic attitude of populists after gaining power. The leaders of this party recognised that the election of judges by the citizens would only strengthen the processes of judicial anarchism and lead to the control of the judiciary by local cliques. Paradoxically, violent social reactions erupt against some populist moves. An example is the revolt described by Rafał

17 See Chapter 7 by Mátyás Bencze in this volume.

18 See Chapter 8 by Peter Čuroš in this volume.

19 Adam Czarnota, 'Constitutional Correction as a Third Democratic Revolutionary Moment in Central Eastern Europe' (2019) 11(2/3) *Hague Journal on the Rule of Law* 397, 404. See also Chapter 4 by Karolina Kocemba and Michał Stambulski, in this volume.

20 Paul Blokker, 'Building Democracy by Legal Means? The Contestation of Human Rights and Constitutionalism in East-Central Europe' (2020) 18(3) *Journal of Modern European History* 335.

21 Nadia Urbinati, *Me the People: How Populism Transforms Democracy* (Cambridge, MA: Harvard University Press, 2019), 4ff.

Mańko in Chapter 5 against the judgment delegalising embryopathological abortion in Poland, handed down by the Constitutional Court controlled by an illiberal majority. Violent reactions and mass protests led to the suspension of the publication of the judgment for a period of three months, which, according to the author, was an example of '*exceptio popularis*,' a "minor" state of exception, conceptually related to the *stato di eccezione* theorised *inter alia* by Giorgio Agamben.[22]

An important element of the specificity of Central and Eastern Europe is the limitation of settling accounts with the past. The implementation of transitional justice was hindered primarily by the scale and long-term nature of totalitarian practices. As Václav Havel convincingly argued,

> We have all become used to the totalitarian system, [...] and accepted it as an immutable fact, thus helping to perpetuate it. We are all – though naturally to various degrees – responsible for the creation of the totalitarian machinery. None of us is just its victim; we are all responsible for it.[23]

However, contrary to Havel's view, populist discourses were able to convince the masses that they could feel themselves victims of the system they participated in building. The imperfections of transitional justice are an important factor in the success of populists. In the populist discourses in the region, a specific combination of post-communism and liberalism took place. According to this narrative, liberalism is a dialectical complement to Marxism, sharing with it the conviction of the need to promote progress and build a "new man" – the practice of liberalism and real socialism is the same – it consists in building, by privileged social groups, unconditional support for the ruling ideology and accumulation of capital. Post-communism in this perspective is a mental effect of transforming the former *homo sovieticus* into the new *homo oeconomicus*. The basis of this mentality is cynicism and slyness, moral relativism and, at the same time, a complex and utopian belief in the possibility of freeing oneself from the "East." From an external perspective, it is also an element of self-destructive naïvety – the attitude of a lemming. The process of propagating the "post-communist" mentality is, according to the illiberal narrative, controlled by local compradors, backed by international plutocrats striving for the disappearance of all authority and factors integrating colonised societies.[24] In other words Soviet colonisation was replaced by a liberal one. The same people are responsible for it – post-communists or their descendants. Traitors who should be punished continue

22 See Chapter 5 by Rafał Mańko in this volume.

23 Quoted in Samuel P. Huntington, *The Third Wave: Democratization in the Late Twentieth Century* (Norman, OK: University of Oklahoma Press, 1991), 214.

24 Andras Lanczi, 'What is Postcommunism?' (2007) 29(1) *Society and Economy* 65.

to live in comfort and corrupt the nation. As Saygun Gökarıksel points out in his chapter, the imperfections of transitional justice are the reason for legitimising and strengthening the victims' discourse, based on the assumption of national innocence and purification of guilt. The niche created by the lack of remembrance practices has been taken over by the essentialist, exclusionary identity politics that right-wing populist groups are fuelling as part of nationalist sovereignty and security policies.[25]

Interestingly, in Russia, which was the former hegemon, populist narratives are similar and different at the same time. On the one hand, the oligarchic elites that are liberal today have a Soviet communist past and therefore cannot be trusted. On the other hand, the saviours must be people with a traditional Soviet mentality, faithful to the state and focused on averting the "greatest geopolitical catastrophe," which was the collapse of the Soviet Union.[26]

What the contributions to this volume have shown, is that semi-peripheral Central and Eastern Europe remains different from the West. The problems here are sometimes rooted in Western concepts, (failed) legal transplants, and local reflections of Western disputes. However, even if they are imported, they take very specific forms that require both specific tests and diagnoses as well as original, region-specific solutions. Referring to Michel Foucault, we could point out that these differences are, above all, caused by different historical experiences. As Foucault explained, genealogy must define a historical ontology in relation to local regimes of truth, to fields of power that are unitary only in a very specific context, and to ethics that are also immersed in a specific *hic et nunc*.[27] In the opinion of Foucault himself, who spent more than a year in Poland in the late 1950s, local historical experiences were much more important for the process of understanding the context than modernising structures, political devices, or even formalised means of control and pressure. The French philosopher wrote that a special 'historical sadness' prevailed in this part of the world, the conviction that history made any changes very difficult. There was no Western historiosophical optimism here.[28] In 1982, when Foucault became involved in helping the Polish opposition after the imposition of martial law, he wrote in Paris 'we are not living in the same time as them.'[29]

25 See Chapter 9 by Saygun Gökarıksel in this volume.
26 See Chapter 10 by Mikhail Antonov in this volume.
27 Michel Foucault, 'Afterword: The Subject and Power' in Hubert L. Dreyfus and Paul Rabinow, *Michel Foucault: Beyond Structuralism and Hermeneutics* (Chicago: University of Chicago Press, 1983), 237.
28 Michel Foucault, 'L'experience morale et sociale des Polonais ne peut plus être effacée', in Michel Foucault *Dits et écrits*, François Ewald and Daniel Defert (eds) vol. 4 (Gallimard: Paris, 1994), 345.
29 Michel Foucault, 'Il n'y a pas de neutralité possible' in *Dits et écrits*, 338.

Pierre Legrand, a philosopher of law and comparative lawyer exceptionally sensitive to the dialectic of sameness and difference pointed out that German, French, or English law can never be the same precisely because of the radically different contexts in which both legal systems are interpreted. Being a German, French, or English lawyer is so deeply imbued in being a German, Frenchman, or Englishman, that even if, on the face, the legal solutions coincide (as the Common Core project tried to show), the actual life of the law remains radically different.[30] Therefore, comparative studies must be particularly sensitive to the differences in perspectives at many levels of analysis. All the more so that comparative studies should play a critical and political role. It should debunk myths instead of perpetuating them. As Legrand notes:

> At a time when the co-presence of the foreign has become a fact of life for every law and for so many lawyers, 'comparative law's' disreputation cannot but give cause for particular concern. In this sense, negativity epitomizes the transformative role that theory must play as counter-discourse. It effectuates a politics of (good) resistance. It is transgressive in as much as it is critically promoting a radical intellectual transformation or re-signification of the field of 'comparative law' operating as what Adorno's aesthetics of negativity styles a '*Nicht-Mitmachen*' (a not-playing-along or a non-participation). It is an undisciplined gesture.[31]

On the other hand, as noted by Richard Rorty, the public functions of theory require the weakening of identity elements in favour of perceiving similarities. After all, left-wing philosophising at least since Marx's famous Eleventh Thesis on Feuerbach is politics. Closing and emphasising otherness limits the cooperative inclinations of theory, privatising it.[32]

Practicing critical theory in the context of Central and Eastern Europe, one must be aware of both the great differences and some similarities necessary for political dialogue with the West. Even if Kaczyński and Orbán resemble, *qua* populists, Western European, US, or South American populists – which, in external and formal traits, they undoubtedly do – the *episteme* in which CEE populisms are grounded is intransigently different from the UK, Venezuela, or Florida. This is not only on account of different languages, but above all on account of very different historical experiences, cultural

30 Pierre Legrand, 'The Impossibility of "Legal Transplants"' (1997) 4 *Maastricht Journal of European and Comparative Law* 111; idem, 'The Same and the Different' in Pierre Legrand and Roderick Munday (eds), *Comparative Legal Studies: Traditions and Transitions* (Cambridge: CUP, 2003).

31 Pierre Legrand, 'Negative Comparative Law' (2015) 10 *Journal of Comparative Law* 450.

32 Richard Rorty, 'Philosophy as Cultural Politics' in *Political Papers* (Cambridge: CUP, 2017), 90.

legacies, and symbolic universes. The symbolic universe of a peasant from Mazovia (Poland) is incomparable to that of a Texas rancher or Venezuelan farmer. It is, however, comparable to a Slovak or Hungarian farmer. The common experience of foreign rule (be it Russian, Austrian, or Ottoman), the common experience of actually existing socialism imposed from above from the USSR, the common experience of a brutal, unexpected, and unplanned transition to a market economy, finally the experience of joining, not really prepared for, the European Union – all these common experiences of Central and Eastern Europe create a common symbolic space, a space of common collective memories, common legal and political experiences, and common predicaments. In objective sociological and historical terms, the commonality of our region, contrasting it to Western Europe but also to other peripheral and semi-peripheral regions of the world, contributes to a common CEE identity.[33]

As critical legal scholars, we would of course be happy to welcome in our region a new CEE version of left-wing populism of the kind described and advocated by Chantal Mouffe.[34] At the same time, however, as historically embedded legal realists, we are aware that, at this conjecture, the advent of a progressive populism in our region is not possible. As Saygun Gökarıksel has shown in his chapter, the negative experiences of Soviet influence during the socialist period have been turned into an entire ideology of anti-communism, effectively blocking progressive political projects on account of their Marxist pedigree. At the same time, however, as Karolina Kocemba and Michał Stambulski have convincingly argued, the government of Law and Justice is selectively picking the pecuniary elements of a leftist programme (social transfers) in order to build an electorate within the working class and the *lumpenproletariat*, thereby effectively annihilating any potential social base for the emergence of a leftist populism.[35] *Mutatis mutandis*, the same diagnosis applies for Hungary.

In these circumstances, as critical legal scholars we need to be political realists and count with a possible *longue durée* of populist rule in our region. It is within the horizon of this specific historical conjecture that the outline of our critical approach should be formulated. After all, as scholars, in contrast to activists, we intend to partake in the moulding of social consciousness

33 Rafał Mańko, Martin Škop, and Markéta Štěpáníková, 'Carving Out Central Europe as a Space of Legal Culture: A Way Out of Peripherality?' (2016) 6(2) *Wroclaw Review of Law, Administration and Economics* 4; Rafał Mańko, 'Delimiting Central Europe as a Juridical Space: A Preliminary Exercise in Critical Legal Geography' (2019) *Acta Universitatis Lodziensis. Folia Iuridica* 63; idem, 'Being Central European, or Some Reflections on Law, Double Peripherality and the Political in Times of Transformation' in Tomás Gábriš and Ján Sombati (eds), *Central and Eastern Europe as a Double Periphery* (Berlin: Peter Lang, 2020).

34 Chantal Mouffe, *For a Left Populism* (London: Verso, 2018).

35 See Chapter 4 by Karolina Kocemba and Michał Stambulski in this volume.

and act as members of ideological intelligentsias, struggling for hegemony. Undoubtedly, the present moment is marked, to an increasing extent, by the hegemony of the illiberal, right-wing, ethnonationalist, and conservative-clerical ideology. As numerous chapters in the book have shown, this ideology increasingly enjoys the upper hand in the shaping of the material content of the law.[36]

Despite a number of affinities with Western Europe, on one hand, and with non-European states troubled by the phenomenon of populism, on the other hand, the CEE region displays a number of particular traits. In the 'Introduction' to this volume, they were identified as the region's semi-peripheral status (as opposed to full peripherality), on one hand, and its historical experiences marked by the short traditions, frequent transitions, and deep traumas. Without repeating the claims made in the 'Introduction,' in the present concluding remarks we would like to draw concrete methodological conclusions from this semi-peripheral status of Central and Eastern Europe, made in hindsight of the onslaught and entrenchment of illiberal populism.

On top of the classical methodological commitments made in the 'Introduction' (emancipation, realism, anti-formalism), drawing on the chapters in this volume, we believe that two other concrete recommendations can be formulated. First, the critique of legal transplants. As it was noted in the introductory chapter, and became visible in the case studies in Chapters 3–10, legal transfers have, indeed, determined the form and outlook of legal life of CEE. This is not to say that legal transplantation is *per se* wrong – after all, Alan Watson praised it for being the prime *spiritus movens* of juridical innovation.[37] What is problematic, however, from a CEE perspective, is that the legal life of the region became, especially as regards constitutional law, virtually colonised by legal transfers. The case-law of the Polish, Hungarian, or Romanian constitutional courts in the neoliberal 1990s and early 2000s all sounded almost the same, as if a symphony of juridified neoliberalism. As many chapters in this volume have shown, these neophitic courts were virtually deaf to any calls for defending social rights, even if the letter of the constitution leant itself easily to such an interpretation (for example, the Polish Constitution mentions "social justice" in its Article 2).[38]

36 See especially chapters by Karolina Kocemba and Michał Stambulski; Rafał Mańko; Màtyàs Bencze, and Saygun Gökarıksel, in this volume.

37 Alan Watson, *Legal Transplants: An Approach to Comparative Law* (2nd ed., Atlanta: University of Georgia Press, 1993).

38 See especially chapters by Adam Sulikowski and Alexandra Mercescu, in this volume. By contrast, see also Chapter 4 by Karolina Kocemba and Michał Stambulski, emphasising the social rights focus of the populists.

Therefore, any reasonable critique of the legal status quo of Central and Eastern Europe cannot shy away from a critique of legal transplants.[39] Whereas American, British, or French constitutionalists can, and probably, do without such a concept, in order to meaningfully study the legal life of the semi-periphery one needs the critical tools offered by theories of peripherality and neocolonialism. Despite all the formal affinities, to criticise a judgment of the Polish, Romanian, or Hungarian Constitutional Court *is essentially different* from subjecting to critique the judgment of the Bundesverfassungsgericht, the Corte Costituzionale, or the Conseil Constitutionnel. Even if *in form* they are the same, the courts of CEE are working with legal transplants which radically changes the entire sense of their enterprise.[40]

Legal transplants are very closely connected to legal survivals, i.e., legal institutions which have survived despite a radical change in the political, social, and economic milieu.[41] As it was noted in section 4 of the 'Introduction,' Central and Eastern Europe has been marked by sharp and traumatic transitions,[42] allowing for little institutional continuity. This thesis can be fairly applied to the entire region, including the entirety of the former USSR, whose statehood represented a deep, programmatic, and pragmatic discontinuity with that of the Russian Empire.

In this general context of institutional discontinuity, there still emerge, from time to time, legal institutions clearly originating in the past.[43] These institutions can be compared to palimpsests.[44] The external layer of the law, its visible form, hides beneath itself earlier epochs (e.g., authoritarian

39 Cf. Hans-Wolfgang Micklitz, 'Prologue: The Westernisation of the East and the Easternisation of the West' in Michal Bobek (ed.), *Central European Judges Under the European Influence: The Transformative Power of the EU Revisited* (Oxford: Hart, 2015); Michał Gałędek, 'Introduction: Modernisation, National Identity, and Legal Instrumentalism' in Michał Gałędek and Anna Klimaszewska (eds), *Modernization, National Identity and Legal Instrumentalism: Studies in Comparative Legal History*, vol. 1: *Private Law* (Leiden-Boston: Brill-Nijhoff, 2020).

40 Cf. Chapter 6 by Alexandra Mercescu in this volume.

41 Rafał Mańko, 'Survival of the Socialist Legal Tradition? A Polish Perspective' (2013) 4(2) *Comparative Law Review* 1; idem, '"Demons of the Past"? Legal Survivals of the Socialist Legal Tradition in Contemporary Polish Private Law' in Mańko, Cercel, and Sulikowski (eds), *Law and Critique*, 66–89; idem, 'Legal Survivals and the Resilience of Juridical Form,' *Law and Critique* (forthcoming).

42 Rafał Mańko, 'Law, Politics and the Economy in Poland's Post-Socialist Transformation: Preliminary Notes Towards an Investigation' in Balázs Fekete and Fruzsina Gárdos-Orosz (eds), *25 Years After Transition in Central and Eastern Europe: Understanding the Transition from an Internal Perspective* (Frankfurt am Main: Peter Lang, 2017).

43 Rafał Mańko, 'Towards a Typology of Dimensions of the Continuity and Discontinuity of Law: The Perspective of Polish Private Law after the 1989 Transformation' (2016) 6(2) *Wroclaw Review of Law, Administration and Economics* 108; idem, 'Form and Substance of Legal Continuity' (2017) 17(2) *Zeszyty Prawnicze* 207.

44 For an application of the metaphor of a palympsest to the law, albeit in a different setting, see, e.g., Bret D. Asbury, 'Law as Palimpsest: Conceptualizing Contingency in Judicial Opinions' (2009) 61 *Alabama Law Review* 121.

traditions of actually existing socialism or the right-wing authoritarianism of the 1930s) and, at the same time, foreign origins of legal transfers. To understand such legal institutions and subject them to a critique, it is necessary to go beyond external appearances, looking for hidden continuities, forgotten foreign origins of "tamed" and "translated" legal transplants, and undisclosed ideological commitments made under the cover of officially recognised hegemonies. Whereas all these features are present in legal cultures of the centre, they obtain a different significance in the semi-periphery, where the discrepancy between the actual lived *nomos* and the formal law has been always greater, the domination of legal transplantation over local legal innovation absolute, and legal continuity was rather the exception than the rule.[45]

45 Cf. Introduction to this volume, 17–25.

Index

Kolibri 360 GmbH
Ferdinand-Jühlke-Straße 7
99095 Erfurt, Deutschland
produktsicherheit@kolibri360.de